SAINT GREGORY OF NYSSA

Catechetical Discourse

T0326709

ST VLADIMIR'S SEMINARY PRESS
Popular Patristics Series
Number 60

The Popular Patristics Series published by St Vladimir's Seminary Press provides readable and accurate translations of a wide range of early Christian literature to a wide audience—students of Christian history to lay Christians reading for spiritual benefit. Recognized scholars in their fields provide short but comprehensive and clear introductions to the material. The texts include classics of Christian literature, thematic volumes, collections of homilies, letters on spiritual counsel, and poetical works from a variety of geographical contexts and historical backgrounds. The mission of the series is to mine the riches of the early Church and to make these treasures available to all.

Series Editor
BOGDAN BUCUR

Associate Editor
IGNATIUS GREEN

* * *

Series Editor
1999–2020
JOHN BEHR

SAINT GREGORY OF NYSSA

Catechetical Discourse

A Handbook for Catechists

Introduction, Translation, Notes, Glossary, and Bibliography by
IGNATIUS GREEN

ST VLADIMIR'S SEMINARY PRESS

YONKERS, NEW YORK

2019

Library of Congress Control Number: 2019943730

COPYRIGHT © 2019 BY
Ignatius Green

ST VLADIMIR'S SEMINARY PRESS
575 Scarsdale Road, Yonkers, NY 10707
1-800-204-2665
www.svspress.com

ISBN 978–088141–648–0 (paper)
ISBN 978–088141–651–0 (electronic)
ISSN 1555–5755

For Aimilia
ἡ ἱερῆος σύζυγος
καὶ τὰ παιδία, ἃ ἡμῖν ἔδωκεν ὁ Θεός
οἷς πόθον ἔχοιμεν ἕνα

Contents

Abbreviations

ANF   The Ante-Nicene Fathers. Edited by Alexander Roberts and James Donaldson. Buffalo, 1885–1887. 10 vols. Repr., Peabody, MA: Hendrickson, 1994.

GNO   Gregorii Nysseni Opera. Edited by Werner Jaeger, et al. Leiden: Brill, 1920–

LSJ   *A Greek-English Lexicon*. Edited by Henry George Liddell, Robert Scott, and Henry Stuart Jones. 9th edition. Oxford: Clarendon Press, 1996.

LXX   Septuagint (the Greek translation of the Old Testament used by the Fathers of the Church)

NPNF¹   The Nicene and Post-Nicene Fathers, Series 1. Edited by Philip Schaff. New York, 1886–1889. 14 vols. Repr., Peabody, MA: Hendrickson, 1994.

NPNF²   The Nicene and Post-Nicene Fathers, Series 2. Edited by Philip Schaff and Henry Wace. New York, 1890. 14 vols. Repr., Peabody, MA: Hendrickson, 1994.

PG   Patrologia Graeca. Edited by J.-P. Migne. 162 vols. Paris, 1857–1886.

PPS   Popular Patristics Series. Yonkers, NY: St Vladimir's Seminary Press, 1996–

Preface

Many people have helped me with this project. I cannot sufficiently thank my wife, Presbytera Aimilia, for her love, patience, and support. I owe a great debt to Fr John Behr for guiding me through my academic career, for sharing his love of grappling with a text, and for accepting this translation in the Popular Patristics Series. I am also deeply grateful for Brittany Lauber's willingness to check my translation against the Greek. The text is surely better for her aid, and any remaining defects or infelicities are mine alone. Finally, I want to thank Fr John and Mat. Brenda Mikitish for their careful proofreading, and Amber Schley Iragui, who took the rough sketch I gave her and created such a striking cover.

I am thankful to have had this opportunity to explore the *Catechetical Discourse* and to immerse myself in St Gregory's other works. The beauty of his theological vision is deep, far ranging, and compelling. He has much to offer our age, which in many ways resembles Julian the Apostate's project: he rejected Christ and the Church, but ended up aping the beauty and love found in the gospel. The answer to an apostate age is both defense and persuasion. St Gregory can be emulated today, both in his adroit defense of the faith, and in the persuasive power of his portrayal of the surpassing beauty of Christ. He shows us how to engage in a discourse that is properly catechetical, "so that the Church may be increased by the 'addition of those being saved'" and that they too may adore Christ on bended knee, knowing him and naming him as the Church teaches us, crying out:

> *O radiant fountain, ever gushing with life, creative power co-eternal with the Father, who with surpassing beauty hast fulfilled*

the whole economy of the salvation of mankind; O Christ our God, who didst burst the indestructible bonds of death and the bolts of hades, and hast trampled down multitudes of evil spirits; who didst offer thyself for us as a blameless victim, giving thine immaculate body as a sacrifice, inviolate and unblemished by any sin, and through that dread and indescribable act of sacrifice, didst bestow eternal life upon us; who didst descend into hades and break down its eternal bars, showing forth the way up to those who sat below; thou who, in thy wisdom, didst bait and hook the ruler of evil, the dragon of the abyss, and with cords of gloom didst bind him in Tartarus, in unquenchable fire, confining him to the outer darkness by thine infinite might; O glorious Wisdom of the Father, who didst manifest thyself as a mighty ally to the oppressed, enlightening those that sat in darkness and in the shadow of death, thou Lord of eternal glory and beloved Son of the Father most high, Light everlasting of Light everlasting, Sun of righteousness…

(Third Kneeling Prayer, Vespers of Pentecost)

To him be all glory, honor, and worship, with his unoriginate Father, and his all-holy, good, and life-giving Spirit, now and ever, and unto the ages of ages. Amen.

Rev. Ignatius Green
Pentecost 2019

Introduction

St Gregory of Nyssa

In the fourth century, St Gregory of Nyssa was a touchstone of Orthodoxy at the heart of the age's theological crisis, and his work was crucial to its resolution. He played a key role in the First Council of Constantinople (AD 381), which named him an exemplar of right belief.[1] In later years, he continued to win praise: the Seventh Ecumenical Council (AD 787) called him the "father of fathers."[2] While parts of his works that touched upon *apokatastasis* required cautious explanation, his reputation was not tarnished in subsequent centuries.[3]

The bishop of Nyssa also fascinates contemporary scholars, but here we find a quite different picture, or, rather, many different and conflicting portraits. Some see him as a sort of patron saint of contemporary concerns: an advocate of human rights (perhaps the first to condemn slavery unequivocally), a proto-feminist who deferred to his ascetic-theologian sister St Macrina, a "sex-positive" theologian who purportedly championed fluid notions of gender. This is not the place for a thorough evaluation of such claims, but this much must be said: Gregory is a complicated writer with great breadth and depth. Selecting isolated elements of his writings can produce startlingly different results: "Gregory can be read in many different ways . . . he appeals to theologians of surprisingly diverse views, from radical feminists to conservative evangelicals."[4]

---

[1]Emperor Theodosius ratified this by imperial decree. *Codex Theodosianus* 16.1.3 (issued July 30, 381).

[2]See Acts of II Nicaea (787), sixth session (Mansi, 13.293e).

[3]See pp. 38–58 below for the reception of his views on apokatastasis.

[4]Morwenna Ludlow, *Gregory of Nyssa, Ancient and (Post)modern* (Oxford: Oxford University Press, 2007), 4.

Gregory was a true son of Cappadocia, a region in central Anatolia (modern-day Turkey), which played a part in the Christian story from the day of Pentecost (Acts 2.9). Near the beginning of the third century, St Alexander was a bishop in Cappadocia before he transferred to Jerusalem, where he supported Origen's work as a teacher and preacher.[5] But it was St Gregory the Wonderworker, a student of Origen, who was credited with converting Cappadocia on a large scale.[6] Gregory of Nyssa drew upon this patrimony: his paternal grandmother, St Macrina the Elder, was a spiritual daughter of the Wonderworker, and his teaching and memory was cherished by her many descendants. Her son St Basil the Elder and his wife St Emmelia had nine or ten children, "like an army of saints."[7] The future of the faith was in large part determined by their lives and teaching.[8]

Gregory of Nyssa was born around AD 335.[9] Macrina was the firstborn, who later became the matriarch of the family even while her mother was alive. St Basil the Great was born second, St Naucratius third, followed by Gregory and four or five sisters (in unknown order), and St Peter was born last. Their father Basil the Elder was a rhetorician and lawyer in Neocaesarea. The younger Basil was able to begin his studies with his father, but Gregory could not. Their father died soon after Peter's birth, around the year 345. After this

[5] Eusebius, *Ecclesiastical History* 6.11.2; 6.23.4; 6.27.

[6] Gregory of Nyssa, *Life of Gregory the Wonderworker* (GNO X/1:16). When he arrived in the region, there were only seventeen Christians. On his deathbed, he was pleased to find that there were now only seventeen remaining pagans.

[7] Gregory of Nazianzus, *Epigram* 161 (trans. Paton). Emmelia calls Peter her tenth or "tithe" (δεκατῷ, ἐπιδέκατος) in *Life of Macrina* 15.3, but this may be a symbolic reference to biblical tithe offerings. The same work lists "four sons and five daughters" (7.4). If the latter is more accurate, perhaps one child did not survive infancy.

[8] Together they curtailed the remaining neo-Arian threat and laid the groundwork for the completion of the Nicene Creed; they established a rule for monastic life; they promoted the veneration of the martyrs and the concomitant development of the Church's liturgical life; they articulated the distinction between God's essence and energies in terms that would receive definitive dogmatic formulation in the work of St Gregory Palamas.

[9] We have no direct evidence for the year of his birth, but we know that he studied under Basil in Caesarea in 356, and rhetorical studies seldom continued much longer than a student's twentieth year.

the family relocated to Annisa in the country, and Basil left to study in Constantinople and Athens in the late 340s. Already their family life began to change from that of conventional landed Christian aristocrats. Macrina became the first ascetic in the family, and in 351 Naucratius likewise took up solitary life. Five years later he tragically died while fishing, caught in his own net at his hermitage on the river Iris in 356.[10] This rocked the family, and it also led to its further transformation. Emmelia became a monastic, and Peter, the youngest, was raised in a domestic monastery from the age of ten.

And where was Gregory in all of this? We know of only one event before the death of Naucratius, a vision or dream he had as a youth during the vigil for the forty martyrs of Sebaste.[11] Gregory studied under his brother Basil for a short time around 356,[12] after the latter had returned from Athens. Soon Basil renounced public life and a promising career, received baptism, and traveled throughout Egypt and Palestine, studying the different forms of monastic life. In 358 he settled down near Annisa on the river Iris, the very place Naucratius had lived. It seems that Gregory joined Basil there for a time.[13] But this was not to last. By around the year 364 Gregory had become a rhetorician, though he too had been baptized by this point, and had been made a reader in the Church, apparently with the intention of becoming a priest.[14] It appears that his life took a detour, and likely at this

[10]Gregory of Nyssa, *Life of St Macrina* 11.1; Gregory of Nazianzus, *Epigrams* 156–58.

[11]Gregory of Nyssa, *On the Forty Martyrs I* (GNO X/1:167–68).

[12]Gregory of Nyssa, Letter 13. Some have exaggerated Gregory's lack of education. Libanius, the greatest rhetorician of the age, spoke highly of the rhetorical education available in Caesarea (Libanius, Letter 1222), and he specifically praised Gregory's style (Gregory of Nyssa, Letter 13.2–6). We must not let the modest reply that he "never had a teacher" obscure the fact that in the same letter Gregory says that Basil was his teacher for a time, and through him lays claim to Libanius himself as his (indirect) teacher (Letter 13.4, 6). His oratorical skill is clear from the prominent addresses he was invited to give at the First Council of Constantinople and at the funerals of Emperor Theodosius' wife and daughter.

[13]See Basil, Letter 223.5.

[14]This could not have happened before 364, when Jovian abrogated Julian's edict of 362, which forbade Christians from teaching rhetoric. We know of Gregory's rhetorical career from Nazianzen's Letter 11, which is a firm rebuke for having forsaken an ecclesiastical career.

point, after he left Annisa, he was married. Much ink has been spilled attempting to determine the bishop of Nyssa's marital status, but in the end the resolution of this question is not particularly important. Whether he was married and had children, or married and celibate (as St Gregory of Nazianen's sister St Gorgonia was), or married and widowed and living as a monastic, or simply a monk for most of his adult life after a brief career in rhetoric (any of these possibilities could be argued, given the evidence we possess),[15] his ecclesiastical and spiritual milieu are clear. His family stood at the fore of the development of the eastern monastic tradition, and married or not, Gregory was in sympathy with the vision and spirituality of this movement.[16]

Once Gregory's career in the Church began, it was marked by the events of his time: "The rest of his history is Church politics."[17] Basil became the archbishop of Caesarea in Cappadocia in 370, and after his diocese was partitioned in 371 he sought to appoint new bishops to shore up neo-Nicene support in the region. To this end, he made his brother Gregory and his best friend Gregory bishops of Nyssa and Sasima, respectively. Little is known of these early years, but in the winter of 375–76 Gregory was exiled, ostensibly for financial mismanagement, but he himself wrote, "The Emperor Valens drove me out on account of the faith."[18] We do not know where he spent his exile, but soon after his return in 378, his brother Basil died on January 1, 379.[19] A heavy burden

[15]The two main sources are Gregory of Nyssa's *On Virginity* 3 and Gregory Nazianzen's Letter 197, but further evidence is found in the latter's Epigram 161 and 164. For a thorough discussion of the question, see Silvas, *Letters*, 15–25.

[16]I do not accept Mark Hart's claim that *On Virginity* is "ironic." Mark Hart, "Gregory of Nyssa's Ironic Praise of the Celibate Life," *Heythrop Journal* 33 (1992): 1–19. For a literary refutation of his argument, see Valerie Karras, "A Re-evaluation of Marriage, Celibacy, and Irony in Gregory of Nyssa's *On Virginity*," *Journal of Early Christian Studies* 13.1 (2005): 111–21.

[17]Harold Fredrik Cherniss, *The Platonism of Gregory of Nyssa* (Berkeley, CA: University of California Press, 1930), 4.

[18]*Life of Macrina* 23.1. The details of this period can be discerned in Basil's Letters 225, 231, 232, 237, 239.

[19]This is the traditional date. Competing theories for revising this date do not concern us here (cf. Silvas, *Letters*, 32–39).

fell on the shoulders of both men named Gregory. The defense of the faith was theirs to wage, especially against the Eunomians and Pneumatomachians.[20] They did this individually in their writings and homilies and corporately in synods. The time leading up to the First Council of Constantinople was politically complicated and eventful for Gregory,[21] but it was the council itself that proved to be the turning point.

Emperor Theodosius, a supporter of the neo-Nicene cause, convened the council in May 381. Gregory figured prominently in the proceedings—he likely preached an opening address[22] and he certainly preached at the funeral of St Meletius, the first president of the council—and he was one of three bishops in the civil diocese of Pontica named as an exemplar of the Orthodox faith. The council also sent him on a special mission to the churches in Arabia and Jerusalem. Gregory returned to Constantinople at Theodosius' request to deliver his *On the Divinity of the Son and the Holy Spirit* in 383, and two years later he preached funeral orations for the emperor's wife and daughter, a few weeks apart. From 387 onward, Theodosius came to spend most of his time in Italy, and Gregory retired from public life, turning inward, and likely at this point he penned many of his spiritual and mystical writings. Most scholars believe that the *Catechetical Discourse* was written before this period,

[20]The followers of Eunomius—who claimed not only that the Son was not consubstantial with the Father (as Nicea defined) but that he was "unlike" him (hence their other name, "Anomoean," from the Greek ἀνόμοιος, "unlike")—and those who "fought against the Spirit," i.e., who denied the divinity of the Holy Spirit.

[21]In May to June of 379 Gregory participated in the neo-Nicene council in Antioch, and soon after arrived at his sister Macrina's deathbed in July 379, which inspired *On the Soul and the Resurrection* and *The Life of Macrina*. He helped in the election of a neo-Nicene bishop in Ibora in Pontus in the winter of 379–80, and sought to do the same in the higher-stakes election of a metropolitan in Sebaste in Febuary of 380. To his chagrin, he himself was elected, and then in the ensuing uproar put into some sort of custody, "whether coercive or protective is uncertain" (Silvas, *Letters*, 43).

[22]Most scholars believe that *On His Own Ordination* was the council's opening address. See *The Brill Dictionary of Gregory of Nyssa*, ed. Lucas Francisco Mateo-Seco, et al. (Leiden: Brill, 2010), 214.

though it evades any certain dating.[23] The last we hear of Gregory is in the list of participants at a council in Constantinople in 394.

The *Catechetical Discourse*

The *Catechetical Discourse* is well known and important both among Gregory's works and in the broader patristic tradition, but it has received little attention from scholars in its own right.[24] In many ways it stands alone, sui generis in the Nyssene corpus.[25] It draws upon important themes in the prior tradition—especially the works of Origen, St Methodius of Olympus, and, above all, St Athanasius' *On the Incarnation*—at times in surprising ways.[26] It touches upon the essential doctrines of the Christian faith:

[23]Twentieth-century scholars assigned dates between 381 and 387; Kees argued more specifically for 386 or 387, while Winling hypothesized a date before 381. See Kees, Reinhard Kees, *Die Lehre von der* Oikonomia *Gottes in der* Oratio catechetica *Gregors von Nyssa* (Leiden: Brill, 1995), 201–208; *Discours catéchétique*, trans. and ed. Raymond Winling (Paris: Les Édition du Cerf, 2000), 125–30; Pierre Maraval, "Chronology of Works," in *Brill Dictionary*, 156.

[24]Kees' is the only monograph written on the *Discourse*, and it is mentioned only once in the *Brill Dictionary of Gregory of Nyssa* (surprisingly not in the entry on the *Discourse*).

[25]Gregory's works are quite varied: they include polemical treatises against heretics (e.g., *Against Eunomius*), speculative works on anthropological and eschatological themes (e.g., *On the Making of Man* and *On the Soul and the Resurrection*), lives of saints (e.g., the *Life of Macrina* and *Life of Gregory the Wonderworker*), works on the ascetical or mystical life (e.g., *On Virginity* and *Life of Moses*), letters on many different themes, and sermons on Scripture (e.g., homilies on the Beatitudes, on the Lord's Prayer, on Ecclesiastes, and on the Song of Songs), on feast days of the Lord or the saints (e.g., on Nativity, Pascha, and Ascension, and *On the Forty Martyrs*), and on important moral themes (e.g., *On Love of the Poor*, *Against Fornication*, and *Against Usury*).

[26]Despite the fact that Methodius was one of the first vocal opponents of Origen's teaching (specifically on the resurrection), Gregory describes our death and resurrection first by using an image drawn from Methodius—fallen man is "dissolved again 'into the earth' [Gen 3.19] like some 'clay vessel,' so that, the filth now shut up within him being separated out, he might be re-formed by the resurrection to the form [he had] from the beginning" (8.3)—and then immediately afterward describes our mortal state in terms of the "garments of skin" (8.4–5; cf. Gen 3.21), an idea drawn from Origen. For verbal echoes and broad structural correspondences between the *Catechetical Discourse* and *On the Incarnation*, see Kees, *Die Lehre*, 87–89.

1) the Trinity (chapters 1–4)

2) Creation, the Image of God, and the Fall (chapters 5–8)

3) Christ's Birth, Life, Death, and Resurrection (chapters 9–32)

4) Baptism and the Eucharist (chapters 33–40)

The broad scope of the work and the order of its presentation have long led scholars to make two important assumptions. Because of the broad scope, they take the work to be a grand work of systematic theology, "a complete and systematic account of his views on Salvation."[27] Because of the order of presentation, they see the work as an exposition of salvation history: "the general scheme of the *Oration* encompasses all of creation history from beginning to end," beginning with the Trinity, "with a special focus on pre-incarnational christology"; it then "progresses to an illustration of the God-intended paradisial state of humanity, its fall from this state and its subsequent salvation in the incarnation of the Son and Logos," culminating in "the method by which we may interiorise this salvation within the Church," i.e., the sacraments of baptism and the Eucharist.[28] But a close reading of the text does not bear out either of these assumptions.

The *Catechetical Discourse* is a handbook for catechists, written with a practical aim. Gregory does not lay out a systematic theology proceeding from first principles. Instead he addresses the concrete contexts of his catechists: "Indeed the same manner of teaching will not be suitable for all who approach the word, but the catechesis must also be made to suit the differences of religions, looking to the same aim of the discourse, but not using proofs in the same manner

---

[27]Jean Riviére, *The Doctrine of the Atonement: A Historical Essay*, trans. Luigi Cappadelta, vol. 1 (London: Kegan, Paul, Trench, Trübner & Co., Ltd., 1909), 179.

[28]Mario Baghos, "Reconsidering *Apokatastasis* in St Gregory of Nyssa's *On the Soul and Resurrection* and the *Catechetical Oration*," in *Cappadocian Legacy: A Critical Appraisal*, ed. Doru Costache and Philip Kariatlis (Sydney, Australia: St Andrew's Orthodox Press, 2013), 400. Previous scholars expressed similar views (e.g., Winling, Kees, Srawley, and Meridier).

for each" (Prol.1). This is the guiding principle throughout the work, and not a historical narrative. The transitions introduced throughout the work all address the current conditions of catechists. The first four chapters do indeed argue for the doctrine of the Trinity, but the argument begins: "Thus when the dialogue is with a Hellenist, it would be good to make this the beginning of the argument: whether he supposes the divine to exist, or if he agrees with the atheists' teaching" (Prol.4). Likewise the transition to the next large section (chapters 5–8) does not move chronologically—from theology to economy, i.e., from God in himself to God's creation, work, and manifestation outside himself[29]—but practically: Jews and Greeks might accept the preceding arguments about the Trinity, but they balk at the incarnation, "accordingly, from a different beginning we will bring gainsayers even to faith in this" (5.1). If history does not explain the connection between the work's four main sections, we must look elsewhere.

Rhetoricians had long divided speeches into four parts, stretching back to Gorgias' *The Encomium of Helen*:[30]

1) Introduction	(*exordium*, προοίμιον)[31]
2) Narrative	(*narratio*, διήγησις)[32]

---

[29]Grillmeier and Kees argue that the theology-economy dichotomy lies at the root of the work's structure, but this is difficult to maintain. Grillmeier himself admitted that theology and economy are often mixed together in the *Discourse*. Most notably, there is a second Trinitarian section in relation to baptism (38–39) after the section on the Eucharist (37).

[30]See Cicero, *De Oratore* 2.76 (though he sometimes acknowledged further subdivisions into five or six parts, cf. *De Oratore* 35; *De Inventione* 2.16, respectively; Quintillian favored a fivefold division, *Institutio Oratoria* 3.9.1–3); Aristotle, *Rhetoric* 3.13.4 (although he goes so far as to say that a speech could be reduced to two parts: the statement of the case and the proof). "The ancients, Aristotle, Cicero, and Quintilian, all write of the 'natural order' of a speech; that is, the four or more separate divisions into which all speeches should be separated. . . . [A]lthough Cicero's and Quintilian's divisions appear to be at variance with Aristotle's, they are actually in perfect accord." Ramon L. Irwin, "The Classical Speech Divisions," *Quarterly Journal of Speech* 25 (1939): 212–213, at 212.

[31]Also called *propositio* and θέσις.

[32]In Aristotle the second part of a speech is called the πρόθεσις (*Rhetoric* 3.13.4).

3) Proof   (*confirmatio*, κατασκευή)[33]

4) Conclusion   (*peroratio*, ἐπίλογος)

This fits perfectly with the *Catechetical Discourse*:

1) Chapters 1–4	Introduction	The Trinity
2) Chapters 5–8	Narrative	Creation, the Image of God, and the Fall
3) Chapters 9–32	Proof	Christ's Birth, Life, Death, and Resurrection
4) Chapters 33–40	Conclusion	Baptism and the Eucharist

As a former rhetorician, Gregory would have been familiar with rhetorical handbooks going back to the time of the pre-Socratics that followed precisely this four-part division, especially in judicial oratory.[34]

In ancient rhetoric we also find a clue to understanding the *Catechetical Discourse*'s unique character amidst fourth-century catechetical literature, which consists primarily of homilies addressed catechumens. St Cyril of Jerusalem and Theodore of Mopsuestia preached a series of catechetical homilies explaining the Nicene Creed for catechumens before their baptism, followed by a shorter series of mystagogical homilies that explained the sacraments of initiation to the newly baptized after they had gone through them. St Ambrose took a more directly scriptural, narrative-driven approach to catechetical instruction (his *On Abraham* is an example), followed by similar mystagogical homilies, while St John Chrysostom

Cicero includes *propositio* in his sixfold division, but when Cicero speaks of five divisions, he removes the *propositio* and includes *narratio*, which remains in his fourfold division. This became the standard order in the handbook tradition that I discuss below.

[33] Also called *probatio* and πίστις.

[34] See George A. Kennedy, "Historical Survey of Rhetoric" in *Handbook of Classical Rhetoric in the Hellenistic Period (330 B.C.–A.D. 400)*, ed. Stanley E. Porter (Leiden: Brill, 1997), 9–10.

took a slightly less orderly approach in the two series of catechetical homilies that come down to us. St Augustine's *De catechizandis
rudibus* is by far the most similar to the *Discourse*. In it, the deacon
Deogratias asks for advice on the narrative section of his catechetical addresses, and Augustine, a former rhetorician like Gregory,
proceeds to give advice, and sketches out two possible narratives for
him. This process of framing new arguments was called "invention"
or "discovery" (εὕρεσις, *inventio*) in classical rhetoric.[35] It was the
first step in composing a speech, the first of the five "canons" (the
others involved subsequent aspects of the process: arrangement,
style, memory, and delivery).

This is precisely what Gregory does in the *Catechetical Discourse*:
he discovers or invents arguments for his catechists. It is then their
task to complete the process, arranging the arguments into a coherent order, and employing the other canons to craft and deliver
catechetical homilies. Gregory explains himself quite clearly: "the
same manner of teaching will not be suitable for all who approach
the word, but the catechesis must also be made to suit the differences
of religions, looking to the same aim of the discourse, but not using
proofs in the same manner for each" (Prol.1). As such, he seeks to
show how this is done in different scenarios. When he uses only one
scriptural argument in the fourth chapter, he says explicitly, "It is
enough to recall one testimony, leaving the discovery [εὕρεσιν] of
more to those who are more industrious" (4.1).

In late antiquity five textbooks, known as the Hermogenic corpus, came to dominate the study of rhetoric, eventually displacing
even Aristotle's *Rhetoric*. The fourth book of the corpus is entitled
On Invention (Περὶ Εὑρέσεως). It is divided into four books, following the fourfold division of ancient speeches, though the last
book concerns rhetorical style, not conclusions.[36] Though Gregory

[35]For more on invention or discovery, see Malcolm Heath, "Invention," in
Handbook of Classical Rhetoric, 89–119; Kennedy, *Greek Rhetoric under Christian
Emperors*, 86–96.

[36]Likewise Gregory's fourth section, while it may be construed as a natural ending for the catechetical process (catechesis ends in mystagogy), is nevertheless not a

may not have known the final redaction as it comes down to us, he may well have known this work in an earlier form (which was likely similar in its overall structure).[37] Even if he never knew this particular work, it is clear that there was an established tradition of writing handbooks "on invention" by Gregory's time, and the four-fold schema was a standard division of rhetorical manuals for nearly a thousand years.

The *Catechetical Discourse* is a Christian appropriation of this "on invention" rhetorical handbook tradition. Of course, the borrowing is not entirely straightforward: the *Discourse* is not devoted to an abstract methodological treatment of invention qua invention. The beginning of the prologue resembles such an approach (Prol.1–3), but it soon gives way to concrete examples. The *Discourse* is not a single treatise for a single audience, and we are now in a position to see it for what it is: an extended series of inventions. Gregory created a handbook that discovers a multitude of arguments for the different parts of a traditional judicial speech (as Augustine invented two narratives of differing lengths for Deogratias in *De catechizandis rudibus*).

This has profound consequences for our understanding of the *Catechetical Discourse*. The work is not systematic theology in the modern sense, in which Gregory propounds his "ransom theory," or his "sacramental theology," etc. This is not to say that he simply does not mean what he says, but it requires a more nuanced reading. Here he provides catechists with winsome arguments by which they can gain the assent of those whom they address.Reading the Nyssene corpus without regard for its rhetorical character can lead to serious

typical conclusion. Winling notes "the absence of a true peroration, which is surprising." Winling, *Discours Catéchétique*, 129.

[37]"*On Invention* might be based to a considerable extent on a work of the mid-second century C.E., though largely written in the third or even fourth century and revised into its present form in the fifth or sixth when it was adapted to fill out the Hermogenic 'Art of Rhetoric.'" *Invention and Method: Two Rhetorical Treatises from the Hermogenic Corpus*, trans. George A. Kennedy (Atlanta, GA: Society of Biblical Literature, 2005), xvi.

distortions.[38] It is essential to consider the rhetorical purpose of a work when we seek to understand Gregory's view on thorny and contested matters. We lack space to analyze the entire *Discourse*, but we will briefly examine four key themes that have been interpreted and misinterpreted over the years: the Trinity, the sacraments, the saving work of Christ, and the question of universalism.

The Trinity

The first section of the *Catechetical Discourse* invents arguments for Greeks and Jews to prove that there is one God, known and distinguished in three persons. This comes first because this is the fundamental change in belief required for the conversion of a polytheist or strict monotheist. The incarnation cannot be defended unless one believes in the divine Word who is incarnate, nor is the catechist's audience ready to die and rise with Christ in baptism until they have come to believe that his death and resurrection are salvific. The order is practical, and directed at the persuasion of potential converts. Different appeals will work for Greeks and for Jews, as Gregory summarizes at the beginning of the next section: "But the Greek [will be convinced] because of common notions [κοινῶν ἐννοιῶν], and the Jew likewise [will be convinced] because of the Scriptures" (5.1). It is clear that scriptural arguments can be used with a Jewish audience, since both Christians and Jews hold the Law and the prophets to be inspired. But what are "common notions," and how can both Christians and Greeks appeal to them?

[38]E.g., marriage and sexual reproduction are treated in opposite ways in the *Discourse*, where he says that through the sexual organs "nature battles death" (28.4), and in *On Virginity*, which makes a bold claim: "the bodily procreation of children . . . is more an embarking upon death than upon life for man," since it does nothing more than "furnish it [death] with fuel and provide it with victims who are like condemned prisoners." *On Virginity* 14 (trans. Callahan). Neither passage is concerned with an objective evaluation of marriage. The former defends the propriety of the incarnation against a Gnostic tendency to devalue the body, while the latter seeks to praise the life of virginity, and in classical rhetoric an encomium necessarily included a diatribe. See Lucas Francisco Mateo-Seco, "Matrimony," in *Brill Dictionary*, 489–92, at 489.

This could seem to point to specific philosophical commitments, but caution must be urged. It is quite difficult to discern Gregory's philosophy of mind.[39] The Stoics used "common notions" (κοιναὶ ἔννοιαι) as a technical term, along with "natural notions" (φυσικαὶ ἔννοιαι) and "preconception" (πρόληψις, translated here in the *Discourse* as "presupposition"), to describe the fundamental structure of the mind common to all people. Gregory uses this last term three times in the *Discourse*, twice in its verbal form and once as a noun. Could this indicate a Stoic influence? Recent research shows that all three terms could be used interchangeably, and all three refer to a fundamental category in Stoic psychology and epistemology, tracing its way back to the early Stoa.[40] But there is scant evidence that Gregory uses "common notions" or πρόληψις with this specific Stoic meaning in the *Discourse* or elsewhere. Each time he uses the latter term, it indicates the uniqueness of the views that a person holds, not at all their commonality with all other people. When used as a noun, Gregory says that catechists must "look to men's presuppositions [προλήψεις]" (Pr.2), which differ "according to the error in which each is involved" (ibid.). Likewise, when the word occurs in verbal form, it describes the Jew, who "has presupposed one set of suppositions [ὑπολήψεσιν . . . προείληπται]" (ibid.), contrasted with the various heresies, "each presupposing their own suppositions [ὑπολήψεσι προειλημμένοι]" (ibid.). Gregory portrays "common notions" as persuasive for Greeks but not to Jews, who require scriptural proof (5.1). Thus they are not seen as truly *common* to all people everywhere. Finally, the word ὑπόληψις, which I translate as "supposition,"

[39]See Michel Barnes, "The Polemical Context and Content of Gregory of Nyssa's Psychology," *Medieval Philosophy and Theology* 4 (1994): 1–24, at 2.

[40]See Henry Dyson, *Prolepsis and Ennoia in the Early Stoa* (Berlin: Walter de Gruyter, 2009), especially pp. 1–22. Dyson engages all the primary material and virtually all the secondary material to reach this conclusion. He differs from the prior judgment of F. H. Sandbach, "Ennoia and Prolepsis in the Stoic Theory of Knowledge," *Classical Quarterly* 24 (1930): 45–51. Cf. Mauro Bonazzi, "The Platonist Appropriation of Stoic Epistemology," in *From Stoicism to Platonism: The Development of Philosophy, 100 BCE–100 CE*, ed. Troels Engberg-Pedersen (Cambridge: Cambridge University Press, 2017), 120–141, at 122–23.

does not carry a technical philosophical sense for Gregory (it occurs once in his *Homilies on the Beatitudes* in a way that could sound epistemological, but upon examination here too ὑπόληψις ought to be understood in a more general sense).[41] So it seems that none of these terms—κοιναὶ ἔννοιαι, πρόληψις, or ὑπόληψις—bear a meaning unique to a particular philosophical school in the *Catechetical Discourse*. "Common notions" had a general meaning common to a broad spectrum of philosophical views—"the term κοιναὶ ἔννοιαι as such was widespread in ancient philosophy as a means to establish a commonly accepted ground before moving on with developing an argument"[42]—which Gregory does play upon, but he commits himself to no specific school or system.

But this does not exhaust all the possible meanings of the term ὑπόληψις. A far more promising technical meaning can be found, once more, in ancient rhetoric. The first book of *On Invention* begins with a chapter on introductions "from Hypolepsis (Suppositions)" (ἐξ ὑπολήψεως).[43] This is called "the finest and most productive method of invention,"[44] and it is rather straightforward and sensible.

---

[41]"It is like the concept [ὑπόληψις] of the Divinity, which is naturally implanted in all human beings [ἔγκειται μὲν πᾶσι φυσικῶς τοῖς ἀνθρώποις], but in ignorance of the God who really is, error arises on the subject." *Homilies on the Beatitudes* 5.2 (GNO VII/2:125; trans. Norris). We must note that this "implanted" (ἔγκειται) "concept" (ὑπόληψις) of God is rather weak, and subject to error; the words quoted above are brought in as an example of our *fallibility*: "The area of our life in which we are most often wrong is this, that we are unable to perceive correctly what is actually good and what is mistakenly supposed to be such." Ibid. As Weiswurm concluded, "What St. Gregory intended to say is that all men have at least a vague idea about God," but that "because of this very vagueness of their notions concerning God, they are ignorant as to the proper and fitting manner of worshipping Him," and this "in no way forces us to interpret it in the sense of an innate idea." Alcuin Alois Weiswurm, *The Nature of Human Knowledge According to Saint Gregory of Nyssa* (Washington, DC: CUA Press, 1952), 163.

[42]Johan Leemans, "Logic and the Trinity: Introducing Text and Context of Gregory of Nyssa's *Ad Graecos*," in *Gregory of Nyssa: The Minor Treatises on Trinitarian Theology and Apollinarism: Proceedings of the 11th International Colloquium on Gregory of Nyssa (Tübingen, 17–20 September 2008)*, ed. Volker Henning Drecoll and Margitta Berghaus (Leiden: Brill, 2011), 111–130, at 115.

[43]Ps.-Hermogenes, *On Invention* 1.1.93–100 (trans. Kennedy).

[44]Ps.-Hermogenes, *On Invention* 1.1.93 (trans. Kennedy).

Speakers should argue from and according to the views, opinions, and attitudes of their audience. This holds true for everyone involved in the courtroom drama: "There is need, then, to consider . . . in turn, hypolepses about the person of each of the following: the judge, the prosecutors, the defendants, those involved in the actions and indictments, [and] those revealed from outside the case[.]"[45] For the judges, "one must look at what sort of thing the action is and what sort of thing it is supposed [ὑπείληπται] to be, good or bad, and what attitude the judges have about it and how they are disposed toward what has been done."[46] This is exactly the sort of "supposition" that Gregory is concerned with in the *Discourse*. It differs among different groups, and each audience must be addressed in accordance with the views that they uniquely suppose.

It is this rhetorical sensitivity that guides both the arguments and the terms that Gregory uses. It is energy poorly spent to compare the Trinitarian terms employed in the *Discourse*'s introduction with Nyssene treatises devoted to Trinitarian theology that address Christian audiences (whether heretics or fellow neo-Nicene believers). Here Gregory is addressing a pagan Greek, who is less fluent in Christian terminology. The use of terms like ὑπόστασις or πρόσωπον, οὐσία or φύσις provides no reliable evidence for the development of his theology. As Winling notes, "Anyone wishing to gauge the *Catechetical Discourse* by the normative formula *mia ousia-treis hupostaseis* risks disappointment if he is not flexible enough to use other parameters."[47] But the use of terms does provide a good example of how carefully Gregory considers his catechists' audience.

---

[45] Ps.-Hermogenes, *On Invention* 1.1.93–94 (trans. Kennedy).

[46] Ps.-Hermogenes, *On Invention* 1.1.94 (trans. Kennedy). Like most rhetorical manuals in late antiquity, the legal model assumed is that of fourth-century BC Athens, regardless of contemporary realities.

[47] Winling, *Discours Catéchétique*, 47. For his treatment of these technical terms in the *Discourse*, see pp. 47–50, and for a comparison with other dogmatic works, see pp. 54–56.

The Sacraments

Gregory employs two analogical explanations of baptism. First he dwells upon baptism as regeneration, with rather vivid and surprising parallels to biological generation (33–34). Then he introduces "another mystery" (35.1): baptism is a mimetic participation in Christ's death and resurrection. Few are tempted to draw out the first set of images as Gregory's "doctrine of baptism." But they are no less grounded in Scripture than the mimetic model. Gregory compares the baptismal waters that give us spiritual rebirth to the semen that gives us biological birth in "carnal begetting" (33.2). This may focus on a different set of scriptural images than most subsequent Fathers chose to emphasize, but it is nevertheless scriptural. The New Testament consistently refers to Christians becoming "sons" or "children" of God. There are two distinct images used to explain this status. While St Paul speaks of "adoption" (Rom 8.14–17; Gal 4.5–7), the apostles John and Peter use the analogy of being begotten by God (cf. Jn 1.13), to the extent that both refer to God's "seed" (1 Jn 3.9; 1 Pet 1.23). Gregory relied on Scripture when he compared the baptismal waters to human semen (an image he also uses in a sermon with his flock).[48] We cannot ignore this explanation merely because it strikes us as odd and jarring. However, there are other compelling reasons to give more attention to his second account (35). In the first place, the initial explanation of baptism (33–34) is explicitly apologetic. Gregory anticipates an objection: "For how, they say, do prayer and calling upon the divine power, performed over water, become the beginning of life to those who are initiated" (33.1). He responds with a question of his own: "Let us ask them in turn about the manner of carnal begetting, which is clear to all, how that which is sown for the origin of the composition of a living thing becomes a man?" (33.2). Gregory was well acquainted with the biological theories of his time, but he apparently remained aloof from the Aristotelian consensus about reproduction.[49] At any rate, he expected his interlocutor to

[48]*On the Baptism of Christ* (NPNF[2] 5:520).

[49]Stoics, Philo, Plutarch, and Galen all accepted Aristotle's account. See Prudence

regard the process as somewhat mysterious: "The answer, then, which is likely to be given to us . . . is . . . that by divine power that [seed] becomes a man, which, when it is not present, it is unchanged and inactive" (33.3). This section does not explain baptismal regeneration; rather, it defends its inexplicability by demonstrating our inability to explain biological generation.[50] To be sure, the passage does not leave baptism completely unexplained: "Prayer to God, and calling upon heavenly grace, and water, and faith are the things through which the mystery of regeneration is fulfilled" (33.1). This provides evidence for the liturgy of baptism in the fourth century: Gregory appears to describe a prayer of blessing over the waters.[51] Theodore of Mopsuestia and Ambrose also speak of such prayers as effectual and even necessary.[52]

The second description of baptism has a different character. First, it is in keeping with contemporary liturgical evidence. Fourth-century liturgical texts show a growing reliance on Pauline imagery of dying and rising with Christ (e.g., it is instructive to compare the second-century *Didache* with the fourth-century *Apostolic Constitutions*). Gregory calls baptism "the imitation" (35.1) of Christ. We follow after him, "for it is not possible to arrive at the same end unless one travels by the same [paths]" (35.2). We are like those trapped in a labyrinth. We must wend our way, following after our leader, who has himself escaped the labyrinth, and is thus able to show us the way out. This image "figuratively [τροπικῶς]" (35.3) refers to the "prison

Allen, *The Concept of Woman: The Aristotelian Revolution, 750 B.C.—A.D. 1250*, 2nd ed. (Grand Rapids, MI: Eerdmans, 1997), 161–63, 187–93, 195–96.

[50]Cf. Gregory's earlier defense of the incarnation (11.1): Since we cannot understand the union of soul and body in man, but are witness to the fact that they are united, we must grant the same in the case of the union of the divine and the human in the God-man. Cf. Gregory of Nazianzus, *Oration* 29.8.

[51]However, this may simply be Gregory's understanding of the dominical formula in baptism. "He may have in mind the blessing of the water, the calling on the threefold divine name at the actual baptism, or both." Everett Ferguson, *Baptism in the Early Church: History, Theology, and Liturgy in the First Five Centuries* (Grand Rapids, MI: William B. Eerdmans Publishing Co., 2009), 606.

[52]Theodore of Mopsuestia, *Mystagogy* 3.9; Ambrose, *On the Sacraments* 1.15; cf. Cyril, *Mystagogy* 3.3.

of death" (ibid.). To follow and imitate Christ, we must undergo what he did: the three-day death and resurrection (35.4). In Christ, "the economy of death" (35.7; cf. 32.6) reached its providential fulfillment. Not only does Christ's resurrection unite his own sundered soul and body, he becomes the "glue" (16.7) that unites what was previously disunited (cf. 16.6–9). However, Gregory admits that our imitation is incomplete. Our participation in Christ's resurrection from the dead will only be complete in the resurrection of our bodies.

Gregory's final discussion of baptism comes after he describes the Eucharist. First, he points to the need for correct faith: "he who confesses the holy Trinity to be uncreated enters into unchangeable and unalterable life," because otherwise, "he who, through a deceptive supposition, sees a created nature in the Trinity, and then is baptized into it, is again begotten into a changeable and alterable life" (38.4), an anti-Eunomian polemic (he is not alone in rejecting Eunomian baptism).[53] Gregory then exhorts the baptized to live lives worthy of their calling. Otherwise, "though it may be daring to say, I will say it and not be deterred, that in these cases the water is water, since the gift of the Holy Spirit is nowhere manifest in what takes place" (40.3). Though Cyril says something similar,[54] it is difficult to understand this as an objective claim (does God withhold grace at the moment of baptism, foreseeing a subsequently unregenerate life?). But when read as a final exhortation for the baptized to "walk in newness of life" (Rom 6.4), his claims are not incongruous or hard to understand. Those who live unrepentant lives fail, in some way,

[53]Gregory of Nazianzus baptized Eunomian converts at the paschal vigil, for which he was stoned by angry opponents (see his Letter 77; in *De vita sua* he calls it his "banquet of stones"); Athanasius wrote, "is not the rite administered by them altogether empty and unprofitable, making a show, but in reality being no help towards religion? For the Arians do not baptize into Father and Son, but into Creator and creature, and into Maker and work. And as a creature is other than the Son, so the Baptism, which is supposed to be given by them, is other than the truth, though they pretend to name the Name of the Father and the Son" (*Against the Arians* 2.18.42; NPNF² 4:371); Cyril of Jerusalem says more generally, "For only heretics are re-baptized, since their former baptism was not really baptism" (*Procatechesis* 7; PPS 57:71).

[54]Cyril, *Procatechesis* 2.

to partake or make good use of baptismal grace (admittedly this is easier to conceive of as a forfeiture than a retroactive invalidation):[55] "For that which you have not become, you are not" (40.4). He then turns to explicit exhortations: "If then you received God and became a child of God, show by your decision the God who is in you, show in yourself him who begot [you]. From these things we recognize God, through them it is fitting for him who has become a son of God to show [his] relationship with God" (40.5).

Gregory's discussion of the Eucharist resembles his first account of baptism. He begins with an already ancient image: it is an antidote to the poison we have all ingested (37.2–3). Ignatius wrote this way at the beginning of the second century: the Eucharist is "the medicine of immortality, the antidote which prevents death, yet enables us to live at all times in Jesus Christ."[56] Here too, the tone is apologetic, as we see when Gregory proposes "to digress a little into the physiology of the body" (37.5). Gregory's extended treatment of physiology and nutrition is meant to make the Eucharist seem more plausible for Greek sensibilities. Gregory describes the transformation of bread into Christ's body in this context. Since our bodies are made of the food we eat, and we eat bread, then we are all bread become body, which makes the transformation of bread into body in the Eucharist less implausible. Of course, the manner in which the change takes place differs: in the Eucharist the Word himself transforms the bread into what he calls it—"This is my body."[57] Gregory uses Aristotelian

---

[55]This cannot be an absolute loss of baptismal grace (or, indeed, a claim that the person is truly unbaptized, so that a second baptism is in order). As Gregory's canonical epistle makes clear, repentance is possible for any sin, however grave, though the therapy needed to find healing may be arduous.

[56]Ignatius, *Epistle to the Ephesians* 20.2 (PPS 49:41).

[57]Perhaps this is evidence for a Logocentric eucharistic epiclesis. In most extant liturgies, the Holy Spirit is called down upon the gifts to change them, though the Word is petitioned to make the change in the Egyptian *Euchologion of Serapion*. But we cannot press this statement too far. The description is dictated by the broader terms of the argument Gregory is sketching. We must not forget that his explanation here resembles what we now call apologetics far more than a systematic exposition of sacramental theology.

terminology, but this need not imply a philosophical commitment. He is quite eclectic in such borrowings. We cannot take this description of the transformation as the Nyssene "doctrine of the Eucharist," though this has happened often in the past (especially in polemics between Protestants and Catholics, both of whom were eager to interpret early patristic evidence—which was articulated in an entirely different context—to support their own positions). Like Justin Martyr, Gregory gives an apologia for the Eucharist, not a theory of eucharistic transformation. Later St John of Damascus drew on this section of the *Discourse* when he described the Eucharist in his *Exact Exposition*, but he did not borrow Gregory's description of the eucharistic change (he refused to offer any account of how the change takes place).[58]

The Saving Work of Christ

Gregory has long been credited with a "ransom theory" of salvation. Ransom had a complicated history in western Christianity. Anselm rejected it, and after this development, western discourse on the atonement became primarily a contest between Anselmian proponents of the "objective" view of a penal substitutionary atonement and the partisans of Abelard's "subjective" model. At least this is how scholars of the late nineteenth and early twentieth century represented the past millennium of soteriological reflection.[59] Then in 1930 Gustaf Aulén published *Christus Victor*, which rehabilitated what he called the "classical" teaching on the atonement. This may have gained a more receptive audience for the account of ransom in

[58]"However, should you inquire as to the manner in which this is done, let it suffice for you to hear that it is done through the Holy Spirit, just as it was through the Holy Spirit that the Lord made flesh subsist for himself and in himself from the blessed Mother of God. And more than this we do not know . . . the manner in which it is so is impossible to find out." John of Damascus, *Exact Exposition* 4.13 (trans. Chase, modified).

[59]Jean Riviére, *The Doctrine of the Atonement: A Historical Essay*, trans. Luigi Cappadelta, Volumes 1 & 2 (London: Kegan, Paul, Trench, Trübner & Co., Ltd., 1909).

the *Catechetical Discourse*, but it did not necessarily lead people to read it more carefully or accurately.

The image of ransom has biblical roots: the word "ransom" (λύτρον, λύτρωσις) occurs frequently in the Septuagint and New Testament. Most often these words are translated as "redemption," and this points to the close connection between the notion of ransom and the fundamental Christian doctrine of redemption. Christ himself said "the Son of Man came . . . to give his life as a ransom for many" (Mt 20.28; Mk 10.45). But why is a ransom necessary? To whom is the ransom given? In the second century, Irenaeus answered the first question in terms of justice, as Gregory does in the *Discourse*, but he does not specify who received the ransom.[60] Origen claimed that the devil did,[61] and it is precisely this form of the ransom theory that so repulsed scholars and theologians at the turn of the twentieth century.[62] Gregory of Nazianzus also objected to the ransom theory in no less uncertain terms: neither the Father nor the devil received the ransom in his estimation.[63] Basil spoke in different ways: in his homily on Psalm 48 he says that the ransom is offered both to the devil and to the Father,[64] while in his anaphora, the ransom is offered to death.[65] The fathers continued to speak of

---

[60]Irenaeus, *Against Heresies* 5.1.1. Irenaeus was "the first of the Catholic writers to anticipate the ransom theme." Eugene Teselle, "The Cross as Ransom," *Journal of Early Christian Studies* 4.2 (1996): 147–70, at 158.

[61]Origen, *Commentary on Romans* 2.13.29.

[62]"Nothing is more common than to find the patristic teaching dismissed with an impatient shrug of the shoulders, as mere puerilities, or sharply rated as ethically intolerable." Gustaf Aulén, *Christus Victor: A Historical Study of the Three Main Types of the Idea of Atonement*, trans. A. G. Herbert. (London: SPCK, 1953), 1963.. However, Aulén himself adds, "It must be admitted that it is not surprising that many features in the patristic teaching should awaken disgust, such as its mythological dress, its naïve simplicity, its grotesque realism." Ibid.

[63]Gregory of Nazianzus, *Oration* 45.22.

[64]Basil the Great, Homily 19.3, 4 on Psalm 48.

[65]"And having cleansed us with water and sanctified us by the Holy Spirit, he gave himself as a ransom to death, in which we were held captive, sold under sin." *Hieratikon: Liturgy Book for Priest and Deacon*, ed. Hieromonk Herman (Majkrzak) and Vitaly Permiakov (New Canaan, PA: St Tikhon's Monastery Press, 2017), 182–83.

Peter Bouteneff leans upon this personified use of death to conclude: "the answer

ransom for a thousand years after Gregory of Nyssa, e.g., John of Damascus and Gregory Palamas.[66] The latter, as in the *Discourse*, sees the ransom as a vehicle to deceive the devil.[67]

If the devil is deceived, he must be capable of ignorance. Though he is a spirit, he is not omniscient, and Scripture itself can lend support to the idea that the devil was ignorant of Christ's identity: in the temptation, the conditional "If you are the Son of God" (Mt 4.3, 6; Lk 4.3, 9) could express genuine doubt,[68] and St Paul did say that "None of the rulers of this age understood this" (1 Cor 2.8), which Origen took to refer to the demons.[69] Just after the completion of the New Testament, this theme was taken up by St Ignatius, who thought that multiple aspects of the incarnation "eluded" (ἔλαθεν) the ruler of this age (cf. Jn 14.30),[70] and here we begin to see the notion of intentional deception. Second-century apocryphal texts also attest to Satan's ignorance, likewise with hints that he was deliberately deceived.[71]

This tradition was in wide circulation in Gregory of Nyssa's time, and it continued throughout the patristic period.[72] But his fishhook that catches the devil with its bait (24.4) is not a formal "theory of atonement," rather, it is a striking image that expresses the notion

from the Greek East was clear from long before: *there is no identifiable party that demanded the sacrifice or ransom of Christ. . . .* So when the Fathers did speak of a 'recipient' of the sacrifice, they spoke metaphorically." Peter Bouteneff, "Christ and Salvation," in *The Cambridge Companion to Orthodox Christian Theology*, ed. Mary B. Cunningham and Elizabeth Theokritoff (Cambridge: Cambridge University Press, 2008), 98.

[66]John of Damascus, *Exact Exposition* 3.27; Gregory Palamas, Homily 16.1, 2, 30–31.

[67]Palamas, Homily 16.4.

[68]Chrysostom takes it this way (*Homilies on Matthew,* Homily 13.3).

[69]Origen, *On First Principles* 3.3.2.

[70]"The virginity of Mary and her giving birth, and likewise the death of the Lord, elude the ruler of this world. Three mysteries of crying out were performed in the quietness of God." Ignatius, *Ephesians* 19.1 (PPS 49:39).

[71]Cf. *Ascension of Isaiah* 9; *Gospel of Bartholomew* 1–33; *Gospel of Nicodemus* 4(20).1–3.

[72]For more on this theme, see Nicholas Constas, "The Last Temptation of Satan: Divine Deception in Greek Patristic Interpretation of the Passion Narrative," *Greek Orthodox Theological Review* 47:1–4 (2002): 237–74

of deception within a complex matrix of scriptural allusions (made explicit in a paschal homily, not in the *Discourse*).[73] As Fr John McGuckin laments: "Poor Gregory of Nyssa is one of the worst examples of a victim of this kind of superficial reading, which takes one of his incidental sermon allusions (Christ's capture of Leviathan) and wholly missing the Leviathan allusion elevates it to make him the originator of the 'Fish-Hook Theory of Atonement.' He would have found this hilarious, but generations of textbook readers since have taken it all too seriously."[74] But we must also remember that many of the church fathers used similar expressions, although none of them—including Gregory of Nyssa—held this to be the primary explanation of Christ's saving work. Nazianzen, his fellow Cappadocian, describes the incarnation as a means of "conversing with us through the mediation of the flesh as through a veil," which led to the devil's deception: the "deceiver . . . was himself cheated by God's assumption of our nature; so that in attacking Adam as he thought, he should really meet with God"; Chrysostom likewise says, "the devil . . . set himself in array against him; or rather not against God unveiled, but God hidden in man's nature"; St Ephrem the Syrian exults in Christ's deception of the devil, and St Romanos the Melodist, who drew deeply from the Semitic poetry of Ephrem and others, like Gregory portrays Christ deceiving death with a baited hook; in commenting on the book of Jonah, St Jerome describes deception in terms strikingly similar to the *Discourse* (though death is deceived, not the devil); Gregory the Great reproduces the *Discourse*'s fishhook image precisely; Maximus the Confessor refers

[73]This is clearer in *On the Three-Day Period* than in the *Discourse*: "having swallowed the bait of the flesh, he was pierced with the fishhook of deity, and so the snake was caught with the fishhook; just as he says to Job . . . 'You shall catch the snake with a fishook' [Job 40.25]." Gregory of Nyssa, *On the Three-Day Space* (GNO IX:281; trans. Hall). In the broader context, he describes the harrowing of hades in a complex intertextual pastiche (reading Isaiah 10.12 with Matthew 12.40, in conjunction with Isaiah 14.12–13, 2 Corinthians 5.4, and 1 Corinthians 15.26).

[74]John McGuckin, "St Gregory of Nyssa on the Dynamics of Salvation," in *Seeing the Glory Studies in Patristic Theology*, Collected Studies of John A. McGuckin, Vol. 2 (Yonkers, NY: St Vladimir's Seminary Press, 2017), 217–48, at 223 n.12

to the devil swallowing the "bait of the flesh," which was poison for the devil but a healing medicine for mankind; John of Damascus reproduces the image of the fishhook (as in Jerome, death is deceived), and he borrows directly from the *Discourse*, invoking the fourfold qualities manifest in God's deception and defeat of the devil; several centuries later, Gregory Palamas insists that deception was not only used, but necessary.[75] Palamas explicitly frames this in terms of justice and wisdom, and when he describes "how the deceiver was deceived," he calls Christ "a ransom for us," and concludes that the "devil was caught by the bait"; just as in the *Discourse*, the deception leads immediately to the harrowing of hades.[76] This is the true heart of Gregory's explanation of Christ's saving work in chapters 20–26.

Gregory does not, in fact, teach the "ransom theory" in the *Catechetical Discourse*, though it has long been read this way by those who view the work as "a complete and systematic account of his views on Salvation."[77] In reality, the *Catechetical Discourse* is a handbook for catechists, a rhetorical text with multiple layers of meaning. The ransom is merely the illusory surface appearance that deceived the devil. The ransom itself is a deception, but neither the ransom nor the deception saves us. They serve as a Trojan horse, that Christ might gain entry to the realm of the dead.[78] There he saves us by harrowing hades.

[75]Gregory of Nazianzus, *Oration* 39.13 (NPNF[2] 7:356–57); Chrysostom, *Homilies on Matthew*, Homily 2.1 (NPNF[1] 10:9); Ephrem the Syrian, *Nisibene Hymns* 38.6; 41.11; Romanos the Melodist, *Kontakion* 44.7; Jerome, *Epistle* 60.2; Gregory the Great, *Forty Gospel Homilies*, Homily 2.25; Maximus the Confessor, *Various Texts on Theology, the Divine Economy, and Virtue and Vice* 1.11; John of Damascus, *Exact Exposition* 3.27 and 3.1 (cf. *Catechetical Discourse* 24); Gregory Palamas, Homily 16.4.

[76]Gregory Palamas, Palamas, Homily 16.22, 30, 31 (trans. Veniamin).

[77]Riviére, *The Doctrine of the Atonement*, 1:179.

[78]Radde-Gallwitz notes this: "Gregory's account is not the same as the so-called 'ransom theory,' in which God, out of respect for the devil's rights, puts forth his Son as a ransom payment. Rather, Gregory maintains that the entire affair of incarnation was a giant ruse intended to trick Satan." Radde-Gallwitz, *Gregory of Nyssa's Doctrinal Works: A Literary Study* (Oxford: Oxford University Press, 2018), 238.

It is ironic that many earlier scholars criticized Gregory for a "mythic" depiction of the ransom theory, when the truly operative event in his account is the harrowing of hades (made possible by deceiving the devil), which is described in strikingly non-mythical terms. Other treatments in apocryphal or pseudo-epigraphical New Testament material and earlier fathers use symbolic language, speaking of "gates," "bars," "chains," "locks," and all the other appurtenances of what St Peter calls a "prison" (1 Pet 3.19; cf. Mt 16.18).[79] Gregory speaks only of "life" and "death," "light" and "darkness." It is here that we see Christ win the victory:

> The divine was hidden by the veil of our nature, in order that, as in the case of greedy fish, the hook of the divinity might be swallowed with the bait of the flesh, and thus when life came to dwell in death and light shone in the darkness, that which is understood as the opposite of light and life might be utterly destroyed. For it is not in the nature of darkness to remain in the presence of light, nor death to exist where life is active. (24.4)

A note of caution must be added. The centrality of the harrowing of hades in this particular account does not imply that Gregory overlooks the importance of the crucifixion (elsewhere he clearly describes its sacrificial and propitiatory character).[80] Gregory is not a systematic theologian composing a treatise on soteriology. He is the bishop of Nyssa, discovering arguments that his catechists may use to defend the fittingness of Christ's birth, death, and resurrection. Here he fashions an argument to uphold four God-befitting qualities: *goodness* in his desire to save us, *justice* at first apparently by means of ransom but then in fact by means of recompensing the deceiver with a deception in turn (and this deception itself shows

---

[79]For extensive quotations of the earliest sources and helpful theological analysis of the harrowing of hell, see Hilarion (Alfeyev), *Christ the Conqueror of Hell: The Descent into Hades from an Orthodox Perspective* (Crestwood, NY: St Vladimir's Seminary Press, 2009).

[80]See *Brill Dictionary*, 697; Riviére, *The Doctrine of the Atonement*, 1:184–85.

wisdom), and *power* by defeating death by his very being: by being life and light in hades, his presence destroys its death and darkness.

Finally, Gregory's emphasis upon the saving character of Christ's resurrection shows that he is not myopic or one-sided in his notion of salvation. Winling is surely right to point to the importance of the resurrection in the *Catechetical Discourse*,[81] and indeed, in Gregory's soteriology in general.[82] But it is striking to note that the resurrection does not receive a single treatment (another blow to the notion of a chronological structure to the work), but rather several: in the narrative, Gregory borrows Methodius' image of the clay vessel that is smashed to be refashioned (8.3, 7), a restorative image of the general resurrection without specific reference to Christ's resurrection; in the proof he describes Christ as the principle of the resurrection that enlivens the whole of humanity (16.6–9, 32.3–4; cf. Rom 5.12–21); in the conclusion our personal participation in Christ's death and resurrection is discussed in terms of baptismal mimesis (35.1–12), and our place in the general resurrection is determined by baptism (35.13–15).

Apokatastasis and the Question of Universalism

Gregory uses the word *apokatastasis* in the *Catechetical Discourse* (26.8.69, 35.13.114),[83] and the work has long been credited with the teaching that the devil will be saved. Many scholars simply cite the twenty-sixth chapter as proof of this position without further analysis or comment. But this is the final flourish of a much longer argu-

[81]Winling, *Discours*, 41–44 and Raymond Winling, "La résurrection du Christ comme principe explicatif et comme élément structurant dans le Discours catéchétique de Grégoire de Nysse," *Studia Patristica* 23 (1989): 74–80.

[82]"The Resurrection of the Lord occupies the primary place in the Nyssen's soteriology." *Brill Dictionary*, 697.

[83]The word occurs once in the New Testament (Acts 3.21), and became associated with Origen and the idea that all will be saved. But it is not always used in a technical sense, or with this meaning. For a good treatment of the word's meaning and different uses in St Gregory of Nyssa, see Morwenna Ludlow, *Universal Salvation: Eschatology in the Thought of Gregory of Nyssa and Karl Rahner* (Oxford: Oxford University Press, 2000), 38–44.

ment: based on God-befitting qualities as laid out in chapter 20 (and a recapitulation of the human condition in chapter 21), Gregory goes on to describe the ransom in 22–23, which chapter 24 reveals was a mere device by which the devil was deceived, which gave Christ access to accomplish the harrowing of hades. After an excursus in chapter 25, Gregory defends the propriety of using deception. Here he makes his famous statement. Christ destroys the devil's works:

> in the same manner, when death, and corruption, and darkness, and any other offspring of vice had grown around the inventor of evil, the approach of the divine power, like fire accomplishing the disappearance of what is against nature, benefits [our] nature by purification, though the separation is painful—therefore even the adversary himself would not dispute that what has come to pass is both just and saving, if indeed he might now come to a perception of the benefit. (26.7)

Earlier English translations rendered "any other offspring of vice had grown around the inventor of evil" (εἴ τι κακίας ἔκγονον τῷ εὑρετῇ τοῦ κακοῦ περιφυέντων) as "every other offshoot of evil had grown into *the nature* of the author of evil" (NPNF) or "all the other products of vice had attached themselves to *the nature* of the author of evil" (Srawley). But the word "nature" (φύσις) is not in the Greek. It is supplied, on etymological grounds: περιφυέντων—the aorist participle of the verb περιφύω "to grow around"—could be related to the word nature. But this is a stretch. Gregory is restating what he said before: Christ's work could claim to be not only "benefitting the one who was destroyed by these things, but also him who worked our destruction himself," because death, darkness, and corruption were destroyed, bringing about "the profit of him who is purified from these things" (26.5). This is nothing other than the harrowing of hades, the destruction of the devil's works. It is not at all obvious that the devil will come to see the destruction of the devil's works in so sanguine a light: "if indeed he might now come to a perception" is a quite weak construction. Further, the "now" situates this subjective statement in the present, focusing upon the past harrowing of hades: it is not the ineluctable future salvation of the devil after long ages of purification, as some would have it.[84] The only certain way in which the "healing of the inventor of vice himself" (26.9) takes place is through the already accomplished destruction of his works—death, darkness, and corruption—in the harrowing of hades. Whether he chooses to see this as saving and beneficial remains in doubt, especially when one reads broadly in the Nyssene corpus: the devil remains completely opposed to the saving will of God, his "one intent and endeavour it is to oppose the divine will in order *that* none *should be saved or come to the knowledge of the truth*."[85]

In chapter 35 Gregory seems to say at first that only the baptized can be saved: "It is not possible, I mean, for man to be in the resurrection without the 'washing of regeneration' [Tit 3.5]" (35.13). But soon he defines resurrection as apokatastasis. This would be a decidedly non-universalist understanding of apokatastasis, if it is limited to the baptized, but he then further clarifies: "For not all who receive a return to existence again by the resurrection return to the same life, but there is a great interval between those who have been purified and those who are in need of purification" (35.14). For those who are not baptized and have not sufficiently repented, "it is also altogether necessary for them to come to be in an appropriate [state]. . . . [T]hose who are not initiates in this purification are necessarily purified by fire" (35.14, 15). This may seem to imply a common fate for all, but we must also place this text alongside the very last words of the *Discourse*, where the author paints a far more dichotomous picture of the last things. He inverts the words of the

[84]It is not clear that the purification "through long periods . . . of those who are now lying in vice" in 26.8 refers to the devil. It clearly refers to human beings (some or all—it is not made clear), but throughout this section Gregory contrasts "the one who was destroyed" with "him who worked our destruction" (25.5). Are both lumped together here? At the close of the argument, he speaks of Christ "freeing man from vice and healing the inventor of vice himself" (26.9). Are the freeing and the healing identical actions? Even if it is one action (the harrowing of hades), does it have the same effect for man and the inventor of vice?

[85]Gregory of Nyssa, Letter 17.3 (trans. Silvas). Cf. 1 Tim 2.4

scriptural promise—"eye has not seen, nor ear heard" (1 Cor 2.9) the good things prepared for the saved—by adding: "Nor indeed is the painful life of transgressors comparable to any of the things that pain the senses here, but even though some of the punishments there are called by the names known here, the difference is not slight" (40.7). Here he describes such punishments by emphasizing their perpetuity: the fire is not quenched and the worm does not die (lit. is "endless"—ἀτελεύτητος). This unending quality is what distinguishes them from earthly fire and worms (40.7–8). Both are scriptural, dominical images. Elsewhere Gregory speaks of both fire and worm as bodily punishments for those in resurrected bodies.[86] It is difficult to harmonize endless bodily torments with universal salvation. Still, the *Catechetical Discourse* does not give an entirely unambiguous picture of Nyssene eschatology. Chapter 26 could be read as teaching the salvation of the devil (though this reading is not so clear and straightforward as many have portrayed it), but the final exhortation seems to stress the unending quality of the post-mortem punishments that are "the corresponding products of decision in [earthly] life" (40.8). Nevertheless, it has become something of a commonplace to assert that Gregory of Nyssa was assuredly a universalist who held that all, including the devil himself, will be saved.[87] To evaluate Gregory's view on apokatastasis and its place among the other fathers and the tradition of the Church, a much broader context is required. We can only sketch such a context in this introduction, briefly considering the reception history of universalism in general and of Gregory's writings in particular, and then

[86] *In Sanctum Pascha* (GNO IX:246; trans. Hall).

[87] The most extended arguments for a universalist reading of Gregory can be found in Ilaria Ramelli, *The Christian Doctrine of Apokatastasis: A Critical Assessment from the New Testament to Eriugena* (Leiden: Brill, 2013), 372–440; Ludlow, *Universal Salvation*, 21–111. But there are also scholars who deny he was a universalist, e.g., Jean Daniélou, "Apocatastase," in *L'être et le temps chez Grégoire de Nysse* (Leiden: Brill, 1970), 205–26; Mario Baghos, "Reconsidering *Apokatastasis* in St Gregory of Nyssa's *On the Soul and Resurrection* and the *Catechetical Oration*," in *Cappadocian Legacy: A Critical Appraisal*, 395–440; Michael Azkoul, *St. Gregory of Nyssa and the Tradition of the Fathers* (Lewiston, NY: The Edwin Mellen Press, 1995), 139–48.

looking at some of the important (and conflicting) evidence in the Nyssene corpus.

The mid-twentieth century witnessed a renewed interest in universalism, and a widespread attempt to rehabilitate it as an acceptable theological position.[88] Since the nineteenth century, scholars have questioned whether the Fifth Ecumenical Council (AD 553) did in fact condemn Origen. The acts, which survive only in Latin, do not describe muh discussion on Origenism, and it seems likely that the fifteen anathemas against Origen were signed beforehand at a preparatory council, which apparently won the approval of all five patriarchs at the time. Some scholars have taken this as sufficient evidence to dismiss the condemnation altogether, but the council itself accepted this pre-synod, the acts of the council include a discussion of Origen's posthumous anathematization on a regional level without disapproval, and, most importantly, the council listed Origen as a heretic in its eleventh canon at its eighth and final session on June 2, 553.[89] Further, the reception of the council is quite clear. In the Definition of Faith of the Sixth Ecumenical Council (AD 680–81) all previous councils are affirmed, including "the last, that is the Fifth holy Synod assembled in this place, against Theodore of

[88]Influential Roman Catholic theologians such as Hans Urs von Balthasar and Karl Rahner defended universalism in the twentieth century, and it continues to be both a popular and controversial subject. For recent works arguing for and against universalism, see David Bentley Hart, *That All Shall Be Saved: Heaven, Hell, and Universal Salvation* (New Haven, CT: Yale University Press, 2019); Michael J. McClymond, *The Devil's Redemption: A New History and Interpretation of Christian Universalism*, 2 vols. (Grand Rapids, MI: Baker Academic, 2018).

[89]The revisionist reading was first proposed by Diekamp in 1899. For a list of those who follow him, see Daniel Hombergen, *The Second Origenist Controversy: A New Perspective on Cyril of Scythopolis' Monastic Biographies as Historical Sources for Sixth-Century Origenism* (Rome: Centro Studi S. Anselmo, 2001), 21 n.2. Richard Price, who translated and commented on the council's acts calls these claims "tendentious" in light of the fact that Origen was "included among the heretics anathematized in the eleventh of the canons formally approved at the end of the council." *Acts of the Council of Constantinople of 553: With Related Texts on the Three Chapters Controversy* (Liverpool: Liverpool University Press, 2012), 2:280. For the text of the canon see *Acts* 2:123–24; for the fifth session's discussion of Origen's condemnation at a local council see *Acts* 1:338.

Mopsuestia, Origen, Didymus, and Evagrius."[90] Before the modern period, no one questioned that the council condemned Origenism. To this evidence we must add the general patristic witness. Brian E. Daley's *The Hope of the Early Church* is a magisterial study of patristic eschatology that includes dozens of authors and writings from the first eight centuries, written in Greek, Latin, Coptic, Syriac, and Armenian. Sixty-eight of these, from every century and in every language, affirm eternal damnation, while the list of universalists is quite short: "Origen (though a few scholars disagree), Gregory of Nyssa (also with some dissenters), Didymus the Blind, and Isaac the Syrian (in all likelihood). . . . To summarize, the support for universalism is paltry compared with opposition to it. There is not much of a universalist tradition during the first centuries of the Christian church."[91] This is a broad and nearly unanimous consensus, from an exceedingly diverse set of historical, geographical, cultural, and linguistic contexts.

Nevertheless, Gregory's purported position is often styled a "licit" universalism: the belief that all shall be saved, divested of the more mythological aspects of Origenism. It is urged that this form of universalism received tacit Church approval because Gregory, unlike Origen, is "an uncondemned universalist."[92] But such a theory must account for the specific positions articulated in the reception of the Nyssene corpus. From the fifth to the fifteenth century, three responses emerge: 1) some hold that Gregory was a universalist but reject this teaching, 2) some hold that he was not a universalist but his works were interpolated with heretical material,

---

[90]NPNF[2] 14:344.

[91]As summarized by Michael J. McClymond, "Ilaria Ramelli's *The Christian Doctrine of* Apokatastasis (2013)," in *The Devil's Ransom*, 2:1098. There are also seven authors or works who are "unclear," and two who are pantheists. Ibid.

[92]Cf. Met. Kallistos Ware, "Dare We Hope for the Salvation of All? Origen, St Gregory of Nyssa and St Isaac the Syrian Bishop" in *The Inner Kingdom,* The Collected Works of Kallistos Ware, Vol. 1 (Crestwood, NY: St Vladimir's Seminary Press, 2001), 193–215, at 205–206. The work's title is a very slightly modified form of Balthasar's *Dare We Hope That All Men Be Saved?*

and 3) some hold that he was not a universalist because apokatastasis ought to be interpreted in a non-universalist sense. No one maintains both that Gregory was a universalist and that this is an acceptable teaching.

Severus of Antioch (AD 465–538) did not accept the things Gregory says about apokatastasis, St Photius records.[93] Likewise, in the letters of Sts Barsanuphius and John, someone poses a question about apokatastasis in the Nyssene corpus (distinguishing it from the mythical aspects of Origenism): "In regard to the subject of *apokatastasis*, the holy Gregory of Nyssa himself clearly speaks about it, but not in the manner in which they say he does, namely: 'When hell ceases, humanity will return to its original condition, namely, that of pure intellects'; rather, he does in fact say that hell will cease and assume an end."[94] Barsanuphius rejects this "de-mythologized" universalism, and most of his reply concerns the question of how a holy person can still believe something false. St Mark of Ephesus likewise admits that some passages sound universalist, but he regards this as pardonable, given Gregory's historical circumstances: "At that time the doctrine was still debatable and not completely settled, and the opposing opinion not absolutely rejected, all of which came to pass during the Fifth [Ecumenical] Council."[95] Rather than trusting to a single authority, Mark seeks to "look to the common opinion of the Church and take the Divine Scriptures for rules of faith, not considering something that an individual has written privately apart from them."[96] His student Theodore Agallianus expresses the same opinion.[97]

---

[93]Photius, *Bibliotheca* 232 (PG 103:1104A). This could mean that Severus does not accept (οὐκ ἀποδέχεται) these passages as authentic, but Photius states this much more clearly in the case of Germanus, so here I take him to mean he rejects the teaching, not the textual integrity.

[94]Letter 604 (trans. Chryssavgis); Letters 600–607 all deal with Origenism.

[95]Mark of Ephesus, *First Discourse on Purgatory 11 (unpublished translation by Protodeacon Jeremiah Davis, used with kind permission). Cf. Second Discourse on Purgatory 16–18 (where he discusses the devil in Catechetical Discourse 26).*

[96]Ibid. This is similar to Photius' remarks on some western fathers who accepted the filioque (*Mystagogy of the Holy Spirit* 68).

[97]"The great teacher and father Gregory of Nyssa was carried away with the

Sts Anastasius of Sinai (died *c.* AD 700) and Germanus of Constantinople (*c.* AD 364–*c.* 740) both claimed that Gregory's works were interpolated, and Mark of Ephesus also mentions this possibility when he discusses apokatastasis.[98]

Finally, some seek to interpret Gregory's notion of apokatastasis in a non-universalist sense. Maximus was asked about apokatastasis in the Nyssene corpus, and he replied that the word had three meanings, and the "third, which Gregory of Nyssa, above all, made use of in his writings, is this, the restoration of the powers of the soul that fell into sin, returning to that for which they were created."[99] By analogy with the restoration of corruptible nature, evil must also be expunged, and "thus, by full knowledge, not by participating in the good things [τῇ ἐπιγνώσει οὐ τῇ μεθέξει τῶν ἀγαθῶν], it must recover again its powers and be restored to its original [form], such that the Creator may also be revealed as not being responsible for sin." This—"full knowledge, not by participating in the good things"—is *not* the condition of the saved, whom Maximus describes in opposite terms elsewhere: "the soul 'will experience' rather than know about [πείσεται μᾶλλον ἢ γνώσεται] 'the divine things.'"[100] St Theodore the Studite was asked a similar question, and he quoted the Confessor's words verbatim (as later Mark of Ephesus did in Florence), and then proceeded to make it

teaching of Origen about apokatastasis and the punishment of sinners . . . but subsequent teachers and the catholic Church condemned those who follow the Origenists . . . but they pardoned [συνέγνωσαν, or 'made allowance for'] the wonderful Gregory." Theodore Agallianus, *De Providentia*, in *Catalogue of the Greek Manuscripts in the Library of the Laura on Mount Athos*, ed. Sophronios Eustratiades and Spyridon, Harvard Theological Studies 12 (Cambridge, MA: Harvard University Press, 1925), 421–34, at 430 (my translation).

[98]Anastasius of Sinai, *Viae Dux* 22.3 (PG 89:289D–292A); Germanus, *apud* Photius, *Bibliotheca* 233 (PG 103:1105B–1108D); Mark of Ephesus, *First Discourse on Purgatory* 11.

[99]Maximus, *Questions and Doubts* 19 (trans. Prassas).

[100]Maximus, *Ecclesiastical Mystagogy* 23 (trans. Armstrong). This is an allusion to the Areopagite's famous phrase: "Not only learning about but experiencing divine things" (οὐ μόνον μαθών, ἀλλὰ καὶ παθών τὰ Θεῖα). *On the Divine Names* 4.22 (my translation).

even clearer in his own words that this is a description of damnation: the knowledge of the damned is "fully knowing the privation of participation."[101] He sharply distinguishes this from Origenism: it is "not Origenist, begone—for there is no communion of light with darkness, no symphony of saints with heresiarchs."[102]

But now we must turn from the reception history to Gregory himself. He makes some statements that sound as if he believes all will be saved, but he also makes others that sound as though he believes in eternal damnation (as we saw above, both occur in the *Catechetical Discourse*). This explains why a great number of scholars, looking to the former set of statements, affirm without reservation that Gregory is a universalist, while a Nyssene scholar of such repute as Daniélou states to the contrary, "One cannot say that he maintains the thesis of universal salvation."[103] As Maspero aptly put it, "The Nyssen's corpus contains explicit affirmations of the eternity of hell. At the same time, Gregory's ἀποκατάστασις appears to tend in the direction of universal salvation. In order to resolve the dilemma, it is necessary to refer to the entirety of his thought"[104] (such an ambiguity is present even in Origen).[105] This introduction is too short to weigh all the evidence, but we will briefly consider a few key examples (we have already examined the well-known passages from the *Catechetical Discourse* itself).

---

[101]Theodore the Studite, Letter 52 (PG 99:1501A; my translation); cf. Mark of Ephesus, *Second Oration on Purgatory* 18.

[102]Theodore, Letter 52 (PG 99:1501B; my translation).

[103]Daniélou, "Apocatastase," in *L'être et le temps*, 224. Daniélou goes on to affirm that "Gregory's personal contribution to the Pauline doctrine of apokatastasis consists in affirming the eschatological συμφωνία of all creatures in the confession of the glory of God [cf. Phil 2.9–11]—and in the disappearance of evil." Ibid.

[104]Maspero, "Apocatastasis," in *Brill Dictionary*, 63.

[105]"In scattered places Origen says quite clearly that he thinks all created intelligence will be restored to God at the end of time. In other places he says, equally clearly, that only souls who make the choice for God and practice the virtues God demands will come to rest in heaven. Those who do not live for God shall suffer eternally in hell or perhaps be annihilated there. If in coming years Origen's treatise on the resurrection is rediscovered, this apparent contradiction may be settled." Frederick W. Norris, "Apokatastasis," in *The Westminster Handbook to Origen*, ed. John Anthony McGuckin (Louisville, KY: Westminster John Knox Press, 2004), 59–62, at 59.

But before we turn to other passages in Gregory's writings, we ought to address those who take a more systematic approach, reading a clear universalism in the Nyssene corpus by applying certain metaphysical or ontological principles that are supposed to lead inexorably to the salvation of all. Gregory's emphasis on divine infinitude and creaturely finitude implies the corollary truth that all creaturely evil, being finite, will be exhausted and depleted in the end, which finds further support in the Nyssene notion that evil is a privation of good (though this lends itself to the doctrine of annihilationism, Gregory denies this possibility).[106] Evil's nonbeing ensures its evanescence, and the inevitable disappearance of evil is also interpreted as universal salvation.[107] But as we will see below, one of Gregory's clearest statements about damnation comes immediately after an equally clear affirmation of evil as a privation. Further, two general cautions ought to be observed. First, the disappearance of evil and the victory of the good is also accepted by those who are not universalists: those who affirm eternal damnation also believe that God will be victorious and evil will be destroyed. It is a mistake to conflate the destruction of evil with universal salvation. Maximus and Theodore the Studite addressed this long ago: evil will indeed be destroyed, but for the damned this will entail only a knowledge of the good things of the age to come, and not a participation in those good things.[108] Second, it is a mistake to attempt to extract systematic principles from the Nyssene corpus and to press them to logical conclusions that Gregory himself does not make explicit. He is not a "systematic" theologian in the modern mold.[109]

---

[106]*On the Inscriptions of the Psalms* 2.16.283 (GNO V:174–75); *In illud: Tunc et ipse* (GNO III/2:26).

[107]"The strongest and perhaps most convincing argument of Gregory in support of universal restoration is the finiteness of evil as non-existent . . . [as opposed to] the infiniteness of goodness and love as God's nature." Constantine Tsirplanis, "The Concept of Universal Salvation in Saint Gregory of Nyssa," *Patristic and Byzantine Review* 28 (2010): 79–94, at 82.

[108]See pp. 45–46 above.

[109]"Ultimately, the factor which makes Gregory neither a 'Platonist' nor an 'eclectic' is a coherent nucleus of theological views most of which are directly dependent

The passages that seem to most clearly articulate universal salvation and eternal damnation are both scripturally grounded. Unsurprisingly, the passages of Scripture that lend themselves to a universalist reading (especially 1 Cor 15.24–28 and Phil 2.10–11) sound universalist in Gregory,[110] and those that seem to speak clearly of eternal damnation (Mt 25.45–46, 26.24; Mk 9.48; Lk 16.24–26) likewise sound this way in the Nyssene corpus.[111]

According to Ilaria Ramelli, the passage that shows "most unequivocally that apokatastasis in his view entails universal salvation"[112] occurs in a treatise that seeks to refute a subordinationist reading of 1 Corinthians 15.28. Here Gregory writes, "And since everything that comes to be in him [i.e., Christ] is saved, salvation is interpreted by subjection, as the psalm instructs us to understand [Ps 61.2–3 LXX]. Accordingly, we learn in this passage of the apostle's letter to believe that nothing is outside what is to be saved" (μηδὲν ἔξω τῶν σῳζομένων).[113] The work is an anti-subordinationist polemic, not an eschatological speculation, but it builds upon Origen's exegesis of the same passage,[114] and its claims must be analyzed at greater length elsewhere. Ludlow lists two most telling passages, the first of which speaks of an eschatological feast of tabernacles:

on Scripture. Philosophical and scientific language . . . may have served an apologetic function. . . . But one can say that Scripture is the foundation of all Gregory's thought and that he used both philosophical and scientific concepts to express, clarify, explain, and (to a certain extent) systematize it. . . . Gregory is above all a theologian: attempts to see him as a philosopher usually end up frustrated by his lack of a philosophical 'system.'" Ludlow, *Universal Salvation*, 26.

[110]E.g., *In illud: Tunc et ipse* and certain sections of *On the Soul and the Resurrection*. Ramelli sees apokatastasis "treated most extensively" in these two works. Ramelli, *Christian Doctrine of* Apokatastasis, 374.

[111]E.g. passages in *On Infants' Early Deaths, On the Soul and the Resurrection, Concerning Almsgiving,* and *On the Beatitudes.*

[112]Ramelli, *The Christian Doctrine of* Apokatastasis, 436.

[113]*In illud: Tunc et ipse Filius* (GNO III/2:20–21; trans. Greer).

[114]For its relation to Origen, see Ilaria Ramelli, "In Illud: Tunc et ipse Filius . . . : Gregory of Nyssa's Exegesis, Its Derivations from Origen, and Early Patristic Interpretations Related to Origen's," *Studia Patristica* 44 (2010): 259–74.

Since all intervening barricades by which our vice has fenced us off from what lies within the veil are eventually to be done away with (cf. Ephesians 2.14), when the tabernacle of our nature is set up again in the resurrection, and all the indwelling corruption of vice has vanished from the things that exist, then the common feast will be instituted around God by those who have thickened again through the resurrection. One and the same gladness will be set before all, with no difference any longer dividing off the rational nature from an equal participation in the good, for those who through vice are now outside shall then be admitted within the inner shrine of the divine blessedness.[115]

This must be weighed along with other statements in the same work, some of which are similar but more tenatative:

And that the Apostle listed this nature [i.e., demons], some say [ἥνπερ φασὶ], among the things under the earth, signifying in that passage that when evil shall some day be made to vanish through the long courses of ages, nothing shall be left outside the good, but that even from these shall arise in one accord the confession of Christ's Lordship [Phil 2.10–11].[116]

Other passages in the same work seem to speak clearly of eternal damnation. The second passage that Ludlow emphasizes is also tentative, reporting what someone *might* say about apokatastasis:

Perhaps someone [τάχα τις], taking his departure from the fact that after three days of distress in darkness the Egyptians did share in the light, might be led [ἀγάγοι] to perceive the final restoration [ἀποκατάστασιν] which is expected to take place

---

[115]*On the Soul and the Resurrection* 10.23–24 (trans. Silvas).

[116]*On the Soul and the Resurrection* 4.17 (trans. Silvas). This is said by Macrina, a further distancing (i.e., Gregory records that his sister affirmed that some held this view). Further, what follows immediately after this in the text seems to indicate that perdition is indeed everlasting. See below, pp. 51–52.

later in the kingdom of heaven of those who have suffered condemnation in Gehenna.[117]

Gregory expresses no analogous reticence when discussing the eternal fate of Judas in his treatise *On Infants' Early Deaths*. This work,
unlike many others, is primarily concerned with the postmortem
fate of different types of people, focusing, as the title makes clear, primarily on infants. Here Gregory contrasts the innocence of infants
who have never sinned with the worst sinners, especially Judas:

> Certainly, in comparison with one who has lived all his life in
> sin, not only the innocent babe but even one who has never
> come into the world at all will be blessed. We learn as much
> too in the case of Judas, from the sentence pronounced upon
> him in the Gospels [Mt 26.24]; namely, that when we think of
> such men, that which never existed is to be preferred to that
> which has existed in such sin. For, as to the latter, on account of
> the depth of the ingrained evil, the chastisement in the way of
> purgation [ἡ διὰ τῆς καθάρσεως κόλασις] will be extended into
> infinity [εἰς ἄπειρον παρατείνεται]; but as for what has never
> existed, how can any torment touch it?[118]

Two things must be observed: 1) Gregory bases this judgment upon
a scriptural, dominical assertion, and 2) he describes Judas' punishment in terms of "infinity" (ἄπειρον). Arguments that ἄπειρον does
not mean "infinity" here do not remedy the situation,[119] because
this is not the only evidence to be weighed. The scriptural reference
can hardly be pressed to support the notion that Judas will be saved
after an indefinite period of purgative chastisement. How can non-

---

[117]*Life of Moses* 2.82 (trans. Ferguson and Malherbe). Recall the tentative language in *Catechetical Discourse* 26.7: "if indeed he might now come to a perception
of the benefit."

[118]*On Infants' Early Deaths* (GNO III/2, 87; NPNF[2] 5:378).

[119]Ludlow accepts a literal meaning of "infinity," but claims that it is intended
as "hyberbole, emphasizing the extreme duration of the punishment" (*Universal
Salvation*, 83), while Ramelli asserts that εἰς ἄπειρον ought to be translated as "to the
unlimited," "to an indefinite duration" (*Apokatastasis*, 440 n.368).

existence be preferable to Judas' fate unless he is forever damned? Surely to be saved is better than not to exist. How can non-existence be preferred to the infinite increase of joy and grace and beatitude from glory to glory that epektasis promises, even if painful purgation marks the beginning of this progress? Gregory could seek to explain the Lord's words—"But woe to that man by whom the Son of Man is betrayed! It would have been better for that man if he had not been born" (Mt 26.24)—in some other way, but he twice paraphrases them accurately, without seeking to mitigate their force or meaning.

In *On the Soul and the Resurrection* Gregory seems to speak quite clearly about the eternal consequences of our freely chosen paths, in a Greek construction that is even more difficult to read otherwise: "In his love for man he [God] gave him the power to choose which of the two he would have, I mean the good or the bad, either in this short and fleeting life or in those endless ages whose boundary is infinity [τοὺς ἀτελευτήτους ἐκείνους αἰῶνας, ὧν πέρας ἡ ἀπειρία ἐστίν]."[120] It is in light of this that some people avail themselves of the better part: "But for those who order their own life here with discerning and sober reasoning, enduring in this brief life things painful to the senses and storing up the good for the age that is to come, the result is that better lot which is co-extensive with eternal life."[121] But the converse is also true. This passage explicates the parable of the rich man and Lazarus, and the present section interprets the words: "You during your life in the flesh received your share of good things" (Lk 16.25, as quoted by Gregory). Here the chasm separating the two postmortem states takes on a decidedly non-universalist meaning:

> This therefore, in my opinion, is the "gulf" [τὸ χάσμα] which does not come of a rift in the earth, but is made of those decisions during this life which are divided into opposing inclinations. For anyone who has once chosen pleasure in this life and has not cured his recklessness through repentance, renders inaccessible

---

[120]*On the Soul and the Resurrection* 5.35 (PG 46:81C; trans. Silvas).
[121]*On the Soul and the Resurrection* 5.38 (PG 46:84A; trans. Silvas).

to himself the country of the good hereafter [ἄβατον ἑαυτῷ μετὰ ταῦτα τὴν τῶν ἀγαθῶν χώραν ἐργάζεται], for he has dug by himself this impassible necessity like a yawning and unbridgeable abyss [τὴν ἀδιάβατον ταύτην ἀνάγκην, καθάπερ τι βάραθρον ἀχανές τε καὶ ἀπαρόδευτον καθ' ἑαυτοῦ διορύξας].[122]

For such people, "The privation of the good now manifest to them becomes a flame slowly burning the soul, so that it craves but does not obtain the consolation of one drop of that sea of the good engulfing the holy."[123] There is no apparent limit to this condition. Or rather, the limitless limit was enunciated a little earlier in the text: "those endless ages whose boundary is infinity [τοὺς ἀτελευτήτους ἐκείνους αἰῶνας, ὧν πέρας ἡ ἀπειρία ἐστίν]."[124]

This is a marked precedent in the Nyssene corpus: the saint's sternest rebukes, which seem to point quite clearly toward the eternality of damnation, are addressed toward those who do not help the poor (he has scriptural, dominical grounds, especially Matthew 25.31–46 and Luke 16.19–31): "Do not despise the offerings of the poor as unworthy. . . . The good which we expect is stored up; the doorkeepers of the kingdom [of heaven] open the gates of divine goodness and close [κλείοντες] them to the intractable and to misanthropes. They are both severe accusers and trustworthy advocates offering pleas and accusations not by words but from the evidence of judgment, for [Christ] scrutinizes the hearts of men and cries out his message with the utmost clarity (Acts 1.24; 15.8). The divine preaching which you have often heard prescribes a fearful judgment."[125] Gregory then dramatically describes the scene, drawing upon the division of the sheep and goats in Matthew 25, and continues: "There the judge speaks, and the King answers those who have been generous: for those who have lived the best life the enjoyment of the kingdom [of heaven], for the misanthropes and the wicked

[122]*On the Soul and the Resurrection* 5.39 (PG 46:84B; trans. Silvas).

[123]*On the Soul and the Resurrection* 5.42 (PG 46:84C; trans. Silvas, modified).

[124]*On the Soul and the Resurrection* 5.35 (PG 46:81C; trans. Silvas).

[125]*On Almsgiving* (GNO XI: 98–99; trans. McCambley)

the punishment of fire and this extending through eternity [τιμωρία πυρὸς καὶ αὕτη διαιωνίζουσα]."[126] He strikes the same tone in a homily against usury: "Love man, not riches, and resist this type of sin. . . . You hinder the road of life [ἀποφράττετε ζωῆς ὁδόν] and close the doors to the kingdom [κλείετε τῆς βασιλείας τὰς θύρας]. Fascination with trivial matters makes your ears tingle and subjects you to eternal grief [αἰωνίου λύπης]."[127] The homily closes with a grim vision: "Then with what eyes will you see what is condemned to death at the resurrection [κατὰ τὸν καιρὸν τῆς ἀναστάσεως... τὸν φονευθέντα]? You will come to the judgment seat of Christ where usuries are not counted but where lives are judged."[128] Gregory then compares usurers to the wicked servant in the parable, who would not forgive his fellow servant's debt (Mt 18.32–34), and concludes, "Then an ineffective repentance [ἀνόνητος μεταμέλεια] accompanied by heavy groans and the inevitability of punishment [κόλασις ἀπαραίτητος] will seize you."[129] Finally, we must consider Gregory's fifth homily on the Beatitudes, an exegesis of Matthew 5.7: "Blessed are the merciful [ἐλεήμονες], for they will receive mercy [ἐλεηθήσονται]." In Greek this is related to almsgiving (ἐλεημοσύνη), and here Gregory plays on this dual sense, reading Matthew 5.7 in light of Matthew 25.31–46. He affirms the converse of the beatitude: cursed are those who are not merciful (who do not give alms), for they shall not receive mercy. Near the halfway point of the homily, Gregory clearly states the principle that evil has no positive being of its own: "evil exists as soon as it is chosen, present in being the moment we choose it. By itself with its own proper being apart from free will, evil is never found to exist."[130] And it is precisely our free will that can cut us off from mercy: we reap what we sow, and all is reflected back to us as clearly and inexorably as a

[126]Ibid. (GNO IX:99–100).
[127]*Against Usury* (GNO IX:196; trans. McCambley, altered).
[128]Ibid. (GNO IX:204).
[129]Ibid.
[130]*Beatitudes* 5.5 (GNO VII/2:129; trans. Hall, modified).

mirror's reflection.[131] The vivid and startling language at the close
of the homily must be carefully weighed when one considers claims
for Gregory's purported universalism: "It is believed, and rightly
believed, that all humanity will stand before the judgment-seat of
Christ, for each to get the consequences of what he has done in the
body, whether good or bad" (2 Cor 5.10), and the criterion is clear:
"In both cases he uses a word which points them out, as if it were
a finger to make the reality known: 'Inasmuch as you did it to one
of these the least of my brothers.'" (Mt 25.40).[132] The application
of this principle is fearful. On the last day, "the whole human race"
will be "all agog with fear and hope about the future, often wavering between one expected outcome and the other . . . [even] those
who have lived with a clear conscience are distrustful of the future,
seeing others dragged off to that miserable darkness by their bad
conscience, which acts as executioner," and those who showed no
mercy will be shown none: "The one however who has assiduously
hidden away his wealth . . . if he is dragged head-first towards the
fire of darkness, while all those who have in this life experienced his
harshness and brutality reproach him with it and say" (in what fol-

---

[131]"Two things clearly demonstrate the power of autonomy and free will . . .
the fact that all depends on the freedom of choice which we possess, whether good
or bad, and that the divine judgment, following with impartial and just verdict the
results of our purpose, confers on each person whatever he has personally provided
as his own. . . . Just as accurate mirrors shew the reflections of faces to be the same
as the faces themselves . . . so the just judgment of God treats our attitudes with total
fairness, using our own to give us back in return the same as it finds in us. 'Come,' he
says, 'ye blessed,' and 'Go, ye accursed' (Mt 25.34, 41). . . . The rich man, relaxing in
luxury, had no mercy on the poor man (Lk 16.19–31). . . . It was not that a single drop
would be missed from the great fountain of paradise, but that *the moisture of mercy
is incompatible with hardness of heart.* 'What has light in common with darkness?' (2
Cor 6.14) 'Whatever a man sows,' it says, 'such shall he also reap; for the one who sows
for the flesh from the flesh shall reap destruction, while the one who sows for the spirit
from the spirit shall reap eternal life' (cf. Gal 6.7–8). The sowing is, I believe, human
choice, and the harvest is what you get back for your choice. Plentiful is the crop of
good things for those who chose such a sowing, irksome the thorn-gathering for those
who planted thorny seeds in their life. A person must reap exactly what he has sown;
it cannot be otherwise." *Beatitudes* 5.5 (GNO VII/2:129–31; Hall trans.).

[132]*Beatitudes* 5.7 (GNO VII/2:133; trans. Hall).

lows, Gregory inverts another of Christ's sayings: those who "make friends with the mammon of unrighteousness," i.e., give alms, will be received into "eternal dwellings" [Lk 16.9], but those who fail to give alms will receive no welcome into the eternal dwellings from those on whom they had no mercy):

> 'Remember that you received your good things in your lifetime [Lk 16.25]. You locked away mercy in your safes along with your wealth and abandoned kindness for the sake of land; you did not acquire the charity you need for life here. You cannot have what you did not get; you do not find what you did not save up; you do not collect what you did not spread about; you do not reap where you planted no seeds. Your harvest matches your sowing; you sowed bitterness, so reap its sheaves. You prized want of mercy, so take what you have loved; you looked not with compassion, you will get no merciful looks; you ignored suffering, you will be ignored as you perish [περιοφθήσῃ ἀπολλύμενος]; you fled from mercy, mercy will flee from you; you shunned the poor, you will be shunned by the one who became poor for my sake.' If this kind of thing should be said, where will be his gold? Where will be his splendid things? Where will be the assurance affixed to treasures with seals? Where will be the guard-dogs assigned to their nightly watch, the weapons made ready against conspirators, the description listed in the books? What use will they be against weeping and grinding of teeth? Who will illuminate the darkness, who quench the flame, who ward off the undying worm? Let us then take note, my brothers, of the voice of the Lord, who has taught us so much about the future in few words, in Christ Jesus our Lord, to whom be glory and power for ever and ever. Amen.[133]

Clearly evidence can be marshaled for more than one Nyssene eschatology. But perhaps this is unsurprising, if we recall that the question of universalism itself was unsettled in his time, as Mark

[133]*Beatitudes* 5.8 (GNO VII/2:134–36; trans. Hall).

of Ephesus noted. This could be compared to Gregory's Christological statements: by later standards they sometimes seem to err
in opposite directions, though at times they do conform to the
Chalcedonian definition. In the late fourth century there was no
officially accepted or rejected articulation of the doctrine, and he
expressed himself rather freely, and perhaps, in the eyes of later ages,
imprecisely. Likewise, when Gregory exegetes every knee bowing
and every tongue confessing in Philippians 2 and God being "all in
all" in 1 Corinthians 15—both of which can sound universalist—he
too sounds universalist, but when he turns to the sheep and the goats
in Matthew 25 or to Lazarus and the rich man in Luke 16—both passages that seem to teach eternal damnation—he too seems to affirm
the everlasting condition of the damned. Perhaps he was untroubled
to sound ambiguous on the matter, since both possibilities remained
open at the time (as we saw above, this was no longer considered
to be the case after the Fifth Ecumenical Council, and the broad
consensus had never regarded the question as open). But this con-
textual argument will not satisfy all. Many urge that Gregory's whole
"system" tends toward salvation. But this is appropriate and to be
expected. He clearly accepts that this is God's will for all people, and
he frequently quotes St Paul to this effect: God "wills for all men to
be saved and come to the knowledge of the truth" (1 Tim 2.4; no one
has ever read Gregory as teaching double predestination). The real
question is: are people free to reject God's will and, consequently,
salvation? Freedom is at the heart of Gregory's notion of the image
of God within us.[134] Some urge that Gregory was a moral intellec-
tualist—i.e., one who holds that people only ever do wrong out of
error, and thus those who understand what is good will choose the
good—and, as such, his notion of freedom precludes the possibility
of rejecting God's saving will once we understand the choice properly (though even Plato's Socrates, who is indelibly associated with
intellectualism, believed some would be eternally damned).[135] But

---

[134]*Catechetical Discourse* 5.9–10; *On the Making of Man* 16.11.

[135]Ramelli, *The Christian Doctrine of* Apokatastasis, 123–24, 178, 272, 305, 306,

in the *Catechetical Discourse* Gregory consistently points to the fact that Adam and Eve "willingly" (ἑκουσίως; 7.4, 21.5, 22.2)[136] chose sin and succumbed to the devil's temptation. They were not simply victims of deception.

Finally, it is possible to reject universalism without rejecting all of Gregory's insights. God wills for all to be saved, and to be saved is to be truly human, to fulfill the image within us and attain to the "measure of the stature of the fullness of Christ" (Eph 4.13). In this sense, all true humanity, the whole *anthropos* foreseen by God at the beginning (as described in *On the Making of Man* 16.16–18), will indeed be saved. Those who reject salvation reject their own humanity, in the deepest sense. God will be all in all, but he is also a consuming fire, and, as Gregory's brother Basil put it: "I believe that the fire prepared in punishment for the devil and his angels [Mt 25.41] is divided by the voice of the Lord [cf. Ps 28.7], in order that, since there are two capacities in fire, the burning and the illuminating, the fierce and punitive part of the fire may wait for those who deserve to burn, while its illuminating and radiant part may be allotted for the enjoyment of those who are rejoicing."[137] God will be all in all: St Peter said that in the apokatastasis, the "times of refreshment" will come "from the presence of the Lord" (Acts 3.20–21), and St Paul affirmed that at the very same time "when the Lord Jesus is revealed from heaven with his mighty angels in flaming fire, inflicting vengeance on those who do not know God and on those who do not obey the gospel of our Lord Jesus, they will suffer the punishment of eternal destruction from the presence of the Lord" (2 Thess 1.8–9). Just as the presence of Christ harrowed hades, his presence itself is heaven or hell to those who accept or reject him. As Gregory put it: "To the

387–88, 427–29, 438 n.365, 481, 820; cf. Ludlow, *Universal Salvation*, 95–111. Cf. Plato, *Republic* 615e3; *Phaedo* 113e2; *Gorgias* 525c2.

[136]He uses the same term to describe those who "willingly" (ἑκουσίως) rejected Peter's preaching on the day of Pentecost, in a section dedictated to defending free will.

[137]Basil the Great, Homily 13.6, On Psalm 28 (PG 29:297A; trans. Way), cf. *Hexameron* 6.3; Gregory Palamas, Homily 24.7.

one who has lived without sin there is no darkness, no worm, no
Gehenna, no fire, nor any other of these fearful names and things. . . .
Since then in the same place evil comes to one but not to the other,
the difference of free choices distinguishing each from the other, it
is evident that nothing evil can come into existence apart from our
free choice."[138]

The Greek Text and the Translation

The first printed edition of the Greek text of *Catechetical Discourse*
was published in Paris in 1615. A 1638 reprint of this edition was
used for Migne's text in *Patrologia Graeca*. It drew on three manuscripts and was quite corrupt, with several lacunae and a large
interpolation at the end. In 1838 Krabinger published a critical text
in Munich, which greatly improved on the editio princeps, using
three manuscripts of the *Catechetical Discourse* and three manuscripts of Euthymius Zigabenus' *Panoplia Dogmatica* (which quotes
the *Discourse* extensively). The Nicene and Post-Nicene Fathers
translation uses this text. In 1903 John Herbert Srawley published a
critical edition with Cambridge, using fourteen manuscripts of the
Discourse and seven of the *Panoplia*. Finally, in 1996 Mühlenberg
published a critical text in the *Gregorii Nysseni Opera* series, using
fifty-nine manuscripts of the *Discourse*, along with material from the
Panoplia, Theodoret of Cyrus, Leontius of Byzantium, Anastasius of
Sinai, and other authors. The Sources Chrétiennes volume uses this
Greek text.

This volume uses Srawley's text, while accepting most of the
readings that Mühlenberg favors in the critical text. Every significant
difference between the two texts is indicated in the apparatus. I provide the PG, Srawley, and GNO page numbers in the margins, and
the line divisions follow the Sources Chrétiennes volume's layout of
Mühlenberg's text (facilitating reference to the *Thesaurus Linguae
Graecae*, which uses the SC text and its line numbers). At times, to

---

[138]Gregory of Nyssa, *Life of Moses* 2.88 (trans. Malherbe and Ferguson).

match the English paragraph divisions, a line of Greek is broken; this is marked with em dashes, and the second half begins in line with where it broke off above (this does not change the numbering—these two halves are still counted as one line). The GNO line numbers are indicated in subscripts within the text (at the beginning of each word that begins a new line). I have retained the division into forty chapters, though it is not original, and I have included the chapter subdivisions used by Méridier in his 1908 Greek-French edition.

This is the fourth English translation of the *Catechetical Discourse*.[139] The translation strives first of all for accuracy, rendering Gregory's complex sentences as directly as possible, and then for ease of reading and comprehension. Finally, I attempt to convey the beauty of the original, worthy of the consummate rhetorician who wrote it. I hope and pray that I have accurately and aptly translated the *Catechetical Discourse*, that strong stream flowing from the great "river of words," "the star of Nyssa."[140]

---

[139] *The Great Catechism*, trans. William Moore and Henry Austin Wilson (NPNF² 5:471–509); *The Catechetical Oration of St. Gregory of Nyssa*, trans. John Herbert Srawley (London: Society for Promoting Christian Knowledge, 1917); *An Address on Religious Instruction*, trans. Cyril C. Richardson, in *Christology of the Later Fathers*, ed. Edward R. Hardy and Cyril C. Richardson (Louisville, KY: The Westminster Press, 1954), 268–325. Richardson is the least literal, by design: "The attempt has been made to present the exact sense in fluent English, by abbreviating the original sentence structure and by occasionally omitting the synonyms." *Christology of the Later Fathers*, 246. I wholeheartedly endorse Richardson's evaluation of Srawley's translation: "Srawley's rendering has been of considerable aid to the present editor. It is extremely accurate, even frequently retaining the lengthy and rhetorical sentence of the original." Ibid., 252.

[140] Sophronius of Jerusalem, quoted by Photius, *Bibliotheca* 231; Nicephorus Callistus, *Historia ecclesiastica* 11.19.

ΤΟΥ ΕΝ ΑΓΙΟΙΣ ΠΑΤΡΟΣ ΗΜΩΝ
ΓΡΗΓΟΡΙΟΥ
ΕΠΙΣΚΟΠΟΥ ΝΥΣΣΗΣ
ΛΟΓΟΣ ΚΑΤΗΧΗΤΙΚΟΣ

ΠΡΟΛΟΓΟΣ

GNO 5; PG 9;
Sr 1) Ὁ τῆς κατηχήσεως λόγος ἀναγκαῖος μέν ἐστι τοῖς
₂προεστηκόσι τοῦ μυστηρίου τῆς εὐσεβείας, ὡς ἂν πληθύ-
₃νοιτο τῇ προσθήκῃ τῶν σῳζομένων ἡ ἐκκλησία, τοῦ κατὰ
₄τὴν διδαχὴν πιστοῦ λόγου τῇ ἀκοῇ τῶν ἀπίστων προσα-
5 γομένου. ₅Οὐ μὴν ὁ αὐτὸς τῆς διδασκαλίας τρόπος ἐπὶ ₆πάντων
(Sr 2) ἁρμόσει τῶν προσιόντων τῷ λόγῳ, ἀλλὰ κατὰ | ₇τὰς τῶν θρησ-
κειῶν διαφορὰς μεθαρμόζειν προσήκει καὶ ₈τὴν κατήχησιν,
πρὸς τὸν αὐτὸν μὲν ὁρῶντας τοῦ λόγου ₉σκοπὸν, οὐχ ὁμοιο-
τρόπως δὲ ταῖς κατασκευαῖς ἐφ᾽ ₁₀ἑκάστου χρωμένους. (2) Ἄλλαις

Title: GNO omits ΤΟΥ ΕΝ ΑΓΙΟΙΣ ΠΑΤΡΟΣ ΗΜΩΝ; PG also includes a
longer reading at the end Ο ΜΕΓΑΣ / ΕΝ ΚΑΦΑΛΑΙΟΙΣ ΤΕΣΣΑΡΑΚΟΝΤΑ
ΔΙΗΡΗΜΕΝΟΣ (the Great [Catechetical Discourse] / divided into forty chapters) |
9 χρωμένους GNO : κεχρημένους Srawley

CATECHETICAL DISCOURSE
OF OUR FATHER AMONG THE SAINTS
GREGORY
THE BISHOP OF NYSSA

PROLOGUE

Catechetical Discourse: One Aim, Different Arguments

The discourse of catechesis is necessary for those who preside[1] over "the mystery of piety,"[2] so that the Church may be increased by the "addition of those being saved,"[3] while "the word of faith in accordance with teaching"[4] is brought to the hearing of unbelievers. Indeed the same manner of teaching will not be suitable for all who approach the word,[5] but the catechesis must also be made to suit the differences of religions, looking to the same aim of the discourse, but not using proofs[6] in the same manner for each. (2) For the Judaizer

[1]I.e., the bishops, who instructed catechumens and the newly illumined, or those appointed by the bishop to do so. In his famous letter on pilgrimages, St Gregory refers to "those who preside [τοῖς προεστῶσι] over the holy churches of Jerusalem" (Letter 2.12). St Justin Martyr (*First Apology* 67) likewise refers to the one who "presides" over the eucharistic assembly (ὁ προεστώς). Sometimes Gregory uses the word in a more general sense (e.g., to describe Jewish leaders below at 19).

[2]1 Tim 3.16
[3]Cf. Acts 2.47
[4]Tit 1.9
[5]Or the "discourse" (τῷ λόγῳ), but here most likely "word" in the New Testament sense: the content of the gospel proclamation (cf. Mt 13.19–23; Mk 2.2, 4.14–20, 4.33, 16.20; Lk 1.2, 5.1, 8.11–15, 11.28; Jn 8.31, 14.24; etc.).

[6]The word is used here as a technical term in classical rhetoric: the proof (κατασκευή) is the heart of an oration or treatise. For more on the *Discourse's* rhetorical background, see introduction pp. 20–24.

10 γὰρ ὑπολήψεσιν ὁ ἰουδαΐζων 11προείληπται καὶ τῷ ἑλληνισμῷ
συζῶν ἑτέραις, ὅτε 12Ἀνόμοιος καὶ ὁ Μανιχαῖος, καὶ οἱ κατὰ
Μαρκίωνα καὶ 13Οὐαλεντῖνον καὶ Βασιλείδην καὶ ὁ λοιπὸς κατά-
λογος τῶν 14κατὰ τὰς αἱρέσεις πλανωμένων ἰδίαις ἕκαστος ὑπο-
λήψει 15προειλημμένοι ἀναγκαίαν ποιοῦσι τὴν πρὸς τὰς ἐκεί-
15 νων 16ὑπονοίας μάχην· κατὰ γὰρ τὸ εἶδος τῆς νόσου καὶ τὸν
(GNO 6) 17τρόπον τῆς θεραπείας προσαρμοστέον. (3) Οὐ τοῖς αὐτοῖς | θερα-
πεύσεις τοῦ Ἕλληνος τὴν πολυθεΐαν καὶ τοῦ Ἰουδαίου 2τὴν περὶ
τὸν μονογενῆ Θεὸν ἀπιστίαν, οὐδὲ ἀπὸ τῶν 3αὐτῶν τοῖς κατὰ
τὰς αἱρέσεις πεπλανημένοις ἀνατρέψεις 4τὰς ἠπατημένας περὶ
20 (Sr 3) τῶν δογμάτων μυθοποιΐας· οὐ γὰρ 5δι’ | ὧν ἄν τις ἐπανορ-
(PG 12) θώσαιτο τὸν | Σαβέλλιον, διὰ τῶν αὐτῶν 6ὠφελήσει καὶ τὸν
Ἀνόμοιον, οὐδὲ ἡ πρὸς τὸν Μανιχαῖον 7μάχη καὶ τὸν Ἰουδαῖον
ὀνίνησιν, ἀλλὰ χρή, καθὼς 8εἴρηται, πρὸς τὰς προλήψεις τῶν
ἀνθρώπων βλέπειν καὶ 9κατὰ τὴν ἐγκειμένην ἑκάστῳ πλάνην
25 ποιεῖσθαι τὸν λόγον, 10ἀρχάς τινας καὶ προτάσεις εὐλόγους ἐφ’
ἑκάστης διαλέξεως 11προβαλλόμενον, ὡς ἂν διὰ τῶν παρ’ ἀμφο-
τέροις 12ὁμολογουμένων ἐκκαλυφθείη κατὰ τὸ ἀκόλουθον ἡ 13ἀλή-
θεια.

has presupposed one set of suppositions[7] and the one living in Hellenism different ones, while the Anomoean and the Manichean, and the followers of Marcion, and of Valentinus, and Basilides, and the remaining catalogue of those erring in heresies, each presupposing their own suppositions, make it necessary to do battle with their conjectures. For the manner of healing must be suited to the form of the illness.[8] (3) You will not heal the Greek's polytheism and the Jew's unbelief regarding "the only-begotten God"[9] with the same [arguments], nor for those who have erred in heresies will you overthrow the delusions about [their] teachings' made-up myths from the same [arguments]. For you will not also profit the Anomoean with the same [arguments] by which someone might correct the Sabellian, nor does the battle with the Manichean benefit the Jew.[10] But it is necessary, as has been said, to look to men's presuppositions, and for the discussion to be made according to the error in which each is involved, putting forward certain principles and reasonable propositions for each dialogue, so that through the things admitted by both sides the truth may be unveiled in order.[11]

[7]For the philosophical and rhetorical senses of the word "supposition" (ὑπόληψις) and "presupposition" (πρόληψις), see introduction, pp. 25–27.

[8]St Gregory frequently refers to the work of the polemicist as both "battle" and "healing" (e.g., *Against Eunomius*, Letter to Peter and 1.9 [NPNF 5:44] that speaks of the "sword" of St Basil healing the heretic). Cf. *Letter to Letoius* (GNO III/5), which sees sin as a sickness that must be healed.

[9]Jn 1.18 (variant reading)

[10]This is a series of pairs of opposite errors.

[11]"Order" consistently translates ἀκολουθία in its various forms. This is an important concept for Gregory. Together with his notion of "aim" (σκοπός), it defines the way he reads and writes. A text follows a certain order to accomplish its aim. Here, the order is primarily logical, and the catechists' aim is refuting objections and convincing potential converts in order to bring them to the faith. See "*Akolouthia*" in *Brill Dictionary*, 14–20; "*Skopos*," ibid., 681–82; Daniélou, "Enchaînement" in *L'être et le temps*, 18–50.

Α’

(4) ₁₄Οὐκοῦν ὅταν πρός τινα τῶν ἑλληνιζόντων ἡ διάλεξις ᾖ,
30 καλῶς ἂν ἔχοι ταύτην ποιεῖσθαι τοῦ λόγου τὴν ἀρχήν, ₁₆πότερον
εἶναι τὸ θεῖον ὑπείληφεν, ἢ τῷ τῶν ἀθέων συμφέρεται ₁₇δόγ-
(Sr 4) ματι. Εἰ μὲν οὖν μὴ εἶναι λέγοι, ἐκ | τῶν **τεχνικῶς** ₁₈**καὶ σοφῶς**
κατὰ τὸν κόσμον οἰκονομουμένων ₁₉προσαχθήσεται πρὸς τὸ διὰ
τούτων εἶναί τινα **δύναμιν** τὴν ₂₀ἐν τούτοις διαδεικνυμένην καὶ
35 τοῦ παντὸς ὑπερκειμένην ₂₁ὁμολογῆσαι· εἰ δὲ τὸ μὲν εἶναι μὴ
ἀμφιβάλλοι, εἰς πλῆθος ₂₂δὲ θεῶν ταῖς ὑπονοίαις ἐκφέροιτο,
(GNO 7) τοιαύτη χρησόμεθα | πρὸς αὐτὸν τῇ ἀκολουθίᾳ, (5) πότερον
τέλειον ἢ ἐλλιπὲς ἡγεῖται ₂τὸ θεῖον. Τοῦ δὲ κατὰ τὸ εἰκὸς τὴν
τελειότητα προσμαρτυροῦντος ₃τῇ θείᾳ φύσει, τὸ διὰ πάντων
40 αὐτὸν τῶν ₄ἐνθεωρουμένων τῇ θεότητι τέλειον ἀπαιτήσομεν,
ὡς ἂν μὴ ₅σύμμικτον ἐκ τῶν ἐναντίων θεωροῖτο τὸ θεῖον, ἐξ
ἐλλιποῦς ₆καὶ τελείου. Ἀλλ’ εἴτε κατὰ τὴν δύναμιν, εἴτε κατὰ
₇τὴν τοῦ ἀγαθοῦ ἐπίνοιαν, εἴτε κατὰ τὸ σοφόν τε καὶ ἄφθαρτον
₈καὶ ἀΐδιον καὶ εἴ τι ἄλλο θεοπρεπὲς νόημα τῇ θεωρίᾳ ₉προσ-

37 χρησόμεθα GNO : χρησώμεθα Srawley | 40 ἀπαιτήσομεν GNO : ἀπαιτήσωμεν
Srawley | 43 ἐπίνοιαν GNO : ἔννοια Srawley

PART 1

INTRODUCTION

One God, Three Persons

How to Begin the Discourse with a Greek
The One God

(4) Thus when the dialogue is with a Hellenist, it would be good to make this the beginning of the argument:[12] whether he supposes the divine to exist, or if he agrees with the atheists' teaching. Thus, if he should say [the divine] does not exist, from the skillful and wise economy[13] of the world he will be led to admit the existence in them of some power displayed by them and transcending all.[14] But if he should not doubt [the divine's] existence, but should be carried off into conjectures of a multitude of gods, let us use against him an order [of argument] such as this: (5) whether he regards the divine as perfect or deficient. And if, as is likely, he bears witness to the perfection of the divine nature, we will require him [to grant] perfection throughout all that is contemplated in the divinity, so that the divine might not be contemplated as a commixture of opposites, of deficiency and perfection. But whether with regard to power, or with regard to the concept of the good, or with regard to wisdom and incorruptibility and eternality or any other God-befitting[15] thought

---

[12]Or "discourse" (λόγου). Here Gregory is about to launch a detailed argument against a prototypical Greek (a timely concern, given the resurgence of Hellenism under Emperor Julian). This is the most detailed invention of logical arguments in the entire discourse.

[13]Or "arrangement," "management" (οἰκονομουμένων). See Giulio Maspero, "Economy," in *Brill Dictionary*, 537–43.

[14]Or "the universe" (τοῦ παντὸς). Cf. Wis 13.1–5; Rom 1.20; cf. Prov 8.22; Ps 103.24 LXX; 1 Cor 1.24.

[15]The concept of what is and is not befitting for God (θεοπρεπής) is essential to St Gregory's arguments in the *Discourse*. This notion had a long history in Christian and pagan philosophical thought. See Anthony Meredith, "God-fittingness in Gregory of Nyssa," *Studia Patristica* 18.3 (1989): 507–15.

45 κείμενον τύχοι, ἐν παντὶ τὴν τελειότητα θεωρεῖσθαι ₁₀περὶ τὴν
(Sr 5) θείαν φύσιν | κατὰ τὸ εὔλογον τῆς ἀκολουθίας ₁₁ταύτης συγκα-
ταθήσεται. (6) Τούτου δὲ δοθέντος ἡμῖν οὐκέτ᾽ ἂν εἴη ₁₂χαλεπὸν τὸ ἐσκε-
δασμένον τῆς διανοίας εἰς πλῆθος θεῶν ₁₃πρὸς μιᾶς θεότητος
περιαγαγεῖν ὁμολογίαν. Εἰ γὰρ τὸ τέλειον ₁₄ἐν παντὶ δοίη περὶ
50 τὸ ὑποκείμενον ὁμολογεῖσθαι, ₁₅πολλὰ δὲ εἶναι τὰ τέλεια διὰ
τῶν αὐτῶν χαρακτηριζόμενα ₁₆λέγοι, ἀνάγκη πᾶσα ἐπὶ τῶν
μηδεμιᾷ παραλλαγῇ διακρινομένων ₁₇ἀλλ᾽ ἐν τοῖς αὐτοῖς θεωρουμένων ἢ ἐπιδεῖξαι τὸ ₁₈ἴδιον, ἤ εἰ μηδὲν ἰδιαζόντως κατα-
λάβοι ἡ ἔννοια ἐφ᾽ ₁₉ὧν τὸ διακρῖνον οὐκ ἔστι, μὴ ὑπονοεῖν
55 τὴν διάκρισιν. (7) Εἰ ₂₀γὰρ μήτε παρὰ τὸ πλέον καὶ ἔλαττον τὴν
διαφορὰν ἐξευρίσκοι, ₂₁διότι τὴν ἐλάττωσιν ὁ τῆς τελειότητος
οὐ παραδέχεται ₂₂λόγος, μήτε τὴν παρὰ τὸ χεῖρον καὶ
προτιμότερον· ₂₃οὐ γὰρ ἂν ἔτι θεότητος σχοίη ὑπόληψιν οὗ ἡ
τοῦ χείρονος ₂₄οὐκ ἄπεστι προσηγορία· μήτε κατὰ τὸ ἀρχαῖον
60 καὶ ₂₅πρόσφατον· τὸ γὰρ μὴ ἀεὶ ὂν ἔξω τῆς περὶ τὸ θεῖον ἔστιν
(Sr 6) ₂₆ὑπολήψεως· | ἀλλ᾽ εἷς καὶ ὁ αὐτὸς τῆς θεότητος λόγος, ₂₇οὐδε-
(GNO 8) μιᾶς ἰδιότητος ἐν οὐδενὶ κατὰ τὸ εὔλογον εὑρισκο-| μένης,
ἀνάγκη πᾶσα πρὸς μιᾶς θεότητος ὁμολογίαν συνθλιβῆναι ₂τὴν
πεπλανημένην περὶ τοῦ πλήθους τῶν θεῶν ₃φαντασίαν. (8) Εἰ γὰρ
65 τὸ ἀγαθὸν καὶ τὸ δίκαιον, τό τε σοφὸν ₄καὶ τὸ δυνατὸν ὡσαύτως
λέγοιτο, ἤ τε ἀφθαρσία καὶ ἡ ἀϊδιότης ₅καὶ πᾶσα εὐσεβὴς διάνοια κατὰ τὸν αὐτὸν ὁμολογοῖτο ₆τρόπον, πάσης κατὰ πάντα
λόγον διαφορᾶς ὑφαιρουμένης, ₇συνυφαιρεῖται κατ᾽ ἀνάγκην τὸ
τῶν θεῶν πλῆθος ₈ἀπὸ τοῦ δόγματος, τῆς διὰ πάντων ταὐ-
70 τότητος εἰς τὸ ἓν ₉τὴν πίστιν περιαγούσης.

that he might happen to cling to in contemplation, he will affirm in every point the perfection that is to be contemplated regarding the divine nature, according to the reasonableness of the order of this [argument]. (6) And if this is granted to us, it should no longer be difficult to bring round [his] thought, which is scattered among a multitude of gods, to the admission of one divinity. For if he should grant perfection to be admitted in every respect about the subject, and should say many perfect [divinities][16] exist, having the same characteristics, it is altogether necessary either—in the case of things distinguished by not even one variation, but which are contemplated with the same [attributes]—to display particularity, or—if thought should grasp nothing particularizing in things for which there is no distinction—not to conjecture the distinction. (7) For if he should not discover a difference with respect to the greater and the deficient (since the principle of perfection does not admit deficiency), nor with respect to the worse and the more valuable (for one would no longer bear the supposition of divinity, whose designation does not exclude the worse), nor with regard to the ancient and the brand new (for that which does not always exist is outside [a proper] supposition about the divine), but rather [he should discover that] the principle itself of divinity is one, not one particularity being found in a single thing, as is reasonable, [then] it is altogether necessary for the erring fantasy about a multitude of gods to be pressed to the admission of one divinity. (8) For if the good and the just, and the wise and the powerful should be asserted in the same way, and incorruptibility and eternality and every pious thought should be admitted in the same manner, every difference being taken away in every respect, the multitude of gods is by necessity taken away from the teaching, the sameness throughout all things bringing him round to faith in the One.

---

[16]Lit. "many perfections" (πολλὰ . . . τὰ τέλεια).

(PG 13; Sr 7) Α’ 10Ἀλλ’ ἐπειδὴ καὶ ὁ τῆς εὐσεβείας λόγος οἶδέ τινα | διά-
κρισιν 11ὑποστάσεων ἐν τῇ ἑνότητι τῆς φύσεως βλέπειν, ὡς ἂν
12μὴ τῇ πρὸς τοὺς Ἕλληνας μάχῃ πρὸς τὸν Ἰουδαϊσμὸν 13ἡμῖν ὁ
λόγος ὑπενεχθείη, πάλιν προσήκει διαστολῇ τινὶ 14τεχνικῇ καὶ
5 τὴν περὶ τοῦτο πλάνην ἐπανορθώσασθαι. (2) 15Οὐδὲ γὰρ τοῖς ἔξω
τοῦ καθ’ ἡμᾶς δόγματος ἄλογον εἶναι 16τὸ θεῖον ὑπείληπται·
τοῦτο δὲ παρ’ ἐκείνων ὁμολογούμενον 17ἱκανῶς διαρθρώσει τὸν
ἡμέτερον λόγον. Ὁ γὰρ ὁμολογῶν 18μὴ ἄλογον εἶναι τὸν Θεὸν
πάντως λόγον ἔχειν τὸν μὴ 19ἄλογον συγκαταθήσεται. Ἀλλὰ
10 μὴν καὶ ὁ ἀνθρώπινος 20ὁμωνύμως λέγεται λόγος. Οὐκοῦν εἰ
(Sr 8) λέγοι καθ’ ὁμοιότητα | 21τοῦ παρ’ ἡμῖν καὶ τὸν τοῦ Θεοῦ λόγον
ὑπονοεῖν, οὕτω 22μεταχθήσεται πρὸς τὴν ὑψηλοτέραν ὑπόληψιν. (3) Ἀνάγκη 23γὰρ πᾶσα κατάλληλον εἶναι πιστεύειν τῇ φύσει
τὸν λόγον, 24ὡς καὶ τὰ ἄλλα πάντα. Καὶ γὰρ δύναμίς τις καὶ ζωὴ
15 καὶ 25σοφία περὶ τὸ ἀνθρώπινον βλέπεται· ἀλλ’ οὐκ ἄν τις ἐκ 26τῆς
ὁμωνυμίας τοιαύτην καὶ ἐπὶ τοῦ Θεοῦ τὴν ζωὴν ἢ τὴν 27δύναμιν
ἢ τὴν σοφίαν ὑπονοήσειεν, ἀλλὰ πρὸς τὸ τῆς 28φύσεως τῆς
(GNO 9) ἡμετέρας μέτρον συνταπεινοῦνται καὶ αἱ τῶν | τοιούτων ὀνο-
μάτων ἐμφάσεις. Ἐπειδὴ γὰρ φθαρτὴ καὶ 2ἀσθενὴς ἡμῶν ἡ

11 τοῦ GNO : τῶν Srawley

Further Arguments for a Greek
The Three Persons: The Word

1 But since the word of piety[17] knows to see some distinction[18] of hypostases[19] in the unity of nature, lest in the battle against the Greek our discourse be carried away into Judaism, again it is proper to correct the error about this also with a certain technical distinction.[20] (2) For not even those outside our doctrine have supposed the divine to be irrational [or "wordless"];[21] this admission by them will sufficiently articulate our discourse.[22] For he who admits that God is not wordless will by all means grant him who is not wordless to have a word. But indeed the human word is also called by the same name. If therefore he should claim to conjecture that the Word of God is similar to the [words used] by us he will thus be led to a loftier supposition. (3) For it is altogether necessary to believe the word corresponds with the nature, like all other things as well. For a certain power and life and wisdom is seen regarding the human; but one would not conjecture from the sameness of the names that in the case of God "life" or "power" or "wisdom" are such as this, but the meanings[23] of such names are lowered to the measure of our nature.

[17]I.e., the faith of the Church.

[18]διάκρισιν.

[19]The Cappadocian Fathers gave the term *hypostasis* (ὑπόστασις) its Trinitarian meaning. Before them, it meant simply "substance," and could be used interchangeably with the word οὐσία (the Council of Nicea condemned those who professed three ὑποστάσεις in this sense). In this section, St Gregory builds from the Hellenistic, pre-Christian notion of "substance" to the Christian notion of "hypostasis" as *person*. To reflect this, the same word is translated at times as "substance" and at times as "hypostasis," depending on how St Gregory uses it, and how his catechists' audience would understand it.

[20]διαστολῇ.

[21]The present argument plays upon the fact that the word λόγος means both "reason" and "word." Cultured Greeks would not believe God to be irrational (ἄλογος); once this is granted, Gregory feels free to use the word broadly to argue that God has a λόγος in the Johannine sense (cf. Jn 1.1–18).

[22]St Gregory plays upon various forms of λόγος here: "irrational [or 'wordless']" (ἄλογον), "admission" (ὁμολογούμενον), and "discourse" (λόγον)—the end of the sentence could be translated: "articulate our Word."

[23]Here St Gregory uses ἔμφασις in its rhetorical sense (see LSJ A.III).

20 φύσις, διὰ τοῦτο ὠκύμορος ἡ ζωή, 3ἀνυπόστατος ἡ δύναμις, ἀπαγὴς ὁ λόγος. (4) Ἐπὶ δὲ τῆς ὑπερκειμένης 4φύσεως τῷ μεγαλείῳ τοῦ θεωρουμένου πᾶν τὸ 5περὶ αὐτῆς λεγόμενον συνεπαίρεται. Οὐκοῦν κἂν λόγος 6Θεοῦ λέγηται, οὐκ ἐν τῇ ὁρμῇ τοῦ φθεγγομένου τὴν ὑπόστασιν 7ἔχειν νομισθήσεται, καθ' ὁμοιό-

25 τητα τοῦ ἡμετέρου 8μεταχωρῶν εἰς ἀνύπαρκτον· ἀλλ' ὥσπερ ἡ ἡμετέρα φύσις 9ἐπίκηρος οὖσα καὶ ἐπίκηρον τὸν λόγον ἔχει, οὕτως ἡ ἄφθαρτος 10καὶ ἀεὶ ἑστῶσα φύσις ἀΐδιον ἔχει καὶ ὑφεστῶτα 11τὸν Λόγον.

(Sr 9)   (5) Εἰ δὲ τοῦτο κατὰ τὸ ἀκόλουθον ὁμολογηθείη | τὸ 12ὑφεστάναι

30 τὸν τοῦ Θεοῦ Λόγον ἀϊδίως, ἀνάγκη πᾶσα ἐν 13ζωῇ τοῦ Λόγου τὴν ὑπόστασιν εἶναι ὁμολογεῖν. Οὐ γὰρ καθ' 14ὁμοιότητα τῶν λίθων ἀψύχως ὑφεστάναι τὸν λόγον εὐαγές 15ἐστιν οἴεσθαι. Ἀλλ' εἰ ὑφέστηκε νοερόν τι χρῆμα καὶ 16ἀσώματον ὤν, ζῇ πάντως· εἰ δὲ τοῦ ζῆν κεχώρισται, οὐδὲ 17ἐν ὑποστάσει πάντως ἐστίν.

35 Ἀλλὰ μὴν ἀσεβὲς ἀπεδείχθη 18τὸν τοῦ Θεοῦ Λόγον ἀνυπόστατον εἶναι. Οὐκοῦν συναπεδείχθη 19κατὰ τὸ ἀκόλουθον τὸ ἐν ζωῇ τοῦτον θεωρεῖσθαι 20τὸν Λόγον. (6) Ἁπλῆς δὲ τῆς τοῦ Λόγου φύσεως κατὰ τὸ εἰκὸς 21εἶναι πεπιστευμένης καὶ οὐδεμίαν διπλόην καὶ σύνθεσιν ἐν 22ἑαυτῇ δεικνυούσης, οὐκέτ' ἄν τις κατὰ

40 μετουσίαν ζωῆς 23τὸν Λόγον ἐν ζωῇ θεωροίη (οὐ γὰρ ἂν ἐκτὸς εἴη συνθέσεως 24ἡ τοιαύτη ὑπόληψις τὸ ἕτερον ἐν ἑτέρῳ λέγειν εἶναι), ἀλλ' 25ἀνάγκη πᾶσα τῆς ἁπλότητος ὁμολογουμένης, αὐτοζωὴν 26εἶναι τὸν Λόγον οἴεσθαι, οὐ ζωῆς μετουσίαν.

24 καὶ after φθεγγομένου Srawley | 29 δὲ GNO : δὴ Srawley

For since our nature is corruptible and weak, because of this the "life" is fleeting, the "power" insubstantial,[24] the "word" unstable.[25] (4) But in the case of the transcendent nature, with the greatness of the one who is contemplated, everything being said about it is elevated. Therefore, though the "Word" of God is spoken of, it will not be deemed to have substance in the rush of utterance,[26] like ours passing into nonexistence;[27] but just as our nature, being perishable, also has a perishable word, so the incorruptible and ever existing nature also has the eternal and subsisting Word.[28]

(5) If this eternal subsistence of the Word of God should be admitted, according to the order [of the argument], it is altogether necessary to admit the substance of the Word to be living.[29] For it is not pious to think of the word subsisting inanimately like stones. But if it subsists, being something noetic and bodiless, by all means it lives; and if it has been separated from living, it is not at all subsisting.[30] But indeed the [idea of the] insubstantiality of the Word of God is demonstrated to be impious. Therefore it is demonstrated, according to the order [of the argument], that this Word is to be contemplated as living. (6) And since the nature of the Word has been believed to be simple, as is likely, and shows no duality or compositeness in itself, one would no longer contemplate the Word as living by some participation in life: for such a supposition would not be without compositeness, to say the one exists in the other. But it is altogether necessary, the simplicity being admitted, to think the Word to be life itself,[31] not a participation in life.[32]

[24]Or "non-hypostatic" (ἀνυπόστατος).

[25]Cf. Athanasius, *Against the Arians* 2.34, 35; cf. Irenaeus, *Against Heresies* 2.13.8.

[26]I.e. the Word of God is not articulated through exhaled air, like human speech.

[27]Cf. Athanasius, *Against the Gentiles* 3.40.4 and 3.45.1–2 (echoing the earlier the Philonic distinction between the "uttered word" [λόγος προφορικός] and the "word that remains within" the mind [λόγος ἐνδιάθετος]); a comparison with human speech was common in other Christian circles as well, e.g., Tertullian, *Against Praxeas* c.5.

[28]St John of Damascus draws upon this argument (*Exact Exposition* 1.6).

[29]Lit. "in life" (ἐν ζωῇ).

[30]Lit. "in substance" (ἐν ὑποστάσει).

[31]Jn 1.4; 9.5, Heb 1.3 (cf. Wis 7.26); 1 Jn 1.5.

[32]Cf. Jn 5.26.

(GNO 10)   (7) Εἰ οὖν ζῇ ὁ Λό- | γος | ὁ ζωὴ ὤν, καὶ προαιρετικὴν πάντως
45 (Sr 10) δύναμιν | ἔχει· οὐδὲν $_2$γὰρ ἀπροαίρετον τῶν ζώντων ἐστί. Τὴν δὲ
προαίρεσιν $_3$ταύτην καὶ δυνατὴν εἶναι κατὰ τὸ ἀκόλουθον εὐ-
σεβές ἐστι $_4$λογίζεσθαι. Εἰ γὰρ μή τις τὸ δυνατὸν ὁμολογοίη, τὸ
ἀδύνατον $_5$πάντως κατασκευάσει. (8) Ἀλλὰ μὴν πόρρω τῆς περὶ
(PG 16) τὸ $_6$θεῖον ὑπολήψεώς ἐστι τὸ | ἀδύνατον. Οὐδὲν γὰρ τῶν ἀπεμ-
50 φαινόντων $_7$περὶ τὴν θείαν θεωρεῖται φύσιν, ἀνάγκη δὲ $_8$πᾶσα
τοσαύτην εἶναι ὁμολογεῖν τοῦ Λόγου τὴν δύναμιν, $_9$ὅση ἐστὶ καὶ
ἡ πρόθεσις, ἵνα μή τις μίξις τῶν ἐναντίων καὶ $_{10}$συνδρομὴ περὶ
τὸ ἁπλοῦν θεωροῖτο, ἀδυναμίας τε καὶ $_{11}$δυνάμεως ἐν τῇ αὐτῇ
προθέσει θεωρουμένων, εἴπερ τὸ μέν $_{12}$τι δύναιτο, πρὸς δέ τι
55 ἀδυνάτως ἔχοι· πάντα δὲ δυναμένην $_{13}$τὴν τοῦ Λόγου προαίρεσιν
πρὸς οὐδὲν τῶν κακῶν τὴν $_{14}$ῥοπὴν ἔχειν (ἀλλότρια γὰρ τῆς
θείας φύσεως ἡ πρὸς κακίαν $_{15}$ὁρμή), ἀλλὰ πᾶν ὅτιπέρ ἐστιν
ἀγαθόν, τοῦτο καὶ βούλεσθαι, $_{16}$βουλομένην δὲ πάντως καὶ
δύνασθαι, δυναμένην δὲ $_{17}$μὴ ἀνενέργητον εἶναι, ἀλλὰ πᾶσαν
60 ἀγαθοῦ πρόθεσιν εἰς $_{18}$ἐνέργειαν ἄγειν.
    (9) Ἀγαθὸν δὲ ὁ κόσμος καὶ τὰ ἐν αὐτῷ πάντα $_{19}$σοφῶς τε καὶ
(Sr 11) τεχνικῶς θεωρούμενα. Ἆρα τοῦ | Λόγου $_{20}$ἔργα τὰ πάντα τοῦ
ζῶντος μὲν καὶ ὑφεστῶτος, ὅτι Θεοῦ $_{21}$Λόγος ἐστί, προαι-
ρουμένου δὲ ὅτι ζῇ, δυναμένου δὲ πᾶν $_{22}$ὅτιπερ ἂν ἕληται, αἱρου-
65 μένου δὲ τὸ ἀγαθόν τε καὶ σοφὸν $_{23}$πάντως, καὶ εἴ τι τῆς
κρείττονος σημασίας ἐστίν. (10) Ἐπεὶ οὖν $_{24}$ἀγαθόν τι ὁ κόσμος

(7) If, then, the Word, being life, lives, he by all means has the power of decision; for of living things, not one is without decision.[33] And it is pious for this decision also to be reckoned to be powerful, according to the order [of the argument]. For if anyone should not admit its power, he will altogether prove its powerlessness. (8) But powerlessness is far from a [proper] supposition about the divine. For nothing incongruous is contemplated about the divine nature, and it is altogether necessary to admit the Word has such power, which is also as great as [its] purpose,[34] so that no sort of mixture and concourse of opposites might be contemplated about the simplicity, both powerlessness and power being contemplated in the same purpose, if indeed he should be able[35] [to do] one thing, but should be unable to do another. And [we must admit] the Word's decision, being powerful in every way, to have an inclination toward nothing evil (for the impulse toward vice is alien to the divine nature), but all that is good, this also it intends, and, intending it is also altogether able to do, and, being able, is not inactive, but leads every good purpose into activity.

(9) Now the world is a good thing and all things in it are seen [to be] wisely and skillfully [made].[36] Therefore all things are the works of the living and subsisting Word; for he is the Word of God, having decision, for he lives, and being able [to do] all that he seizes upon, and deciding [to do] both the good and the wise, and anything that is a sign of the superior. (10) Whereas, then, the world is

---

[33]This is a rather egalitarian view, or at least not an Aristotelian one. Aristotle thought that women, children, slaves, and even animals were capable of a lower sort of volition (τὸ ἑκούσιον), but not true decision (προαίρεσις): decision is voluntary, but not everything voluntary is true decision (*Nicomachean Ethics* 1111b 6–7; *Rhetoric* 1368b 10–12). This was important for Aristotle, because the good life, or happiness (εὐδαιμονία), was "life with decision" (ζῆν κατὰ προαίρεσιν, *Politics* 1280a 31–34).

[34]I.e., the Word of God is able to do whatever he decides to do: the power (of decision) is equal to the purpose (what he has proposed to do—the root of the Greek word used here: πρόθεσις).

[35]In Greek "to be able" (δύναμαι) is related to the word "power" (δύναμις), which can also mean "ability" (likewise δυνατός can mean "powerful" or "able," "capable").

[36]Cf. Wis 13.1–5; Rom 1.20; Prov 8.22; Ps 103.24 LXX; 1 Cor 1.24.

ὁμολογεῖται, ἀπεδείχθη δὲ διὰ τῶν [25]εἰρημένων τοῦ Λόγου ἔργον τὸν κόσμον εἶναι τοῦ τὸ ἀγαθὸν [26]καὶ αἱρουμένου καὶ (GNO 11) δυναμένου, ὁ δὲ Λόγος οὗτος | ἕτερός ἐστι παρὰ τὸν οὗ ἐστι 70 Λόγος.

Τρόπον γάρ τινα τῶν [2]πρός τι λεγομένων καὶ τοῦτό ἐστιν, ἐπειδὴ χρὴ πάντως τῷ [3]Λόγῳ καὶ τὸν Πατέρα τοῦ Λόγου συνυπακούεσθαι· οὐ γὰρ [4]ἂν εἴη Λόγος, μή τινος ὢν Λόγος. Εἰ οὖν διακρίνει τῷ [5]σχετικῷ τῆς σημασίας ἡ τῶν ἀκουόντων 75 διάνοια αὐτόν τε [6]τὸν Λόγον καὶ τὸν ὅθεν ἐστίν, οὐκέτ᾽ ἂν ἡμῖν κινδυνεύοι τὸ [7]μυστήριον ταῖς Ἑλληνικαῖς μαχόμενον ὑπολή- ψεσι τοῖς [8]τὰ τῶν Ἰουδαίων πρεσβεύουσι συνενεχθῆναι· ἀλλ᾽ ἐπ᾽ [9]ἴσης ἑκατέρων τὴν ἀτοπίαν ἐκφεύξεται, τόν τε ζῶντα τοῦ (Sr 12) [10]Θεοῦ Λόγον καὶ ἐνεργὸν καὶ | ποιητικὸν ὁμολογῶν, ὅπερ [11]Ἰου- 80 δαῖος οὐ δέχεται, καὶ τὸ μὴ διαφέρειν κατὰ τὴν φύσιν [12]αὐτόν τε τὸν Λόγον καὶ τὸν ὅθεν ἐστίν.—

—(11) Ὥσπερ γὰρ ἐφ᾽ [13]ἡμῶν ἐκ τοῦ νοῦ φαμὲν εἶναι τὸν λόγον, οὔτε δι᾽ ὅλου τὸν [14]αὐτὸν ὄντα τῷ νῷ, οὔτε παντάπασιν ἕτερον· (τῷ μὲν γὰρ ἐξ [15]ἐκείνου εἶναι ἄλλο τι καὶ οὐκ ἐκεῖνό ἐστι, τῷ δὲ αὐτὸν τὸν [16]νοῦν εἰς τὸ ἐμφανὲς ἄγειν 85 οὐκέτ᾽ ἂν ἕτερόν τι παρ᾽ ἐκεῖνον [17]ὑπονοοῖτο, ἀλλὰ κατὰ τὴν φύσιν ἓν ὢν ἕτερον τῷ ὑποκειμένῳ [18]ἐστίν)· οὕτω καὶ ὁ τοῦ Θεοῦ Λόγος τῷ μὲν ὑφεστάναι [19]καθ᾽ ἑαυτὸν διῄρηται πρὸς ἐκεῖνον παρ᾽ οὗ τὴν ὑπόστασιν [20]ἔχει, τῷ δὲ ταῦτα δεικνύειν ἐν ἑαυτῷ, ἃ περὶ τὸν [21]Θεὸν καθορᾶται, ὁ αὐτός ἐστι κατὰ τὴν 90 φύσιν ἐκείνῳ τῷ [22]διὰ τῶν αὐτῶν γνωρισμάτων εὑρισκομένῳ· εἴτε γὰρ ἀγαθότης, [23]εἴτε δύναμις, εἴτε σοφία, εἴτε τὸ ἀϊδίως (Sr 13) εἶναι, εἴτε τὸ [24]κακίας καὶ θανάτου | καὶ φθορᾶς ἀνεπίδεκτον, εἴτε (GNO 12) τὸ ἓν | παντὶ τέλειον, εἴτε τι τοιοῦτον ὅλως σημεῖόν τις ποιοῖτο [2]τῆς τοῦ Πατρὸς καταλήψεως, διὰ τῶν αὐτῶν εὑρήσει [3]σημείων 95 καὶ τὸν ἐξ ἐκείνου ὑφεστῶτα Λόγον. |

86 οὕτω GNO : οὕτως Srawley

admitted to be something good, and the world was demonstrated by what was said to be a work of the Word, who both chooses and is able [to do] the good, but this Word is different from him whose Word he is.

For this is also a sort of relational manner of speaking, since it is altogether necessary for the Father of the Word to be heard of together with the Word; for he would not be the Word if he is not someone's Word. If, then, the thought of [our] hearers distinguishes the Word himself and him from whom he is with a relational sign, our mystery will no longer be in danger of being carried off with those who advocate the [teachings] of the Jews while battling Greek suppositions; but it will equally escape the absurdity of each, confessing the living Word of God as both active and creative, which the Jew does not admit, and the lack of difference in nature between the Word himself and him from whom he is.

(11) For just as in our case, we say the word is from the mind, neither being wholly the same as the mind, nor in all ways different (for by being from it, it is something other and is not it, but by making the mind manifest it is no longer understood as something different, apart from it, but being one in nature, it is [nonetheless] different from the subject), thus also the Word of God by his own subsistence is distinguished from him from whom he has hypostasis,[37] but by showing these things in himself, which are seen about God, he is the same in nature as him who is discovered by the same characteristics: for whether [it be] goodness, or power, or wisdom, or eternal existence, or inaccessibility to vice and death and corruption, or perfection in everything, or any such thing that someone may consider a sign of apprehending the Father, by the same signs he will discover the Word, having his hypostasis from him.

[37]Here ὑπόστασις, by being carefully defined in the context of the relationship of the persons of the Trinity, begins to take on its proper Christian sense of "hypostasis" (person). Thus when "τὴν ὑπόστασιν" occurs in this sentence, it is rendered as "hypostasis." See n. 19 on p. 64 above.

(PG 17) Β' ₄Ὥσπερ δὲ τὸν Λόγον ἐκ τῶν καθ' ἡμᾶς ἀναγωγικῶς ἐπὶ ₅τῆς ὑπερκειμένης ἔγνωμεν φύσεως, κατὰ τὸν αὐτὸν τρόπον ₆καὶ τῇ περὶ τοῦ Πνεύματος ἐννοίᾳ προσαχθησόμεθα, ₇σκιάς τινας καὶ μιμήματα τῆς ἀφράστου δυνάμεως ἐν τῇ ₈καθ' ἡμᾶς 5 θεωροῦντες φύσει. Ἀλλ' ἐφ' ἡμῶν μὲν τὸ πνεῦμα ₉ἡ τοῦ ἀέρος ἐστὶν ὁλκή, ἀλλοτρίου πράγματος πρὸς ₁₀τὴν τοῦ σώματος σύστασιν ἀναγκαίως εἰσελκομένου τε ₁₁καὶ προχεομένου, ὅπερ ἐν (Sr 14) τῷ καιρῷ τῆς ἐκφωνήσεως τοῦ ₁₂λόγου | φωνὴ γίνεται, τὴν τοῦ λόγου δύναμιν ἐν ἑαυτῇ φανεροῦσα. (2) ₁₃Ἐπὶ δὲ τῆς θείας φύσεως 10 τὸ μὲν εἶναι Πνεῦμα Θεοῦ ₁₄εὐσεβὲς ἐνομίσθη, καθὼς ἐδόθη καὶ Λόγον εἶναι Θεοῦ διὰ ₁₅τὸ μὴ δεῖν ἐλλιπέστερον τοῦ ἡμετέρου λόγου τὸν τοῦ Θεοῦ ₁₆εἶναι Λόγον, εἴπερ τούτου μετὰ πνεύματος θεωρουμένου ₁₇ἐκεῖνος δίχα Πνεύματος εἶναι πιστεύοιτο. Οὐ μὴν ἀλλότριόν ₁₈τι καθ' ὁμοιότητα τοῦ ἡμετέρου πνεύματος 15 ἔξωθεν ₁₉ἐπεισρεῖν τῷ Θεῷ καὶ ἐν αὐτῷ γίνεσθαι τὸ Πνεῦμα θεοπρεπές ₂₀ἐστιν οἴεσθαι· ἀλλ' ὡς Θεοῦ Λόγον ἀκούσαντες οὐκ ₂₁ἀνυπόστατόν τι πρᾶγμα τὸν Λόγον ᾠήθημεν οὐδὲ ἐκ μαθήσεως ₂₂ἐγγινόμενον, οὔτε διὰ φωνῆς προφερόμενον, οὔτε ₂₃μετὰ τὸ προενεχθῆναι διαλυόμενον, οὐδὲ ἄλλο τι πάσχοντα ₂₄τοιοῦτον, 20 οἷα περὶ τὸν ἡμέτερον λόγον θεωρεῖται πάθη, ₂₅ἀλλ' οὐσιωδῶς ὑφεστῶτα, προαιρετικόν τε καὶ ἐνεργὸν ₂₆καὶ παντοδύ- (GNO 13) ναμον, (3) οὕτω καὶ Πνεῦμα μεμαθηκότες Θεοῦ, | τὸ συμπαρομαρτοῦν τῷ Λόγῳ καὶ φανεροῦν αὐτοῦ τὴν ₂ἐνέργειαν, οὐ πνοὴν ἄσθματος ἐννοοῦμεν (ἢ γὰρ ἂν καθαιροῖτο ₃πρὸς ταπει- 25 (Sr 15) νότητα τὸ μεγαλεῖον τῆς θείας δυνάμεως, ₄εἰ | καθ' ὁμοιότητα τοῦ ἡμετέρου καὶ τὸ ἐν αὐτῷ ₅Πνεῦμα ὑπονοοῖτο), ἀλλὰ

---

15 ἐπεισρεῖν GNO : ἐπιρρεῖν Srawley | 18 προφερόμενον GNO : προφαινόμενον Srawley | 22 οὕτω GNO : οὕτως Srawley

Further Arguments for a Greek
The Spirit: An Argument by Ascent

2 For just as by way of ascent[38] we came to know the transcendent nature of the Word from the things that relate to us, in the same manner we will also be led to the notion of the Spirit, contemplating in our nature some shadows and imitations of the unutterable power. But in our case the inhalation of air is the "spirit" [i.e., breath],[39] an alien thing, necessarily being inhaled and exhaled to sustain the body, the thing that becomes the voice at the time the word is voiced out loud, manifesting the meaning of the word in itself. (2) And in the case of the divine nature, [to affirm] the existence of the Spirit of God is deemed pious, even as the existence of the Word of God was also granted, because the Word of God must not be more deficient than our word, [as would be the case] if, indeed, while this [human word] is contemplated with spirit [i.e., breath], that [divine Word] would be believed to be without Spirit. Indeed it is not befitting God to think some alien thing like our spirit [i.e., breath] streams into God from outside and becomes the Spirit in him; but as when we heard of the Word of God we did not deem him an insubstantial sort of thing, and not born from learning, nor brought forth by a voice, nor dissolved after being brought forth, and not experiencing any other such thing, such as the experiences that are contemplated about our word, but essentially subsisting, both capable of decision and active and all powerful, (3) so too having learned of a Spirit of God, the one accompanying the Word and manifesting his activity, we do not think [he is] a panting breath (for the greatness of the divine power would be cast down to baseness if the Spirit in him were understood to be like ours), but contemplated as an essential

---

[38]Literally "anagogically" (ἀναγωγικῶς). Here Gregory applies the hermeneutical practice of Origen, seeking a higher sense in a text of Scripture, to his trinitarian contemplation of man.

[39]This sense of "spirit" is uncommon in English, though an echo survives in the expression "gave up the ghost" (cf. Mt 27:50; Mk 15:37; Lk 23:46; Jn 19:30).

δύναμιν οὐσιώδη αὐτὴν ἐφ' ₆ἑαυτῆς ἐν ἰδιαζούσῃ ὑποστάσει
θεωρουμένην, οὔτε χωρισθῆναι ₇τοῦ Θεοῦ, ἐν ᾧ ἔστιν, ἢ τοῦ
Λόγου τοῦ Θεοῦ, ᾧ παρομαρτεῖ ₈δυναμένην, οὔτε πρὸς τὸ ἀνύ-
30 παρκτον ἀναχεομένην, ₉ἀλλὰ καθ' ὁμοιότητα τοῦ Θεοῦ Λόγου
καθ' ὑπόστασιν ₁₀οὖσαν, προαιρετικήν, αὐτοκίνητον, ἐνεργόν,
πάντοτε τὸ ₁₁ἀγαθὸν αἱρουμένην καὶ πρὸς πᾶσαν πρόθεσιν
σύνδρομον ₁₂ἔχουσαν τῇ βουλήσει τὴν δύναμιν.

Γ' Ὥστε τὸν ἀκριβῶς τὰ ₁₃βάθη τοῦ μυστηρίου διασκοπού-
μενον ἐν μὲν τῇ ψυχῇ κατὰ ₁₄τὸ ἀπόρρητον μετρίαν τινὰ κατα-
νόησιν τῆς κατὰ τὴν ₁₅θεογνωσίαν διδασκαλίας λαμβάνειν, μὴ
μέντοι δύνασθαι ₁₆λόγῳ διασαφεῖν τὴν ἀνέκφραστον ταύτην τοῦ
5 μυστηρίου ₁₇βαθύτητα. Πῶς τὸ αὐτὸ καὶ ἀριθμητόν ἐστι καὶ
(Sr 16) διαφεύγει ₁₈τὴν ἐξαρίθμησιν, | καὶ διῃρημένως ὁρᾶται καὶ ἐν
μονάδι ₁₉καταλαμβάνεται, καὶ διακέκριται τῇ ὑποστάσει καὶ οὐ
διώρισται ₂₀τῷ ὑποκειμένῳ; (2) Ἄλλο γάρ τι τῇ ὑποστάσει τὸ
₂₁Πνεῦμα καὶ ἕτερον ὁ Λόγος, καὶ ἄλλο πάλιν ἐκεῖνο οὗ καὶ ₂₂ὁ
10 Λόγος ἐστὶ καὶ τὸ Πνεῦμα. Ἀλλ' ἐπειδὰν τὸ διακεκριμένον ₂₃ἐν
τούτοις κατανοήσῃς, πάλιν ἡ τῆς φύσεως ἑνότης ₂₄τὸν δια-
μερισμὸν οὐ προσίεται, ὡς μήτε τὸ τῆς μοναρχίας ₂₅σχίζεσθαι
κράτος εἰς θεότητας διαφόρους κατατεμνόμενον, ₂₆μήτε τῷ
(GNO 14) Ἰουδαϊκῷ δόγματι συμβαίνειν τὸν λόγον, | ἀλλὰ διὰ μέσου τῶν
15 (Sr 17) δύο ὑπολήψεων χωρεῖν τὴν ἀλήθειαν, | ₂ἑκατέραν τε τῶν
αἱρέσεων καθαιρούσαν καὶ ἀφ' ἑκάτερας ₃παραδεχομένην τὸ
(PG 20) χρήσιμον. Τοῦ μὲν γὰρ Ἰουδαίου ₄καθαιρεῖ-| ται τὸ δόγμα τῇ τε
τοῦ Λόγου παραδοχῇ καὶ τῇ ₅πίστει τοῦ Πνεύματος, τῶν δὲ
Ἑλληνιζόντων ἡ πολύθεος ₆ἐξαφανίζεται πλάνη, τῆς κατὰ φύσιν
20 ἑνότητος παραγραφομένης ₇τὴν πληθυντικὴν φαντασίαν. (3) Πάλιν δὲ αὖ ἐκ μὲν ₈τῆς Ἰουδαϊκῆς ὑπολήψεως ἡ τῆς φύσεως ἑνότης
παραμενέτω· ₉ἐκ δὲ τοῦ Ἑλληνισμοῦ ἡ κατὰ τὰς ὑποστάσεις
₁₀διάκρισις μόνη, θεραπευθείσης ἑκατέρωθεν καταλλήλως ₁₁τῆς
ἀσεβοῦς ὑπονοίας· ἔστι γὰρ ὥσπερ θεραπεία τῶν μὲν ₁₂περὶ τὸ
25 ἓν πλανωμένων ὁ ἀριθμὸς τῆς Τριάδος, τῶν δὲ εἰς ₁₃πλῆθος
ἐσκεδασμένων ὁ τῆς ἑνότητος λόγος.

power himself, in himself, in an individuating hypostasis, neither
able to be separated from God, in whom he is, nor from the Word
of God, whom he accompanies, nor poured out into non-existence,
but being like the Word of God in hypostasis, capable of decision,
self-moved, active, altogether choosing the good and having power
concurrent with intention for every purpose.

The Depth of the Mystery and the Truth as a Mean

3 And thus he who looks precisely into the depths of the mystery
grasps in secret in [his own] soul some measure of understanding of
the teaching of the knowledge of God, yet is not able to make clear
in speech this unutterable depth of the mystery. How is it that the
same thing is both numbered and escapes enumeration, is both seen
separately and apprehended in unity, is both distinguished in hypostasis and not divided in underlying subject?[40] (2) For in hypostasis
the Spirit is one thing and the Word another, and another again is he
to whom the Word and the Spirit belong. But whenever you understand the distinction in these, again the unity of nature does not
admit partition, so that neither is the might of the monarchy split,
being cut up into differing divinities, nor does the discourse agree
with Jewish teaching, but the truth passes through the mean of the
two suppositions, casting down each of the heresies and accepting
what is useful from each. For the teaching of the Jew is overturned
both by the acceptance of the Word and by faith in the Spirit, while
the Hellenists' polytheistic error is destroyed, the unity of nature
abolishing the fantasy of multiplicity. (3) And again, once more,
from the Jewish supposition let the unity of the nature remain, and
from Hellenism only the distinction of hypostases, each correspondingly healing the other's impious conjecture: for just as the number
of the Trinity is a healing for those in error about the one [nature],
the principle of unity [is a healing] for those [whose thought is] scattered in a multitude [of gods].

[40]Here the "underlying subject" (τῷ ὑποκειμένῳ) is the divine essence (οὐσία)
or nature (φύσις).

(Sr 18) Δ' [14]Εἰ δὲ ἀντιλέγοι τούτοις ὁ Ἰουδαῖος, οὐκέτ' ἂν ἡμῖν | ἐκ [15]τοῦ ἴσου δύσκολος ὁ πρὸς ἐκεῖνον γενήσεται λόγος. Ἐκ [16]γὰρ τῶν συντρόφων αὐτῷ διδαγμάτων ἡ τῆς ἀληθείας [17]ἔσται φανέρωσις. Τὸ γὰρ εἶναι Λόγον Θεοῦ καὶ Πνεῦμα Θεοῦ, [18]οὐσιωδῶς
5 ὑφεστώσας δυνάμεις, ποιητικάς τε τῶν γεγενημένων [19]καὶ περιεκτικὰς τῶν ὄντων, ἐκ τῶν θεοπνεύστων [20]Γραφῶν ἐναργέστερον δείκνυται. Ἀρκεῖ δὲ μιᾶς μαρτυρίας [21]ἐπιμνησθέντας τοῖς φιλοπονωτέροις καταλιπεῖν τῶν πλειόνων [22]τὴν εὕρεσιν. (2) Τῷ λόγῳ τοῦ Κυρίου, φησίν, οἱ οὐρανοὶ [23]ἐστερεώθησαν καὶ τῷ
10 πνεύματι τοῦ στόματος αὐτοῦ πᾶσα [24]ἡ δύναμις αὐτῶν. Ποίῳ λόγῳ καὶ ποίῳ πνεύματι; Οὔτε γὰρ [25]ῥῆμα ὁ λόγος, οὔτε ἄσθμα τὸ πνεῦμα. Ἢ γὰρ ἂν καθ' ὁμοιότητα [26]τῆς ἡμετέρας φύσεως καὶ τὸ θεῖον ἐξανθρωπίζοιτο, [27]εἰ τοιούτῳ κεχρῆσθαι λόγῳ καὶ
(GNO 15; τοιούτῳ πνεύματι τὸν τοῦ | παντὸς ποιητὴν δογματίζοι. (3) | Τίς
Sr 19) 15 δὲ καὶ δύναμις ἀπὸ [2]ῥημάτων καὶ ἄσθματος τηλικαύτη, ὡς ἐξαρκεῖν πρὸς [3]οὐρανῶν σύστασιν καὶ τῶν ἐν τούτοις δυνάμεων; Εἰ γὰρ [4]ὅμοιος τῷ ἡμετέρῳ ῥήματι καὶ ὁ τοῦ Θεοῦ Λόγος καὶ τὸ [5]Πνεῦμα τῷ πνεύματι, ὁμοία πάντως ἐκ

---

8 φιλοπονωτέροις GNO : φιλοτιμοτέροις Srawley | 14 δογματίζοιε GNO : δογματίζοιεν Srawley | 18 <καὶ> after πνεύματι GNO

Convincing a Jew
Scriptural Arguments for the Word and the Spirit

4 If the Jew should contradict these [conclusions], the discourse for him shall no longer be as difficult for us. For the manifestation of the truth will be from the teachings in which he was brought up.[41] For the existence of a Word of God and a Spirit of God, powers subsisting essentially,[42] who made all that has come to be and who embrace [all] existing things, is demonstrated more clearly from the Scriptures, inspired by God. It is enough to recall one testimony,[43] leaving the discovery[44] of more to those who are more industrious.[45] (2) "By the Word of the Lord," it says, "the heavens were established, and by the Spirit of his mouth all their host."[46] By what kind of "word" and what kind of "spirit"? For the Word is not a saying, nor is the Spirit mere breathing. For the divine would be anthropomorphized in the likeness of our nature if the teaching were proclaimed that the maker of all things used such a word and such a spirit. (3) And further, what power from speaking and mere breathing is able to suffice for the constitution of the heavens and the hosts in them? For if the Word of God is similar to our saying and the Spirit also [is similar to our] spirit, then the power from such similarities is altogether

[41]I.e., from Old Testament Scripture.

[42]I.e., they are distinct hypostases.

[43]By St Gregory's time there was a long-established genre of *testimonia* (Gr. μαρτυρία) that proved Jesus to be the Messiah, and demonstrated Christian doctrine from the Old Testament, e.g., St Justin Martyr's *Dialogue with Trypho*. Because this is so well established, Gregory only needs to use one example.

[44]Gregory clearly indicates that he is thinking in rhetorical terms: he is giving one example of the "discovery" of scriptural arguments for the Word and the Spirit. For the rhetorical meaning of "discovery," see p. xxx.

[45]The comparative form of φιλόπονος (lit. "lover of labor"). For Gregory, this word is associated with scriptural research and exegesis, and specifically with Origen's exegesis. Twice Gregory speaks of Origen by name, both times praising his interpretation of the Song of Songs and describing him as an "industrious [φιλόπονος]" exegete (*Life of Gregory the Wonderworker* 13.11; *Song of Songs* 13.3). This was already a traditional description: Athanasius calls Origen "very learned and industrious [φιλόπονος]" multiple times (e.g., *Letter to Serapion* 4.4.9–10 [PG 26:649]; *On the Decrees of the Council of Nicea* 27 [PG 25:466]).

[46]Ps 32.6 LXX.

τῶν ὁμοίων $_6$ἡ δύναμις, καὶ ὅσην ὁ ἡμέτερος τοσαύτην καὶ ὁ τοῦ
Θεοῦ $_7$Λόγος τὴν ἰσχὺν ἔχει. Ἀλλὰ μὴν ἀνενέργητά τε καὶ
20 ἀνυπόστατα $_8$τὰ παρ' ἡμῖν ῥήματα καὶ τὸ τοῖς ῥήμασι συνδιεξ-
ερχόμενον $_9$πνεῦμα. (4) Ἄπρακτα πάντως καὶ ἀνυπόστατα
$_{10}$κἀκεῖνα κατασκευάσουσιν οἱ πρὸς τὴν ὁμοιότητα τοῦ $_{11}$παρ'
ἡμῖν λόγου τὸ θεῖον κατάγοντες. Εἰ δέ, καθὼς λέγει $_{12}$Δαβίδ,
ἐστερεώθησαν τῷ λόγῳ Κυρίου οἱ οὐρανοὶ καὶ αἱ $_{13}$δυνάμεις
25 αὐτῶν ἐν τῷ πνεύματι τοῦ Θεοῦ τὴν σύστασιν $_{14}$ἔσχον, ἄρα
συνέστηκε τὸ τῆς ἀληθείας μυστήριον, Λόγον $_{15}$ἐν οὐσίᾳ καὶ
Πνεῦμα ἐν ὑποστάσει λέγειν ὑφηγούμενον.

Β'

E' $_{16}$Ἀλλὰ τὸ μὲν εἶναι Λόγον Θεοῦ καὶ Πνεῦμα διά τε | τῶν
(Sr 20) $_{17}$κοινῶν ἐννοιῶν ὁ Ἕλλην καὶ διὰ τῶν γραφικῶν ὁ Ἰουδαῖος $_{18}$ἴσως
οὐκ ἀντιλέξει· τὴν δὲ κατὰ ἄνθρωπον οἰκονομίαν $_{19}$τοῦ Θεοῦ
Λόγου κατὰ τὸ ἴσον ἑκάτερος αὐτῶν ἀποδοκιμάσει $_{20}$ὡς ἀπί-
θανόν τε καὶ ἀπρεπῆ περὶ Θεοῦ λέγεσθαι. $_{21}$Οὐκοῦν ἐξ ἑτέρας
5 ἀρχῆς καὶ εἰς τὴν περὶ τούτου πίστιν $_{22}$τοὺς ἀντιλέγοντας προσ-
αξόμεθα.—

similar, and the Word of God has just as much strength as ours. But indeed our sayings and the spirit that goes out with the sayings are both inactive and insubstantial.[47] (4) They will be proved[48] to be altogether inert and insubstantial by the ones dragging the divine down to a likeness to our word. But if, even as David says, "By the Word of the Lord the heavens were established, and their hosts by the Spirit of God" had their composition, then the mystery of the truth has been established, guiding [us] to speak of the Word in essence and the Spirit in hypostasis.

PART 2

THE NARRATIVE

Creation, the Image of God, the Fall, the Nature of Evil, and Death

Creation reflects God's reason and power

5 But the Greek, because of common notions,[49] and the Jew likewise, because of the Scriptures, will not contradict the existence of a Word of God and a Spirit; but each of them will equally reject the economy of the Word of God as man[50] as both unbelievable and not fitting to be said about God. Accordingly, from a different beginning[51] we will bring gainsayers even to faith in this.

---

[47]Or "non-hypostatic."

[48]Again, the rhetorical meaning of κατασκευάζω (see n. 6 on p. 60).

[49]While "common notions" had a technical meaning in Stoic thought, here Gregory seems to mean the common ground that he used above in his arguments (i.e., what is befitting for God? e.g., perfection, incorruptibility, etc.). See introduction, p. xxx.

[50]Or "with respect to man" (κατὰ ἄνθρωπον), but this refers to the incarnation. See Silvas, *Letters*, 127 n. 89.

[51]Or "premise" (ἀρχῆς). He is referring to another premise for a logical demonstration.

—(2) Λόγῳ τὰ πάντα γεγενῆσθαι ₂₃καὶ Σοφίᾳ παρὰ τοῦ τὸ
(Sr 21) πᾶν | συστησαμένου πιστεύουσιν, ₂₄ἢ καὶ πρὸς ταύτην
(GNO 16) δυσπειθῶς ἔχουσι τὴν ὑπόληψιν. | Ἀλλ᾽ εἰ μὴ δοῖεν λόγον
10 καθηγεῖσθαι καὶ σοφίαν τῆς τῶν ὄντων ₂συστάσεως, ἀλογίαν τε
(PG 21) καὶ ἀτεχνίαν τῇ ἀρχῇ | τοῦ ₃παντὸς ἐπιστήσουσιν. Εἰ δὲ τοῦτο
ἄτοπόν τε καὶ ἀσεβές, ₄ὁμολογεῖται πάντως ὅτι λόγον τε καὶ
σοφίαν ἡγεμονεύειν ₅τῶν ὄντων ὁμολογήσουσιν. [Ἀλλὰ μὴν ἐν
τοῖς φθάσασιν ₆ἀποδέδεικται μὴ αὐτὸ τοῦτο ῥῆμα ὢν ὁ τοῦ
15 Θεοῦ Λόγος, ἢ ₇ἕξις ἐπιστήμης τινὸς ἢ σοφίας, ἀλλὰ κατ᾽
οὐσίαν τις ₈ὑφεστῶσα δύναμις, προαιρετική τε παντὸς ἀγαθοῦ
καὶ ἐν ₉ἰσχύϊ πᾶν τὸ κατὰ προαίρεσιν ἔχουσα], ἀγαθοῦ δὲ ὄντος
₁₀τοῦ κόσμου τὴν τῶν ἀγαθῶν προεκτικήν τε καὶ ποιητικὴν
₁₁δύναμιν αἰτίαν εἶναι. Εἰ δὲ τοῦ κόσμου παντὸς ἡ ὑπόστασις ₁₂τῆς
20 τοῦ Λόγου δυνάμεως ἐξῆπται, καθὼς ἡ ἀκολουθία ₁₃παρέδειξεν,
ἀνάγκη πᾶσα καὶ τῶν τοῦ κόσμου μερῶν μὴ ₁₄ἄλλην ἐπινοεῖν
αἰτίαν τινὰ τῆς συστάσεως ἀλλ᾽ ἢ τὸν Λόγον ₁₅αὐτόν, δι᾽ οὗ τὰ
πάντα τὴν εἰς τὸ γενέσθαι πάροδον ₁₆ἔσχε.

(3) Τοῦτον δὲ εἴτε Λόγον, εἴτε Σοφίαν, εἴτε Δύναμιν, εἴτε
25 ₁₇Θεόν, εἴτε ἄλλο τι τῶν ὑψηλῶν τε καὶ τιμίων ὀνομάζειν τις
₁₈ἐθέλοι, οὐ διοισόμεθα· ὅ τι γὰρ ἂν εὑρεθῇ δεικτικὸν τοῦ ₁₉ὑπο- |
(Sr 22) κειμένου ῥῆμα ἢ ὄνομα, ἕν ἐστι τὸ διὰ τῶν φωνῶν σημαι-
νόμενον· ₂₀ἡ ἀΐδιος τοῦ Θεοῦ δύναμις, ἡ ποιητικὴ τῶν ὄντων, ₂₁ἡ
εὑρετικὴ τῶν μὴ ὄντων, ἡ συνεκτικὴ τῶν γεγονότων, ₂₂ἡ
30 προορατικὴ τῶν μελλόντων. Οὗτος τοίνυν ὁ Θεὸς ₂₃Λόγος, ἡ

13–17 GNO places Ἀλλὰ through ἔχουσα in brackets

(2) Either they believe that all things have come into being by Reason[52] and by Wisdom from him who constituted all, or they stubbornly hold [their] supposition even about this. But if they do not grant Reason and Wisdom to be guiding the constitution of existing things, they will set up both irrationality and lack of skill as the beginning[53] of all. And if this is both absurd and impious, they will altogether agree that both Reason and Wisdom guide existing things. But indeed it has been demonstrated in the previous [arguments] that the Word of God is not the same as this saying, or the possession of some knowledge or wisdom, but it is a kind of power subsisting by essence, both capable of deciding all good and having everything in his strength in accordance with [his] decision; and [it was demonstrated that] since the world is good, [its] cause is a power that is both able to decide and able to make all good things. And if the substance[54] of all the world depends on the power of the Word, as the order [of the argument] demonstrated, it is by all means necessary to conceive of no other cause of the constitution of the parts of the cosmos than the Word himself, through whom all things had [their] passage into being.[55]

(3) And this, whether someone should want to name it Word, or Wisdom, or Power, or God, or any other one of the lofty and honorable [names], we will not quarrel; for whatever saying or name is discovered that can demonstrate the subject, one thing is signified by the [different] expressions: the eternal power of God, the maker of existing things, the inventor of things that do not exist,[56] the sustainer of things that have come into being, the foreseer of things to come. This one therefore is God the Word, the Wisdom, the Power,

[52]Λόγῳ, the same word translated as "Word" above (i.e., the Word of God).

[53]Or "principle" (ἀρχῇ).

[54]Here Gregory uses ὑπόστασις in its older, non-trinitarian sense.

[55]More literally, their "passage into becoming." In Greek philosophy, a fundamental distinction was made between "being" and "becoming," stretching back to the two great pre-Socratic philosophers Parmenides and Heraclitus.

[56]A reference to the teaching of creation ex nihilo. Cf. Athanasius, *On the Incarnation* 3 (which in turn quotes *Shepherd of Hermas*, Mandate 1.1.); for biblical precedents see 2 Mac 7.28; Rom 4.17; Heb 11.3.

(GNO 17) Σοφία, ἡ Δύναμις, ἀπεδείχθη κατὰ τὸ ἀκόλουθον | τῆς ἀνθρω-
πίνης φύσεως ποιητής, οὐκ ἀνάγκῃ τινὶ πρὸς ₂τὴν τοῦ ἀνθρώπου κατασκευὴν ἐναχθείς, ἀλλ' ἀγάπης ₃περιουσίᾳ τοῦ τοιούτου ζῴου δημιουργήσας τὴν γένεσιν. ₄Ἔδει γὰρ μήτε τὸ φῶς
35 ἀθέατον, μήτε τὴν δόξαν ἀμάρτυρον, ₅μήτε ἀναπόλαυστον
αὐτοῦ εἶναι τὴν ἀγαθότητα, μήτε τὰ ₆ἄλλα πάντα ὅσα περὶ τὴν
θείαν καθορᾶται φύσιν ἀργὰ ₇κεῖσθαι, μὴ ὄντος τοῦ μετέχοντός
τε καὶ ἀπολαύοντος.

(4) Εἰ ₈τοίνυν ἐπὶ τούτοις ὁ ἄνθρωπος εἰς γένεσιν ἔρχεται, ἐφ'
40 ᾧτε ₉μέτοχος τῶν θείων ἀγαθῶν γενέσθαι, ἀναγκαίως τοιοῦτος
₁₀κατασκευάζεται, ὡς ἐπιτηδείως πρὸς τὴν τῶν ἀγαθῶν ₁₁μετου-
(Sr 23) σίαν ἔχειν. Καθάπερ γὰρ ὁ ὀφθαλμὸς διὰ | τῆς ἐγκειμένης ₁₂αὐτῷ
φυσικῶς αὐγῆς ἐν κοινωνίᾳ τοῦ φωτὸς γίνεται, ₁₃διὰ τῆς
ἐμφύτου δυνάμεως τὸ συγγενὲς ἐφελκόμενος, οὕτως ₁₄ἀναγ-
45 καῖον ἦν ἐγκραθῆναί τι τῇ ἀνθρωπίνῃ φύσει συγγενὲς ₁₅πρὸς τὸ
θεῖον, ὡς ἂν διὰ τοῦ καταλλήλου πρὸς τὸ ₁₆οἰκεῖον τὴν ἔφεσιν
ἔχοι. (5) Καὶ γὰρ καὶ ἐν τῇ τῶν ἀλόγων ₁₇φύσει, ὅσα τὸν ἔνυδρον καὶ
ἐναέριον ἔλαχε βίον, καταλλήλως ₁₈ἕκαστον τῷ τῆς ζωῆς εἴδει
κατεσκευάσθη, ὡς οἰκεῖον ₁₉ἑκατέρῳ καὶ ὁμόφυλον διὰ τῆς
50 ποιᾶς τοῦ σώματος ₂₀διαπλάσεως τῷ μὲν τὸν ἀέρα, τῷ δὲ τὸ

36 αὐτοῦ om. Srawley | 49 κατεσκευάσθη GNO : κατεσκευάσθη Srawley | ἑκατέρῳ
GNO : ἑκατέρου Srawley

demonstrated according to the order [of the argument] as the maker of human nature, not led by some necessity to the fashioning of man, but rather crafting[57] the genesis[58] of such a living thing out of an excess of love. For it was necessary that the light not be unseen, nor the glory be without witness, nor his goodness be unenjoyed, nor for all the other things seen about the divine nature to lie idle, there being no one partaking of or enjoying [them].

The Image of God

(4) Therefore, if man comes to genesis for these [reasons], for him to become a partaker of divine good things, he is necessarily fashioned like this, so as to suitably have a participation in good things. For just as the eye, because of the sunbeam naturally enclosing it, shares something in common with the light, drawing what is akin [to it] by an innate power,[59] so it was necessary for some kinship with the divine to be mixed with human nature, so that by the mutual relationship, [human nature] might have a propensity for what is proper [to it].[60] (5) For even with the nature of irrational things, of all that have been allotted life in the water and in the air, each was fashioned in a way that corresponds to [its] form of life, so that by the type of the body's formation what is proper and of the same stock

---

[57]Or "creating" (δημιουργήσας—the verb form of "demiurge"). The term "demiurge" was associated with the creation of the world at least since Plato's *Timaeus* (its original meaning is "craftsman").

[58]In this section, γένεσις is transliterated to retain in English the echo of the title of the book of Genesis. It could simply mean "birth," "coming into being."

[59]Competing theories of vision were proposed by thinkers from before Socrates until the early modern period: the two dominant views throughout history belonged to those who believed that light beams enter into the eye and cause us to see, and to those who believed that something extends out from the eye to apprehend the object of vision (the debate was no more settled in the age of Descartes than in that of the pre-Socratics).

[60]"What is proper [to it]" translates τὸ οἰκεῖον, which is often a synonym of ἴδιος (in 36.1.9 and 36.2.9 Gregory uses the two words interchangeably in a single line).

ὕδωρ εἶναι. Οὕτως ₂₁οὖν καὶ τὸν ἄνθρωπον ἐπὶ τῇ τῶν θείων ἀγαθῶν ἀπολαύσει ₂₂γενόμενον ἔδει τι συγγενὲς ἐν τῇ φύσει πρὸς τὸ μετεχόμενον ₂₃ἔχειν. (6) Διὰ τοῦτο καὶ ζωῇ καὶ λόγῳ καὶ σοφίᾳ καὶ πᾶσι ₂₄τοῖς θεοπρεπέσιν ἀγαθοῖς κατεκοσμήθη, ὡς 55 ἂν δι᾽ ἑκάστου ₂₅τούτων πρὸς τὸ οἰκεῖον τὴν ἐπιθυμίαν ἔχοι. Ἐπεὶ οὖν ₂₆ἓν τῶν περὶ τὴν θείαν φύσιν ἀγαθῶν καὶ ἡ ἀϊδιότης (GNO 18) ἐστίν, | ἔδει πάντως μηδὲ τούτου τὴν κατασκευὴν εἶναι τῆς ₂φύσεως ἡμῶν ἀπόκληρον, ἀλλ᾽ ἔχειν ἐν ἑαυτῇ τὸ ἀθάνατον, ₃ὡς (Sr 24) ἂν διὰ τῆς ἐγκειμένης | δυνάμεως γνωρίζοι τε τὸ ₄ὑπερκείμενον 60 καὶ ἐν ἐπιθυμίᾳ τῆς θείας ἀϊδιότητος εἴη.

(7) ₅Ταῦτά τοι περιληπτικῇ φωνῇ δι᾽ ἑνὸς ῥήματος ὁ τῆς κοσμογονίας ₆ἐνεδείξατο λόγος, κατ᾽ εἰκόνα Θεοῦ τὸν ἄνθρωπον ₇γεγενῆσθαι λέγων· ἐν γὰρ τῇ ὁμοιώσει τῇ κατὰ τὴν ₈εἰκόνα (PG 24) πάντων | ἐστὶ τῶν τὸ θεῖον χαρακτηριζόντων ἡ ₉ἀπαρίθμησις 65 καὶ ὅσα περὶ τούτων ἱστορικώτερον ὁ Μωϋσῆς ₁₀διεξέρχεται ἐν διηγήσεως εἴδει δόγματα ἡμῖν παρατιθέμενος, ₁₁τῆς αὐτῆς ἔχεται διδασκαλίας. Ὁ γὰρ παράδεισος ₁₂ἐκεῖνος καὶ ἡ τῶν καρπῶν ἰδιότης, ὧν ἡ βρῶσις οὐ ₁₃γαστρὸς πλησμονήν, ἀλλὰ γνῶσιν καὶ ἀϊδιότητα ζωῆς τοῖς ₁₄γευσαμένοις δίδωσι, πάντα 70 ταῦτα συνᾴδει τοῖς προτεθεωρημένοις ₁₅περὶ τὸν ἄνθρωπον, ὡς | (Sr 25) ἀγαθῆς τε καὶ ἐν ₁₆ἀγαθοῖς οὔσης κατ᾽ ἀρχὰς ἡμῖν τῆς φύσεως.

(8) ₁₇Ἀλλ᾽ ἀντιλέγει τυχὸν τοῖς εἰρημένοις ὁ πρὸς τὰ παρόντα ₁₈βλέπων καὶ οἴεται διελέγχειν τὸν λόγον οὐκ ἀληθεύοντα ₁₉τῷ μὴ

65 Μωϋσῆς GNO : Μωσῆς Srawley

[is provided] for each one (for the one to be in the air, and for the other in the water). Therefore in this way man also, who was born for the enjoyment of divine good things, must have in [his] nature some kinship with that of which he partakes. (6) Because of this he was adorned with life and reason and wisdom and all God-befitting good things, so that through each of them he might have the desire for what is proper [to him]. Since then one of the good things about the divine nature is eternality, it is altogether necessary for the fashioning of our nature not to be without this inheritance, but to have immortality in itself, so that by [this] inherent power one might both recognize the transcendent and desire the divine eternality.

(7) The account of the cosmogony[61] indicated these things through one saying in a comprehensive expression, saying that man has come into being "according to the image of God."[62] For the enumeration of all the things that characterize the divine is "in the likeness," "according to the image," and all that Moses goes through in a more historical [manner],[63] setting out teachings for us in the form of a narrative, which holds the same teaching. For that paradise and the property of [its] fruits, the eating of which do not give fullness of the belly, but knowledge and eternality of life to those who taste [them], all these things accord with what was previously seen about man, that in our origins [human] nature was both good and existing among good things.

OBJECTION: *Man is not in such conditions, but in the midst of evils. Thus claims about the image are untrue.*

(8) But perhaps one who looks at present things contradicts what has been said and thinks to refute the discourse as not being true,

[61]I.e., Genesis.
[62]Gen 1.27, 5.1. Cf. *On the Making of Man* 16.
[63]Here "more historical" (ἱστορικώτερον) refers less to "history" in the contemporary sense, i.e., "events that happened in the past," and more to a "narrative" or "account." (In other words, St Gregory is not discussing historicity so much as claiming that a narratival account also conveys more abstract spiritual teachings, as he says in the next clause.)

ἐν ἐκείνοις νῦν, ἀλλ' ἐν πᾶσι σχεδὸν τοῖς ὑπεναντίοις [20]ὁρᾶσθαι
75 τὸν ἄνθρωπον—ποῦ γὰρ τῆς ψυχῆς τὸ [21]θεοειδές; Ποῦ δὲ ἡ
ἀπάθεια τοῦ σώματος; Ποῦ τῆς ζωῆς τὸ [22]ἀΐδιον; —ὠκύ-
(GNO 19) μορον, ἐμπαθές, ἐπίκηρον, πρὸς πᾶσαν παθη- | μάτων ἰδέαν
κατά τε σῶμα καὶ ψυχὴν ἐπιτήδειον. Ταῦτα [2]καὶ τὰ τοιαῦτα
λέγων καὶ κατατρέχων τῆς φύσεως, [3]ἀνατρέπειν τὸν ἀποδοθέντα περὶ τοῦ ἀνθρώπου λόγον [4]οἰήσεται.—

80   —Ἀλλ' ὡς ἂν μηδα-
μοῦ τῆς ἀκολουθίας ὁ λόγος [5]παρατραπείη, καὶ περὶ τούτων ἐν
ὀλίγοις διαληψόμεθα. (9) [6]Τὸ νῦν ἐν ἀτόποις εἶναι τὴν ἀνθρωπίνην
ζωὴν οὐχ ἱκανός [7]ἐστιν ἔλεγχος τοῦ μηδέποτε τὸν ἄνθρωπον ἐν
ἀγαθοῖς [8]γεγενῆσθαι· ἐπειδὴ γὰρ Θεοῦ ἔργον ὁ ἄνθρωπος, τοῦ
85 δι' [9]ἀγαθότητα τὸ ζῷον τοῦτο παραγαγόντος εἰς γένεσιν, οὐκ
[10]ἄν τις εὐλόγως, οὗ ἡ αἰτία τῆς συστάσεως ἀγαθότης ἐστί,
[11]τοῦτον ἐν κακοῖς γεγενῆσθαι παρὰ τοῦ πεποιηκότος [12]καθυ-
ποπτεύσειεν, ἀλλ' ἕτερόν ἐστιν αἴτιον τοῦ ταῦτά τε [13]νῦν περὶ
(Sr 26) ἡμᾶς εἶναι καὶ | τῶν προτιμοτέρων ἐρημωθῆναι. [14]Ἀρχὴ δὲ πάλιν
90 καὶ πρὸς τοῦτον ἡμῖν τὸν λόγον οὐκ ἔξω [15]τῆς τῶν ἀντιλεγόντων
ἐστὶ συγκαταθέσεως. Ὁ γὰρ ἐπὶ [16]μετουσίᾳ τῶν ἰδίων ἀγαθῶν
ποιήσας τὸν ἄνθρωπον καὶ [17]πάντων αὐτῷ τῶν καλῶν τὰς ἀφορμὰς ἐγκατασκευάσας [18]τῇ φύσει, ὡς ἂν δι' ἑκάστου καταλλήλως πρὸς τὸ ὅμοιον [19]ἡ ὄρεξις φέροιτο, οὐκ ἂν τοῦ καλλίστου
95 τε καὶ τιμιωτάτου [20]τῶν ἀγαθῶν ἀπεστέρησε, λέγω δὴ τῆς κατὰ
τὸ ἀδέσποτον [21]καὶ αὐτεξούσιον χάριτος. (10) Εἰ γάρ τις ἀνάγκη τῆς
ἀνθρωπίνης [22]ἐπεστάτει ζωῆς, διεψεύσθη ἂν ἡ εἰκὼν κατ' ἐκεῖνο
[23]τὸ μέρος, ἀλλοτριωθεῖσα τῷ ἀνομοίῳ πρὸς τὸ ἀρχέτυπον· |
(GNO 20) τῆς γὰρ βασιλευούσης φύσεως ἡ ἀνάγκαις τισὶν ὑπεζευγμένη

for man is not seen in those [circumstances] now, but in all things that are nearly opposite—for where is the godlikeness of the soul? where is the impassibility[64] of the body? where is the eternality of life?—fleeting, impassioned, perishable, both body and soul fit for every form of suffering. Saying these things and the like, and running down [our] nature, he will think to overturn the discourse that has been given about man.

RESPONSE: *It was not always thus. Man was created in the midst of good things, and with free will.*

But so the discourse may be in no way be diverted from [its] order, we will also take up these things in a few [words]. (9) The present existence of human life in absurdities is not a sufficient refutation that man has never come into being among good things; for since man is a work of God, who led this living thing to genesis by [his] goodness, someone would not reasonably suspect this: that he, for whom the cause of [his] constitution is goodness, was brought into being among evil things by him who has made [him], but there is a different cause of these things now existing around us and of our being deprived of more honorable things. And again the beginning of this discourse of ours is also not beyond the assent of the naysayers. For he who made man for participation in his own good things, and who fashioned in his nature the means[65] for all things that are good for him, so that the appetite might in each case be carried appropriately toward what is similar, did not rob [man] of the best and most honorable of good things, I mean the grace of independence and self-determination. (10) If some necessity presided over human life, the image would have been false in that part, being alien to the archetype by [its] dissimilarity; for how would it be called the image of the kingly nature if it were under yoke to and enslaved by

---

[64]Or "passionlessness" (ἀπάθεια). In patristic writings "passions" are often identified with sin, but "passion" (πάθος) can also refer more generally to "suffering" or simply the state of being "passive," as opposed to active. Just below, we find two related words, translated as "impassioned" (ἐμπαθές) and "suffering" (παθημάτων).

[65]Or "the origins [τὰς ἀφορμὰς] of all things that are good for him."

[100] [2]τε καὶ δουλεύουσα πῶς ἂν εἰκὼν ὀνομάζοιτο; Οὐκοῦν [3]τὸ διὰ
(Sr 27) πάντων πρὸς τὸ | θεῖον ὡμοιωμένον ἔδει πάντως [4]ἔχειν ἐν τῇ
φύσει τὸ αὐτοκρατὲς καὶ ἀδέσποτον, ὥστε [5]ἆθλον ἀρετῆς εἶναι
τὴν τῶν ἀγαθῶν μετουσίαν.

(11) Πόθεν [6]οὖν, ἐρεῖς, ὁ διὰ πάντων τοῖς καλλίστοις τετιμημένος
τὰ [7]χείρω τῶν ἀγαθῶν ἀντηλλάξατο;—

[105]   —Σαφὴς καὶ ὁ περὶ τούτου
[8]λόγος· οὐδεμία κακοῦ γένεσις ἐκ τοῦ θείου βουλήματος [9]τὴν
ἀρχὴν ἔσχεν—ἢ γὰρ ἂν ἔξω μέμψεως ἦν ἡ κακία, θεὸν [10]ἑαυτῆς
ἐπιγραφομένη ποιητὴν καὶ πατέρα—ἀλλ' ἐμφύεταί [11]πως τὸ
κακὸν ἔνδοθεν, τῇ προαιρέσει τότε συνιστάμενον, [12]ὅταν τις ἀπὸ
[110] τοῦ καλοῦ γένηται τῆς ψυχῆς ἀναχώρησις. [13]Καθάπερ γὰρ ἡ
ὅρασις φύσεώς ἐστιν ἐνέργεια, ἡ δὲ πήρωσις [14]στέρησίς ἐστι τῆς
(Sr 28) φυσικῆς ἐνεργείας, οὕτω καὶ ἡ ἀρετὴ [15]πρὸς τὴν κακίαν | ἀντι-
(PG 25) καθέστηκεν. Οὐ γὰρ ἔστιν ἄλλως [16]κακίας γένεσιν ἐν-| νοῆσαι ἢ
ἀρετῆς ἀπουσίαν. (12) Ὥσπερ γὰρ [17]τοῦ φωτὸς ὑφαιρεθέντος ὁ
[115] ζόφος ἐπηκολούθησε, παρόντος [18]δὲ οὐκ ἔστιν, οὕτως, ἕως ἂν
παρῇ τὸ ἀγαθὸν ἐν τῇ [19]φύσει, ἀνύπαρκτόν τί ἐστι καθ' ἑαυτὴν ἡ
κακία, ἡ δὲ τοῦ [20]κρείττονος ἀναχώρησις τοῦ ἐναντίου γίνεται
γένεσις. Ἐπεὶ [21]οὖν τοῦτο τῆς αὐτεξουσιότητός ἐστι τὸ ἰδίωμα,
τὸ κατ' [22]ἐξουσίαν αἱρεῖσθαι τὸ καταθύμιον, οὐχ ὁ θεός σοι τῶν
[120] [23]παρόντων ἐστὶν αἴτιος κακῶν, ἀδέσποτόν τε καὶ ἄνετόν [24]σοι
κατασκευάσας τὴν φύσιν, ἀλλ' ἡ ἀβουλία τὸ χεῖρον [25]ἀντὶ τοῦ
κρείττονος προελομένη.

(GNO 21) ΣΤ'   Ζητεῖς δὲ καὶ τὴν αἰτίαν τυχὸν τῆς κατὰ τὴν βουλὴν
διαμαρτίας· [2]εἰς τοῦτο γὰρ ἡ ἀκολουθία τὸν λόγον φέρει.—

                                                  —[3]Οὐκ-
οῦν πάλιν ἀρχή τις ἡμῖν κατὰ τὸ εὔλογον εὑρεθήσεται, [4]ᾗ καὶ

some necessities? Therefore what is similar to the divine in all things must by all means have self-mastery and independence by nature, so that the prize for virtue may be participation in good things.

OBJECTION: *Why did we fall?*

(11) "Whence is it, then," you ask, "that he who was honored with the best of all things exchanged good things for inferior ones?"

RESPONSE: *We chose evil through our free will.*

The discourse is also clear about this: the genesis of evil in no way had [its] beginning from the divine will—for vice would be without blame if God was claimed to be its maker and father—but the evil is somehow implanted within, being composed by decision then, when there is any withdrawal of the soul from the good. For just as sight is an activity of nature, and blindness is a privation of a natural activity, so too virtue is opposed to vice. For the genesis of vice is to be understood in no other way than as an absence of virtue. (12) For just as when the light is taken away darkness follows, but when [light] is present [darkness] does not exist, so as long as good is present in a nature vice is in itself something nonexistent, but the withdrawal of what is superior is the genesis of the opposite. Since, therefore, this is the property of self-determination, to choose at will what is desired, it is not God who is the cause of your present evils, who fashioned your nature both independent and uncontrolled, but [your] thoughtlessness, which chose the inferior in place of the superior.

OBJECTION: *What is the cause of this error in judgment?*

6 But perhaps you also seek the cause of the error in judgment; for the order [of the argument] leads the discourse to this.

RESPONSE: *The devil fell through envy, then he tempted man.*

Therefore, again, some reasonable beginning[66] will be discovered

---

[66]Or "principle" (ἀρχή). St Gregory is speaking of the premise for further argumentation.

τοῦτο σαφηνίσει τὸ ζήτημα. Τοιοῦτόν τινα λόγον $_5$παρὰ τῶν
5 (Sr 29) πατέρων διεδεξάμεθα· ἔστι δὲ ὁ λόγος οὐ | μυθώδης $_6$διήγη-
σις, ἀλλ' ἐξ αὐτῆς τῆς φύσεως ἡμῶν τὸ πιστὸν $_7$ἐπαγόμενος.
(2) Διπλῆ τίς ἐστιν ἐν τοῖς οὖσιν ἡ κατανόησις, $_8$εἰς τὸ νοητόν
τε καὶ αἰσθητὸν τῆς θεωρίας διῃρημένης· καὶ $_9$οὐδὲν ἂν παρὰ
ταῦτα καταληφθείη ἐν τῇ τῶν ὄντων φύσει $_{10}$τῆς διαιρέσεως
10 ταύτης ἔξω φερόμενον. Διῄρηται δὲ ταῦτα $_{11}$πρὸς ἄλληλα πολ-
λῷ τῷ μέσῳ, ὡς μήτε τὴν αἰσθητὴν ἐν $_{12}$τοῖς νοητοῖς εἶναι
γνωρίσμασι, μήτε ἐν τοῖς αἰσθητοῖς ἐκείνην, $_{13}$ἀλλ' ἀπὸ τῶν
ἐναντίων ἑκατέραν χαρακτηρίζεσθαι. $_{14}$Ἡ μὲν γὰρ νοητὴ φύσις
ἀσώματόν τι χρῆμά ἐστι καὶ ἀναφὲς $_{15}$καὶ ἀνείδεον· ἡ δὲ αἰσθη-
15 τὴ κατ' αὐτὸ τὸ ὄνομα ἐντός $_{16}$ἐστι τῆς διὰ τῶν αἰσθητηρίων
κατανοήσεως. (3) Ἀλλ' ὥσπερ $_{17}$ἐν αὐτῷ τῷ αἰσθητῷ κόσμῳ, πολ-
(Sr 30) λῆς πρὸς ἄλληλα τῶν $_{18}$στοιχείων οὔσης ἐναντιώσεως, | ἐπινε-
νόηταί τις ἁρμονία $_{19}$διὰ τῶν ἐναντίων ἁρμοζομένη παρὰ τῆς τοῦ
παντὸς ἐπιστατούσης $_{20}$σοφίας, καὶ οὕτω πάσης γίνεται πρὸς
20 ἑαυτῇ $_{21}$συμφωνία τῆς κτίσεως, οὐδαμοῦ τῆς φυσικῆς ἐναντιό-
τητος $_{22}$τὸν τῆς συμπνοίας εἱρμὸν διαλυούσης· κατὰ τὸν αὐτὸν
(GNO 22) $_{23}$τρόπον καὶ τοῦ αἰσθητοῦ πρὸς τὸ νοητὸν γίνεταί τις | κατὰ
θείαν σοφίαν μίξις τε καὶ ἀνάκρασις, ὡς ἂν πάντα $_2$τοῦ καλοῦ
κατὰ τὸ ἴσον μετέχοι καὶ μηδὲν τῶν ὄντων $_3$ἀμοιροίη τῆς τοῦ
25 κρείττονος φύσεως. Διὰ τοῦτο τὸ μὲν $_4$κατάλληλον τῇ νοητῇ
φύσει χωρίον ἡ λεπτὴ καὶ εὐκίνητός $_5$ἐστιν οὐσία, κατὰ τὴν
ὑπερκόσμιον λῆξιν πολλὴν ἔχουσα $_6$τῷ ἰδιάζοντι τῆς φύσεως
πρὸς τὸ νοητὸν τὴν συγγένειαν, $_7$προμηθείᾳ δὲ κρείττονι πρὸς
(Sr 31) τὴν αἰσθητὴν κτίσιν γίνεται $_8$τις τοῦ | νοητοῦ συνανάκρασις, ὡς
30 ἂν μηδὲν ἀπόβλητον εἴη $_9$τῆς κτίσεως, καθώς φησιν ὁ ἀπόστολος, μηδὲ τῆς θείας $_{10}$κοινωνίας ἀπόκληρον. (4) Τούτου χάριν ἐκ

---

19 οὕτω GNO : οὕτως Srawley

for us, which will also clarify this inquiry. We have received such an account from the fathers, and the account is not a mythical narrative,[67] but one that urges belief from our nature itself. (2) [Our] observation of existing things is something twofold, [our] contemplation [of them] being divided into the noetic[68] and the sensory; and nothing beside these, falling outside this division, may be grasped in the nature of existing things. And these are divided from one another by a great interval, so that the sensory is not among the characteristics of noetic things, nor are the latter among sensory things, but each is characterized by its opposite. For while the noetic nature is some bodiless thing, impalpable, and formless, the sensory, by its very name, is within the understanding through the senses. (3) But just as in the sensory world itself, though there is much opposition of the elements with each other, a certain harmony has been contrived by the Wisdom that presides over all, harmonizing through opposites, and thus the symphony of all creation with itself comes about, nothing of the opposite nature dissolving the chain of agreement; in the same manner also a certain mixture and mingling of the sensory with the noetic comes about by the divine wisdom, so that all might partake equally of the good, and none of the things that exist might be without a portion of the superior nature. Because of this, the realm that corresponds to the noetic nature is a subtle and agile essence, by supercosmic allotment having in the distinctiveness of [its] nature much kinship with the noetic, but by superior forethought there is a certain commixture of the noetic with the sensory creation, so that nothing of creation would be "rejected," as the Apostle says,[69] nor disinherited from the divine communion. (4) For

[67] St Gregory is responding to Julian the Apostate, who called the Genesis account "altogether mythical" (μυθῶδη). Julian, *Against the Galileans* 75b (trans. Paton). Julian readily admitted that "the Hellenes invented their myths," but he criticized Christians for not making a similar concession: "Unless every one of these is a myth having an ineffable contemplation [θεωρίαν], as I indeed believe, they are filled with many blasphemous sayings about God." Ibid., 44a, 75b.

[68] Or "intelligible" (νοητόν). Throughout the translation, "noetic" is used for both νοητός and νοερός.

[69] 1 Tim 4.4.

νοητοῦ τε καὶ ₁₁αἰσθητοῦ τὸ κατὰ τὸν ἄνθρωπον μίγμα παρὰ τῆς
θείας ₁₂ἀναδείκνυται φύσεως, καθὼς διδάσκει τῆς κοσμογενείας
₁₃ὁ λόγος· Λαβὼν γὰρ ὁ θεός, φησίν, χοῦν ἀπὸ τῆς γῆς τὸν |
35 (PG 28) ₁₄ἄνθρωπον ἔπλασε καὶ διὰ τῆς ἰδίας ἐμπνεύσεως τῷ πλάσ-
ματι ₁₅τὴν ζωὴν ἐνεφύτευσεν, ὡς ἂν συνεπαρθείη τῷ θείῳ τὸ
₁₆γήϊνον καὶ μία τις κατὰ τὸ ὁμότιμον διὰ πάσης τῆς κτίσεως ₁₇ἡ
χάρις διήκοι, τῆς κάτω φύσεως πρὸς τὴν ὑπερκόσμιον ₁₈συγκιρ-
ναμένης.

40   (5) Ἐπεὶ οὖν τῆς νοητῆς κτίσεως προϋποστάσης, ₁₉καὶ ἑκάστῃ
(Sr 32) τῶν ἀγγελικῶν δυνάμεων πρὸς | τὴν ₂₀τοῦ παντὸς σύστασιν ἐνερ-
γείας τινὸς παρὰ τῆς τῶν πάντων ₂₁ἐπιστατούσης ἐξουσίας
προσνεμηθείσης, ἥν τις δύναμις ₂₂καὶ ἡ τὸν περίγειον τόπον
(GNO 23) (συνέχειν τε καὶ περικρατεῖν | τεταγμένη, εἰς αὐτὸ τοῦτο
45 δυναμωθεῖσα παρὰ τῆς τὸ πᾶν ₂₀οἰκονομούσης δυνάμεως· εἶτα
κατεσκευάσθη τὸ γήϊνον ₃πλάσμα, τῆς ἄνω δυνάμεως ἀπεικόνισμα—τοῦτο δὴ τὸ ₄ζῷον ὁ ἄνθρωπος—καὶ ἦν ἐν αὐτῷ τὸ
θεοειδὲς τῆς νοητῆς ₅φύσεως κάλλος ἀρρήτῳ τινὶ δυνάμει
συγκεκραμένον· δεινὸν ₆ποιεῖται καὶ οὐκ ἀνεκτὸν ὁ τὴν περί-
50 γειον οἰκονομίαν ₇λαχών, εἰ ἐκ τῆς ὑποχειρίου αὐτῷ φύσεως
ἀναδειχθήσεταί ₈τις οὐσία πρὸς τὴν ὑπερέχουσαν ἀξίαν ὡμοιω-
μένη.

        (6) Τὸ δ' ₉ὅπως ἐπὶ τὸ πάθος κατερρύη τοῦ φθόνου ὁ ἐπὶ μηδενὶ
₁₀κακῷ κτισθεὶς παρὰ τοῦ τὸ πᾶν ἐν ἀγαθότητι συστησαμένου,
55 (Sr 33) ₁₁τὸ μὲν δι' ἀκριβείας ἐπεξιέναι | οὐ τῆς παρούσης πραγματείας
₁₂ἐστί, δυνατὸν δ' ἂν εἴη καὶ δι' ὀλίγου τοῖς εὐπειθεστέροις
₁₃παραθέσθαι τὸν λόγον. Τῆς γὰρ ἀρετῆς καὶ τῆς ₁₄κακίας οὐχ ὡς
δύο τινῶν καθ' ὑπόστασιν φαινομένων ἡ ₁₅ἀντιδιαστολὴ θεω-
ρεῖται· ἀλλ' ὥσπερ ἀντιδιαιρεῖται τῷ ₁₆ὄντι τὸ μὴ ὂν καὶ οὐκ
60 ἔστι καθ' ὑπόστασιν εἰπεῖν τὸ μὴ ὂν ₁₇ἀντιδιαστέλλεσθαι πρὸς τὸ

33 κοσμογενείας GNO : κοσμογονίας Srawley

this reason the mixture of noetic and sensory in man is shown forth
by the divine nature, as the account of the genesis of the cosmos[70]
teaches. For "God," it says, "taking dust from the earth, formed man"
and by his own inbreathing he implanted life in what he formed,[71]
so that the earthly might be raised up to the divine and one certain
grace of equal honor might pervade all of creation, the lower nature
being mingled with the supercosmic.

(5) Since, then, the noetic creation existed beforehand, and the
authority presiding over all things assigned a certain activity to each
of the angelic powers for the maintenance of the universe, there was
a certain power also assigned to hold together and to have command
over the region around the earth, empowered for this very thing by
the power that arranges the economy of the universe, [and] then
an earthen creature[72] was fashioned, a representation of the higher
power—now man is this living thing—and there was in him the
godlike beauty of the noetic nature commingled with some ineffable power, [and] he who was allotted the economy of the [region]
around the earth deems it terrible and unbearable if, of the nature
under his control, some being should be shown as having a likeness
to the transcendent dignity.

(6) Now it does not belong to the present treatise to go over
with precision how the one who was in no way created for evil by
him who constituted all in goodness sank down into the passion of
envy,[73] but it would be possible for an account to be provided briefly
for those who are open to being persuaded. For the distinction[74]
between virtue and vice is not seen[75] as between some two substan-

---

[70]Perhaps an allusion to Genesis using an unusual word: κοσμογενείας. A textual
variant uses "cosmogony" (κοσμογονίας), a word more familiar to pagan audiences
(recalling Hesiod's *Theogony*).

[71]Gen 2.7.

[72]Lit. "formation," "formed thing" (πλάσμα).

[73]Wis 2.23–24 (likewise influential in the account of the devil's fall in *On the
Incarnation* 5).

[74]ἀντιδιαστολὴ.

[75]Or "contemplated" (θεωρεῖται).

ὄν, ἀλλὰ τὴν ἀνυπαρξίαν ₁₈ἀντιδιαιρεῖσθαι λέγομεν πρὸς τὴν
ὕπαρξιν, κατὰ τὸν ₁₉αὐτὸν τρόπον καὶ ἡ κακία τῷ τῆς ἀρετῆς
ἀντικαθέστηκε ₂₀λόγῳ, οὐ καθ' ἑαυτήν τις οὖσα, ἀλλὰ τῇ ἀπουσίᾳ νοουμένη ₂₁τοῦ κρείττονος· καὶ ὥσπερ φαμὲν ἀντιδιαι-
65 ρεῖσθαι τῇ ὁράσει ₂₂τὴν πήρωσιν, οὐ καθ' ἑαυτὴν οὖσαν τῇ φύσει
τὴν πήρωσιν, ₂₃ἀλλὰ προλαβούσης ἕξεως στέρησιν, οὕτω καὶ
τὴν ₂₄κακίαν ἐν τῇ τοῦ ἀγαθοῦ στερήσει θεωρεῖσθαι λέγομεν,
(GNO 24) ₂₅οἷόν τινα σκιὰν τῇ ἀναχωρήσει τῆς ἀκτῖνος ἐπισυμβαίνου- | σαν.
(Sr 34) (7) Ἐπειδὴ τοίνυν ἡ | ἄκτιστος φύσις τῆς κινήσεως τῆς ₂κατὰ
70 τροπὴν καὶ μεταβολὴν καὶ ἀλλοίωσίν ἐστιν ἀνεπίδεκτος, ₃πᾶν
δὲ τὸ διὰ κτίσεως ὑποστὰν συγγενῶς πρὸς ₄τὴν ἀλλοίωσιν ἔχει,
διότι καὶ αὐτὴ τῆς κτίσεως ἡ ὑπόστασις ₅ἀπὸ ἀλλοιώσεως
ἤρξατο τοῦ μὴ ὄντος εἰς τὸ εἶναι θείᾳ ₆δυνάμει μετατεθέντος·
κτιστὴ δὲ ἦν καὶ ἡ μνημονευθεῖσα ₇δύναμις, αὐτεξουσίῳ κινή-
75 ματι τὸ δοκοῦν αἱρουμένη, ἐπειδὴ ₈πρὸς τὸ ἀγαθόν τε καὶ
ἄφθονον ἐπέμυσεν ὄμμα, ὥσπερ ₉ὁ ἐν ἡλίῳ τοῖς βλεφάροις τὰς
ὄψεις ἀποβαλὼν σκότος ₁₀ὁρᾷ, οὕτω κἀκεῖνος αὐτῷ τῷ μὴ
θελῆσαι τὸ ἀγαθὸν κατανοῆσαι ₁₁τὸ ἐναντίον τῷ ἀγαθῷ κατενόησε. Τοῦτο δέ ἐστιν ₁₂ὁ φθόνος.
80 (Sr 35)   (8) Ὁμολογεῖται δὲ παντὸς πράγματος ἀρχὴν τῶν | ₁₃μετ' αὐτὴν
κατὰ τὸ ἀκόλουθον ἐπισυμβαινόντων αἰτίαν ₁₄εἶναι· οἷον τῇ
ὑγείᾳ τὸ εὐεκτεῖν, τὸ ἐργάζεσθαι, τὸ καθ' ἡδονὴν ₁₅βιοτεύειν, τῇ
δὲ νόσῳ τὸ ἀσθενεῖν, τὸ ἀνενέργητον ₁₆εἶναι, τὸ ἐν ἀηδίᾳ τὴν
(PG 29) ζωὴν ἔχειν. Οὕτω | καὶ τὰ ἄλλα πάντα ₁₇ταῖς οἰκείαις ἀρχαῖς
85 κατὰ τὸ ἀκόλουθον ἕπεται. Ὥσπερ ₁₈οὖν ἡ ἀπάθεια τῆς κατ'
ἀρετὴν ζωῆς ἀρχὴ καὶ ὑπόθεσις ₁₉γίνεται, οὕτως ἡ διὰ τοῦ
φθόνου γενομένη πρὸς κακίαν ₂₀ῥοπὴ τῶν μετ' αὐτὴν πάντων
ἀναδειχθέντων κακῶν ὁδὸς ₂₁κατέστη. (9) Ἐπειδὴ γὰρ ἅπαξ πρὸς
(GNO 25) τὸ κακὸν τὴν ῥοπὴν | ἔσχεν ὁ τῇ ἀποστροφῇ τῆς ἀγαθότητος ἐν
90 ἑαυτῷ γεννήσας ₂τὸν φθόνον, ὥσπερ λίθος ἀκρωρείας ἀπορ-
ραγεὶς ὑπὸ τοῦ ₃ἰδίου βάρους πρὸς τὸ πρανὲς συνελαύνεται,
οὕτω κἀκεῖνος, ₄τῆς πρὸς τὸ ἀγαθὸν συμφυῖας ἀποσπασθεὶς καὶ

77 ὄφεις ἀποβαλὼν GNO : ὄψεις ὑποβαλὼν Srawley | 78 κατανοῆσαι GNO : νοῆσαι
Srawley

tial phenomena; but just as nonbeing is distinguished[76] from being (and this is not to say that nonbeing is distinguished from being in substance, but we say nonexistence is distinguished from existence), in the same manner vice is also opposed to virtue in principle; [it is] not some being in itself, but understood as an absence of what is better; and just as we say that blindness is logically opposed to sight—blindness is not by nature a being in itself, but a privation of a former faculty—so we also say vice is to be seen in the privation of the good, just as some shadow follows upon the withdrawal of the sun's ray. (7) Since, then, the uncreated nature does not admit of motion by way of change or alteration, and all that subsists through creation has an affinity[77] with alteration, since even the substance of creation itself began from alteration, nonbeing passing into existence by divine power, and the abovementioned power was also created, choosing by a free-willed movement[78] what pleased him,[79] he then closed his eyes to what is good and not envious, just as he who closes his eyes in the sun sees darkness, so too he by the very fact that he did not will to perceive the good, perceived the opposite of the good. And this is envy.

(8) Now it is agreed that the beginning of every matter is the cause of the things that follow after it in order: as upon health [there follows] a good bodily state, activity, a pleasant life; upon sickness [there follows] weakness, inactivity, an unpleasant life. So too all other things follow from their own causes in order. Therefore just as dispassion is the beginning and foundation of a life in accordance with virtue, so the inclination toward vice that came about through envy became the way to all the evils that have shown up after it. (9) For then, once he who begot envy in himself by turning away from goodness came to have an inclination to evil, just as a stone torn from a mountain ridge is forced down headlong by its own weight, so too he was torn from an innate affinity with the good and weighed down

[76]ἀντιδιαιρεῖται.
[77]Or "kinship" (συγγενῶς).
[78]Or "self-determination" (αὐτεξουσίῳ).
[79]Or "seemed good" (τὸ δοκοῦν) to him.

πρὸς ₅κακίαν βρίσας αὐτομάτως οἷόν τινι βάρει πρὸς τὸν
ἔσχατον ₆τῆς πονηρίας ὅρον συνωσθεὶς ἀπηνέχθη, καὶ τὴν
95 διανοητικὴν ₇δύναμιν, ἣν εἰς συνέργειαν τῆς τοῦ κρείττονος
₈μετουσίας ἔσχε παρὰ τοῦ κτίσαντος, ταύτην εἰς εὕρεσιν ₉τῶν
(Sr 36) κατὰ κακίαν ἐπινοουμένων συνεργὸν ποιησάμενος, | ₁₀εὐμηχά-
νως περιέρχεται δι' ἀπάτης τὸν ἄνθρωπον, αὐτὸν ₁₁ἑαυτοῦ
γενέσθαι πείσας φονέα τε καὶ αὐτόχειρα.—

—(10) Ἐπειδὴ ₁₂γὰρ διὰ τῆς
100 θείας εὐλογίας δυναμωθεὶς ὁ ἄνθρωπος ὑψηλὸς ₁₃μὲν ἦν τῷ
ἀξιώματι—βασιλεύειν γὰρ ἐτάχθη τῆς γῆς τε ₁₄καὶ τῶν ἐπ'
αὐτῆς πάντων, καλὸς δὲ τὸ εἶδος (ἀπεικόνισμα ₁₅γὰρ τοῦ
ἀρχετύπου ἐγεγόνει κάλλους, ἀπαθὴς δὲ τὴν ₁₆φύσιν, τοῦ
γὰρ ἀπαθοῦς μίμημα ἦν)—ἀνάπλεως δὲ παρρησίας, ₁₇αὐτῆς
105 κατὰ πρόσωπον τῆς θείας ἐμφανείας κατατρυφῶν· ₁₈ταῦτα δὲ
τῷ ἀντικειμένῳ τοῦ κατὰ τὸν φθόνον ₁₉πάθους ὑπεκκαύματα ἦν.
(11) Ἰσχύϊ δέ τινι καὶ βίᾳ δυνάμεως ₂₀κατεργάσασθαι τὸ κατὰ
γνώμην οὐχ οἷός τε ἦν (ὑπερίσχυε ₂₁γὰρ ἡ τῆς εὐλογίας τοῦ
Θεοῦ δύναμις τῆς τούτου βίας)· διὰ ₂₂τοῦτο ἀποστῆσαι τῆς
110 ἐνισχυούσης αὐτὸν δυνάμεως μηχανᾶται, ₂₃ὥς ἂν εὐάλωτος
αὐτῷ πρὸς τὴν ἐπιβουλὴν κατασταίη. ₂₄Καὶ ὥσπερ ἐπὶ λύχνου
(GNO 26) τοῦ πυρὸς τῆς θρυαλλίδος | περιδεδραγμένου, εἴ τις ἀδυνατῶν
(Sr 37) τῷ φυσήματι σβέσαι ₂τὴν φλόγα ὕδωρ ἐμμίξειε τῷ ἐλαίῳ, | διὰ
τῆς ἐπινοίας ₃ταύτης ἀμαυρώσει τὴν φλόγα, οὕτω δι' ἀπάτης
115 τῇ προαιρέσει ₄τοῦ ἀνθρώπου τὴν κακίαν ἐμμίξας ὁ ἀντικεί-
μενος ₅σβέσιν τινὰ καὶ ἀμαύρωσιν τῆς εὐλογίας ἐποίησεν, ἧς
₆ἐπιλειπούσης ἐξ ἀνάγκης τὸ ἀντικείμενον ἀντεισέρχεται.
₇Ἀντίκειται δὲ τῇ ζωῇ μὲν ὁ θάνατος, ἡ ἀσθένεια δὲ τῇ

114 οὕτω GNO : οὕτως Srawley

toward vice on his own initiative, as if by some weight he was forced and carried away to the last boundary of wickedness, and the power of thought, which he had from the creator to aid participation in what is superior, this was made an aid in the discovery[80] of vicious devices,[81] [and] cunningly he cheats man by deceit, persuading him to become his own murderer and executioner.

(10) For since man was exalted in dignity, empowered through the divine blessing—he was appointed to reign over the earth and all things on it, and [his] form was beautiful (for he had come into being as a representation of the archetypal beauty, and [he had] an impassible nature, for he was a copy[82] of the impassible one)—he was full of confidence,[83] delighting in the presence of the divine manifestation itself. But these things were fuel for the passion of envy in the adversary.

(11) But this intention was not able to be accomplished by any strength or by force of power (for the power of God's blessing was stronger than this force); because of this he devises to withdraw him [i.e., man] from the Power that strengthened him, so that he might render him easy prey to the plot against him. And just as in the case of a lamp—when the fire has caught the wick, if someone who is unable to quench the flame by blowing mixes water with the oil, he will dim the flame by this artifice—so the adversary, mixing vice in man's will[84] by deception, somewhat quenched and dimmed the blessing, [and] when this [i.e., the blessing] failed, by necessity the opposite entered in. Now death is opposed to life, weakness to

---

[80]Or "invention" (εὕρεσιν).

[81]Lit. "of things devised in accordance with vice" (τῶν κατὰ κακίαν ἐπινοουμένων).

[82]Or "imitation" (μίμημα).

[83]Or "boldness," "frankness," "candor" (παρρησίας). This connotes the confidence of free citizens in their city, the frankness of one friend with another, and the filial boldness of a son with his father (in the Byzantine liturgy the priest prays for such boldness, that he and the people may address God as Father in the Lord's Prayer). This confidence was enjoyed in paradise, lost in the fall, and regained for us by the Son, through whom we become adopted children of God (Jn 1.12; Rom 8.15; Gal 4.6).

[84]Or "faculty of decision" (προαιρέσει).

δυνάμει, ₈τῇ εὐλογίᾳ δὲ ἡ κατάρα, τῇ παρρησίᾳ δὲ ἡ αἰσχύνη,
120 ₉καὶ πᾶσι τοῖς ἀγαθοῖς τὰ κατὰ τὸ ἐναντίον νοούμενα. Διὰ
₁₀τοῦτο ἐν τοῖς παροῦσι κακοῖς ἐστὶ νῦν τὸ ἀνθρώπινον, τῆς
₁₁ἀρχῆς ἐκείνης τοῦ τοιούτου τέλους τὰς ἀφορμὰς παρα-
₁₂σχούσης.

Ζ' ₁₃Καὶ μηδεὶς ἐρωτάτω, εἰ προειδὼς τὴν ἀνθρωπίνην
συμφορὰν ₁₄ὁ Θεὸς τὴν ἐκ τῆς ἀβουλίας αὐτῷ συμβησομένην
₁₅ἦλθεν εἰς τὸ κτίσαι τὸν ἄνθρωπον, ᾧ τὸ μὴ γενέσθαι μᾶλλον
₁₆ἴσως ἢ τὸ ἐν κακοῖς εἶναι λυσιτελέστερον ἦν. Ταῦτα ₁₇γὰρ οἱ τοῖς
5 Μανιχαϊκοῖς δόγμασι δι' ἀπάτης παρασυρέντες ₁₈εἰς σύστασιν
(Sr 38) τῆς ἑαυτῶν πλάνης προβάλ- | λουσιν, ὡς ₁₉διὰ τούτου πονηρὸν
(PG 32) εἶναι τὸν τῆς ἀνθρωπίνης φύσεως ₂₀κτίστην ἀποδει-| κνύοντες. Εἰ
γὰρ ἀγνοεῖ μὲν τῶν ὄντων ₂₁οὐδὲν ὁ Θεός, ἐν κακοῖς δὲ ὁ
ἄνθρωπος, οὐκέτ' ἂν ὁ τῆς ₂₂ἀγαθότητος τοῦ Θεοῦ διασῴζοιτο
10 λόγος, εἴπερ ἐν κακοῖς ₂₃μέλλοντα τὸν ἄνθρωπον ζήσεσθαι πρὸς
τὸν βίον παρήγαγεν· ₂₄εἰ γὰρ ἀγαθῆς φύσεως ἡ κατὰ τὸ ἀγαθὸν
ἐνέργεια ₂₅πάντως ἐστίν, ὁ λυπηρὸς οὗτος καὶ ἐπίκηρος βίος
οὐκέτ' ₂₆ἄν, φησίν, εἰς τὴν τοῦ ἀγαθοῦ δημιουργίαν ἀνάγοιτο,
(GNO 27) ἀλλ' | ἕτερον χρὴ τῆς τοιαύτης ζωῆς αἴτιον οἴεσθαι, ᾧ πρὸς
15 ₂πονηρίαν ἡ φύσις ἐπιρρεπῶς ἔχει.

(2) Ταῦτα γὰρ πάντα καὶ τὰ ₃τοιαῦτα τοῖς μὲν ἐν βάθει καθάπερ
τινὰ δευσοποιὸν βαφὴν ₄τὴν αἱρετικὴν παραδεδεγμένοις ἀπάτην ἰσχύν τινα διὰ τῆς ₅ἐπιπολαίου πιθανότητος ἔχειν δοκεῖ,
τοῖς δὲ διορατικωτέροις ₆τῆς ἀληθείας σαθρὰ ὄντα καὶ πρό-
20 χειρον τὴν τῆς ₇ἀπάτης ἀπόδειξιν ἔχοντα σαφῶς καθορᾶται.
Καί μοι ₈δοκεῖ καλῶς ἔχειν τὸν ἀπόστολον ἐν τούτοις συνή-

power, curse to blessing, shame to boldness, and to all good things those that are understood as their opposite. Because of this humanity is now in the midst of present evils, that beginning affording the origins of such an end.

God's Foresight and the Origin of Evil

OBJECTION: *If God foresaw human sin and misery, why did he create man? It would be better not to come into being than to exist amidst evils.*

7 And let no one ask if, having foreknown the human calamity, which befell him because of [his] thoughtlessness, God came to create man, since perhaps it was more profitable not to come into being than to exist in the midst of evils. For these things are proposed by those who are deceptively misled by the Manichean teaching for the confirmation of their own error, so as to demonstrate by this that the creator of human nature is wicked. "For if God is ignorant of none of the things that exist, but man is in the midst of evils, the argument for God's goodness can no longer be maintained, if indeed he brought man into a life that is destined to be lived in the midst of evils; for if activity in the good is altogether [characteristic] of a good nature, this painful and transient life," they say, "can no longer be referred to the creation[85] of the Good, but it is necessary to think of another cause of such a life, whose nature is inclined to wickedness."

RESPONSE: *We must judge things correctly. God created everything that exists in goodness. Evil is a privation of being, freely chosen by man. God is not to blame.*

(2) All these and similar [arguments] seem, through [their] superficial plausibility, to have a certain force for those who have received the heretical deceit deeply like some indelible dye, but those who have a keener perception of the truth clearly see these [arguments] are unsound and have a proof of the deception ready to hand. And

[85]Or "workmanship" (δημιουργίαν).

γορον ₉τῆς κατ' αὐτῶν κατηγορίας προστήσασθαι. Διαιρεῖ γὰρ
ἐν ₁₀τῷ πρὸς Κορινθίους λόγῳ τάς τε σαρκώδεις καὶ τὰς
πνευματικὰς ₁₁τῶν ψυχῶν καταστάσεις, δεικνύς, οἶμαι, διὰ |
25 (Sr 39) τῶν ₁₂λεγομένων ὅτι οὐ δι' αἰσθήσεως τὸ καλὸν ἢ τὸ κακὸν
₁₃κρίνειν προσήκει, ἀλλ' ἔξω τῶν κατὰ τὸ σῶμα φαινομένων ₁₄τὸν
νοῦν ἀποστήσαντας, αὐτὴν ἐφ' ἑαυτῆς τοῦ καλοῦ ₁₅τε καὶ τοῦ
ἐναντίου διακρίνειν τὴν φύσιν. Ὁ γὰρ πνευματικός, ₁₆φησίν,
ἀνακρίνει τὰ πάντα. —

—(3) Ταύτην οἶμαι τὴν ₁₇αἰτίαν τῆς τῶν δογ-
30 μάτων τούτων μυθοποιΐας τοῖς τὰ τοιαῦτα ₁₈προφέρουσιν ἐγγε-
γενῆσθαι, ὅτι πρὸς τὸ ἡδὺ τῆς ₁₉σωματικῆς ἀπολαύσεως τὸ
ἀγαθὸν ὁριζόμενοι διὰ τὸ ₂₀πάθεσι καὶ ἀρρωστήμασιν ὑποκεῖ-
σθαι κατ' ἀνάγκην τὴν ₂₁τοῦ σώματος φύσιν σύνθετον οὖσαν καὶ
εἰς διάλυσιν ῥεοῦσαν, ₂₂ἐπακολουθεῖν δέ πως τοῖς τοιούτοις
35 παθήμασιν ἀλγεινήν ₂₃τινα αἴσθησιν, πονηροῦ θεοῦ τὴν ἀνθρω-
(GNO 28) ποποιΐαν | ἔργον εἶναι νομίζουσιν, ὡς, εἴγε πρὸς τὸ ὑψηλότερον
ἔβλεπεν ₂αὐτοῖς ἡ διάνοια καὶ τῆς περὶ τὰς ἡδονὰς διαθέσεως
(Sr 40) ₃τὸν νοῦν ἀποικίσαντες ἀπαθῶς ἐπεσκόπουν | τὴν τῶν ὄντων
₄φύσιν, οὐκ ἂν ἄλλο τι κακὸν εἶναι παρὰ τὴν πονηρίαν ₅ᾠήθησαν.
40 Πονηρία δὲ πᾶσα ἐν τῇ τοῦ ἀγαθοῦ στερήσει ₆χαρακτηρίζεται,
οὐ καθ' ἑαυτὴν οὖσα οὐδὲ καθ' ὑπόστασιν ₇θεωρουμένη· κακὸν
γὰρ οὐδὲν ἔξω προαιρέσεως ἐφ' ₈ἑαυτοῦ κεῖται, ἀλλὰ τὸ μὴ
εἶναι [τὸ ἀγαθὸν] οὕτω κατονομάζεται· ₉τὸ δὲ μὴ ὂν οὐχ ὑφέστηκε, τοῦ δὲ μὴ ὑφεστῶτος ₁₀δημιουργὸς ὁ τῶν ὑφεστώτων
45 δημιουργὸς οὐκ ἔστιν.

(4) Οὐκοῦν ₁₁ἔξω τῆς τῶν κακῶν αἰτίας ὁ Θεός, ὁ τῶν ὄντων οὐχ
ὁ ₁₂τῶν μὴ ὄντων ποιητὴς ὤν, ὁ τὴν ὅρασιν οὐ τὴν πήρωσιν
₁₃δημιουργήσας, ὁ τὴν ἀρετὴν οὐ τὴν στέρησιν αὐτῆς ἀναδείξας,
₁₄ὁ ἆθλον τῆς προαιρέσεως τὸ τῶν ἀγαθῶν γέρας ₁₅τοῖς κατ'
50 ἀρετὴν πολιτευομένοις προθείς, οὐκ ἀνάγκη τινὶ ₁₆βιαίᾳ πρὸς τὸ
ἑαυτῷ δοκοῦν ὑποζεύξας τὴν ἀνθρωπίνην ₁₇φύσιν καθάπερ τι
σκεῦος ἄψυχον ἀκουσίως πρὸς τὸ καλὸν ₁₈ἐφελκόμενος. Εἰ δὲ
τοῦ φωτὸς ἐξ αἰθρίας καθαρῶς ₁₉περιλάμποντος ἑκουσίως τις |

42 τὸ GNO : τῷ Srawley

it seems good to me to put forward the apostle in these [matters] as an advocate for their condemnation. For in the discourse to the Corinthians he distinguishes between the carnal and spiritual states of souls, showing, I think, by what he says that it is not fitting to judge good or evil by sense perception, but, withdrawing the mind beyond bodily phenomena, [it is necessary] to distinguish the nature of the good and its opposite itself by itself. For "the spiritual man," he says, "judges all things."[86]

(3) This, I think, is the cause of these teachings' made-up myths for those who bring forward such things: that defining the good as the enjoyment of bodily pleasure—because the body's nature, which is composite and rushing on to dissolution, is by necessity subject to suffering and sickness, and following upon such sufferings there is a certain painful sensation—they deem the making of man to be the work of a wicked God, since, if their thought saw what is higher and, banishing a disposition to pleasure from the mind, looked upon the nature of existing things dispassionately, they would not think evil is anything other than wickedness. Now all wickedness is characterized as a privation of the good, not being contemplated[87] as a being in itself nor according to substance, for nothing evil lies by itself, outside [our] decision, but the non-existence of the good is so named; nonbeing does not subsist, and the creator of subsisting things is not the creator of what does not subsist.

(4) Therefore God is outside the cause of evil, he who is the maker of beings and not of nonbeings, he who created sight, not blindness, he who manifested virtue, not its privation, he who set forth as the prize for the contest of free will[88] the privilege of good things for those live according to virtue; he did not put human nature under the yoke of some necessary compulsion to his own good pleasure, dragging it to the good as if it were an inanimate, unwilling vessel. But if someone, while the light is shining freely

[86]1 Cor 2.15.
[87]Or "seen" (θεωρουμένη).
[88]Or "decision" (προαιρέσεως).

(Sr 41) ἀποβάλοι τοῖς βλεφάροις [20]τὴν ὅρασιν, ἔξω τῆς τοῦ μὴ βλέπειν
55 αἰτίας ὁ ἥλιος. |

(GNO 29; PG 33) Η' Ἀλλ' ἀγανακτεῖ πάντως ὁ πρὸς τὴν διάλυσιν βλέπων [2]τοῦ σώματος, καὶ χαλεπὸν ποιεῖται τῷ θανάτῳ τὴν ζωὴν [3]ἡμῶν διαλύεσθαι, καὶ τοῦτό φησι τῶν κακῶν ἔσχατον εἶναι, [4]τὸ τὸν βίον ἡμῶν τῇ νεκρότητι σβέννυσθαι.—

—Οὐκοῦν ἐπισκεψάσθω [5]διὰ
5 τοῦ σκυθρωποῦ τούτου τὴν ὑπερβολὴν τῆς [6]θείας εὐεργεσίας· τάχα γὰρ ἂν μᾶλλον διὰ τούτου προσαχθείη [7]θαυμάσαι τὴν χάριν τῆς περὶ τὸν ἄνθρωπον τοῦ [8]Θεοῦ κηδεμονίας. (2) Τὸ ζῆν διὰ
(Sr 42) τὴν τῶν καταθυμίων | ἀπόλαυσιν [9]αἱρετόν ἐστι τοῖς τοῦ βίου μετέχουσιν, ὡς εἴ γέ τις ἐν [10]ὀδύναις διαβιῴη, παρὰ πολὺ τῷ
10 τοιούτῳ τὸ μὴ εἶναι τοῦ [11]ἀλγεινῶς εἶναι προτιμότερον κρίνεται. Οὐκοῦν ἐξετάσωμεν [12]εἰ ὁ τῆς ζωῆς χορηγὸς πρὸς ἄλλο τι βλέπει, καὶ οὐχ [13]ὅπως ἂν ἐν τοῖς καλλίστοις βιώημεν.

(3) Ἐπειδὴ γὰρ τῷ αὐτεξουσίῳ [14]κινήματι τοῦ κακοῦ τὴν κοινω-νίαν ἐπεσπασάμεθα, [15]διά τινος ἡδονῆς οἷόν τι δηλητήριον
15 μέλιτι παραρτυθὲν τῇ [16]φύσει τὸ κακὸν καταμίξαντες, καὶ διὰ τοῦτο τῆς κατὰ τὸ [17]ἀπαθὲς νοουμένης μακαριότητος ἐκπεσόν-τες πρὸς τὴν [18]κακίαν μετεμορφώθημεν, τούτου ἕνεκεν οἷόν τι σκεῦος [19]ὀστράκινον πάλιν ὁ ἄνθρωπος εἰς γῆν ἀναλύεται, ὅπως ἂν [20]τῆς νῦν ἐναπειλημμένης αὐτῷ ῥυπαρίας ἀποκριθείσης

54 ἀποβάλοι GNO : ὑποβάλοι Srawley | βλέπειν GNO : βλέποντος Srawley |
6 τούτου GNO : τούτων Srawley

on a clear day, should willingly close his eyes, the sun is outside the cause of [his] not seeing.

Death—Both Wound and Cure

OBJECTION: *Death is the greatest of evils.*

8 But he feels altogether indignant who looks at the dissolution of the body, and reckons it a hardship that our life is dissolved by death, and says, "This is the worst[89] of evils, for our life to be quenched by death."

RESPONSE: *Death is used by God for the reformation and purification of our nature, through the resurrection. Both pain and death are therapeutic. Those who doubt this make pleasure the criterion of good and evil.*

Then let him observe the excess of the divine beneficence through this sad [state]; for perhaps by this he might be all the more brought to wonder at the grace of God's care for man. (2) Living is choice for those who partake of life because of the enjoyment of the things that are to their mind, so that if someone should pass his life in pains, he judges it more dignified not to exist than to exist in so much pain. Therefore let us carefully examine if the giver of life looks to anything else, and not how we might live amid the best things.

(3) For since by a movement of free will[90] we gained fellowship with evil, by a certain pleasure mixing evil into [our] nature like something poisonous[91] sweetened with honey, and by this falling away from the blessedness of a dispassionate understanding we were transformed to vice, on account of this man is dissolved again "into the earth"[92] like some "clay vessel,"[93] so that, the filth now shut

[89] Lit. "limit" or "last" (ἔσχατον).
[90] Or "self-determination" (αὐτεξουσίῳ).
[91] Or "harmful," lit. "deleterious" (δηλητήριον).
[92] Gen 3.19.
[93] 2 Cor 4.7. The image of the clay vessel that follows is drawn from St Methodius of Olympus, *On the Resurrection* 1.44. He in turn drew on Scripture (e.g. Jer 18.1–6; Is 64.8; Rom 9.21–23; etc.).

20 εἰς ₂₁τὸ ἐξ ἀρχῆς σχῆμα διὰ τῆς ἀναστάσεως ἀναπλασθείη, εἴ
₂₂γε τὸ κατ' εἰκόνα ἐν τῇ παρούσῃ ζωῇ διεσώσατο.—

(GNO 30; —(4) Τὸ δὲ |
Sr 43) τοιοῦτον δόγμα ἱστορικώτερον μὲν | καὶ δι' αἰνιγμάτων ὁ
₂Μωϋσῆς ἡμῖν ἐκτίθεται, πλὴν ἔκδηλον καὶ τὰ αἰνίγματα ₃τὴν
διδασκαλίαν ἔχει. Ἐπειδὴ γάρ, φησίν, ἐν τοῖς ἀπηγορευμένοις
25 ₄ἐγένοντο οἱ πρῶτοι ἄνθρωποι καὶ τῆς μακαριότητος ₅ἐκείνης
ἀπεγυμνώθησαν, δερματίνους ἐπιβάλλει χιτῶνας ₆τοῖς πρωτο-
πλάστοις ὁ κύριος· οὔ μοι δοκεῖ πρὸς τὰ ₇τοιαῦτα δέρματα τοῦ
λόγου τὴν διάνοιαν φέρων—ποίων ₈γὰρ ἀποσφαγέντων τε καὶ
δαρέντων ζῴων ἐπινοεῖται αὐτοῖς ₉ἡ περιβολή; —ἀλλ', ἐπειδὴ
30 πᾶν δέρμα χωρισθὲν τοῦ ₁₀ζῴου νεκρόν ἐστι, πάντως οἶμαι τὴν
πρὸς τὸ νεκροῦσθαι ₁₁δύναμιν, ἣ τῆς ἀλόγου φύσεως ἐξαίρετος
ἦν, ἐκ προμηθείας ₁₂μετὰ ταῦτα τοῖς ἀνθρώποις ἐπιβεβληκέναι
τὸν ₁₃τὴν κακίαν ἡμῶν ἰατρεύοντα, οὐχ ὡς εἰς ἀεὶ παραμένειν·
₁₄ὁ γὰρ χιτὼν τῶν ἔξωθεν ἡμῖν ἐπιβαλλομένων ἐστί, πρόσκαιρον
35 ₁₅τὴν ἑαυτοῦ χρῆσιν παρέχων τῷ σώματι, οὐ συμπεφυκὼς ₁₆τῇ
φύσει.

(5) Οὐκοῦν ἐκ τῆς τῶν ἀλόγων φύσεως ἡ ₁₇νεκρότης οἰκονο-
(Sr 44) μικῶς περι- | ετέθη τῇ εἰς ἀθανασίαν κτισθείσῃ ₁₈φύσει, τὸ ἔξωθεν
αὐτῆς περικαλύπτουσα, οὐ τὸ ₁₉ἔσωθεν, τὸ αἰσθητὸν τοῦ ἀνθρώ-
40 που μέρος διαλαμβάνουσα, ₂₀αὐτῆς δὲ τῆς θείας εἰκόνος οὐ προσαπτομένη. Λύεται ₂₁δὲ τὸ αἰσθητόν, οὐκ ἀφανίζεται. Ἀφανισμὸς μὲν γάρ ἐστιν ₂₂ἡ εἰς τὸ μὴ ὂν μεταχώρησις, λύσις δὲ ἡ εἰς τὰ

up within him being separated out, he might be re-formed by the resurrection to the form [he had] from the beginning, if indeed he preserves what is according to the image in the present life.

(4) Moses sets out such a teaching for us in a more historical [manner] through enigmas, yet the enigmas also have a quite clear teaching. For since he says the first human beings[94] came to be amid forbidden things and were stripped naked of that blessedness, the Lord puts "garments of skin"[95] on the first-formed ones.[96] It does not seem to me that "skins" such as these bear the [literal] meaning of the word—for from what sort of slaughtered and skinned animals was the clothing contrived for them?—but, since every skin separated from the animal is dead, I certainly think that he who heals our vice, out of forethought, has clothed men after these [events] with the power[97] to be dead, which was a special [characteristic] of irrational nature, [but] not to remain so forever. For a garment is one of the things put on us externally, handing over the use of itself to the body for a time,[98] not having grown together[99] with [us] by nature.

(5) Therefore mortality, [taken] from the nature of irrational [animals], economically enveloped [our] nature, [which was] created for immortality,[100] enfolding the external, not the internal, embracing the sense perceptible part of man, but not fastening upon[101] the divine image itself. But what is sensory is dissolved; it does not disappear.[102] For disappearance is a departure into nonbeing, but dissolution is a diffusion again into the elements of

[94]Or "men" (ἄνθρωποι), here referring to Adam and Eve.

[95]Gen 3.21.

[96]Cf. 1 Tim 2.13.

[97]Or "ability" (δύναμιν).

[98]Perhaps Gregory's garment imagery is inspired not only by the image of the "garments of skin," but also the Pauline description of "the corruptible" and "the mortal" "putting on" "incorruptibility" and "immortality" (1 Cor 15.53—this chapter is important to Gregory's eschatological thought).

[99]Or "having had an innate affinity" (συμπεφυκώς).

[100]Cf. Wis 2.23.

[101]Or "touching" (προσαπτομένη).

[102]Or "it is not destroyed" (ἀφανίζεται); likewise "disappearance" (ἀφανισμός) at the beginning of the next sentence can also mean "destruction."

τοῦ κόσμου $_{23}$στοιχεῖα πάλιν, ἀφ' ὧν τὴν σύστασιν ἔσχε διά-
χυσις. Τὸ δὲ $_{24}$ἐν τούτοις γενόμενον οὐκ ἀπόλωλε, κἂν ἐκφεύγῃ
45 τὴν $_{25}$κατάληψιν τῆς ἡμετέρας αἰσθήσεως. (6) Ἡ δὲ αἰτία τῆς
(GNO 31) λύ- | σεως δήλη διὰ τοῦ ῥηθέντος ἡμῖν ὑποδείγματος. Ἐπειδὴ
(PG 36) $_2$γὰρ ἡ αἴσθησις πρὸς τὸ παχύ τε καὶ | γήϊνον οἰκείως ἔχει,
$_3$κρείττων δὲ καὶ ὑψηλοτέρα τῶν κατ' αἴσθησιν κινημάτων $_4$ἡ
νοερὰ φύσις, διὰ τοῦτο τῆς περὶ τὸ καλὸν κρίσεως ἐν τῇ
50 $_5$δοκιμασίᾳ τῶν αἰσθήσεων ἁμαρτηθείσης, τῆς δὲ τοῦ $_6$καλοῦ
διαμαρτίας τὴν τῆς ἐναντίας ἕξεως ὑπόστασιν $_7$ἐνεργησάσης,
τὸ ἀχρειωθὲν ἡμῶν μέρος τῇ παραδοχῇ τοῦ $_8$ἐναντίου λύεται. Ὁ
δὲ τοῦ ὑποδείγματος λόγος τοιοῦτός $_9$ἐστι· (7) δεδόσθω τι σκεῦος
ἐκ πηλοῦ συνεστηκέναι, τοῦτο δὲ $_{10}$πλῆρες ἔκ τινος ἐπιβουλῆς
55 (Sr 45) γεγενῆσθαι τετηκότος μολίβδου, $_{11}$τὸν δὲ μόλιβδον | ἐγχεθέντα
παγῆναι καὶ μένειν ἀπρόχυτον· $_{12}$ἀντιποιεῖσθαι δὲ τοῦ σκεύους
τὸν κεκτημένον, $_{13}$ἔχοντα δὲ τοῦ κεραμεύειν τὴν ἐπιστήμην
περιθρύψαι τῷ $_{14}$μολίβδῳ τὸ ὄστρακον, εἶθ' οὕτω πάλιν κατὰ τὸ
πρότερον $_{15}$σχῆμα πρὸς τὴν ἰδίαν ἑαυτοῦ χρῆσιν ἀναπλάσαι τὸ
60 $_{16}$σκεῦος, κενὸν τῆς ἐμμιχθείσης ὕλης γενόμενον. Οὕτως οὖν $_{17}$καὶ
ὁ τοῦ ἡμετέρου σκεύους πλάστης, τῷ αἰσθητικῷ μέρει $_{18}$(τῷ
κατὰ τὸ σῶμά φημι), τῆς κακίας καταμιχθείσης, διαλύσας
$_{19}$τὴν παραδεξαμένην τὸ κακὸν ὕλην, πάλιν ἀμιγὲς τοῦ $_{20}$ἐναντίου
διὰ τῆς ἀναστάσεως ἀναπλάσας, πρὸς τὸ ἐξ ἀρχῆς $_{21}$κάλλος
65 ἀναστοιχειώσει τὸ σκεῦος.

(8) Ἐπειδὴ δὲ σύνδεσίς $_{22}$τις καὶ κοινωνία τῶν κατὰ ἁμαρτίαν
παθημάτων γίνεται $_{23}$τῇ τε ψυχῇ καὶ τῷ σώματι, καί τις ἀνα-
λογία τοῦ σωματικοῦ $_{24}$θανάτου πρὸς τὸν ψυχικόν ἐστι θάνα-
τον· ὥσπερ γὰρ $_{25}$ἐν σαρκὶ τὸ τῆς αἰσθητῆς χωρισθῆναι ζωῆς
70 (Sr 46) προσαγορεύομεν | $_{26}$θάνατον, οὕτω καὶ ἐπὶ τῆς ψυχῆς τὸν τῆς
(GNO 32) ἀληθοῦς | ζωῆς χωρισμὸν θάνατον ὀνομάζομεν. Ἐπεὶ οὖν μία
τίς $_2$ἐστιν ἡ τοῦ κακοῦ κοινωνία, καθὼς προείρηται, ἐν ψυχῇ $_3$τε
θεωρουμένη καὶ σώματι—δι' ἀμφοτέρων γὰρ πρόεισι τὸ

58 οὕτω GNO : οὕτως Srawley | 70 οὕτω GNO : οὕτως Srawley | 73 πρόεισι GNO :
πρόεισιν Srawley

the cosmos, from which it had [its] composition. What comes into being among these [elements] does not utterly disappear, although it might escape the grasp of our senses. (6) The cause of dissolution [was made] clear by the illustration mentioned by us [earlier]. For since sensory perception has a kinship with the dense and earthy, but the noetic nature is better and higher than the movements of sensory perception, because of this, since it was by the examination of the senses that the judgment of the good went astray,[103] and straying from the good produced the substance of the opposite state, the part of us rendered useless by the reception of the opposite is dissolved. The account of the illustration is something like this: (7) let us suppose[104] some vessel to have been made out of clay, and this has become full of molten lead by some treachery, and the lead that was poured in hardens and remains impossible to pour out, but the vessel's owner lays claim [to it], and, having a knowledge of ceramics, he smashes the earthen vessel around the lead, and in this way he re-forms the vessel again, according to [its] former form for his very own use, empty of the matter that had been mixed into it. So too, then, he who formed our vessel, when vice was mingled in our sensory (I mean the bodily) part, by dissolving the matter that received evil, [and] again re-forming [it] through the resurrection, unmixed with [its] opposite, he will restore[105] [it] to the beauty [it had] from the beginning.

(8) And since there is some bond and fellowship with sinful passions for both soul and body, there is also some analogy between bodily death and the soul's death; for just as in [the case of] the flesh we call "death" the separation from sensory life, so too in the case of the soul we name the separation from true life "death." Therefore, since fellowship with evil is one thing, as has been said before, con-

---

[103]The words translated as "went astray" (ἀμαρτηθείσης) and "straying" (διαμαρτίας) are related to the word "sin" (ἀμαρτία), which etymologically means "missing the mark" or "going astray."

[104]Lit. "let it be granted" (δεδόσθω), reminiscent of an ancient geometric proof. The illustration is taken from St Methodius, *On the Resurrection* 1.6–7.

[105]Lit. "re-element" (ἀναστοιχειώσει).

[4]πονηρὸν εἰς ἐνέργειαν—διὰ τοῦτο ὁ μὲν τῆς διαλύσεως [5]θάνα-
75 τος ἐκ τῆς τῶν νεκρῶν δερμάτων ἐπιβολῆς τῆς [6]ψυχῆς οὐχ
ἅπτεται (πῶς γὰρ ἂν διαλυθείη τὸ μὴ συγκείμενον;), (9) [7]ἐπεὶ
δὲ χρεία τοῦ κἀκείνης τὰς ἐμφυείσας ἐξ ἁμαρτιῶν [8]κηλῖδας διά
τινος ἰατρείας ἐξαιρεθῆναι, τούτου ἕνεκεν [9]ἐν μὲν τῇ παρούσῃ
ζωῇ τὸ τῆς ἀρετῆς φάρμακον εἰς [10]θεραπείαν τῶν
80 τοιούτων προσετέθη τραυμάτων· εἰ δὲ ἀθεράπευτος [11]μένοι, ἐν
τῷ μετὰ ταῦτα βίῳ τεταμίευται ἡ θεραπεία.—

   —(10) [12]Ἀλλ’ ὥσπερ εἰσί
τινες κατὰ τὸ σῶμα τῶν παθημάτων [13]διαφοραί, ὧν αἱ μὲν ῥᾷον,
αἱ δὲ δυσκολώτερον τὴν [14]θεραπείαν προσίενται, ἐφ’ ὧν καὶ
(Sr 47) τομαὶ καὶ καυτήρια καὶ | [15]πικραὶ φαρμακοποσίαι πρὸς τὴν
85 ἀναίρεσιν τοῦ ἐνσκήψαντος [16]τῷ σώματι πάθους παραλαμβά-
νονται, τοιοῦτόν τι [17]καὶ ἡ μετὰ ταῦτα κρίσις εἰς θεραπείαν τῶν
τῆς ψυχῆς [18]ἀρρωστημάτων κατεπαγγέλλεται, ὃ τοῖς μὲν χαυ-
νοτέροις [19]ἀπειλὴ καὶ σκυθρωπῶν ἐστιν ἐπανάστασις, ὡς ἂν
φόβῳ [20]τῆς τῶν ἀλγεινῶν ἀντιδόσεως πρὸς τὴν φυγὴν τῆς κα-
90 κίας [21]σωφρονισθείημεν, τοῖς δὲ συνετωτέροις ἰατρεία καὶ θεραπεία [22]παρὰ τοῦ τὸ ἴδιον πλάσμα πρὸς τὴν ἐξ ἀρχῆς ἐπανάγοντος
(GNO 33) [23]χάριν εἶναι πιστεύεται. (11) Ὡς γὰρ οἱ τοὺς ἥλους τε καὶ | τὰς
ἀκροχορδόνας παρὰ φύσιν ἐπιγενομένας τῷ σώματι [2]διὰ τομῆς
ἢ καύσεως ἀποξύοντες οὐκ ἀνώδυνον ἐπάγουσι [3]τῷ εὐεργε-
95 τουμένῳ τὴν ἴασιν—πλὴν οὐκ ἐπὶ βλάβῃ τοῦ ὑπομένοντος [4]τὴν
τομὴν ἄγουσιν—οὕτω καὶ ὅσα ταῖς ψυχαῖς [5]ἡμῶν διὰ τῆς τῶν
(Sr 48; PG 37) παθημάτων κοινωνίας | ἀποσαρκωθείσαις [6]ὑλώδη πε-| ριττώ-
ματα ἐπιπωροῦται, ἐν τῷ καιρῷ τῆς [7]κρίσεως τέμνεταί τε καὶ
ἀποξύεται τῇ ἀρρήτῳ ἐκείνῃ [8]σοφίᾳ καὶ δυνάμει τοῦ, καθὼς
100 λέγει τὸ εὐαγγέλιον, τοὺς [9]κακοὺς ἰατρεύοντος. Οὐ χρείαν
γὰρ ἔχουσι, φησίν, οἱ [10]ὑγιαίνοντες ἰατροῦ, ἀλλ’ οἱ κακῶς
ἔχοντες. —

---

75 GNO supplies ὁ after θάνατος | 88 ἐπανάστασις GNO : ἐπανόρθωσις Srawley |
91 Srawley includes Θεοῦ after τοῦ | 96 οὕτω GNO : οὕτως Srawley

templated[106] both in soul and body—for wickedness proceeds into activity through both of them—because of this the death of dissolution, [which comes] from the covering of dead skins, does not touch the soul (for how could it dissolve what is not composite?), (9) and since it was necessary for its stains, implanted by sins, to be removed by some sort of healing, on account of this, in the present life the medicine of virtue is applied for the therapy of such wounds; but if it should remain without therapy, the therapy is dispensed in the afterlife.[107]

(10) But just as there are different sorts of bodily sufferings[108]— some of which admit of therapy with ease, while [others are] more difficult, and for these cutting, cautery, and bitter medicine is taken for the removal of the suffering[109] that befell the body—the judgment [to come] after these things promises some such things for the therapy of the soul's sicknesses, which to the more frivolous is a threat and the emergence of dark things, so that by fear of the pains of recompense we might gain the prudence to flee vice, but for those with more understanding it is believed to be healing and therapy [dispensed] by him who leads his own formation back to the grace [it had] from the beginning. (11) For as those who by cutting or cautery remove calluses and warts, which grow on the body against nature, do not lead those who are treated[110] to healing by benefitting them without pain—although they do not bring on the cutting in order to harm the patient—so too as many material excrescences as have hardened on our souls, which have become fleshly through fellowship with the passions, in the time of judgment are cut and scraped off by that ineffable wisdom and power of him who, as the gospel says, heals those who are evil. For he says, "Those who are healthy have no need of a physician, but those who are sick."[111]

---

[106]Or "seen" (θεωρουμένη).
[107]Lit. "life after these things" (τῷ μετὰ ταῦτα βίῳ).
[108]Or "passions" (παθημάτων).
[109]Or "passion" (πάθους).
[110]Lit. "those [whose calluses or warts] are scraped off" (ἀποξύοντες).
[111]Lk 5.31 (cf. Mt 9.12; Mk 2.17). In Greek, the connection is clearer. St Gregory

—(12) Διὰ δὲ τὸ ₁₁πολλὴν γεγενῆσθαι τῇ ψυχῇ πρὸς τὸ κακὸν συμφυῖαν ₁₂ὥσπερ ἡ τῆς μυρμηκίας τομὴ δριμύσσει τὴν ἐπιφάνειαν—₁₃τὸ γὰρ παρὰ φύσιν ἐμφυὲν τῇ φύσει διά τινος
105 συμπαθείας ₁₄τῷ ὑποκειμένῳ προσίσχεται, καί τις γίνεται τοῦ ἀλλοτρίου ₁₅πρὸς τὸ ἡμέτερον παράλογος συνανάκρασις, ὡς λυπεῖσθαι ₁₆καὶ δάκνεσθαι τοῦ παρὰ φύσιν χωριζομένην τὴν αἴσθησιν—₁₇οὕτω καὶ τῆς ψυχῆς ἀπολεπτυνομένης τε καὶ
(Sr 49) ἐκτηκομένης ₁₈ἐν τοῖς ὑπὲρ τῆς ἁμαρτίας ἐλεγμοῖς, | καθώς
110 ₁₉φησί που ἡ προφητεία, διὰ τὴν ἐν βάθει γενομένην πρὸς τὸ ₂₀κακὸν οἰκειότητα κατ' ἀνάγκην ἐπακολουθοῦσιν ἄρρητοί ₂₁τινες καὶ ἀνέκφραστοι ἀλγηδόνες, ὧν ἡ διήγησις ἐκ τοῦ ₂₂ἴσου τὸ
(GNO 34) ἄφραστον ἔχει τῇ τῶν ἐλπιζομένων ἀγαθῶν φύσει· | οὔτε γὰρ ταῦτα, οὔτε ἐκεῖνα τῇ δυνάμει τῶν λόγων ἢ τῷ ₂στοχασμῷ
115 τῆς διανοίας ὑπάγεται.

(13) Οὐκοῦν πρὸς τὸ πέρας ₃τις ἀποσκοπῶν τῆς σοφίας τοῦ τὸ πᾶν οἰκονομοῦντος ₄οὐκέτ' ἂν εὐλόγως κακῶν αἴτιον τὸν τῶν ἀνθρώπων δημιουργὸν ₅ὑπὸ μικροψυχίας κατονομάζοι, ἢ ἀγνοεῖν αὐτὸν τὸ ₆ἐσόμενον λέγων, ἢ εἰδότα καὶ πεποιηκότα μὴ ἔξω
120 τῆς πρὸς ₇τὸ πονηρὸν ὁρμῆς εἶναι. Καὶ γὰρ ᾔδει τὸ ἐσόμενον καὶ τὴν ₈πρὸς τὸ γινόμενον ὁρμὴν οὐκ ἐκώλυσεν· ὅτι γὰρ ἐκτραπήσεται ₉τοῦ ἀγαθοῦ τὸ ἀνθρώπινον, οὐκ ἠγνόησεν ὁ ₁₀πάντα

110 φησί που GNO : πού φησιν Srawley

(12) And since a strong innate affinity toward evil has come about in the soul, just as the cutting of warts sharply pains the skin—for the unnatural ingrowth[112] in [our] nature attaches to the subject by some sympathy, and there is an unexpected[113] commingling of what is alien with what is ours, so that sensory perception, which is separated from what is against nature, is distressed and stings—so too the soul pines and melts with reproofs for sin, as prophecy says somewhere,[114] because it has a close relationship with evil in [its] depth, certain ineffable and unspeakable pains follow[115] by necessity, whose description[116] is equally unspeakable as the nature of the good things that are hoped for;[117] for neither the former nor the latter is subject to the power of words or the conjecture of thought.

(13) Therefore anyone who looks at the purpose of the wisdom of the one who arranges the economy of the universe[118] would no longer reasonably call the creator of men the cause of evils out of narrowmindedness,[119] saying that either he is ignorant of the future,[120] or that having known and having made, he is not outside the impulse to wickedness. For he both knew the future and did not prevent the impulse from coming into existence; for he was not ignorant that

---

paraphrases the verse: Christ "heals those who are evil [τοὺς κακοὺς]." The scriptural phrase "those who are sick" translates a Greek idiom, which contains the adverbial form of the same word: οἱ κακῶς ἔχοντες.

[112]There is a play on words in the Greek: an "innate affinity [συμφυῖαν] toward evil" is an "unnatural ingrowth" (παρὰ φύσιν ἐμφυὲν).

[113]Or "unreasonable" (παράλογος).

[114]Cf. Ps 38.12 (LXX).

[115]Here "follow" (ἐπακολουθοῦσιν) is related to the word for "order" (ἀκολουθία) that St Gregory consistently uses. There is a set order at work: deeply rooted evil necessarily causes pain as it is rooted out.

[116]Or "narration" (διήγησις).

[117]Cf. 1 Cor 2.9 (cf. Is 64.4), quoted later at 40.7.

[118]Or "of all" (τὸ πᾶν).

[119]Lit. "littleness" or "meanness of soul" (μικροψυχίας), unlike the "great-souled" or "magnanimous" (μεγαλόψυχος) person, whom Aristotle praises in the *Nicomachean Ethics* 4.3. This is a cutting criticism for a cultured Greek of Gregory's time.

[120]Lit. "of what will be" (τὸ ἐσόμενον).

ἐμπερικρατῶν τῇ γνωστικῇ δυνάμει καὶ τὸ ἐφεξῆς ₁₁τῷ παρῳ-
χηκότι κατὰ τὸ ἴσον βλέπων. (14) Ἀλλ᾽ ὥσπερ τὴν ₁₂παρατροπὴν
125 ἐθεάσατο, οὕτω καὶ τὴν ἀνάκλησιν αὐτοῦ ₁₃πάλιν τὴν πρὸς τὸ
ἀγαθὸν κατενόησε. Τί οὖν ἄμεινον ἦν; ₁₄καθ᾽ ὅλου μὴ ἀγαγεῖν
τὴν φύσιν ἡμῶν εἰς γένεσιν, ἐπειδὴ ₁₅τοῦ καλοῦ διαμαρτήσεσθαι
προεώρα τὸν γενησόμενον, ἢ ₁₆ἀγαγόντα καὶ <τὸν> νενοσηκότα |
(Sr 50) πάλιν πρὸς τὴν ἐξ ἀρχῆς ₁₇χάριν διὰ μετανοίας ἀνακαλέσασθαι;
130 (15) Τὸ δὲ διὰ τὰς σωματικὰς ₁₈ἀλγηδόνας, αἳ τῷ ῥευστῷ τῆς φύσεως κατ᾽ ἀνάγκην ₁₉ἐπισυμβαίνουσι κακῶν ποιητὴν τὸν Θεὸν
ὀνομάζειν ἢ μηδὲ ₂₀ὅλως ἀνθρώπου κτίστην αὐτὸν οἴεσθαι, ὡς
ἂν μὴ καὶ τῶν ₂₁ἀλγυνόντων ἡμᾶς αἴτιος ὑπονοοῖτο, τοῦτο τῆς
ἐσχάτης ₂₂μικροψυχίας ἐστὶ τῶν τῇ αἰσθήσει τὸ καλὸν καὶ τὸ
135 κακὸν ₂₃διακρινόντων, οἳ οὐκ ἴσασιν ὅτι ἐκεῖνο τῇ φύσει μόνον
₂₄ἐστὶν ἀγαθὸν οὗ ἡ αἴσθησις οὐκ ἐφάπτεται, καὶ μόνον ₂₅ἐκεῖνο
κακὸν ἡ τοῦ ἀληθινοῦ ἀγαθοῦ ἀλλοτρίωσις. (16) Πόνοις ₂₆δὲ καὶ
(GNO 35) ἡδοναῖς τὸ καλὸν καὶ τὸ μὴ καλὸν κρίνειν τῆς | ἀλόγου φύσεως
ἴδιόν ἐστιν, ἐφ᾽ ὧν τοῦ ἀληθῶς καλοῦ ἡ ₂κατανόησις διὰ τὸ μὴ
140 μετέχειν αὐτὰ νοῦ καὶ διανοίας χώραν ₃οὐκ ἔχει. Ἀλλ᾽ ὅτι μὲν
Θεοῦ ἔργον ὁ ἄνθρωπος, καλόν ₄τε καὶ ἐπὶ καλλίστοις γενόμενον, οὐ μόνον ἐκ τῶν εἰρημένων ₅δῆλόν ἐστιν, ἀλλὰ καὶ ἐκ
μυρίων ἑτέρων, ὧν τὸ πλῆθος ₆διὰ τὴν ἀμετρίαν παραδρα-
μούμεθα. —
(PG 40)   —(17) Θεὸν δὲ | ἀνθρώπου ₇ποιητὴν ὀνομάσαντες οὐκ
145 ἐπιλελήσμεθα τῶν ἐν τῷ προοιμίῳ ₈πρὸς τοὺς Ἕλληνας ἡμῖν
διευκρινηθέντων, ἐν οἷς ἀπεδείκνυτο ₉ὁ τοῦ Θεοῦ Λόγος οὐσιώ-
δης [τις] καὶ ἐνυπόστατος ₁₀ὢν αὐτὸς εἶναι καὶ Θεὸς καὶ Λόγος,
πᾶσαν δύναμιν ₁₁ποιητικὴν ἐμπεριειληφώς, μᾶλλον δὲ αὐτο-
δύναμις ὢν καὶ ₁₂πρὸς πᾶν ἀγαθὸν τὴν ὁρμὴν ἔχων καὶ πᾶν

128 GNO supplies τὸν after καὶ | 147 GNO places τις in brackets

humanity would turn away from the good, he who embraces all things by [his] knowledge[121] and who sees what is to come equally with the past.[122] (14) But just as he saw the turning aside, so too he perceived his recall to the good once more. What, then, was better? Not to lead our nature to genesis at all, since he foresaw that he who would come into being would err[123] from the good; or having led [him into being] also to recall him who has become sick to the grace [he had] from the beginning once more through repentance. (15) But to call God the maker of evils or to think he is not wholly the creator of man[124] because of bodily pains, which result by necessity from [our] nature's instability,[125] so they might not suspect him as the cause of our pains—this is the extreme of the narrow-mindedness of those who distinguish good and evil by sensory perception, who do not know that that only is good by nature which sensory perception does not touch, and that only is evil which is alienation from the true good. (16) But to judge the good and what is not good by pains and pleasures is a property of an irrational nature, of those whose understanding has no room for the truly good, since they do not partake of the things of the mind and thought. But that man is the work of God, made[126] good and for the best things, is clear not only from what has been said, but also from countless other things, the multitude of which we will pass over, because [they are] without measure.

(17) Now when we call God the maker of man we do not forget the things we carefully distinguished in our introduction [addressed] to the Greeks,[127] in which the Word of God, being something essential and hypostatic, was demonstrated to be himself both God and Word, who has embraced all creative power, and even more is power itself,

[121]Lit. "knowing power," or "gnostic ability" (γνωστικῇ δυνάμει).

[122]Cf. Is 46.10.

[123]"Err" (διαμαρτήσεσθαι) is related to the word for "sin" (see p. 85, n. 103 above).

[124]In some dualist systems of belief, God *partially* created human beings (i.e., the spirit was of divine origin, but the body was not).

[125]Or "fluctuation," "state of flux" (ῥευστῷ).

[126]Lit. "coming into being" (γενόμενον).

[127]See Prol. 4 through Chapter 2.

150 ὅτιπερ ἂν θελήσῃ [13]κατεργαζόμενος τῷ σύνδρομον ἔχειν τῇ
βουλήσει [14]τὴν δύναμιν, οὗ καὶ θέλημα καὶ ἔργον ἐστὶν ἡ τῶν
(Sr 51) ὄντων [15]ζωή, παρ' οὗ καὶ ὁ | ἄνθρωπος εἰς τὸ ζῆν παρήχθη, πᾶσι
τοῖς [16]καλλίστοις θεοειδῶς κεκοσμημένος.

(18) Ἐπειδὴ δὲ μόνον [17]ἀναλλοίωτόν ἐστι κατὰ τὴν φύσιν τὸ μὴ
155 διὰ κτίσεως ἔχον [18]τὴν γένεσιν, τὰ δ' ὅσα παρὰ τῆς ἀκτίστου
φύσεως ἐκ τοῦ [19]μὴ ὄντος ὑπέστη, εὐθὺς ἀπὸ τροπῆς τοῦ εἶναι
ἀρξάμενα [20]πάντοτε δι' ἀλλοιώσεως πρόεισιν, εἰ μὲν κατὰ φύσιν
πράττοι [21]πρὸς τὸ κρεῖττον αὐτοῖς τῆς ἀλλοιώσεως εἰς ἀεὶ
γιγνομένης, [22]εἰ δὲ παρατραπείη τῆς εὐθείας, τῆς πρὸς τὸ
160 ἐναντίον [23]αὐτὰ διαδεχομένης κινήσεως. —

—(19) Ἐπεὶ οὖν ἐν τούτοις
καὶ [24]ὁ ἄνθρωπος ἦν, ᾧ τὸ τρεπτὸν τῆς φύσεως πρὸς τὸ ἐναντίον
[25]παρώλισθεν, ἅπαξ δὲ τῆς τῶν ἀγαθῶν ἀναχωρήσεως [26]δι' ἀκο-
(GNO 36) λούθου πᾶσαν ἰδέαν κακῶν ἀντεισαγούσης, ὡς τῇ | μὲν
ἀποστροφῇ τῆς ζωῆς ἀντεισαχθῆναι τὸν θάνατον, τῇ [2]δὲ στε-
165 ρήσει τοῦ φωτὸς ἐπιγενέσθαι τὸ σκότος, τῇ δὲ τῆς [3]ἀρετῆς
ἀπουσίᾳ τὴν κακίαν ἀντεισαχθῆναι καὶ πάσῃ τῇ [4]τῶν ἀγαθῶν
ἰδέᾳ τὸν τῶν ἐναντίων ἀνταριθμηθῆναι κατάλογον· [5]τὸν ἐν
τούτοις καὶ τοῖς τοιούτοις ἐξ ἀβουλίας ἐμπεπτωκότα [6](οὐδὲ
γὰρ ἦν δυνατὸν ἐν φρονήσει εἶναι τὸν [7]ἀπεστραμμένον τὴν
170 φρόνησιν καὶ σοφόν τι βουλεύσασθαι [8]τὸν τῆς σοφίας
ἀναχωρήσαντα), διὰ τίνος ἔδει πάλιν πρὸς [9]τὴν ἐξ ἀρχῆς
χάριν ἀνακληθῆναι;

(20) Τίνι διέφερεν ἡ τοῦ πεπτωκότος [10]ἀνόρθωσις, ἡ τοῦ ἀπολω-
(Sr 52) λότος ἀνά- | κλησις, ἡ [11]τοῦ πεπλανημένου χειραγωγία; Τίνι ἄλλῳ
175 ἢ τῷ κυρίῳ πάντως [12]τῆς φύσεως; Τῷ γὰρ ἐξ ἀρχῆς τὴν ζωὴν
δεδωκότι [13]μόνῳ δυνατὸν ἦν καὶ πρέπον ἅμα καὶ ἀπολομένην
ἀνακαλέσασθαι, [14]ὃ παρὰ τοῦ μυστηρίου τῆς ἀληθείας ἀκούο-
μεν, [15]Θεὸν πεποιηκέναι κατ' ἀρχὰς τὸν ἄνθρωπον καὶ σεσω-
κέναι [16]διαπεπτωκότα μανθάνοντες.

and has an impulse to all good, and accomplishes all that he wills by
having power concurrent with his intention, whose will and work is
the life of existing things, by whom man was also led into life, having
been adorned in godlike manner with all the best things.

(18) And since the only thing that is unalterable by nature is that
which does not come into being[128] through creation, but as many
things as are brought into substantial being out of nonbeing by the
uncreated nature, as soon as they begin to be as a result of change,
always proceed by alteration, if they should act according to nature
the alteration is always for the better for them, but if they should turn
aside from the straight path, a movement toward opposite things
takes its place.

(19) Since, then, man was also in the midst of these things,
the changeable [part] of his nature fell to the opposite, and once
the withdrawal of good things introduced every form of evil in
order—so that by turning away from life death was introduced, and
by the privation of light darkness resulted, and by the absence of
virtue vice was introduced, and for every form of good a catalogue
of opposites replaced them; having fallen among these things and
the like out of thoughtlessness (for it was not possible for him who
had turned away from prudence to be prudent, and for him who
withdrew from wisdom to take any wise counsel)—by whom was it
necessary for [man] to be recalled once more to the grace [he had]
from the beginning?

(20) To whom belonged the setting upright of him who had
fallen, the recall of him who had perished, the leading back by the
hand of him who had gone astray? To whom other than to him who
is altogether the Lord of nature? For it was at once both possible and
fitting for him alone who had given life from the beginning also to
recall him who perished, which we hear from the mystery of the
truth, learning that God made man at the beginning and has saved
him who has fallen.

---

[128]Lit. "have [its] genesis [γένεσιν]."

Γ'

Θ'   17Ἀλλὰ μέχρι μὲν τούτων συνθήσεται τυχὸν τῷ λόγῳ ὁ
18πρὸς τὸ ἀκόλουθον βλέπων διὰ τὸ μὴ δοκεῖν ἔξω τι τῆς
19θεοπρεποῦς ἐννοίας τῶν εἰρημένων εἶναι, πρὸς δὲ τὰ 20ἐφεξῆς
οὐχ ὁμοίως ἕξει, δι' ὧν μάλιστα τὸ μυστήριον τῆς 21ἀληθείας
5 κρατύνεται· γένεσις ἀνθρωπίνη καὶ ἡ ἐκ νηπίου 22πρὸς
(GNO 37) τελείωσιν αὔξησις, βρῶσίς τε καὶ πόσις, καὶ κόπος, | καὶ
ὕπνος, καὶ λύπη, καὶ δάκρυον, συκοφαντία τε καὶ
(Sr 53) δικα- | στήριον, 2σταυρός, καὶ θάνατος, καὶ ἡ ἐν μνη-
μείῳ θέσις· 3ταῦτα γὰρ συμπαραλαμβανόμενα τῷ μυστηρίῳ
10 ἀμβλύνει 4πως τῶν μικροψυχοτέρων τὴν πίστιν, ὡς μηδὲ τὸ
ἐφεξῆς 5τῶν λεγομένων διὰ τὰ προειρημένα συμπαραδέχεσθαι.
Τὸ 6γὰρ θεοπρεπὲς τῆς ἐκ νεκρῶν ἀναστάσεως διὰ τὸ περὶ τὸν
7θάνατον ἀπρεπὲς οὐ προσίενται.

(2) Ἐγὼ δὲ πρότερον οἶμαι 8δεῖν μικρὸν τῆς σαρκικῆς παχύ-
15 (PG 41) τητος | τὸν λογισμὸν 9ἀποστήσαντας, αὐτὸ τὸ καλὸν ἐφ' ἑαυτοῦ
καὶ τὸ μὴ τοιοῦτον 10κατανοῆσαι, ποίοις γνωρίσμασιν ἑκάτερον
τούτων 11καταλαμβάνεται. Οὐδένα γὰρ ἀντερεῖν οἶμαι τῶν λε-
λογισμένων, 12ὅτι ἓν κατὰ φύσιν μόνον τῶν πάντων ἐστὶν αἰσχρὸν 13τὸ κατὰ κακίαν πάθος· τὸ δὲ κακίας ἐκτὸς παντὸς

8 καὶ before σταυρός Srawley

PART 3

THE PROOF

Defending the Economy of the Incarnation

OBJECTION: *The various stages of human life are not befitting for God.*

9 But up to this point, perhaps he who looks to the order will go along with the argument, since the things that have been said do not seem to be anything outside a God-befitting notion, but he will not have the same opinion about the things that follow, through which the mystery of the truth is confirmed most of all: human birth and growth from infancy to adulthood, eating and drinking, and fatigue, and sleep, and grief, and tears, the false accusation and the judgment hall, and the cross, and death, and deposition in the tomb; for these things that are associated with the mystery somehow blunt the belief of those who are narrow-minded, so that they do not accept the following statements along with the things that have been said before. For they do not admit that the resurrection from the dead is befitting for God,[129] because of the unbefittingness of the death.

RESPONSE: *They do not employ the proper criterion of shame and moral beauty. The economy cannot be criticized if the criterion is properly applied.*

(2) Now first I think it is necessary, while withdrawing [our] thought a little from the grossness of the fleshly, to understand the good itself in itself and that which is not like it, [and] by what sort of characteristics each of these is comprehended. For no one, I think, who has reflected will gainsay that of all things only one is

---

[129]Lit. "the God-befittingness of the resurrection" (Τὸ ... θεοπρεπὲς τῆς ἐκ νεκρῶν ἀναστάσεως).

20 14αἴσχους ἐστὶν ἀλλότριον· ᾧ δὲ μηδὲν αἰσχρὸν καταμέμικται,
15τοῦτο πάντως ἐν τῇ τοῦ καλοῦ μοίρᾳ καταλαμβάνεται· 16τὸ δὲ
ἀληθῶς καλὸν ἀμιγές ἐστι τοῦ ἐναντίου· πρέπει 17δὲ Θεῷ πᾶν
ὅτιπερ ἂν ἐν τῇ τοῦ καλοῦ θεωρῆται χώρᾳ. (3) Ἡ 18τοίνυν δειξά-
τωσαν κακίαν εἶναι τὴν γέννησιν, τὴν ἀνατροφήν, 19τὴν αὔξησιν,
25 (Sr 54) τὴν πρὸς τὸ τέλειον τῆς | φύσεως 20πρόοδον, τὴν τοῦ θανάτου
πεῖραν, τὴν ἐκ τοῦ θανάτου 21ἐπάνοδον, ἤ, εἰ ἔξω κακίας εἶναι τὰ
εἰρημένα συντίθενται, 22οὐδὲν αἰσχρὸν εἶναι τὸ κακίας ἀλλότριον
(GNO 38) ἐξ ἀνάγκης ὁμο- | λογήσουσι. Καλοῦ δὲ πάντως ἀναδεικνυμένου
τοῦ πάσης 2αἰσχρότητος καὶ κακίας ἀπηλλαγμένου, πῶς οὐκ
30 ἐλεεινοὶ 3τῆς ἀλογίας οἱ τὸ καλὸν μὴ πρέπειν ἐπὶ Θεοῦ δογματί-
4ζοντες;

Γʹ   5Ἀλλὰ μικρόν, φησί, καὶ εὐπερίγραπτον ἡ ἀνθρωπίνη
6φύσις, ἄπειρον δὲ ἡ θεότης, καὶ πῶς ἂν περιελήφθη τῷ 7ἀτόμῳ
τὸ ἄπειρον;

Καὶ τίς τοῦτό φησιν ὅτι τῇ περιγραφῇ 8τῆς σαρκὸς
καθάπερ ἀγγείῳ τινὶ ἡ ἀπειρία τῆς θεότητος 9περιελήφθη;
5 Οὐδὲ γὰρ ἐπὶ τῆς ἡμετέρας ζωῆς ἐντὸς κατακλείεται 10τῶν τῆς
(Sr 55) σαρκὸς ὅρων ἡ νοερὰ φύσις. | (2) Ἀλλ᾽ ὁ μὲν 11ὄγκος τοῦ σώματος τοῖς
οἰκείοις μέρεσι περιγράφεται, ἡ 12δὲ ψυχὴ τοῖς τῆς διανοίας
κινήμασι πάσῃ κατ᾽ ἐξουσίαν 13ἐφαπλοῦται τῇ κτίσει, καὶ μέ-
χρις οὐρανῶν ἀνιοῦσα, καὶ 14τῶν ἀβύσσων ἐπιβατεύουσα, καὶ τῷ

shameful by nature: vicious passion; but that which is outside of vice is alien to all shame; and that with which nothing shameful is mixed, this is altogether comprehended with the lot of the good; and the truly good is unmixed with its opposite; and all that is contemplated in the realm of the good is befitting for God. (3) Either, then, demonstrate that the birth, the nourishment, the growth, the advance to adulthood,[130] the experience of death, [and] the return from death is vice, or, if they concede that the things that have been mentioned are without vice, by necessity they will agree that nothing is shameful that is alien to vice. And since what is free from all shamefulness and vice is altogether demonstrated to be good, how are they not to be pitied for irrationality, who teach that the good is not befitting for God?

OBJECTION: *Human nature, small and circumscribed, is incompatible with the infinite divine nature.*

10 "But," it is said, "human nature is small and easily circumscribed, but the divinity is infinite, and how can the infinite be encompassed by the atom?"

RESPONSE: *Even the human mind is not confined by the flesh. Further, in man we see the union of soul and body, an analogy for the union of God with man.*

And who says this, that the infinity of the divinity is encompassed by the circumscription of the flesh as if in some vessel? For not even in the case of our life is the noetic nature confined within the boundaries of the flesh.[131] (2) But while the body's mass is circumscribed by its own parts, the soul spreads over all creation at will by the movements of thought,[132] going up as far as the heavens, and setting foot

---

[130]Lit. "nature's completion" (τὸ τέλειον τῆς φύσεως).

[131]Cf. *On the Making of Man* 15.3: "The union of the mental with the bodily presents a connection unspeakable and inconceivable—not being *within* it (for the incorporeal is not enclosed in a body), nor yet surrounding it without (for that which is incorporeal does not include anything), but the mind approaching our nature in some inexplicable and incomprehensible way" (NPNF[2] 5:404).

[132]See Plato, *Phaedrus* 246b.

10 πλάτει τῆς οἰκουμένης 15ἐπερχομένη, καὶ πρὸς τὰ καταχθόνια
διὰ τῆς πολυπραγμοσύνης 16εἰσδύνουσα, πολλάκις δὲ καὶ τῶν
ὑπερουρανίων 17θαυμάτων ἐν περινοίᾳ γίνεται, οὐδὲν βαρυνο-
μένη 18τῷ ἐφολκίῳ τοῦ σώματος.—

                                              —(3) Εἰ δὲ ἀνθρώπου ψυχὴ κατὰ
    τὴν 19τῆς φύσεως ἀνάγκην συγκεκραμένη τῷ σώματι πανταχοῦ
15 20κατ' ἐξουσίαν γίνεται, τίς ἀνάγκη τῇ φύσει τῆς σαρκὸς 21τὴν
    θεότητα λέγειν ἐμπεριείργεσθαι καὶ μὴ διὰ τῶν χωρητῶν 22ἡμῖν
(Sr 56) ὑποδειγμάτων στοχασμόν τινα πρέ- | ποντα περὶ 23τῆς θείας
    οἰκονομίας λαβεῖν; Ὡς γὰρ τὸ πῦρ ἐπὶ τῆς λαμπάδος 24ὁρᾶται
    τῆς ὑποκειμένης περιδεδραγμένον ὕλης, καὶ 25λόγος μὲν δια-
20 26κρίνει τό τε ἐπὶ τῆς ὕλης πῦρ καὶ τὴν τὸ πῦρ 26ἐξάπτουσαν ὕλην,
    ἔργῳ δὲ οὐκ ἔστιν ἀπ' ἀλλήλων ταῦτα 27διατεμόντας, ἐφ' ἑαυτῆς
(GNO 39) δεῖξαι τὴν φλόγα διεζευγμένην | τῆς ὕλης, ἀλλ' ἓν τὰ συναμ-
    φότερα γίνεται. (4) Καί μοι μηδεὶς 2τὸ φθαρτικὸν τοῦ πυρὸς
    συμπαραλαμβανέτω τῷ ὑποδείγματι, 3ἀλλ' ὅσον εὐπρεπές ἐστι
25 μόνον ἐν τῇ εἰκόνι δεξάμενος, 4τὸ ἀπεμφαῖνον ἀποποιείσθω—
(Sr 57) τὸν αὐτὸν οὖν τρόπον, 5ὡς ὁρῶμεν καὶ ἐξημμένην τοῦ | ὑποκει-
    μένου τὴν φλόγα καὶ 6οὐκ ἐναποκλειομένην τῇ ὕλῃ, τί κωλύει
    θείας φύσεως ἕνωσίν 7τινα καὶ προσεγγισμὸν κατανοήσαντας
    πρὸς τὸ ἀνθρώπινον, 8τὴν θεοπρεπῆ διάνοιαν καὶ ἐν τῷ προσ-
30 (PG 44) εγγισμῷ 9διασώσασθαι, | πάσης περιγραφῆς ἐκτὸς εἶναι τὸ
    θεῖον 10πιστεύοντας, κἂν ἐν ἀνθρώπῳ ᾖ;

ΙΑ'   11Εἰ δὲ ζητεῖς πῶς κατακιρνᾶται θεότης πρὸς τὸ ἀνθρώπινον,—

                              —12ὥρα σοι πρὸ τούτου ζητεῖν τίς πρὸς τὴν σάρκα τῆς
13ψυχῆς ἡ συμφυΐα. Εἰ δὲ τῆς σῆς ἀγνοεῖται ψυχῆς ὁ τρόπος,
14καθ' ὃν ἑνοῦται τῷ σώματι, μηδὲ ἐκεῖνο πάντως οἴου δεῖν 15ἐντὸς
5 γενέσθαι τῆς σῆς καταλήψεως. Ἀλλ' ὥσπερ ἐνταῦθα 16καὶ

---

12 ὑπερουρανίων GNO : οὐρανίων Srawley | 23 Srawley includes οὕτω καὶ ἐπὶ
τούτου after γίνεται.

in the depths, traversing the breadth of the inhabited world, and entering into subterranean places out of curiosity, and often it is also in thought about supercelestial wonders, not at all being weighed down by the appendage of the body.

(3) Now if man's soul, which is commingled with the body by the necessity of nature, is everywhere at will, what necessity is there to say the divinity is confined by the nature of the flesh, and why may we not grasp some befitting conjecture about the divine economy through illustrations that we can understand? For as fire is seen on a lamp, taking hold of the underlying matter, and reason distinguishes between the fire on the matter and the matter kindling the fire, but in action these cannot be severed from one another, to show the flame by itself, disjoined from the matter, but both together are one. (4) And let no one, I pray, latch onto the corruptible [nature] of the fire in the illustration, but, accepting only whatever is well-fitting in the image, let him disregard what is dissimilar—in the same manner, then, as we see the flame that was fastened on the underlying [matter] and not enclosed by the matter, what prevents us from understanding a sort of union and approximation of the divine nature with human [nature], and yet in the approximation preserving a God-befitting thought, believing all circumscription to be outside the divine, even if he should be in man?

OBJECTION: *How is the divine mixed with the human in the incarnation?*

11 And if you ask how the divinity is mixed with the human,

RESPONSE: *Even the union of the soul and body in man is a mystery.*

before this it is time for you to ask what the innate affinity[133] is between flesh and soul. And if the manner in which your soul is united to the body is unknown, do not in any way think that that ought to be within your comprehension. But just as here too we have

[133]Lit. "connaturality" (ἡ συμφυΐα).

ἕτερον εἶναί τι παρὰ τὸ σῶμα τὴν ψυχὴν πεπιστεύκαμεν, ₁₇ἐκ
τοῦ μονωθεῖσαν τῆς ψυχῆς τὴν σάρκα νεκράν τε ₁₈καὶ ἀνενέργητον γίνεσθαι, καὶ τὸν τῆς ἑνώσεως οὐκ ἐπιγινώσκομεν ₁₉τρό-
πον, οὕτω κἀκεῖ διαφέρειν μὲν ἐπὶ τὸ μεγαλοπρεπέστερον ₂₀τὴν
10 θείαν φύσιν πρὸς τὴν θνητὴν καὶ ἐπίκηρον ₂₁ὁμολογοῦμεν, τὸν δὲ
τῆς ἀνακράσεως τρόπον τοῦ ₂₂θείου πρὸς τὸν ἀνθρώπινον συνιδεῖν
οὐ χωροῦμεν.—

—(2) Ἀλλὰ τὸ μὲν ₂₃γεγενῆσθαι Θεὸν ἐν ἀνθρώπου φύσει
διὰ τῶν ἱστορουμένων ₂₄θαυμάτων οὐκ ἀμφιβάλλομεν, τὸ δ'
(Sr 58) ὅπως, ὡς | μεῖζον ₂₅ἢ κατὰ λογισμῶν ἔφοδον, διερευνᾶν παραι-
5 (GNO 40) τούμεθα. Οὐδὲ | γὰρ πᾶσαν τὴν σωματικήν τε καὶ νοητὴν
κτίσιν παρὰ τῆς ₂ἀσωμάτου τε καὶ ἀκτίστου φύσεως ὑποστῆναι
πιστεύοντες, ₃τὸ πόθεν ἢ τὸ πῶς τῇ περὶ τούτων πίστει συνεξ-
ετάζομεν. ₄Ἀλλὰ τὸ γεγενῆσθαι παραδεχόμενοι, ἀπολυπραγ-
μόνητον ₅τὸν τρόπον τῆς τοῦ παντὸς συστάσεως καταλείπομεν
20 ₆ὡς ἄρρητον παντάπασιν ὄντα καὶ ἀνερμήνευτον.

IB' Τοῦ δὲ ₇Θεὸν ἐν σαρκὶ πεφανερῶσθαι ἡμῖν ὁ τὰς
ἀποδείξεις ἐπιζητῶν—

—₈πρὸς τὰς ἐνεργείας βλεπέτω· καὶ γὰρ
τοῦ ὅλως εἶναι ₉Θεὸν οὐκ ἄν τις ἑτέραν ἀπόδειξιν ἔχοι πλὴν τῆς
δι' αὐτῶν ₁₀τῶν ἐνεργειῶν μαρτυρίας. Ὥσπερ τοίνυν εἰς τὸ πᾶν
5 ₁₁ἀφορῶντες καὶ τὰς κατὰ τὸν κόσμον οἰκονομίας ἐπισκο-
₁₂ποῦντες καὶ τὰς εὐεργεσίας τὰς θεόθεν κατὰ τὴν ζωὴν ₁₃ἡμῶν
ἐνεργουμένας, ὑπερκεῖσθαί τινα δύναμιν ποιητικὴν ₁₄τῶν γινο-

believed the soul is something different from the body, because the
flesh apart from the soul becomes both dead and inactive, and we do
not know the manner of union, so too in the other case we admit that
the divine nature differs from the mortal and transient in its greater
majesty, but we do not have the capacity to perceive the manner of
the mingling of the divine with the human.

(2) But that God has come to be in man's nature we cannot doubt,
because of the wonders that are recorded,[134] but *how* we decline to
search out, since it is greater than what is accessible to reasoning.
For while we believe that all creation, both bodily and noetic, was
given substance by the bodiless and uncreated nature, we do not
examine the whence and the how for [our] faith in these things. But
accepting what has come into being, we leave aside meddling curiosity[135] about the manner of the constitution of the universe as being
altogether ineffable and unexplainable.

OBJECTION: *Give proof that God was manifest in the flesh.*

12 Let him who is seeking proofs[136] of God having been made manifest to us in the flesh[137]

RESPONSE: *Christ's activity is proof.*

look to [God's] activities;[138] for he would also have no other proof
of God's existence at all except the testimony of the activities themselves. Therefore even as when looking at the universe and considering the economy of the cosmos and the benefits wrought[139] by God

---

[134]This is the participial form of the word "history" (ἱστορουμένων), and it
introduces St Gregory's historical arguments (18.1–3 and 18.4–5).

[135]Though many regard St Gregory as a speculative theologian, in more than one
place he puts a definite limit to the licit exercise of theological curiosity (cf. *On the
Soul and the Resurrection* 3.8–15).

[136]Or "demonstrations" (ἀποδείξεις).

[137]1 Tim 3.16.

[138]Or "energies" (ἐνεργείας). Both St Gregory and his brother St Basil articulated
God's essential unknowability in opposition to Aetius' claim to know God's essence
better than he knew himself; the Cappadocian brothers asserted that God is unknow-
able in essence but known in his activities or energies.

[139]In Greek all these words are related: the "benefits" (εὐεργεσίας) "wrought"

μένων καὶ συντηρητικὴν τῶν ὄντων καταλαμβάνομεν, ₁₅οὕτω
καὶ ἐπὶ τοῦ διὰ σαρκὸς ἡμῖν φανερωθέντος ₁₆Θεοῦ ἱκανὴν
10 (Sr 59) ἀπόδειξιν τῆς ἐπιφανείας τῆς | θεότητος τὰ ₁₇κατὰ τὰς ἐνεργείας
θαύματα πεποιήμεθα, πάντα τοῖς ₁₈ἱστορηθεῖσιν ἔργοις, δι' ὧν ἡ
θεία χαρακτηρίζεται φύσις, ₁₉κατανοήσαντες.—

—(2) Θεοῦ τὸ ζωο-
ποιεῖν τοὺς ἀνθρώπους, Θεοῦ ₂₀τὸ συντηρεῖν διὰ προνοίας τὰ
ὄντα, Θεοῦ τὸ βρῶσιν καὶ ₂₁πόσιν τοῖς διὰ σαρκὸς τὴν ζωὴν
15 εἰληχόσι χαρίζεσθαι, Θεοῦ ₂₂τὸ εὐεργετεῖν τὸν δεόμενον, Θεοῦ
τὸ παρατραπεῖσαν ἐξ ₂₃ἀσθενείας τὴν φύσιν πάλιν δι' ὑγείας
(GNO 41) πρὸς ἑαυτὴν ἐπανά- | γειν, Θεοῦ τὸ πάσης ἐπιστατεῖν ὁμοιο-
τρόπως τῆς κτίσεως, ₂γῆς, θαλάσσης, ἀέρος, καὶ τῶν ὑπὲρ τὸν
ἀέρα τόπων, Θεοῦ ₃τὸ πρὸς πάντα διαρκῆ τὴν δύναμιν ἔχειν καὶ
20 πρό γε πάντων ₄τὸ θανάτου καὶ φθορᾶς εἶναι κρείττονα. (3) Εἰ μὲν
οὖν τινος ₅τούτων καὶ τῶν τοιούτων ἐλλιπὴς ἦν ἡ περὶ αὐτὸν
₆ἱστορία, εἰκότως τὸ μυστήριον ἡμῶν οἱ ἔξω τῆς πίστεως ₇παρε-
(PG 45) γράφοντο· εἰ δὲ δι' ὧν νοεῖται Θεός, πάντα ἐν | τοῖς περὶ ₈αὐτοῦ
διηγήμασι καθορᾶται, τί τὸ ἐμποδίζον τῇ πίστει;

(Sr 60) ΙΓ'   ₉Ἀλλά, φησί, γέννησίς τε καὶ θάνατος ἴδιον τῆς | σαρκι-
κῆς ₁₀ἐστι φύσεως.—

—Φημὶ κἀγώ. Ἀλλὰ τὸ πρὸ τῆς γεννήσεως
₁₁καὶ τὸ μετὰ τὸν θάνατον τὴν τῆς φύσεως ἡμῶν ἐκφεύγει
₁₂κοινότητα. Εἰς γὰρ ἑκάτερα τῆς ἀνθρωπίνης ζωῆς ₁₃τὰ πέρατα
5 βλέποντες, ἴσμεν καὶ ὅθεν ἀρχόμεθα καὶ εἰς τί ₁₄καταλήγομεν·
ἐκ πάθους γὰρ ἀρξάμενος τοῦ εἶναι ὁ ἄνθρωπος ₁₅πάθει συν-

οὕτως GNO : οὕτω Srawley

in our life, we comprehend some overarching power producing what comes into being and preserving what exists, so too in the case of God being made manifest to us through the flesh we have regarded the wonders in [his] activities as sufficient proof of the manifestation of the divinity, understanding all by the works that are recorded, through which the divine nature is characterized.

(2) It belongs to God to give life to men; it belongs to God to preserve what exists by providence;[140] it belongs to God to bestow food and drink on those who have received life through the flesh; it belongs to God to benefit those in need; it belongs to God to lead nature, which was led astray by infirmity, back to itself again through health; it belongs to God to preside over all creation in the same manner, the earth, the sea, the air, and the places above the air; it belongs to God to have power sufficient for all things and above all to be superior to death and corruption. (3) If, then, the record[141] about him was lacking any of these things and the like, those outside the faith would fairly take exception to our mystery; but if everything by which God is perceived is clearly seen in the narratives about him, what is the impediment to faith?

OBJECTION: *Birth and death are proper to the fleshly nature.*

13 "But," it is said, "both birth and death are proper to the fleshly nature."

RESPONSE: *Christ's virginal conception and resurrection exceed fleshly nature.*

And I agree. But what was before the birth and what is after the death exceeds[142] our shared nature. For looking at either of the limits of human life, we know both whence we begin and in what we end; for man, who begins existing out of suffering,[143] meets his end with

(ἐνεργουμένας) by God are his "activities" (τὰς ἐνεργείας; τῶν ἐνεργειῶν).

   [140]Or "foreknowledge" (προνοίας).

   [141]Lit. "history" (ἱστορία); the verb form is rendered "to record" above.

   [142]Lit. "escapes" (ἐκφεύγει).

   [143]In this section the word πάθος (*pathos*) is sometimes translated as "suffer-

απαρτίζεται. Ἐκεῖ δὲ οὔτε ἡ γέννησις ₁₆ἀπὸ πάθους ἤρξατο, οὔτε ὁ θάνατος εἰς πάθος κατέληξεν· ₁₇οὔτε γὰρ τῆς γεννήσεως ἡδονὴ καθηγήσατο οὔτε τὸν ₁₈θάνατον φθορὰ διεδέξατο.

10 (2) Ἀπιστεῖς τῷ θαύματι; Χαίρω ₁₉σου τῇ ἀπιστίᾳ· ὁμολογεῖς γὰρ πάντως δι' ὧν ὑπὲρ πίστιν ₂₀ἤγῇ τὸ λεγόμενον ὑπὲρ τὴν φύσιν εἶναι τὰ θαύματα. Αὐτὸ ₂₁οὖν τοῦτο τῆς θεότητος ἔστω σοι τοῦ φανέντος ἀπόδειξις ₂₂τὸ μὴ διὰ τῶν κατὰ φύσιν προϊέναι |
(Sr 61) τὸ κήρυγμα. Εἰ γὰρ ἐντὸς ₂₃ἦν τῶν τῆς φύσεως ὅρων τὰ περὶ τοῦ
15 Χριστοῦ διηγήματα, ₂₄ποῦ τὸ θεῖον; Εἰ δὲ ὑπερβαίνει τὴν φύσιν
(GNO 42) ὁ λόγος, ἐν | οἷς ἀπιστεῖς, ἐν τούτοις ἐστὶν ἡ ἀπόδειξις τοῦ θεὸν εἶναι ₂τὸν κηρυσσόμενον.—

—(3) Ἄνθρωπος μὲν γὰρ ἐκ συνδυασμοῦ ₃τίκτεται καὶ μετὰ θάνατον ἐν διαφθορᾷ γίνεται. Εἰ ταῦτα ₄περιεῖχε τὸ κήρυγμα, οὐκ ἂν θεὸν εἶναι πάντως ᾠήθης τὸν ₅ἐν
20 τοῖς ἰδιώμασι τῆς φύσεως ἡμῶν μαρτυρούμενον. Ἐπεὶ δὲ ₆γεγενῆσθαι μὲν αὐτὸν ἀκούεις, ἐκβεβηκέναι δὲ τῆς φύσεως ₇ἡμῶν τὴν κοινότητα τῷ τε τῆς γενέσεως τρόπῳ καὶ ₈τῷ ἀνεπι- δέκτῳ τῆς εἰς φθορὰν ἀλλοιώσεως, καλῶς ἂν ₉ἔχοι κατὰ τὸ ἀκόλουθον ἐπὶ τὸ ἕτερον τῇ ἀπιστίᾳ χρήσασθαι, ₁₀εἰς τὸ μὴ
25 ἄνθρωπον αὐτὸν ἕνα τῶν ἐν τῇ φύσει ₁₁δεικνυμένων οἴεσθαι·

(4) Ἀνάγκη γὰρ πᾶσα τὸν μὴ πιστεύοντα ₁₂τὸν τοιοῦτον ἄνθρωπον εἶναι εἰς τὴν περὶ τοῦ θεὸν αὐτὸν ₁₃εἶναι πίστιν ἐναχθῆναι. Ὁ γὰρ γεγενῆσθαι αὐτὸν ἱστορήσας ₁₄καὶ τὸ οὕτως γεγενῆσθαι συν- διηγήσατο. Εἰ οὖν ₁₅πιστόν ἐστι διὰ τῶν εἰρημένων τὸ γεγε-
30 νῆσθαι αὐτόν, διὰ ₁₆τῶν αὐτῶν τούτων πάντως οὐδὲ τὸ οὕτως
(Sr 62) αὐτὸν γεγενῆσθαι ₁₇ἀπίθανον· (5) ὁ | γὰρ τὴν γέννησιν εἰπὼν καὶ τὸ ἐκ παρθενίας ₁₈προσέθηκε, καὶ ὁ τοῦ θανάτου μνησθεὶς καὶ τὴν

---

28 τὸ οὕτως GNO : τὸ ἐκ παρθένου Srawley | 30 γεγενῆσθαι GNO : γεγεννῆσθαι Srawley | 32 προσέθηκε GNO : προσέθηκεν Srawley

suffering. But there [i.e., in Christ's life] neither did the birth begin out of suffering, nor did death end in passibility: for neither did pleasure precede the birth nor did corruption succeed after death.

(2) Do you disbelieve the miracle? I rejoice in your disbelief; for through the things that lead you [to think] that what is said surpasses belief, you altogether admit the miracles are above nature. Let this itself then be proof for you of the divinity of him who was made manifest: the fact that the preaching does not proceed through things in accordance with nature. For if the narratives about Christ were within the boundaries of nature, where is the divine? But if the account, in which things you disbelieve, transcends nature, in these is the proof that he who is preached is God.

(3) For man is born from copulation and after death is in corruption. If the preaching contained these, you would not have thought him to be God at all, who was witnessed with the properties of our nature. But since you hear he was born, but went beyond our shared nature both in the manner of birth and in not admitting alteration into corruption [after death], it would be good, according to the order [of the argument], to direct disbelief in the other direction, not to think of him as [merely] one man among those that appear in nature.

(4) For he who does not believe that someone like this is a man, it is altogether necessary to be led to the belief that he is God; for he who recorded his birth also narrated the way[144] he was born. If, then, his birth is believable because of what has been said, because of these same things the way he was born is not at all unbelievable; (5) for he who spoke of the birth added that it was from a virgin,[145]

---

ing" and sometimes as "passion." It is impossible to convey the various shades of this word's meaning with a single English word. (Once it is translated as "passibility," when it refers to Christ's death, since it certainly cannot be said that he died without "suffering"—but here St Gregory refers to the fact that after his death he did not suffer corruption: "You will not allow your holy one to see corruption" [Acts 13.35; Ps 15.10 LXX]). Gregory will address the proper meaning of the word πάθος below (16.1).

[144]St Gregory seems to have St Matthew in mind in particular: "the way" (τὸ οὕτως) echoes Mt 1.18—"the birth of Jesus Christ took place this way [οὕτως ἦν, lit. 'was thus']."

[145]Lit. "from virginity" (ἐκ παρθενίας).

₁₉ἀνάστασιν τῷ θανάτῳ προσεμαρτύρησεν. Εἰ οὖν ἀφ' ὧν ₂₀ἀκούεις καὶ τεθνάναι καὶ γεγεννῆσθαι δίδως, ἐκ τῶν αὐτῶν 35 ₂₁δώσεις πάντως καὶ τὸ ἔξω πάθους εἶναι καὶ τὴν γέννησιν ₂₂αὐτοῦ (GNO 43) καὶ τὸν θάνατον· ἀλλὰ μὴν ταῦτα μείζω τῆς | φύσεως· οὐκοῦν οὐδὲ ἐκεῖνος πάντως ἐντὸς τῆς φύσεως ὁ ₂ἐν τοῖς ὑπὲρ τὴν φύσιν γεγενῆσθαι ἀποδεικνύμενος.

ΙΔ' ₃Τίς οὖν αἰτία, φησί, τοῦ πρὸς τὴν ταπεινότητα ταύτην ₄καταβῆναι τὸ θεῖον, ὡς ἀμφίβολον εἶναι τὴν πίστιν, εἰ ₅Θεός, τὸ ἀχώρητον καὶ ἀκατανόητον καὶ ἀνεκλάλητον ₆πρᾶγμα, τὸ ὑπὲρ πᾶσαν δόξαν καὶ πᾶσαν μεγαλειότητα, ₇τῷ λύθρῳ τῆς ἀνθρω- 5 (PG 48) πίνης φύσεως καταμίγνυται, ὡς καὶ ₈τὰς ὑψηλὰς ἐνερ-| γείας αὐτοῦ τῇ πρὸς τὸ ταπεινὸν ἐπιμιξίᾳ ₉συνευτελίζεσθαι; |

(Sr 63) ΙΕ' Οὐκ ἀποροῦμεν καὶ πρὸς τοῦτο θεοπρεποῦς ₁₀ἀποκρί- σεως. (2) Ζητεῖς τὴν αἰτίαν τοῦ γενέσθαι Θεὸν ἐν ₁₁ἀνθρώποις; Ἐὰν ἀφέλῃς τοῦ βίου τὰς θεόθεν γινομένας εὐεργεσίας, ₁₂ἐκ ποίων ἐπιγνώσῃ τὸ θεῖον οὐκ ἂν εἰπεῖν ἔχοις. ₁₃Ἀφ' ὧν γὰρ εὖ 5 πάσχομεν, ἀπὸ τούτων τὸν εὐεργέτην ἐπιγινώσκομεν· ₁₄πρὸς γὰρ τὰ γινόμενα βλέποντες, διὰ τούτων ₁₅τὴν τοῦ ἐνεργοῦντος ἀναλογιζόμεθα φύσιν. Εἰ οὖν ἴδιον ₁₆γνώρισμα τῆς θείας φύσεως ἡ φιλανθρωπία, ἔχεις ὃν ἐπεζήτησας ₁₇λόγον, ἔχεις τὴν αἰτίαν τῆς ἐν ἀνθρώποις τοῦ ₁₈Θεοῦ παρουσίας.—

—(3) Ἐδεῖτο γὰρ τοῦ ἰα- 10 τρεύοντος ἡ φύσις ἡμῶν ₁₉ἀσθενήσασα, ἐδεῖτο τοῦ ἀνορθοῦντος

and he who made mention of the death bore witness to the resurrection also along with the death. If, then, you grant the dying and the being born from the things you hear, from the same things you will also by all means grant both his birth and death to be without passibility;[146] but indeed these are greater than nature; therefore he is not at all within nature who is shown to have been born among things that are above nature.

> OBJECTION: *What is the cause of the divine condescension to our humiliation?*

14 "What, then, is the cause," it is said, "of the divine descending to this humiliation, so that belief is wavering, if God—the uncontainable and incomprehensible and unutterable reality, that which is above all glory and all greatness—is mixed with the defilement of human nature, so that his lofty activities are also degraded by admixture with humiliation?"

> RESPONSE: *God's love for man and our need for a savior are the causes.*

15 We are also not at a loss for a God-befitting answer to this. (2) You ask the cause of God being born among men? If you take away from life the benefits that come from God, you would not be able to say by what means you would recognize the divine. For from the good things we experience, from these we recognize the benefactor; for looking at the things that happened, through these we reckon the nature of him who is at work [in them]. If, then, love for man[147] is the characteristic property of the divine nature, you have the reason which you sought, you have the cause of God's presence among men.

(3) For our infirm nature stood in need of a healer, man in the fall stood in need of someone to set him upright, he who was

---

[146]Or "suffering" (πάθους). See p. 75, n. 64 above.
[147]Lit. "philanthropy" (φιλανθρωπίαν); a biblical word (Acts 28.2; Tit 3.4), it is ubiquitous in the writings of the fathers and in Orthodox liturgical texts.

ὁ ἐν τῷ πτώματι ₂₀ἄνθρωπος, ἐδεῖτο τοῦ ζωοποιοῦντος ὁ ἀφα-
μαρτὼν τῆς ₂₁ζωῆς, ἐδεῖτο τοῦ πρὸς τὸ ἀγαθὸν ἐπανάγοντος ὁ
ἀπορρυεὶς ₂₂τῆς τοῦ ἀγαθοῦ μετουσίας, ἔχρῃζε τῆς τοῦ φωτὸς
₂₃παρουσίας ὁ καθειργμένος τῷ σκότῳ, ἐπεζήτει τὸν λυτρωτὴν
15 ₂₄ὁ αἰχμάλωτος, τὸν συναγωνιστὴν ὁ δεσμώτης, ₂₅τὸν ἐλευθε-
(GNO 44; ρωτὴν ὁ τῷ ζυγῷ τῆς δουλείας ἐγκατεχόμενος. | Ἆρα μικρὰ |
Sr 64) ταῦτα καὶ ἀνάξια τοῦ Θεὸν δυσωπῆσαι πρὸς ₂ἐπίσκεψιν τῆς
ἀνθρωπίνης φύσεως καταβῆναι, οὕτως ἐλεεινῶς ₃καὶ ἀθλίως
τῆς ἀνθρωπότητος διακειμένης;

20 (4) ₄Ἀλλ' ἐξῆν, φησί, καὶ εὐεργετηθῆναι τὸν ἄνθρωπον καὶ ₅ἐν
ἀπαθείᾳ τὸν Θεὸν διαμεῖναι. Ὁ γὰρ τῷ βουλήματι τὸ πᾶν ₆συ-
στησάμενος καὶ τὸ μὴ ὂν ὑποστήσας ἐν μόνῃ τῇ ὁρμῇ ₇τοῦ
θελήματος, τί οὐχὶ καὶ τὸν ἄνθρωπον δι' αὐθεντικῆς ₈τινὸς καὶ
θεϊκῆς ἐξουσίας τῆς ἐναντίας δυνάμεως ἀποσπάσας ₉πρὸς τὴν
25 ἐξ ἀρχῆς ἄγει κατάστασιν, εἰ τοῦτο φίλον ₁₀αὐτῷ, ἀλλὰ μακρὰς
περιέρχεται περιόδους, σώματος ₁₁ὑπερχόμενος φύσιν, καὶ διὰ
γεννήσεως παριὼν εἰς τὸν βίον, ₁₂καὶ πᾶσαν ἀκολούθως ἡλικίαν
διεξιών, εἶτα θανάτου ₁₃γευόμενος, καὶ οὕτω διὰ τῆς τοῦ ἰδίου
σώματος ἀναστάσεως ₁₄τὸν σκοπὸν ἀνύων, ὡς οὐκ ἐξὸν αὐτῷ
30 μένοντι ἐπὶ ₁₅τοῦ ὕψους τῆς θεϊκῆς δόξης, διὰ προστάγματος
σῶσαι τὸν ₁₆ἄνθρωπον, τὰς δὲ τοιαύτας περιόδους χαίρειν ἐᾶ-
σαι;

16 ἐγκατεχόμενος GNO : κατεχόμενος Srawley | 28 οὕτω GNO : οὕτως Srawley

deprived of life stood in need of the giver of life,[148] he who declined from participation in the good stood in need of him who leads back to the good, he who was shut up in darkness needed the presence of light, the captive sought the redeemer,[149] the one in bondage the fellow struggler, he who was held fast in the yoke of slavery the liberator; were these small and unworthy things to importune God to descend to visit[150] human nature, since humanity was in so pitiful and wretched a state?

OBJECTION: *It was possible to save man by fiat, without the incarnation.*

(4) "But it was possible," it is said, "both for man to be benefitted and for God to remain in impassibility. For why did he who constituted the universe by [his] intention and brought nonbeing into subsistence by the impulse of will alone not also lead man to the state [he had] from the beginning, tearing him away from the power of the adversary by some commanding and divine authority, if this was dear to him?[151] But instead he goes round long periods [of time], assuming the nature of the body, entering into life through birth, going through each stage of life in order, then 'tasting of death,'[152] and so by the resurrection of his own body accomplishing [his] aim, as if it were not possible for him to save man by a command while remaining in the height of divine glory, rejecting such roundabout ways as these."

---

[148]Cf. 1 Cor 15.45.
[149]Or "ransomer" (λυτρωτὴν). This lays the groundwork for the account of the ransom in Chapters 22–23.
[150]Cf. Ex 3.16; 4.31 LXX.
[151]St Athanasius addresses this objection in *On the Incarnation* 44.
[152]Heb 2.9.

(Sr 65) Οὐκοῦν $_{17}$ἀνάγκη καὶ ταῖς τοιαύταις | τῶν ἀντιθέσεων ἀντικαταστῆναι $_{18}$παρ' ἡμῶν τὴν ἀλήθειαν, ὡς ἂν διὰ μηδενὸς $_{19}$ἡ πίστις κωλύοιτο τῶν ἐξεταστικῶς ζητούντων τοῦ $_{20}$μυστηρίου τὸν λόγον.—

35   —(5) Πρῶτον μὲν οὖν ὅπερ καὶ ἐν τοῖς $_{21}$φθάσασιν ἤδη μετρίως ἐξήτασται, τί τῇ ἀρετῇ κατὰ τὸ $_{22}$ἐναντίον ἀντικαθέστηκεν, ἐπισκεψώμεθα. Ὡς φωτὶ σκότος $_{23}$καὶ θάνατος τῇ ζωῇ, οὕτω τῇ ἀρετῇ ἡ κακία δηλονότι $_{24}$καὶ οὐδὲν παρὰ ταύτην ἕτερον. Καθάπερ γὰρ πολλῶν ὄντων $_{25}$τῶν ἐν τῇ κτίσει θεωρου-
40 μένων οὐδὲν ἄλλο πρὸς τὸ $_{26}$φῶς ἢ τὴν ζωὴν τὴν ἀντιδιαίρεσιν
(GNO 45) ἔχει, οὐ λίθος, οὐ ξύλον, | οὐχ ὕδωρ, οὐκ ἄνθρωπος, οὐκ ἄλλο τι τῶν ὄντων οὐδέν, $_{2}$πλὴν ἰδίως τὰ κατὰ τὸ ἐναντίον νοούμενα, οἷον σκότος καὶ $_{3}$θάνατος, οὕτω καὶ ἐπὶ τῆς ἀρετῆς οὐκ ἄν τις κτίσιν τινὰ $_{4}$κατὰ τὸ ἐναντίον αὐτῇ νοεῖσθαι λέγοι, πλὴν τὸ κατὰ
45 κακίαν $_{5}$νόημα.

(6) Οὐκοῦν εἰ μὲν ἐν κακίᾳ γεγενῆσθαι τὸ θεῖον ὁ $_{6}$ἡμέτερος ἐπρέσβευε λόγος, καιρὸν εἶχεν ὁ ἀντιλέγων $_{7}$κατατρέχειν ἡμῶν
(PG 49) τῆς πίστεως, ὡς ἀνάρμοστά τε καὶ $_{8}$ἀπεμφαίνοντα | περὶ τῆς θείας φύσεως δοξαζόντων. Οὐ γὰρ $_{9}$δὴ θεμιτὸν ἦν αὐτοσοφίαν,
50 καὶ ἀγαθότητα, καὶ ἀφθαρσίαν, $_{10}$καὶ εἴ τι ὑψηλόν ἐστι νόημά τε
(Sr 66) καὶ ὄνομα, πρὸς | τὸ ἐναντίον $_{11}$μεταπεπτωκέναι λέγειν. (7) Εἰ οὖν Θεὸς μὲν ἡ ἀληθὴς ἀρετή, $_{12}$φύσις δέ τις οὐκ ἀντιδιαιρεῖται τῇ ἀρετῇ, ἀλλὰ κακία, Θεὸς $_{13}$δὲ οὐκ ἐν κακίᾳ, ἀλλ' ἐν ἀνθρώπου γίνεται φύσει, μόνον δὲ $_{14}$ἀπρεπὲς καὶ αἰσχρὸν τὸ κατὰ κακίαν
55 πάθος, ἐν ᾧ οὔτε $_{15}$γέγονεν ὁ Θεὸς, οὔτε γενέσθαι φύσιν ἔχει, τί ἐπαισχύνονται $_{16}$τῇ ὁμολογίᾳ τοῦ Θεὸν ἀνθρωπίνης ἅψασθαι φύσεως, οὐδεμιᾶς $_{17}$ἐναντιότητος ὡς πρὸς τὸν τῆς ἀρετῆς λόγον ἐν τῇ $_{18}$κατασκευῇ τοῦ ἀνθρώπου θεωρουμένης; Οὔτε γὰρ τὸ λογικόν, $_{19}$οὔτε τὸ διανοητικόν, οὔτε τὸ ἐπιστήμης δεκτικόν,

49 δοξαζόντων GNO : δογματιζόντων Srawley

RESPONSE: *Only vice is shameful, and the incarnation exhibits virtue, the opposite of vice.*

Therefore it is also necessary for the truth to be set forth by us against these sorts of objections, so the faith might be hindered by nothing for those who seek the rationale of the mystery with exactitude.

(5) First, then, let us consider what has been placed in opposition to virtue (the very thing that has already also been moderately examined in the previous [sections]). As darkness [is opposed] to light and death to life, so clearly vice—and nothing other from this—[is opposed] to virtue. For just as of the many existing things seen in creation nothing else is distinguished over against light or life—not stone, not wood, not water, not man—no other thing among what exists, except the things properly understood as the opposite, such as darkness and death, so too in the case of virtue someone would not say that any created thing is to be thought of as opposite to it, except the thought of vice.

(6) Therefore if our account[153] maintained that the divine was born in vice, the naysayer would have an opportunity to run down our faith, as that of those who hold opinions about the divine nature that are both unfitting and incongruous. For it would indeed be impious[154] to say that Wisdom himself—and Goodness, and Incorruption, and every other lofty thought and name—had fallen to the opposite. (7) If, then, God is true virtue, and there is not any nature distinguished from virtue but vice, and God is born not in vice, but in man's nature, and the only unfitting and shameful thing is the passion of vice, in which neither was God born, nor does he have a nature [able] to be born [in it], why are they ashamed at the confession of God being joined[155] to human nature, seeing in the fashioning of man nothing of opposition to the idea[156] of virtue? For neither rationality, nor discursive thought, nor the capacity for exact

[153]Or "argument" (λόγος).
[154]Or "not lawful" (οὐ . . . θεμιτὸν).
[155]Or "touching" (ἄψασθαι).
[156]Λόγον.

60 οὔτε $_{20}$ἄλλο τι τοιοῦτον, ὃ τῆς ἀνθρωπίνης ἴδιον οὐσίας ἐστί, τῷ $_{21}$λόγῳ τῆς ἀρετῆς ἠναντίωται.

ΙΣΤ' $_{22}$Ἀλλ' αὐτή, φησίν, ἡ τροπὴ τοῦ ἡμετέρου σώματος |
(Sr 67) πάθος $_{23}$ἐστίν. Ὁ δὲ ἐν τούτῳ γεγονὼς ἐν πάθει γίνεται· ἀπαθὲς $_{24}$δὲ τὸ θεῖον. Οὐκοῦν ἀλλοτρία περὶ Θεοῦ ἡ ὑπόληψις, εἴπερ |
(GNO 46) τὸν ἀπαθῆ κατὰ τὴν φύσιν πρὸς κοινωνίαν πάθους ἐλθεῖν
5 $_{2}$διορίζονται.

Ἀλλὰ καὶ πρὸς ταῦτα πάλιν τῷ αὐτῷ λόγῳ $_{3}$χρησόμεθα, ὅτι τὸ πάθος τὸ μὲν κυρίως, τὸ δὲ ἐκ καταχρήσεως $_{4}$λέγεται. Τὸ μὲν οὖν προαιρέσεως ἁπτόμενον καὶ $_{5}$πρὸς κακίαν ἀπὸ τῆς ἀρετῆς μεταστρέφον ἀληθῶς πάθος $_{6}$ἐστί· τὸ δ' ὅσον ἐν τῇ φύσει κατὰ τὸν ἴδιον εἱρμὸν πορευομένη $_{7}$διεξοδικῶς θεωρεῖται,
10
(Sr 68) τοῦτο κυριώτερον | ἔργον ἂν $_{8}$μᾶλλον ἢ πάθος προσαγορεύοιτο, οἷον ἡ γέννησις, ἡ αὔξησις, $_{9}$ἢ διὰ τοῦ ἐπιρρύτου τε καὶ ἀπορρύτου τῆς τροφῆς τοῦ $_{10}$ὑποκειμένου διαμονή, ἡ τῶν στοιχείων περὶ τὸ σῶμα συνδρομή, $_{11}$ἢ τοῦ συντεθέντος πάλιν διάλυσίς τε
15 καὶ πρὸς τὰ $_{12}$συγγενῆ μεταχώρησις.

(2) Τίνος οὖν λέγει τὸ μυστήριον ἡμῶν $_{13}$ἧφθαι τὸ θεῖον; Τοῦ κυρίως λεγομένου πάθους, ὅπερ κακία $_{14}$ἐστίν, ἢ τοῦ κατὰ τὴν φύσιν κινήματος; Εἰ μὲν γὰρ ἐν τοῖς $_{15}$ἀπηγορευμένοις γεγενῆσθαι τὸ θεῖον ὁ λόγος διισχυρίζετο, $_{16}$φεύγειν ἔδει τὴν ἀτοπίαν

knowledge, nor any other such thing that is proper to the essence of humanity is opposed to the idea[157] of virtue.

OBJECTION: *Bodily change is a passion.*

16 "But," it is said, "the change of our body itself is a passion. He who has been born in this [state] is in passion; but the divine is impassible; therefore the supposition about God is alien, if indeed they determine that he who is impassible by nature comes into fellowship with passion."

RESPONSE: *"Passion," in its proper sense, is vice. Thus the incarnation is free of passion.*

But we will also respond to these things with the same argument again, that "passion" is said at times in a proper sense, but at other times in a less correct sense.[158] Therefore what is joined to the will[159] and turns it from virtue to vice is truly passion; but whatever is seen in nature, which proceeds successively in its proper sequence, this would much more properly be called a "work" than a passion, such as birth, growth, the continuance of the subject through the inflow and outflow of nourishment, the concourse of the elements of the body, the dissolution of the composition again, and [its] departure to kindred [elements].

(2) What then does our mystery say has been joined to the divine? "Passion," properly speaking, which is vice, or a movement in accordance with nature? For if the argument affirmed that the divine was born among forbidden things, it would be necessary to

---

[157]Λόγῳ.

[158]Lit. "by catechresis" (ἐκ καταχρήσεως). This was a technical rhetorical term that implied the misuse of a word: "Aristotle (cited in Cic. *Orat.* 94) terms it a kind of metaphor involving a misuse of words (*abusio*). . . . Quint. *Inst.* 8.6.34–36 (*abusio*) gives similar examples. . . . How is this then distinguished from metaphor? It would seem only by a use that strikes one as incorrect." R. Dean Anderson, Jr., *Glossary of Greek Rhetorical Terms Connected to Methods of Argumentation, Figures and Tropes from Anaximenes to Quintilian* (Leuven: Peeters, 2000), 66.

[159]Or "faculty of decision" (προαιρέσεως).

20 τοῦ δόγματος ὡς οὐδὲν ὑγιὲς [17]περὶ τῆς θείας φύσεως διεξι-
όντος· εἰ δὲ τῆς φύσεως ἡμῶν [18]αὐτὸν ἐφῆφθαι λέγει, ἧς καὶ ἡ
πρώτη γένεσίς τε καὶ ὑπόστασις [19]παρ᾽ αὐτοῦ τὴν ἀρχὴν ἔσχε,
(Sr 69) ποῦ τῆς Θεῷ | πρεπούσης [20]ἐννοίας διαμαρτάνει τὸ κήρυγμα,
μηδεμιᾶς παθητικῆς [21]διαθέσεως ἐν ταῖς περὶ Θεοῦ ὑπολήψεσι
25 τῇ πίστει συνεισιούσης; [22]Οὐδὲ γὰρ τὸν ἰατρὸν ἐν πάθει γίνε-
(GNO 47) σθαι λέγομεν, | ὅταν θεραπεύῃ τὸν ἐν πάθει γενόμενον· ἀλλὰ
κἂν προσάψηται [2]τοῦ ἀρρωστήματος, ἔξω πάθους ὁ θερα-
πευτὴς [3]διαμένει.—
—(3) Εἰ ἡ γένεσις αὐτὴ καθ᾽ ἑαυτὴν πάθος οὐκ
ἔστιν, [4]οὐδ᾽ ἂν τὴν ζωήν τις πάθος προσαγορεύσειεν· ἀλλὰ τὸ
30 [5]καθ᾽ ἡδονὴν πάθος τῆς ἀνθρωπίνης καθηγεῖται γενέσεως, [6]καὶ
ἡ πρὸς κακίαν τῶν ζώντων ὁρμή—τοῦτο τῆς φύσεως [7]ἡμῶν
ἐστιν ἀρρώστημα—ἀλλὰ μὴν ἀμφοτέρων αὐτὸν [8]καθαρεύειν
φησὶ τὸ μυστήριον. Εἰ οὖν ἡδονῆς μὲν ἡ γένεσις [9]ἠλλοτρίωται,
κακίας δὲ ἡ ζωή, ποῖον ὑπολέλειπται πάθος, [10]οὗ τὸν Θεὸν
35 (PG 52) κεκοινωνηκέναι φησὶ τὸ τῆς εὐσεβείας [11]μυστήριον; |(4) Εἰ δέ τις
τὴν τοῦ σώματος καὶ τῆς ψυχῆς διάζευξιν [12]πάθος προσαγο-
ρεύοι, πολὺ πρότερον δικαῖος ἂν [13]εἴη τὴν συνδρομὴν ἀμφοτέρων
οὕτω κατονομάσαι. Εἰ γὰρ [14]ὁ χωρισμὸς τῶν συνημμένων
πάθος ἐστί, καὶ ἡ συνάφεια [15]τῶν διεστώτων πάθος ἂν εἴη·
40 (Sr 70) κίνησις γάρ τίς | ἐστιν ἕν τε [16]τῇ συγκράσει τῶν διεστώτων καὶ ἐν
τῇ διακρίσει τῶν [17][συμπεπλεγμένων ἢ] ἠνωμένων. (5) Ὅπερ τοίνυν
ἡ τελευταία [18]κίνησις ὀνομάζεται, τοῦτο προσήκει καλεῖσθαι
καὶ τὴν [19]προάγουσαν. Εἰ δὲ ἡ πρώτη κίνησις ἦν γένεσιν ὀνο-
μάζομεν, [20]πάθος οὐκ ἔστιν, οὐδ᾽ ἂν ἡ δευτέρα κίνησις, ἣν θάνα-
45 (GNO 48) [21]τον ὀνομάζομεν, πάθος [ἂν] κατὰ τὸ ἀκόλουθον λέγοιτο, | καθ᾽

34 ὑπολέλειπται GNO : ὑπολείπεται Srawley | 35 Srawley omits τις |
40 συγκράσει GNO : συγκρίσει Srawley

flee the absurdity of the teaching, in order to remain aloof from an unsound [idea] about the divine nature; but if [the argument] says he has been joined to our nature, whose first genesis and substance had [its] beginning from him, where does the preaching stray from a notion befitting for God, since no passionate state enters into the suppositions about God along with the faith? For we do not say the physician is in "passion" when he treats one who is suffering,[160] but, although he touches illness, the healer remains without suffering.

(3) If birth itself in itself is not a passion, neither does anyone call life a passion; but pleasurable passion precedes human birth, and living things' impulse to vice—this is an infirmity[161] of our nature—but indeed the mystery says he is pure of both. If, then, the birth is alien to pleasure, and the life to vice, what sort of passion has remained, with which "the mystery of piety"[162] says God had fellowship? (4) But if someone should call the disjoining of body and soul a passion, he would be much more justified to name the concourse of both such. For if the separation of things that are joined together is a passion, the joining of disparate things[163] would also be a passion; for change[164] is something [found] both in the commixture of disparate things and in the separation of things that have been entwined or united; (5) therefore what the last change is named, this it is appropriate to call the preceding [change] also. And if the first change, which we name birth, is not a passion, neither would the second change—which we name death, in which the concourse of

[160]In this sentence both "passion" and "suffering" translate ἐν πάθει, but in the first instance Gregory is using the word in its proper sense (true "passion" is vice, which is shameful), and in the second instance he uses it in the less proper sense (bodily "suffering," which is neither a vice nor shameful).

[161]Or "illness" (ἀρρώστημα).

[162]1 Tim 3.16.

[163]The participial form of διάστημα (διεστώτων), an important term for St Gregory. See "*Diastêma*," in *Brill Dictionary*, 227–28.

[164]Elsewhere "motion" or "movement" (κίνησις). Ancient physics and philosophy conceived of various types of "motion" that were not "locomotion," i.e., a motion with respect to location (the most common modern meaning of the term "motion" or "movement"). "Change" conveys this broader sense of κίνησις.

ἦν ἡ συνδρομὴ τοῦ σώματος καὶ τῆς ψυχῆς διακρίνεται.—

—(6) [2]Τὸν δὲ
Θεόν φαμεν ἐν ἑκατέρᾳ γεγενῆσθαι τῇ τῆς [3]φύσεως ἡμῶν
κινήσει, δι' ἧς ἥ τε ψυχὴ πρὸς τὸ σῶμα συντρέχει, [4]τό τε σῶμα
τῆς ψυχῆς διακρίνεται, καταμιχθέντα [5]δὲ πρὸς ἑκάτερον τού-
50 των—πρός τε τὸ αἰσθητόν φημι καὶ [6]τὸ νοερὸν τοῦ
ἀνθρωπίνου συγκρίματος—διὰ τῆς ἀρρήτου [7]ἐκείνης καὶ
ἀνεκφράστου συνανακράσεως τοῦτο οἰκονομήσασθαι [8]τὸ τῶν
ἅπαξ ἑνωθέντων (ψυχῆς λέγω καὶ σώματος), [9]καὶ εἰς ἀεὶ
διαμεῖναι τὴν ἕνωσιν.
55 (7) Τῆς γὰρ φύσεως [10]ἡμῶν διὰ τῆς ἰδίας ἀκολουθίας καὶ ἐν
ἐκείνῳ πρὸς διάκρισιν [11]τοῦ σώματος καὶ τῆς ψυχῆς κινηθείσης,
(Sr 71) πάλιν | συνῆψε [12]τὰ διακριθέντα, καθάπερ τινὶ κόλλῃ—τῇ θείᾳ
λέγω δυνάμει—[13]πρὸς τὴν ἄρρηκτον ἕνωσιν τὸ διασχισθὲν
συναρμόσας. [14]Καὶ τοῦτό ἐστιν ἡ ἀνάστασις, ἡ τῶν συνεζευγ-
60 μένων μετὰ [15]τὴν διάλυσιν ἐπάνοδος εἰς ἀδιάλυτον ἕνωσιν,
ἀλλήλοις [16]συμφυομένων, ὡς ἂν ἡ πρώτη περὶ τὸ ἀνθρώπινον
χάρις [17]ἀνακληθείη καὶ πάλιν ἐπὶ τὴν ἀΐδιον ἐπανέλθοιμεν ζωήν,
[18]τῆς ἐμμιχθείσης τῇ φύσει κακίας διὰ τῆς διαλύσεως ἡμῶν
[19]ἐκρυείσης, οἷον ἐπὶ τοῦ ὑγροῦ συμβαίνει, περιτρυφθέντος [20]αὐ-
65 τῷ τοῦ ἀγγείου, σκεδαννυμένου τε καὶ ἀφανιζομένου, [21]μηδενὸς
ὄντος τοῦ περιστέγοντος.
(8) Καθάπερ δὲ ἡ ἀρχὴ τοῦ [22]θανάτου ἐν ἑνὶ γενομένη πάσῃ
συνδιεξῆλθε τῇ ἀνθρωπίνῃ [23]φύσει, κατὰ τὸν αὐτὸν τρόπον καὶ ἡ
ἀρχὴ τῆς ἀναστάσεως [24]δι' ἑνὸς ἐπὶ πᾶσαν διατείνει τὴν
70 ἀνθρωπότητα. Ὁ γὰρ [25]τὴν ἀναληφθεῖσαν παρ' ἑαυτοῦ ψυχὴν
πάλιν ἑνώσας τῷ [26]οἰκείῳ σώματι διὰ τῆς δυνάμεως ἑαυτοῦ τῆς
(GNO 49) ἑκατέρῳ τού- | των παρὰ τὴν πρώτην σύστασιν ἐμμιχθείσης
(Sr 72) οὕτω γενικωτέρῳ | [2]τινὶ λόγῳ τὴν νοερὰν οὐσίαν τῇ αἰσθητῇ
συγκατέμιξε, [3]τῆς ἀρχῆς κατὰ τὸ ἀκόλουθον ἐπὶ τὸ πέρας
75 [4]εὐοδουμένης.—

74 συγκατέμιξε GNO : συγκατέμιξεν Srawley

body and soul is separated—be said to be a passion, according to the order [of the argument].

(6) And we say God has come to be in each change of our nature, through which soul meets body, and body is separated from soul, and mixing with each of these (I mean the sensory and noetic [parts] of the human composite) through that ineffable and inexpressible commingling, he arranged this economy so that once these things were united (I mean soul and body), the union might also remain forever.

(7) For when our nature, through its own proper order, was changed in him [i.e., Christ] also, in the division of soul and body, he again joined together what was divided as if with some sort of glue—I mean by divine power—fitting together what was torn apart in an unbreakable union. And this is the resurrection: the return, after dissolution, of things that had been conjoined into an indissoluble union, so they grow together with each other, so that humanity's first grace might be recalled and that we might return again to eternal life, the vice mixed in [our] nature having flowed out through dissolution, as happens in the case of a liquid when the vessel holding it is broken—it is dispersed and disappears, since there is nothing to contain it.

(8) And just as the principle[165] of death came about in one [man], [and then] passed through into all human nature, in the same manner also the principle of the resurrection, through one [man] extends to all humanity.[166] For he—who united to his own body the soul he himself assumed by his own power, which was mixed with each of them at [their] first composition—thus on a more general scale commingled noetic being with the sensory, the principle [of the resurrection] successfully making its way in order to the end.[167]

[165]Or "origin," "beginning," "source" (ἀρχὴ); "principle" translates the same word through the rest of this chapter.

[166]See Rom 5.12–20; 1 Cor 15.20–23.

[167]Or "to the limit" (ἐπὶ τὸ πέρας), i.e., the resurrection of Christ leads to the resurrection of the entire human race.

—(9) Ἐν γὰρ τῷ ἀναληφθέντι παρ' αὐτοῦ ἀνθρώπῳ
₅πάλιν μετὰ τὴν διάλυσιν πρὸς τὸ σῶμα τῆς ψυχῆς ₆ἐπανελ-
θούσης, οἷον ἀπό τινος ἀρχῆς εἰς πᾶσαν τὴν ἀνθρωπίνην
₇φύσιν τῇ δυνάμει κατὰ τὸ ἴσον ἡ τοῦ διακριθέντος ₈ἔνωσις
διαβαίνει. Καὶ τοῦτό ἐστι τὸ μυστήριον τῆς τοῦ ₉Θεοῦ περὶ τὸν
80 θάνατον οἰκονομίας καὶ τῆς ἐκ νεκρῶν ₁₀ἀναστάσεως, τὸ δια-
λυθῆναι μὲν τῷ θανάτῳ τοῦ σώματος ₁₁τὴν ψυχὴν κατὰ τὴν
ἀναγκαίαν τῆς φύσεως ἀκολουθίαν ₁₂μὴ κωλῦσαι, εἰς ἄλληλα δὲ
πάλιν ἐπαναγαγεῖν διὰ τῆς ₁₃ἀναστάσεως, ὡς ἂν αὐτὸς γένοιτο
μεθόριον ἀμφοτέρων, ₁₄θανάτου τε καὶ ζωῆς, ἐν ἑαυτῷ μὲν
85 στήσας διαιρουμένην ₁₅τῷ θανάτῳ τὴν φύσιν, αὐτὸς δὲ γενό-
μενος ἀρχὴ τῆς τῶν ₁₆διῃρημένων ἑνώσεως. |

(Sr 73; PG 53) ΙΖ'   ₁₇Ἀλλ' οὔπω φήσει τις λελύσθαι τὴν ὑπενεχθεῖσαν ἡμῖν
₁₈ἀντίθεσιν, ἰσχυροποιεῖσθαι δὲ μᾶλλον ἐκ τῶν εἰρημένων ₁₉τὸ
παρὰ τῶν ἀπίστων ἡμῖν προφερόμενον. Εἰ γὰρ τοσαύτη ₂₀δύ-
ναμίς ἐστιν ἐν αὐτῷ ὅσην ὁ λόγος ἐπέδειξεν, ὡς θανάτου ₂₁τε
5 καθαίρεσιν καὶ ζωῆς εἴσοδον ἐπ' αὐτῷ εἶναι, τί οὐχὶ ₂₂θελήματι
μόνῳ τὸ κατὰ γνώμην ποιεῖ, ἀλλ' ἐκ περιόδου ₂₃τὴν σωτηρίαν
ἡμῶν κατεργάζεται, τικτόμενός τε καὶ ₂₄τρεφόμενος, καὶ τῇ τοῦ
θανάτου πείρᾳ σῴζων τὸν ἄνθρωπον, ₂₅ἐξὸν μήτε ἐν τούτοις
(GNO 50) γενέσθαι καὶ ἡμᾶς περισώσα- | σθαι;—

(9) For when, after dissolution, the soul returned again to the body in the man[168] assumed by him, the union of what was separated passes over in potential into all human nature equally,[169] as if from some new principle. And this is the mystery of God's economy regarding death and the resurrection from the dead: he did not prevent the soul from being loosed by the death of the body in the necessary order of nature, but led [them] back to each other again by the resurrection, so that he himself might become the meeting-point[170] of both, of both death and life, in himself establishing the nature that had been divided by death, and himself becoming the principle of the union of what had been divided.

OBJECTION: *God could save man by fiat.*[171] *Why did he not do so?*

17 But, someone will say, the objection against us has not yet been removed, but rather the [charge] brought by the unbelievers against us is strengthened by what has been said. For if such great power is in him as the argument proved, so that the destruction of death and the entrance to life depend on him, why does he not do what is in accordance with [his] intention by will alone? But he accomplished our salvation in a roundabout way, both being born and nourished and by the experience of death saving man, when it was possible not to have been born among these things and to have saved us.

RESPONSE: *The sick do not set the course of treatment; the doctor does.*

---

[168]By the standards of the christological formulations of the next century, this would no longer be admissible. But given St Gregory's context, "man" (ἀνθρώπῳ) can be read simply as "the humanity" or "human nature." At times Gregory uses the language of two natures in a manner entirely consonant with Chalcedon (see Letter 32.13).

[169]Or, "with equal power" (τῇ δυνάμει κατὰ τὸ ἴσον) instead of "in potential . . . equally."

[170]Or "boundary between" (μεθόριον) both life and death.

[171]This objection was already raised in 15.4.

—(2) Πρὸς δὲ τὸν τοιοῦτον
10 λόγον ἱκανὸν μὲν ἦν πρὸς τοὺς ₂εὐγνώμονας τοσοῦτον εἰπεῖν,
ὅτι καὶ τοῖς ἰατροῖς οὐ νομοθετοῦσι ₃τὸν τρόπον τῆς ἐπιμελείας
οἱ κάμνοντες, οὐδὲ ₄περὶ τοῦ τῆς θεραπείας εἴδους πρὸς τοὺς
εὐεργέτας ἀμφισβητοῦσι, ₅διὰ τί προσήψατο τοῦ πονοῦντος
μέρους ὁ θεραπεύων ₆καὶ τόδε τι πρὸς τὴν τοῦ κακοῦ λύσιν
15 ἐπενόησεν, ₇ἕτερον δέον, ἀλλὰ πρὸς τὸ πέρας ὁρῶντες τῆς
εὐεργεσίας ₈ἐν εὐχαριστίᾳ τὴν εὐποιΐαν ἐδέξαντο.—

—(3) Ἀλλ᾿ ἐπειδή,
καθὼς ₉φησιν ἡ προφητεία, Τὸ πλῆθος τῆς χρηστότητος τοῦ
Θεοῦ ₁₀κεκρυμμένην ἔχει τὴν ὠφέλειαν καὶ οὔπω διὰ τοῦ
(Sr 74) παρόντος ₁₁βίου τηλαυγῶς | καθορᾶται—ἢ γὰρ ἂν περιῄρητο
20 πᾶσα ₁₂τῶν ἀπίστων ἀντίρρησις, εἰ τὸ προσδοκώμενον ἐν
ὀφθαλμοῖς ₁₃ἦν· νυνὶ δὲ ἀναμένει τοὺς ἐπερχομένους αἰῶνας,
₁₄ὥστε ἐν αὐτοῖς ἀποκαλυφθῆναι τὰ νῦν διὰ τῆς πίστεως ₁₅μόνης
ὁρώμενα—ἀναγκαῖον ἂν εἴη λογισμοῖς τισι κατὰ τὸ
₁₆ἐγχωροῦν καὶ τῶν ἐπιζητουμένων ἐξευρεῖν τὴν λύσιν τοῖς
25 ₁₇προλαβοῦσι συμβαίνουσαν.

ΙΗ'   Καίτοι περιττὸν ἴσως ἐστὶ ₁₈Θεὸν ἐπιδεδημηκέναι τῷ
βίῳ πιστεύσαντας διαβάλλειν τὴν ₁₉παρουσίαν ὡς οὐκ ἐν σοφίᾳ
τινὶ καὶ λόγῳ γενομένην τῷ ₂₀κρείττονι· τοῖς γὰρ μὴ λίαν
ἀντιμαχομένοις πρὸς τὴν ₂₁ἀλήθειαν οὐ μικρὰ τῆς θείας ἐπι-
5 δημίας ἀπόδειξις ἡ καὶ ₂₂πρὸ τῆς μελλούσης ζωῆς ἐν τῷ παρόντι
(Sr 75) βίῳ φανερωθεῖσα, ₂₃ἡ διὰ τῶν πραγμάτων αὐτῶν, | φημί, μαρ-
τυρία.

(2) Τίς γὰρ οὐκ ₂₄οἶδεν ὅπως πεπλήρωτο κατὰ πᾶν μέρος τῆς
οἰκουμένης ₂₅ἡ τῶν δαιμόνων ἀπάτη, διὰ τῆς εἰδωλομανίας τῆς
10 (GNO 51) ζωῆς | τῶν ἀνθρώπων κατακρατήσασα; ὅπως τοῦτο νόμιμον
₂πᾶσι τοῖς κατὰ τὸν κόσμον ἔθνεσιν ἦν, τὸ θεραπεύειν διὰ ₃τῶν
εἰδώλων τοὺς δαίμονας ἐν ταῖς ζωοθυσίαις καὶ τοῖς ₄ἐπιβωμίοις
μιάσμασιν; (3) Ἀφ᾿ οὗ δέ, καθὼς φησιν ὁ ἀπόστολος, ₅Ἐπεφάνη
ἡ χάρις τοῦ Θεοῦ ἡ σωτήριος πᾶσιν ἀνθρώποις, ₆διὰ τῆς

(2) For such an argument, it is sufficient to say something like this to reasonable people: that those who are sick do not legislate the manner of care for physicians, nor do they dispute about the form of therapy with their benefactors—"Why did the therapist touch the pained part, and why did he contrive this cure for the illness, when something different was necessary?"—but looking to the purpose of the benefit, they receive the good deed with thanks.

(3) But since, as the prophecy says, "the multitude of God's goodness" has a "hidden"[172] profit and is not yet seen conspicuously in the present life—for all the unbelievers' gainsaying would have been removed if what is expected was before [their] eyes, but now it awaits the coming ages, so that in them the things now seen only by faith might be revealed—it would be necessary to discover the solution to the things that are sought by certain arguments, as much as possible, in accordance with what preceded.

Historical Proof I: Idolatry has ceased among the gentiles.

18 And yet perhaps it is superfluous for those who believe that God has sojourned in [human] life to object to [his] presence[173] as not taking place with wisdom and superior reason; for those who are not violent in fighting against the truth there is no small proof of the divine sojourn, one that is manifest in the present life even before the life to come—I mean the testimony of the facts themselves.

(2) For who does not know how the deceit of demons had filled every part of the inhabited world, having mastered the life of men through the madness of idolatry? [Or] how this was customary for all the peoples in the world, worshipping demons by means of idols,[174] with animal sacrifice and pollutions upon [their] altars?[175]

---

[172]Cf. Ps 30.20 LXX.
[173]Or "coming" (παρουσίαν).
[174]Cf. Ps 95.5 LXX.
[175]In the historical arguments in his chapter, the words used to describe a pagan "altar" (ἐπιβώμιος, βωμός), "shrine" (ἀφίδρυμα), "oracles"/"soothsayers" (χρηστήριον/μαντεῖον), and "worship"/"worshipper" (τὸ θεραπεύειν/θεραπευτής) are different from the ones used to describe a Jewish or Christian "altar" (θυσιαστήριον), "temple"

15 ἀνθρωπίνης ἐπιδημήσασα φύσεως, πάντα ₇καπνοῦ δίκην εἰς τὸ
μὴ ὂν μετεχώρησεν, ὥστε ₈παύσασθαι μὲν τὰς τῶν χρηστηρίων
τε καὶ μαντειῶν μανίας, ₉ἀναιρεθῆναι δὲ τὰς ἐτησίους πομπὰς
καὶ τὰ δι' αἱμάτων ₁₀ἐν ταῖς ἑκατόμβαις μολύσματα, ἐν δὲ τοῖς
πολλοῖς ₁₁τῶν ἐθνῶν ἀφανισθῆναι καθ' ὅλου βωμοὺς καὶ προπύ-
20 λαια ₁₂καὶ τεμένη καὶ ἀφιδρύματα καὶ ὅσα ἄλλα τοῖς θερα-
πευταῖς ₁₃τῶν δαιμόνων ἐπὶ ἀπάτη σφῶν αὐτῶν καὶ τῶν ἐντυγ-
χανόντων ₁₄ἐπετηδεύετο, ὡς ἐν πολλοῖς τῶν τόπων μηδὲ εἰ
(PG 56) ₁₅γέγονε ταῦτά ποτε, μνημονεύεσθαι, | ἀντεγερθῆναι δὲ κατὰ
₁₆πᾶσαν τὴν οἰκουμένην ἐπὶ τῷ τοῦ Χριστοῦ ὀνόματι ναοὺς ₁₇καὶ
25 (Sr 76) θυσιαστήρια, καὶ τὴν σεμνήν τε καὶ | ἀναίμακτον ἱερωσύνην ₁₈καὶ
τὴν ὑψηλὴν φιλοσοφίαν, ἔργῳ μᾶλλον ἢ λόγῳ ₁₉κατορθουμένην,
καὶ τῆς σωματικῆς ζωῆς τὴν ὑπεροψίαν ₂₀καὶ τοῦ θανάτου τὴν
καταφρόνησιν, ἣν οἱ μεταστῆναι τῆς ₂₁πίστεως παρὰ τῶν
τυράννων ἀναγκαζόμενοι φανερῶς ₂₂ἐπεδείξαντο, ἀντ' οὐδενὸς
30 δεξάμενοι τὰς τοῦ σώματος αἰκίας, ₂₃καὶ τὴν ἐπὶ θανάτῳ ψῆφον,

24 τε before καὶ Srawley

(3) But from when, as the apostle says, "the saving grace of God appeared to all men"[176] by sojourning in human nature, all like smoke departed[177] into nonbeing, so that the madness of oracles and soothsayers ceased, annual processions and the blemishes of the blood of hecatombs was abolished, and among most of the peoples altars and temple gateways and sacred precincts and shrines entirely disappeared, and everything else practiced by the worshippers of demons to the deception both of themselves and of those who chanced upon them, so that in many of the places it is not even remembered if these things had ever happened, but in all the inhabited world temples and altars have arisen in Christ's name, and the august and bloodless priesthood, and the lofty philosophy,[178] which is directed more by deed than by word,[179] and contempt for bodily life and disdain for death, which those who were compelled by tyrants to abandon the faith manifestly exhibited, accepting the body's torments and the sentence of death as if it were nothing.

(ναός), "worship" (θρησκεία), and "prophet" (προφήτης); while pagan worship concerns "pollutions" (μιάσματα) and "blemishes" (μολύσματα), both Jewish and Christian worship are described as "august" (σεμνός). It is clear why: St Gregory asserts that pagan worship was demonic and inherently false (hence he uses non-biblical, classical terminology), while Jewish worship was right and God-pleasing until the coming of Christ, but "from now on [after Christ's incarnation, Jewish worship became] an erroneous superstition" (18.5). In this chapter Gregory argues that pagan temples were destroyed because evil had to be uprooted; the Jewish temple, in contrast, was destroyed because the greater, long-awaited good had arrived (a notion with many biblical precedents, cf. Jn 4.23; Heb 10.1–18; etc.).

[176]Tit 2.11.

[177]Cf. Ps 67.3 LXX.

[178]This might refer to the faith in general, but it may refer specifically to monasticism. This was a characteristic way of referring to monasticism at the time, and it would echo St Athanasius' argument in *On the Incarnation* that the destruction of pagan and Jewish worship, along with the courage of martyrs and the witness of the monastic life, was used as proof of the resurrection (and more broadly of the incarnation).

[179]A common claim and aspiration in Christianity (e.g., Jas 1.22; Ignatius of Antioch, *Ephesians* 15.1), also found in pagan philosophical circles. For more on the continuity between classical philosophy and Christianity, see Alan Brown, *The Life of Wisdom: An Introduction to Classical Philosophy and Early Christianity* (London: I. B. Tauris, 2015).

οὐκ ἂν ὑποστάντες ₂₄δηλαδὴ ταῦτα μὴ σαφῆ τε καὶ ἀναμφίβολον
(GNO 52) τῆς θείας | ἐπιδημίας ἔχοντες τὴν ἀπόδειξιν.

(4) Τὸ δὲ αὐτὸ τοῦτο καὶ ₂πρὸς τοὺς Ἰουδαίους ἱκανόν ἐστι
σημεῖον εἰπεῖν τοῦ ₃παρεῖναι τὸν παρ' αὐτῶν ἀπιστούμενον.
35 Μέχρι μὲν γὰρ τῆς ₄τοῦ Χριστοῦ θεοφανείας λαμπρὰ παρ'
αὐτοῖς ἦν τὰ ἐν ₅Ἱεροσολύμοις βασίλεια, ὁ διώνυμος ἐκεῖνος
(Sr 77) ναός, αἱ νενο- | μισμέναι ₆δι' ἔτους θυσίαι, πάντα ὅσα παρὰ τοῦ
νόμου ₇δι' αἰνιγμάτων τοῖς μυστικῶς ἐπαΐειν ἐπισταμένοις
διήρηται, ₈μέχρι τότε κατὰ τὴν ἐξ ἀρχῆς νομισθεῖσαν αὐτοῖς
40 τῆς ₉εὐσεβείας θρησκείαν ἀκώλυτα ἦν. (5) Ἐπεὶ δὲ εἶδον τὸν
προσδοκώμενον, ₁₀ὃν διὰ τῶν προφητῶν τε καὶ τοῦ νόμου
προεδιδάχθησαν, ₁₁καὶ προτιμοτέραν ἐποιήσαντο τῆς εἰς τὸν
₁₂φανέντα πίστεως τὴν λοιπὸν ἐσφαλμένην ἐκείνην δεισιδαι-
μονίαν, ₁₃ἦν κακῶς ἐκλαβόντες, τὰ τοῦ νόμου ῥήματα ₁₄διεφύ-
45 λασσον, συνηθείᾳ μᾶλλον ἢ διανοίᾳ δουλεύοντες, ₁₅οὔτε τὴν
ἐπιφανεῖσαν ἐδέξαντο χάριν, καὶ τὰ σεμνὰ τῆς ₁₆παρ' αὐτοῖς
θρησκείας ἐν διηγήμασι ψιλοῖς ὑπολείπεται, ₁₇τοῦ ναοῦ μὲν οὐδὲ
ἐξ ἰχνῶν ἔτι γινωσκομένου, τῆς δὲ λαμπρᾶς ₁₈ἐκείνης πόλεως ἐν
ἐρειπίοις ὑπολειφθείσης, <ὡς> ₁₉μεῖναι [δὲ] τοῖς Ἰουδαίοις τῶν
50 κατὰ τὸ ἀρχαῖον νενομισμένων ₂₀μηδέν, ἀλλὰ καὶ αὐτὸν τὸν
σεβάσμιον αὐτοῖς ἐν ₂₁Ἱεροσολύμοις τόπον ἄβατον προστάγματι
τῶν δυναστευόντων ₂₂γενέσθαι. |

49 ὡς supplied in GNO | GNO puts δὲ in brackets

Obviously they would not withstand these things unless they had a clear and indisputable proof of the divine sojourn.

Historical Proof II—Jewish Temple and Sacrifice Abolished

(4) And this is itself a sufficient further sign to address to the Jews, of the presence of him who is disbelieved by them. For until Christ's theophany, the splendid palaces in Jerusalem were with them, that far-famed Temple, the sacrifices that had been customary[180] each year, everything whatsoever distinguished by the law in enigmas for those who know to understand [it] mystically—until then these things were unhindered in the pious worship enjoined by law for them from the beginning. (5) But when they saw him whom they expected, who was taught beforehand both by the prophets and by the law, they considered more valuable than faith in him who appeared [i.e., Christ] what was from then on an erroneous super-stition, which they understood wrongly, keeping the letter of the law, being slaves of custom more than the spirit,[181] and they did not accept the grace that appeared, and the august things of their wor-ship remain in mere tales, and the temple is no longer known even by traces, and that splendid city was left in ruins, so that nothing remains to the Jews of what had been customary[182] from antiquity, but even the revered place itself in Jerusalem became inaccessible to them by the command of those in power.[183]

[180]Or "that had been enjoined by law" (νενομισμέναι), i.e., the law of Moses.

[181]The words translated as "letter" and "spirit" would more literally be translated as "sayings" (ῥήματα) and "meaning" (διανοίᾳ). Modern English is influenced by St Paul (2 Cor 3.6), and St Gregory likely has St Paul in mind here, though he uses more general words, given the audience he is presuming his catechists will face.

[182]Or "had been enjoined by law" (νενομισμένων), i.e., the law of Moses.

[183]Jerusalem was sacked twice between the time of Christ and the *Catechetical Discourse*: (1) the first destruction of the temple in AD 70, recorded by Josephus, and (2) the Roman reprisal for the Bar Kokhba revolt (AD 132–36). After the latter, Hadrian expelled the Jews from Jersualem by decree, as Gregory says. It seems the decree was not lifted even by the time Gregory was writing (see Jerome, *In Sophoniam* 1.15–16). For background on Hadrian's decree and the various primary accounts, see J. Rendel Harris, "Hadrian's Decree of Expulsion of the Jews from Jerusalem," *Harvard Theological Review* 19 (1926): 199–206.

(Sr 78) ΙΘ' ₂₃Ἀλλ' ὅμως, ἐπειδὴ μήτε τοῖς Ἑλληνίζουσι μήτε τοῖς
τῶν ₂₄ Ἰουδαϊκῶν προεστῶσι δογμάτων δοκεῖ ταῦτα θείας
(GNO 53) παρ- | ουσίας ποιεῖσθαι τεκμήρια, καλῶς ἂν ἔχοι περὶ τῶν
ἀνθυπενεχθέντων ₂ἡμῖν ἰδίᾳ τὸν λόγον διαλαβεῖν, ὅτου χάριν ₃ἡ
5 θεία φύσις πρὸς τὴν ἡμετέραν συμπλέκεται, δι' ἑαυτῆς ₄σώ-
ζουσα τὸ ἀνθρώπινον, οὐ διὰ προστάγματος κατεργαζομένη
₅τὸ κατὰ πρόθεσιν. Τίς οὖν ἂν γένοιτο ἡμῖν ἀρχὴ ₆πρὸς τὸν
προκείμενον σκοπὸν ἀκολούθως χειραγωγοῦσα ₇τὸν λόγον;
Τίς ἄλλη ἢ τὸ τὰς εὐσεβεῖς περὶ τοῦ Θεοῦ ὑπολήψεις ₈ἐπὶ
10 κεφαλαίων διεξελθεῖν;

Κ' Οὐκοῦν ὁμολογεῖται ₉παρὰ πᾶσι μὴ μόνον δυνατὸν εἶναι
δεῖν πιστεύειν τὸ θεῖον, ₁₀ἀλλὰ καὶ δίκαιον, καὶ ἀγαθόν, καὶ
σοφόν, καὶ πᾶν ὅ τι πρὸς ₁₁τὸ κρεῖττον τὴν διάνοιαν φέρει.
Ἀκόλουθον τοίνυν ἐπὶ τῆς ₁₂παρούσης οἰκονομίας μὴ τὸ μέν τι
5 (Sr 79) βούλεσθαι τῶν τῷ Θεῷ ₁₃πρεπόντων ἐπιφαίνεσθαι | τοῖς γεγε-
νημένοις, τὸ δὲ μὴ παρεῖναι. ₁₄Καθ' ὅλου γὰρ οὐδὲν ἐφ' ἑαυτοῦ
τῶν ὑψηλῶν τούτων ₁₅ὀνομάτων διεζευγμένον τῶν ἄλλων ἀρετὴ

The God-Befittingness of the Incarnation

19 But all the same, since neither the Hellenizers nor those who preside over the Jewish teachings think to consider these things tokens[184] of the divine presence, it would be good, regarding the [objections] brought against us, to treat in particular the reason why the divine nature is intertwined with ours, saving humanity by itself, not accomplishing [his] purpose by a command. What then should be our beginning[185] to guide the argument to the proposed aim in order?[186] What other than to go through the pious suppositions about God, in summary?

The Four God-Befitting Qualities

God is Good, Just, Wise, and Powerful

20 Therefore it is agreed by all that it is necessary to believe the divine to be not only powerful, but also just,[187] and good, and wise, and all that brings to mind the superior. Therefore it follows in the case of the present economy, that any one of the things that are fitting for God is not willingly manifest in what takes place, while something [else that is fitting] is not present. For on the whole none of these lofty names by itself, disjoined from the others, is virtue on

---

[184]Or "signs" (τεκμήρια). While Aristotle used this word in a more precise sense—"in the Logic of Aristotle, *demonstrative proof*, opp. to the fallible σημεῖον and εἰκός, *APr.70b2, Rh.1357b4, 1402b19*, cf. *Phld.Rh.1.369 S.*" (LSJ Lexicon)—it was often treated as a synonym of σημεῖον/*signum*, to mean "non-verbal tokens that stand in need of rhetorical elaboration." *The Cambridge Companion to Ancient Rhetoric*, ed. Erik Gunderson (Cambridge: Cambridge University Press, 2009), 295.

[185]Or "premise" (ἀρχή), i.e., the beginning of an argument.

[186]This is a short and technical description of Gregory's method: an "argument," "discourse," or "account" (λόγον) that proceeds "in order" (ἀκολούθως) to the intended "aim" (σκοπὸν).

[187]Or "righteous" (δίκαιον), but here St Gregory has distributive and retributive justice in mind, much in line with Aristotle's definition of justice (see p. 118, n. 233 below).

κατὰ μόνας $_{16}$ἐστίν· οὔτε τὸ ἀγαθὸν ἀληθῶς ἐστὶν ἀγαθόν, μὴ
μετὰ τοῦ $_{17}$δικαίου τε καὶ σοφοῦ καὶ τοῦ δυνατοῦ τεταγμένον—
10 (PG 57) τὸ γὰρ $_{18}$ἄδικον, ἢ ἄσοφον, ἢ | ἀδύνατον ἀγαθὸν οὐκ ἔστιν—
οὔτε ἡ $_{19}$δύναμις τοῦ δικαίου τε καὶ σοφοῦ κεχωρισμένη ἐν ἀρετῇ
$_{20}$θεωρεῖται—θηριῶδες γάρ ἐστι τὸ τοιοῦτον καὶ τυραννικὸν
$_{21}$τῆς δυνάμεως εἶδος.

(2) Ὡσαύτως δὲ καὶ τὰ λοιπά, εἰ ἔξω τοῦ
$_{22}$δικαίου τὸ σοφὸν φέροιτο, ἢ τὸ δίκαιον εἰ μὴ μετὰ τοῦ $_{23}$δυνατοῦ
15 τε καὶ τοῦ ἀγαθοῦ θεωροῖτο, κακίαν ἄν τις μᾶλλον $_{24}$κυρίως τὰ
τοιαῦτα κατονομάσειε· τὸ γὰρ ἐλλιπὲς τοῦ $_{25}$κρείττονος πῶς ἄν
τις ἐν ἀγαθοῖς ἀριθμήσειεν;

(3) Εἰ δὲ πάντα $_{26}$προσήκει συνδραμεῖν ἐν ταῖς περὶ Θεοῦ δόξαις,
(GNO 54) σκοπήσω- | μεν εἴ τινος ἡ κατὰ ἄνθρωπον οἰκονομία λείπεται
20 τῶν $_{2}$θεοπρεπῶν ὑπολήψεων. Ζητοῦμεν πάντως ἐπὶ τοῦ Θεοῦ
τῆς $_{3}$ἀγαθότητος τὰ σημεῖα. Καὶ τίς ἂν γένοιτο φανερωτέρα
τοῦ $_{4}$ἀγαθοῦ μαρτυρία ἢ τὸ μεταποιηθῆναι αὐτὸν τοῦ πρὸς τὸ
$_{5}$ἐναντίον αὐτομολήσαντος, μηδὲ συνδιατεθῆναι τῷ εὐμετα-
βλήτῳ $_{6}$τῆς ἀνθρωπίνης προαιρέσεως τὴν παγίαν ἐν τῷ $_{7}$ἀγαθῷ
25 καὶ ἀμετάβλητον φύσιν; Οὐ γὰρ ἂν ἦλθεν εἰς τὸ $_{8}$σῶσαι ἡμᾶς,
(Sr 80) καθώς φησιν ὁ Δαβίδ, | μὴ ἀγαθότητος τὴν $_{9}$τοιαύτην πρόθεσιν
ἐμποιούσης.—

—(4) Ἀλλ᾽ οὐδὲν ἂν ὤνησε τὸ $_{10}$ἀγαθὸν τῆς προθέ-
σεως, μὴ σοφίας ἐνεργὸν τὴν φιλανθρωπίαν $_{11}$ποιούσης. Καὶ γὰρ
ἐπὶ τῶν ἀρρώστως διακειμένων $_{12}$πολλοὶ μὲν ἴσως οἱ βουλόμενοι
30 μὴ ἐν κακοῖς εἶναι τὸν $_{13}$κείμενον, μόνοι δὲ τὴν ἀγαθὴν ὑπὲρ τῶν
καμνόντων $_{14}$προαίρεσιν εἰς πέρας ἄγουσιν, οἷς τεχνική τις
δύναμις $_{15}$ἐνεργεῖ πρὸς τὴν τοῦ κάμνοντος ἴασιν. Οὐκοῦν τὴν
σοφίαν $_{16}$δεῖ συνεζεῦχθαι πάντως τῇ ἀγαθότητι. (5) Πῶς τοίνυν ἐν
τοῖς $_{17}$γεγενημένοις τὸ σοφὸν τῷ ἀγαθῷ συνθεωρεῖται; Ὅτι οὐ

---

16 κατονομάσειε GNO : κατονομάσειεν Srawley

its own;[188] neither is the good truly good, if it is not ranked with the just and the wise and the powerful—for the unjust, or unwise, or powerless is not good—nor is power, when it is separated from the just and wise, contemplated as a virtue, for a form of power such as this is bestial and tyrannical. (2) And in the same way also with the rest, if the wise is carried beyond the just, or the just, if it is not contemplated with the powerful and the good, such things someone would more properly call vice. For how can something lacking in what is superior be counted among good things?

(3) And if it is fitting to combine all [of these qualities] in [our] opinions about God, let us see if the economy as man[189] lacks any of the suppositions that are befitting for God. In the case of God, we seek above all the signs of his goodness. And what would be a more manifest testimony of goodness than reclaiming him who had deserted to the adversary, while [God's] nature, firm and unchanged in the good, was not influenced by the easily changed human will?[190] For he would not have come to save us, as David says, had goodness not produced such a purpose in [him].[191]

(4) But the goodness of [his] purpose would have profited nothing, had wisdom not made love for man active. For also in the case of those who are in a sickly state, perhaps there are many who wish the sick one was not ill, but the only ones who bring their good will[192] on the suffering one's behalf to completion are those in whom a certain technical ability is active for the healing of the suffering one. Accordingly wisdom must by all means be joined with goodness. (5) How then is wisdom seen with[193] goodness in the things that have come to pass? For it is not possible to see goodness of purpose in the abstract.[194] For how would the purpose be manifest, were it not

[188]On the recirocity of the virtues, see Andrew Radde-Gallwitz, "Gregory of Nyssa on the Reciprocity of the Virtues," *Journal of Theological Studies* 58.2 (2007): 537–52.

[189]Or "with respect to man" (see p. 71, n. 50).

[190]Or "faculty of decision" (προαιρέσεως).

[191]Cf. Ps 105.4–5; 118.65, 66, 68 LXX.

[192]Or "decision" (προαίρεσιν).

[193]Or "contemplated with" (συνθεωρεῖται).

[194]Lit. "naked" or "bare" (γυμνὸν).

35 18γυμνὸν τὸ κατὰ πρόθεσιν ἀγαθόν ἐστιν ἰδεῖν. Πῶς γὰρ ἂν
   19φανείη ἡ πρόθεσις, μὴ διὰ τῶν γιγνομένων φανερουμένη; Τὰ
   20δὲ πεπραγμένα εἱρμῷ τινι καὶ τάξει δι' ἀκολούθου προϊόντα 21τὸ
   σοφόν τε καὶ τεχνικὸν τῆς οἰκονομίας τοῦ Θεοῦ διαδείκνυσιν.
      (6) 22Ἐπεὶ δέ, καθὼς ἐν τοῖς φθάσασιν εἴρηται, πάντως 23τῷ δικαίῳ
40 τὸ σοφὸν συνεζευγμένον ἀρετὴ γίγνεται, εἰ 24δὲ χωρισθείη, μὴ
(GNO 55) ἂν ἐφ' ἑαυτοῦ κατὰ μόνας ἀγαθὸν εἶναι, | καλῶς ἂν ἔχοι καὶ ἐπὶ
(Sr 81) τοῦ λόγου | τῆς κατὰ ἄνθρωπον οἰκονομίας 2τὰ δύο μετ' ἀλλήλων
   κατανοῆσαι, τὸ σοφόν φημι 3καὶ τὸ δίκαιον.

ΚΑ'   4Τίς οὖν ἡ δικαιοσύνη; Μεμνήμεθα πάντως τῶν κατὰ
   τὸ 5ἀκόλουθον ἐν τοῖς πρώτοις τοῦ λόγου διῃρημένων ὅτι 6μί-
   μημα τῆς θείας φύσεως κατεσκευάσθη ὁ ἄνθρωπος, 7τοῖς τε
   λοιποῖς τῶν ἀγαθῶν καὶ τῷ αὐτεξουσίῳ τῆς προαιρέσεως 8τὴν
5 πρὸς τὸ θεῖον διασῴζων ὁμοίωσιν, τρεπτῆς 9δὲ φύσεως ὢν κατ'
   ἀνάγκην· οὐ γὰρ ἐνεδέχετο τὸν ἐξ ἀλλοιώσεως 10τὴν ἀρχὴν τοῦ
   εἶναι σχόντα μὴ τρεπτὸν εἶναι 11πάντως· ἡ γὰρ ἐκ τοῦ μὴ ὄντος
   εἰς τὸ εἶναι πάροδος ἀλλοίωσίς 12τίς ἐστι, τῆς ἀνυπαρξίας κατὰ
   θείαν δύναμιν εἰς οὐσίαν 13μεθισταμένης, καὶ ἄλλως δὲ τῆς
10 (Sr 82) τροπῆς | ἀναγκαίως 14ἐν τῷ ἀνθρώπῳ θεωρουμένης, ἐπειδὴ μί-
   μημα τῆς θείας 15φύσεως ὁ ἄνθρωπος ἦν, τὸ δὲ μιμούμενον, εἰ
   μὴ ἐν ἑτερότητι 16τύχοι τινί, ταὐτὸν ἂν εἴη πάντως ἐκείνῳ ᾧ
   ἀφωμοίωται.—
(PG 60)   —(2) 17Ἐν τούτῳ τοίνυν τῆς ἑτερότητος τοῦ | κατ'
   εἰκόνα γενομένου 18πρὸς τὸ ἀρχέτυπον οὔσης, ἐν τῷ τὸ μὲν
15 ἄτρεπτον 19εἶναι τῇ φύσει, τὸ δὲ μὴ οὕτως ἔχειν, ἀλλὰ δι'
   ἀλλοιώσεως 20μὲν ὑποστῆναι κατὰ τὸν ἀποδοθέντα λόγον,
   ἀλλοιούμενον 21δὲ μὴ πάντως ἐν τῷ εἶναι μένειν· (3) ἡ δὲ

manifested by the things that took place? And the things that have
been done, proceeding by a certain sequence and arrangement in
order, plainly demonstrate both the wisdom and the artfulness of
God's economy.

(6) And since, as it has been said in the preceding [arguments],
wisdom joined with the just is in all ways virtue, but if it is separated
[from it], it is not good alone by itself, it would be good in the case
of the account of the economy as man to consider the two with each
other, I mean the wise and the just.

*Created beings are by nature changeable. This continual change is
rightly directed toward the good, but the devil deceived us and we
pursued a false good.*

21 What, then, is justice?[195] By all means we remember the distinctions [made] in order in the first parts of the discourse, that man was
fashioned as a copy of the divine nature, preserving the likeness to
the divine both in the remaining good things and in the possession
of free will,[196] but by necessity being of a changeable nature; for it
was not possible for him who had the beginning of [his] being from
alteration not to be changeable at all; for the passage from nonbeing
into existence is a sort of alteration, nonexistence being changed into
being[197] by divine power, and in another way also changeability is
necessarily seen in man, since man was a copy of the divine nature,
and a copy, unless there happens to be some difference, would be
altogether the same as that which it was made to resemble.

(2) Therefore the difference between what was made "in the
image"[198] and the archetype is in this: in that the one is unchangeable by nature, and the other is not so, but gained substance through
alteration, according to the account that was given, and being

---

[195]This is the central question of Plato's *Republic*, a point not lost on the cultured
pagans St Gregory's catechists will face.

[196]Lit. "in the self-determination of the faculty of decision" (τῷ αὐτεξουσίῳ τῆς
προαιρέσεως).

[197]Or "essence" (οὐσίαν).

[198]Gen 1.27, 5.1.

ἀλλοίωσις κίνησίς ₂₂τίς ἐστιν εἰς ἕτερον ἀπὸ τοῦ ἐν ᾧ ἐστὶν εἰς
ἀεὶ προϊοῦσα· ₂₃δύο δὲ τῆς τοιαύτης εἴδη κινήσεως· τὸ μὲν πρὸς
20 τὸ ἀγαθὸν ₂₄ἀεὶ γινόμενον, ἐν ᾧ ἡ πρόοδος στάσιν οὐκ ἔχει, διότι
(GNO 56; πέρας | οὐδὲν τοῦ διεξο- | δευομένου καταλαμβάνεται, τὸ δὲ πρὸς
Sr 83) τὸ ₂ἐναντίον, οὗ ἡ ὑπόστασις ἐν τῷ μὴ ὑφεστάναι ἐστίν· ἡ γὰρ
₃τοῦ ἀγαθοῦ ἐναντίωσις, καθὼς ἐν τοῖς ἔμπροσθεν εἴρηται,
₄τοιοῦτόν τινα νοῦν κατὰ τὴν ἀντιδιαστολὴν ἔχει, καθάπερ
25 ₅φαμὲν τῷ μὴ ὄντι τὸ ὂν ἀντιδιαιρεῖσθαι καὶ τῇ ἀνυπαρξίᾳ ₆τὴν
ὕπαρξιν—· ἐπειδὴ τοίνυν κατὰ τὴν τρεπτήν τε καὶ ἀλ-
λοιώτην ₇ὁρμήν τε καὶ κίνησιν οὐκ ἐνδέχεται τὴν φύσιν ἐφ᾽
₈ἑαυτῆς μένειν ἀκίνητον, ἀλλ᾽ ἐπί τι πάντως ἡ προαίρεσις ₉ἵεται,
τῆς πρὸς τὸ καλὸν ἐπιθυμίας αὐτὴν φυσικῶς ἐφελκομένης ₁₀εἰς
κίνησιν.—

30 　—(4) Καλὸν δὲ τὸ μέν τι ἀληθῶς κατὰ τὴν ₁₁φύσιν ἐστί, τὸ
δὲ οὐ τοιοῦτον, ἀλλ᾽ ἐπηνθισμένον τινὶ ₁₂καλοῦ φαντασίᾳ·
κριτήριον δὲ τούτων ἐστὶν ὁ νοῦς ἔνδοθεν ₁₃ἡμῖν ἐνιδρυμένος, ἐν
ᾧ κινδυνεύεται ἢ τὸ ἐπιτυχεῖν τοῦ ₁₄ὄντως καλοῦ ἢ τὸ παρα-
τραπέντας αὐτοῦ διά τινος τῆς ₁₅κατὰ τὸ φαινόμενον ἀπάτης ἐπὶ
35 τὸ ἐναντίον ἡμᾶς ἀπορρυῆναι, ₁₆οἷόν τι παθεῖν ὁ ἔξωθεν μῦθός
φησιν ἀπιδοῦσαν ἐν ₁₇τῷ ὕδατι τὴν κύνα πρὸς τὴν σκιὰν οὐ διὰ
στόματος ἔφερε ₁₈μεθεῖναι μὲν τὴν ἀληθῆ τροφήν, περιχανοῦσαν
(Sr 84) δὲ τὸ τῆς ₁₉τροφῆς εἴδωλον ἐν λιμῷ γενέσθαι· | (5) ἐπεὶ οὖν τῆς
πρὸς τὸ ₂₀ὄντως ἀγαθὸν ἐπιθυμίας διαψευσθεὶς ὁ νοῦς πρὸς τὸ

alterable does not at all remain in existence; (3) and alteration is a sort of motion always proceeding from the [state] in which it is to a different [state]; and there are two forms of such motion: the one is always toward the good, in which the advance has no rest, since no limit is reached in setting out along this course,[199] and the other is toward the opposite, whose substance is in non-subsistence; for opposition to the good, as was said before, brings to mind some distinction such as this, just as we say being is distinguished from nonbeing and existence from nonexistence—therefore, since by reason of the impulse and motion toward what is changeable and alterable it is not possible for nature in itself to remain motionless, but the will[200] is altogether eager for something, desire for the good[201] naturally draws it into motion.

(4) Now in one case the "good" is something truly in accordance with nature, but in the other it is not so, but decked out with a certain mere appearance of good; and the mind that is established within us is the criterion of these, in which the risk is run either of attaining to the really good or of being turned aside from it by some deceptive appearance that carries us off to the opposite, the sort of thing the outsiders'[202] fable says happened to the dog who looked in the water at the reflection of what he carried in [his] mouth, [who] let go of the true food, and opening his mouth wide to swallow the image of food, remained hungry; (5) since, then, the mind, being deceived in its desire for what is really good, was turned aside to nonbeing, being

---

[199]This notion that God (here, "the good") is infinite, and that the pursuit of him is endless, is one of St Gregory's great contributions to theology (Origen, in contrast, had not conceived of God as infinite), which he stresses in his spiritual writings, especially *The Life of Moses* (this concept of infinite progress is referred to as "*epektasis*"); see "*Epektasis*" in *Brill Dictionary*, 263–68.

[200]Or "faculty of decision" (προαίρεσις).

[201]The word "good" (καλός) in this section may also mean "beautiful." This section deals with true and illusory good *and* beauty, though it is impossible to convey both with a single word in English.

[202]Gregory regularly refers to pagans as those who are "outside" (ἔξωθεν), which has biblical precedent (1 Tim 3.7). Here he is referring to one of Aesop's fables.

40 μὴ ὂν 21παρηνέχθη, δι' ἀπάτης τοῦ τῆς κακίας συμβούλου τε καὶ
22εύρετοῦ καλὸν ἀναπεισθεὶς εἶναι τὸ τῷ καλῷ ἐναντίον—οὐ
23γὰρ ἂν ἐνήργησεν ἡ ἀπάτη, μὴ δελέατος δίκην τῷ τῆς 24κακίας
(GNO 57) ἀγκίστρῳ τῆς τοῦ καλοῦ φαντασίας περιπλασθεί- | σης—ἐν
ταύτῃ τοίνυν γεγονότος ἑκουσίως τῇ συμφορᾷ τοῦ 2ἀνθρώπου
45 τοῦ ἑαυτὸν δι' ἡδονῆς τῷ ἐχθρῷ τῆς ζωῆς ὑποζεύξαντος,
3πάντα μοι κατὰ ταὐτὸν ἀναζήτει τὰ ταῖς θείαις 4ὑπολήψεσι
πρέποντα, τὸ ἀγαθόν, τὸ σοφόν, τὸ δίκαιον, τὸ 5δυνατόν, τὸ
ἄφθαρτον καὶ εἴ τι τῆς τοῦ κρείττονος σημασίας 6ἐστίν. (6) Οὐκοῦν
ὡς ἀγαθὸς οἶκτον λαμβάνει τοῦ διαπεπτωκότος, 7ὡς σοφὸς οὐκ
50 ἀγνοεῖ τὸν τρόπον τῆς ἀνακλήσεως. 8Σοφίας δ' ἂν εἴη καὶ ἡ τοῦ
δικαίου κρίσις· οὐ 9γὰρ ἄν τις ἀφροσύνῃ τὴν ἀληθῆ δικαιο-
σύνην προσάψειεν.

(Sr 85) **ΚΒ'** 10Τί οὖν ἐν τούτοις τὸ δίκαιον; Τὸ μὴ τυραννικῇ | τινι
χρήσασθαι 11κατὰ τοῦ κατέχοντος ἡμᾶς αὐθεντίᾳ, μηδὲ τῷ 12πε-
ριόντι τῆς δυνάμεως ἀποσπάσαντα τοῦ κρατοῦντος 13καταλι-
πεῖν τινα δικαιολογίας ἀφορμὴν τῷ δι' ἡδονῆς 14καταδουλω-
5 σαμένῳ τὸν ἄνθρωπον. Καθάπερ γὰρ οἱ χρημάτων 15τὴν ἑαυτῶν
ἐλευθερίαν ἀποδόμενοι δοῦλοι τῶν 16ὠνησαμένων εἰσίν, αὐτοὶ
πρατῆρες ἑαυτῶν καταστάντες, 17καὶ οὔτε αὐτοῖς οὔτε ἄλλῳ τινὶ
ὑπὲρ ἐκείνων ἔξεστι τὴν 18ἐλευθερίαν ἐπιβοήσασθαι, κἂν εὐπα-
τρίδαι τινὲς ὦσιν οἱ 19πρὸς τὴν συμφορὰν ταύτην αὐτομο-
10 (PG 61) λήσαντες· (2) εἰ δέ τις 20κηδόμενος τοῦ ἀπεμπολη-| θέντος βίᾳ κατὰ
τοῦ ὠνησαμένου 21χρῷτο, ἄδικος εἶναι δόξει τὸν νόμῳ κτηθέντα
τυραννικῶς 22ἐξαιρούμενος· ἐξωνεῖσθαι δὲ πάλιν εἰ βούλοιτο τὸν

persuaded by the deceit of the advocate and inventor of vice that the good is what is opposite to the good—for the deception would not have been effective, had not the mere appearance of good been spread around the hook of vice like bait—therefore man willingly has come to be in this misfortune, through pleasure putting himself under the yoke [of slavery] to the enemy of life; investigate with me in the same way all the things that are fitting for suppositions about the divine: the good, the wise, the just, the powerful, the incorruptible, and anything else that signifies the superior. (6) Therefore, as good he takes pity on him who has fallen; as wise he is not ignorant of the manner of recall. And, further, the judgment of what is just[203] belongs to wisdom; for no one would associate true justice with foolishness.

The Ransom

A ransom satisfies justice in these circumstances: the devil has a claim on us, so God does not steal us back by violence. He provides a just ransom.

22 What, then, is the just in these [circumstances]? In not using some tyrannical authority against him who held us, and not tearing us away by an excess of power from him who held sway [over us], leaving some pretext for a justification for him who enslaved man through pleasure. For just as those who give up their own freedom for money are the slaves of those who bought [them], appointing themselves as their own auctioneers, and it is not possible[204] either for them or for anyone else to cry out for freedom on their behalf, even if those who came to such misfortune of their own accord were from a good family; (2) and if someone concerned for him who was sold were to use violence against the buyer, he would seem to be unjust for tyrannically taking away him who was acquired lawfully; but if he wanted to buy such a one back again, there is no law

---

[203]Cf. Jn 7.24.
[204]Or "allowed" (ἔξεστι).

₂₃τοιοῦτον, οὐδεὶς ὁ κωλύων νόμος ἐστί· κατὰ τὸν αὐτὸν ₂₄τρό-
πον, ἑκουσίως ἡμῶν ἑαυτοὺς ἀπεμπολησάντων, ἔδει ₂₅παρὰ τοῦ
15 (GNO 58) δι' ἀγαθότητα πάλιν ἡμᾶς εἰς ἐλευθερίαν ἐξαι- | ρουμένου μὴ τὸν
τυραννικόν, ἀλλὰ τὸν δίκαιον τρόπον ₂ἐπινοηθῆναι τῆς ἀνακλήσεως. Οὗτος δέ ἐστί τις τὸ ἐπὶ τῷ ₃κρατοῦντι ποιήσασθαι πᾶν
ὅπερ ἂν ἐθέλοι λύτρον ἀντὶ τοῦ ₄κατεχομένου λαβεῖν.

(Sr 86) ΚΓ'   Τί τοίνυν εἰκὸς ἦν μᾶλλον τὸν κρατοῦντα ₅λαβεῖν |
ἑλέσθαι; Δυνατόν ἐστι δι' ἀκολούθου στοχασμόν ₆τινα τῆς
ἐπιθυμίας αὐτοῦ λαβεῖν, εἰ τὰ πρόδηλα ₇γένοιτο ἡμῖν τῶν
ζητουμένων τεκμήρια. Ὁ τοίνυν κατὰ τὸν ₈ἐν ἀρχῇ τοῦ συγ-
5 γράμματος προαποδοθέντα λόγον τῷ ₉πρὸς τὸν εὐημεροῦντα
φθόνῳ πρὸς μὲν τὸ ἀγαθὸν ἐπιμύσας, ₁₀τὸν δὲ τῆς κακίας ζόφον
ἐν ἑαυτῷ γεννήσας, ἀρχὴν ₁₁δὲ τῆς πρὸς τὰ χείρω ῥοπῆς καὶ
ὑπόθεσιν καὶ οἱονεὶ ₁₂μητέρα τῆς λοιπῆς κακίας τὴν φιλαρχίαν
νοσήσας, τίνος ₁₃ἂν ἀντηλλάξατο τὸν κατεχόμενον, εἰ μὴ δη-
10 λαδὴ τοῦ ὑψηλοτέρου ₁₄καὶ μείζονος ἀνταλλάγματος, ὡς ἂν
μᾶλλον ₁₅ἑαυτοῦ τὸ κατὰ τὸν τῦφον θρέψειε πάθος, τὰ μείζω τῶν
₁₆ἐλαττόνων διαμειβόμενος;

(2) Ἀλλὰ μὴν ἐν τοῖς ἀπ' αἰῶνος ₁₇ἱστορουμένοις, ἐν οὐδενὶ
συνεγνώκει τοιοῦτον οὐδέν, οἷα ₁₈καθεώρα περὶ τὸν τότε φαινό-
15 μενον, κυοφορίαν ἀσυνδύαστον, ₁₉καὶ γέννησιν ἄφθορον, καὶ
(Sr 87) θήλην ἐκ παρθενίας, | καὶ ₂₀ἄνωθεν ἐπιμαρτυρούσας τῷ ὑπερ-
φυεῖ τῆς ἀξίας ἐκ τῶν ₂₁ἀοράτων φωνάς, καὶ τῶν τῆς φύσεως

---

11 θρέψειε GNO : θρέψειεν Srawley

preventing it; in the same manner, since we sold ourselves willingly, it was necessary for him who through goodness sought to take us back again to freedom not to devise a tyrannical, but a just manner of recall. And it is something like this: to make it within the power of him who held sway [over us] to receive whatever ransom he might want in exchange for the one held [captive].

Christ was an attractive ransom, given the power manifest in his miracles.

23 What then was he who held sway [over us] most likely to choose to receive? It is possible to take some guess about his desire, according to the order [of the argument], if there should be evidences of the things sought by us. Therefore, he who, according to the account given previously in the beginning of the text, shut [his eyes] to the good in envy at him who lived in happiness,[205] and begot in himself the darkness of vice, and became sick with love of power, the beginning of the inclination to the worse and the mother, as it were, of the rest of vice—what would he exchange for the one who was held [captive], unless what he received in exchange was clearly loftier and greater, so that he might engorge his own passion of pride the more, by receiving greater things for lesser things?

(2) But surely among those whom history records from [the beginning of] the world, he had not known any such thing in anyone. He saw such things as these around him who then appeared: childbearing without union;[206] and birth without corruption;[207] and nursing from a virgin;[208] voices from the invisible ones above

[205]I.e., man (cf. Wis 2.24).

[206]Is 7.14; Mt 1.18–25; Lk 1.26–38.

[207]This teaching dates back to the second-century *Infancy Gospel of James* 19–20, and was continually affirmed in subsequent patristic thought and hymnody. St Gregory began a long tradition of interpreting the burning bush as a type of the incorrupt birth of Christ: "From this we learn also the mystery of the Virgin: The light of divinity which through birth shone from her into human life did not consume the burning bush, even as the flower of her virginity was not withered by giving birth" (*Life of Moses* 2.21; trans. Malherbe and Ferguson).

[208]Lit. "from virginity" (ἐκ παρθενίας).

ἀρρωστημάτων ₂₂διόρθωσιν ἀπραγμάτευτόν τινα καὶ ψιλήν, ἐν
(GNO 59) ῥήματι μόνῳ | καὶ ὁρμῇ τοῦ θελήματος παρ᾽ αὐτοῦ γινο-
20 μένην, τήν τε τῶν ₂τεθνηκότων ἐπὶ τὸν βίον ἀνάλυσιν, καὶ τὸν
[κατὰ] τῶν δαιμόνων ₃φόβον, καὶ τῶν κατὰ τὸν ἀέρα παθῶν
τὴν ἐξουσίαν, ₄καὶ τὴν διὰ θαλάσσης πορείαν, οὐ διαχω-
(Sr 88) ροῦντος ἐφ᾽ ἑκάτερα ₅τοῦ | πελάγους, καὶ τὸν πυθμένα γυμνοῦν-
τος τοῖς ₆παροδεύουσι κατὰ τὴν ἐπὶ Μωϋσέως θαυματουρ-
25 γίαν, ₇ἀλλ᾽ ἄνω τῆς ἐπιφανείας τοῦ ὕδατος ὑποχερσουμένης
τῇ ₈βάσει, καὶ διά τινος ἀσφαλοῦς ἀντιτυπίας ὑπερειδούσης τὸ
₉ἴχνος, τήν τε τῆς τροφῆς ὑπεροψίαν ἐφ᾽ ὅσον βούλοιτο καὶ ₁₀τὰς
ἐν ἐρημίᾳ δαψιλεῖς ἑστιάσεις τῶν ἐν πολλαῖς χιλιάσιν
₁₁εὐωχουμένων, οἷς οὔτε οὐρανὸς ἐπέρρει τὸ μάννα, οὔτε ἡ ₁₂γῆ
30 κατὰ τὴν ἰδίαν αὐτῆς φύσιν σιτοποιοῦσα τὴν χρείαν ₁₃ἐπλήρου,
ἀλλ᾽ ἐκ τῶν ἀρρήτων ταμείων τῆς θείας δυνάμεως ₁₄ἡ φιλοτιμία
προήει, ἕτοιμος ἄρτος ταῖς χερσὶ τῶν ₁₅διακονούντων ἐγγεωρ-
γούμενος καὶ διὰ τοῦ κόρου τῶν ₁₆ἐσθιόντων πλείων γιγνόμενος,
ἥ τε διὰ τῶν ἰχθύων ὀψοφαγία, ₁₇οὐ θαλάσσης αὐτοῖς πρὸς τὴν
35 χρείαν συνεισφερούσης, ₁₈ἀλλὰ τοῦ καὶ τῇ θαλάσσῃ τὸ γένος τῶν
ἰχθύων ἐγκατασπείραντος.—
                                   —(3) ₁₉ Καὶ πῶς ἄν τις τὸ καθ᾽ ἕκαστον
(GNO 60) τῶν | εὐαγγελικῶν διεξίοι θαυμάτων; Ταύτην τοίνυν τὴν
(Sr 89) δύναμιν ₂καθορῶν, ὁ ἐχθρὸς ἐν ἐκείνῳ πλεῖον | τοῦ κατεχομένου
τὸ ₃προκείμενον εἶδεν ἐν τῷ συναλλάγματι. Τούτου χάριν αὐτὸν
40 ₄αἱρεῖται λύτρον τῶν ἐν τῇ τοῦ θανάτου φρουρᾷ καθειργμένων
₅γενέσθαι.

20 καὶ τὴν τῶν καταδίκων ἀνάρρυσιν after ἀνάλυσιν Srawley | 21 GNO brackets
κατὰ¹ | 24 Μωϋσέως GNO : Μωσέως

bearing witness to exceeding worth;[209] and the treatment of natural illnesses without any sort of means and simple, done by him by [his] word alone and by the impulse of [his] will; the release to life of those who had died,[210] and the demons' fear;[211] authority over what happens in the air[212] and walking across the sea[213] (the sea not withdrawing on either side, and laying bare the bottom for those who passed through, as in the case of Moses' wonderworking,[214] but the upper surface of the water became as dry land to [his] foot, and by a certain firm resistance supporting his step); both disdain for food as long as he wanted[215] and bountiful banquets in the wilderness in which many thousands fared sumptuously[216] (neither did manna stream down from heaven for them,[217] nor did the earth fill their need, making bread in accordance with its own nature, but the munificence proceeded out of the ineffable treasuries of divine power, bread ready [to eat] growing in the hands of those who served it, and becoming more while those who ate were satisfied), and the feast of fish[218] (the sea did not contribute to their need, but he who also stocked the different kinds of fish[219] in the sea).

(3) And how could someone go through each of the gospel miracles in detail? The enemy, therefore, observing this power, saw that in him more was proposed in exchange than what he held. Because of this he chooses him to become the ransom for those who were shut up in the prison of death.

---

[209]I.e., the angels (Lk 2.13–14). The Greek (ἐκ τῶν ἀοράτων) may also mean "from the invisible [places]," which could refer to the voice of the Father ((Mt 3.17, 17.5; Mk 1.11, 9.7; Lk 3.22, 9.35; Jn 12.28; 2 Pet 1.17).

[210]Mt 9.18–26; Mk 5.21–43; Lk 7.11–17, 8.40–56.

[211]Mt 8.29; Mk 5.7; Lk 4.34.

[212]Mt 8.23–27; Mk 4.35–41; Lk 8.22–25.

[213]Mt 14.22–36; Mk 6.45–56; Jn 6.16–24.

[214]Ex 14.15–29.

[215]Mt 4.1–11; Lk 4.1–13.

[216]Mt 14.13–21, 15.29–39; Mk 6.30–44, 8.1–9; Lk 9.10–17; Jn 6.1–13.

[217]Ex 16.

[218]Lk 5.1–11; Jn 21.1–14 (although fish are also present in the multiplication miracles, see n. 216 above).

[219]Lit. "the kind of fishes" (τὸ γένος τῶν ἰχθύων); cf. Gen 1.21.

Ἀλλὰ μὴν ἀμήχανον ἦν αὐτὸν γυμνῇ ₆προσβλέψαι τῇ τοῦ
(PG 64) Θεοῦ φαντασίᾳ, μὴ σαρκός τινα μοῖραν ₇ἐν αὐτῷ | θεωρήσαντα,
ἣν ἤδη διὰ τῆς ἁμαρτίας κεχείρωτο. ₈Διὰ τοῦτο περικαλύπ-
45 τεται τῇ σαρκὶ ἡ θεότης, ὡς ἂν πρὸς ₉τὸ σύντροφόν τε καὶ
(Sr 90) συγγενὲς αὐτῷ βλέπων, μὴ πτοηθείη ₁₀τὸν | προσεγγισμὸν τῆς
ὑπερεχούσης δυνάμεως, καὶ τὴν ₁₁ἠρέμα διὰ τῶν θαυμάτων ἐπὶ
τὸ μεῖζον διαλάμπουσαν ₁₂δύναμιν κατανοήσας, ἐπιθυμητὸν
μᾶλλον ἢ φοβερὸν τὸ ₁₃φανὲν εἶναι νομίσῃ.—
—(4) Ὁρᾷς ὅπως τὸ ἀγαθὸν
50 τῷ δικαίῳ ₁₄συνέζευκται καὶ τὸ σοφὸν τούτων οὐκ ἀποκέκριται.
Τὸ ₁₅γὰρ διὰ τῆς τοῦ σώματος περιβολῆς χωρητὴν τὴν θείαν
₁₆δύναμιν ἐπινοῆσαι γενέσθαι, ὡς ἂν ἡ ὑπὲρ ἡμῶν οἰκονομία ₁₇μὴ
παραποδισθείη τῷ φόβῳ τῆς θεϊκῆς ἐπιφανείας, πάντων ₁₈κατὰ
ταὐτὸν τὴν ἀπόδειξιν ἔχει, τοῦ ἀγαθοῦ, τοῦ ₁₉σοφοῦ, τοῦ δι-
55 καίου. Τὸ μὲν γὰρ ἑλέσθαι σῶσαι τῆς ἀγαθότητος ₂₀ἐστι
μαρτυρία· τὸ δὲ συναλλαγματικὴν ποιήσασθαι ₂₁τὴν τοῦ
κρατουμένου λύτρωσιν τὸ δίκαιον δείκνυσι· τὸ δὲ ₂₂χωρητὸν δι'
ἐπινοίας ποιῆσαι τῷ ἐχθρῷ τὸ ἀχώρητον τῆς ₂₃ἀνωτάτω σοφίας
τὴν ἀπόδειξιν ἔχει.

ΚΔ' ₂₄Ἀλλ' ἐπιζητεῖν εἰκὸς τὸν τῇ ἀκολουθίᾳ τῶν εἰρημέ-
(Sr 91) νων ₂₅προσέχοντα, ποῦ τὸ δυνατὸν τῆς θεότητος, ποῦ ἡ |
(GNO 61) ἀφθαρ- | σία τῆς θείας δυνάμεως ἐν τοῖς εἰρημένοις ὁρᾶται.—

—Ἵνα
₂τοίνυν καὶ ταῦτα γένηται καταφανῆ, τὰ ἐφεξῆς τοῦ μυστηρίου
5 ₃διασκοπήσωμεν, ἐν οἷς μάλιστα δείκνυται συγκεκραμένη ₄τῇ
φιλανθρωπίᾳ ἡ δύναμις.—

But surely he was unable to look at the naked manifestation of God, had he not seen in him some portion of the flesh which he had already conquered through sin. Because of this the divinity is covered all around with the flesh, so that, in looking at what is both habitual and akin to him, he might not be terrified at the near approach of the transcendent power, and considering the quiet power shining through the miracles more and more, he might deem what appeared to be more desirable than frightening.

(4) You see how the good is joined with the just, and the wise is not divided from them. For the divine power devised to become perceptible through the covering of the body, so that the economy on our behalf might not be impeded by fear of the divine manifestation. This is a demonstration of all these at once: of the good, the wise, the just. For choosing to save is testimony of goodness; making the ransom of him who was held [captive] a matter of exchange demonstrates the just; and making what is imperceptible perceptible to the enemy by artifice[220] is a demonstration of the highest wisdom.

OBJECTION: *Where is God's power in this saving work?*

24 But one who attends to the order of what has been said is likely to ask, "Where is the power of the divinity? Where is the incorruptibility of the divine power seen in the things that have been said?"

RESPONSE: *Power is demonstrated in the incarnation itself, and in the harrowing of hades, which is accomplished by Christ's divine presence.*

Therefore, so that these things might also be clear, let us consider the things that followed after the mystery,[221] in which power commingled with love for man is most of all demonstrated.

---

[220]This word (ἐπίνοια) is often a technical term for Gregory, used in his polemic *Against Eunomius*. But here he uses the word to mean "device" or "artifice," having used the verb form "devised" (ἐπινοῆσαι) just above.

[221]Often "the mystery" refers to the faith in general (and in Chapters 33–40 it usually means "sacrament"). Here it is specifically Christ's death.

—(2) Πρῶτον μὲν οὖν τὸ ₅τὴν παντοδύναμον φύσιν καὶ πρὸς τὸ ταπεινὸν τῆς ἀνθρωπότητος ₆καταβῆναι ἰσχῦσαι πλείονα τῆς δυνάμεως ₇τὴν ἀπόδειξιν ἔχει ἢ τὰ μέγαλά τε καὶ ὑπερφυῆ τῶν θαυμάτων. ₈Τὸ μὲν γὰρ μέγα τι καὶ ὑψηλὸν ₁₀ ἐξεργασθῆναι παρὰ ₉τῆς θείας δυνάμεως κατὰ φύσιν πώς ἐστι καὶ ἀκόλουθον, ₁₀καὶ οὐκ ἄν τινα ξενισμὸν ἐπάγοι τῇ ἀκοῇ τὸ λέγειν πᾶσαν ₁₁τὴν ἐν τῷ κόσμῳ κτίσιν καὶ πᾶν ὅτιπερ ἔξω τῶν φαινομένων ₁₂καταλαμβάνεται, ἐν τῇ δυνάμει τοῦ Θεοῦ συστῆναι, ₁₃αὐτοῦ τοῦ θελήματος πρὸς τὸ δοκοῦν οὐσιωθέντος· ἡ 15 δὲ ₁₄πρὸς τὸ ταπεινὸν κάθοδος περιουσία τίς ἐστι τῆς δυνάμεως
(Sr 92) ₁₅οὐδὲν ἐν τοῖς | παρὰ φύσιν κωλυομένης.—

—(3) Ὡς γὰρ ἴδιόν ₁₆ἐστι τῆς τοῦ πυρὸς οὐσίας ἡ ἐπὶ τὸ ἄνω φορά, καὶ οὐκ ἄν ₁₇τις θαύματος ἄξιον ἐπὶ τῆς φλογὸς ἡγήσαιτο τὸ φυσικῶς ₁₈ἐνεργούμενον, εἰ δὲ ῥέουσαν ἐπὶ τὸ κάτω καθ᾽ ὁμοιότητα ₁₉τῶν ἐμβριθῶν σωμάτων 20 ἴδοι τὴν φλόγα, τὸ τοιοῦτον ἐν ₂₀θαύματι ποιεῖται, πῶς τὸ πῦρ

(2) First, then, the all-powerful nature being strong to descend even to the humiliation of humanity is more proof of power than great and supernatural miracles. For accomplishing something great and lofty by the divine power is somehow natural and in order, and it would not sound strange to say that every created thing in the world and all that is comprehended beyond [sensory] phenomena is constituted by the power of God, [his] will itself given being according to his good pleasure;[222] but the descent to [our] humiliation is a superabundant example of power in no way hindered by things contrary to [its] nature.

(3) For as it is a property of the essence of fire to tend upward,[223] and someone would not deem the natural activity of a flame worthy of wonder, but if he should see the flame flowing downward like

---

[222]Gregory seems to be saying that created things *are* the will of God, given being. This may be a somewhat poetic image, but it also seems to comport with St Gregory's speculations about the nature of matter elsewhere (though here he is not only discussing sensory reality but also the noetic realm—though perhaps even this has some component of materiality in St Gregory's thought, cf. St John of Damascus, *Exact Exposition* 2.3, quoted below in p. 122, n. 251). Gregory seems to say the same thing in *In illud: Tunc et ipse* (GNO III/2:11).

[223]In ancient Greek thought, there were four elements: earth, water, air, and fire. The modern conception of gravity did not exist. The ancients believed that each element tended toward its proper place. Earth and water tend downward (toward the center of the earth, and hence the center of the universe in a geocentric cosmology), while air and fire tend upward (outward from the center of the earth, and of the universe). The earth was, of course, made up of its eponymous element; water rested upon the surface of the earth; air made up the atmosphere around the earth, and it was believed that a sphere of fire encircled the earth before the sphere of the moon and the larger heavenly spheres. This vision of the four elements enclosed within one another like a Russian nesting doll was first formulated by Empedocles, further developed by Aristotle (e.g., *De caelo* 2.14), and accepted by Ptolemy.

καὶ διαμένει πῦρ ὂν καὶ ἐν ₂₁τῷ τρόπῳ τῆς κινήσεως ἐκβαίνει τὴν
φύσιν, ἐπὶ τὸ κάτω ₂₂φερόμενον· οὕτω καὶ τὴν θείαν τε καὶ
ὑπερέχουσαν δύναμιν ₂₃οὐκ οὐρανῶν μεγέθη καὶ φωστήρων
αὐγαὶ καὶ ἡ τοῦ ₂₄παντὸς διακόσμησις καὶ ἡ διηνεκὴς τῶν ὄντων
25 οἰκονομία ₂₅τοσοῦτον ὅσον ἡ ἐπὶ τὸ ἀσθενὲς τῆς φύσεως ἡμῶν
συγκατάβασις ₂₆δείκνυσι, πῶς τὸ ὑψηλὸν ἐν τῷ ταπεινῷ
(GNO 62) γενό- | μενον καὶ ἐν τῷ ταπεινῷ καθορᾶται καὶ οὐ καταβαίνει τοῦ
₂ὕψους, πῶς θεότης ἀνθρωπίνῃ συμπλακεῖσα φύσει καὶ ₃τοῦτο
γίνεται καὶ ἐκεῖνό ἐστιν.—

—(4) Ἐπειδὴ γάρ, καθὼς ἐν τοῖς
30 ₄ἔμπροσθεν εἴρηται, φύσιν οὐκ εἶχεν ἡ ἐναντία δύναμις ₅ἀκράτῳ
προσμῖξαι τῇ τοῦ Θεοῦ παρουσίᾳ καὶ γυμνὴν ὑποστῆναι ₆αὐτοῦ
τὴν ἐμφάνειαν, ὡς ἂν εὔληπτον γένοιτο τῷ ₇ἐπιζητοῦντι ὑπὲρ
(Sr 93; PG 65) ἡμῶν τὸ | ἀντάλ-| λαγμα, τῷ προκαλύμματι ₈τῆς φύσεως ἡμῶν
ἐνεκρύφθη τὸ θεῖον, ἵνα κατὰ τοὺς λίχνους ₉τῶν ἰχθύων τῷ
35 δελέατι τῆς σαρκὸς συγκατασπασθῇ ₁₀τὸ ἄγκιστρον τῆς θεότητος, καὶ οὕτω τῆς ζωῆς τῷ θανάτῳ ₁₁εἰσοικισθείσης καὶ τῷ
σκότῳ τοῦ φωτὸς ἐπιφανέντος ₁₂ἐξαφανισθῇ τὸ τῷ φωτὶ καὶ τῇ
ζωῇ κατὰ τὸ ἐναντίον ₁₃νοούμενον· οὐ γὰρ ἔχει φύσιν οὔτε
σκότος διαμένειν ἐν ₁₄φωτὸς παρουσίᾳ, οὔτε θάνατον εἶναι ζωῆς
ἐνεργούσης.—

40 —(5) ₁₅Οὐκοῦν ἐπὶ κεφαλαίων τοῦ μυστηρίου τὴν ἀκολουθίαν ₁₆ἀναλαβόντες ἐντελῆ ποιησόμεθα τὴν ἀπολογίαν πρὸς
₁₇τοὺς κατηγοροῦντας τῆς θείας οἰκονομίας, ὅτου χάριν δι'
₁₈ἑαυτῆς ἡ θεότης τὴν ἀνθρωπίνην κατεργάζεται σωτηρίαν. ₁₉Δεῖ
γὰρ διὰ πάντων τὸ θεῖον ἐν ταῖς πρεπούσαις ὑπολήψεσιν ₂₀εἶναι
45 καὶ μὴ τὸ μὲν ὑψηλῶς ἐπ' αὐτοῦ νοεῖσθαι, τὸ δὲ ₂₁τῆς θεο-
(Sr 94) πρεποῦς ἀξίας ἐκβάλλεσθαι· ἀλλὰ πᾶν ὑψηλόν τε ₂₂καὶ | εὐσεβὲς

22 οὕτω GNO : οὕτως Srawley

heavy bodies, such a thing is regarded with wonder, how fire both remains fire and exceeds nature in the manner of [its] motion, being carried downward; so too the greatness of the heavens and the rays of [its] luminaries and the arrangement of the universe and the continuous economy of existing things do not demonstrate the divine and transcendant power so much as condescension to the infirmity of our nature, how the lofty came to be in humiliation, and is seen in humiliation, and does not descend from the lofty,[224] how divinity, entwining with human nature, both becomes this and is that.[225]

(4) For since, as has been said before, the opposing power did not have a nature [able] to come into contact with the unalloyed presence of God and to withstand his naked manifestation, so that the exchange for us might be easily grasped by him who sought [it], the divine was hidden by the veil of our nature, in order that, as in the case of greedy fish, the hook of the divinity might be swallowed with the bait of the flesh, and thus when life came to dwell in death and light shone in the darkness, that which is understood as the opposite of light and life might be utterly destroyed. For it is not in the nature of darkness to remain in the presence of light, nor death to exist where life is active.

Summary—The Economy is Befitting for God

(5) Therefore, let us, by way of summary, resume the order [of the argument] about the mystery, and complete the defense[226] of the divine economy against those who speak against it, because the divinity accomplishes human salvation by itself. In all things it is necessary for the divine to be among fitting suppositions, and not to think highly of one [attribute] while rejecting the worth of [other] God-befitting [attributes]. But it is altogether necessary to believe

---

[224]Cf. Jn 3.13b (longer reading, not present in critical editions).

[225]I.e., he becomes human and remains divine.

[226]St Gregory calls this work both a defense—literally an "apology" (ἀπολογίαν)—and a catechesis (Pr.1, 7; 40.2). For a consideration of the work's rhetorical character, see introduction, pp. 20–24.

νόημα δεῖ πάντως ἐπὶ Θεοῦ πιστεύεσθαι καὶ $_{23}$συνηρτῆσθαι δι' ἀκολουθίας τῷ ἑτέρῳ τὸ ἕτερον.—

—(6) Δέδεικται $_{24}$τοίνυν τὸ ἀγαθόν, τὸ σοφόν, τὸ δίκαιον, τὸ δυνατόν, τὸ $_{25}$φθορᾶς ἀνεπίδεκτον, 50 (GNO 63) πάντα τῷ λόγῳ τῆς καθ' ἡμᾶς οἰ- | κονομίας ἐπιδεικνύμενα· ἡ ἀγαθότης ἐν τῷ προελέσθαι $_2$σῶσαι τὸν ἀπολωλότα καταλαμβάνεται, ἡ σοφία καὶ ἡ $_3$δικαιοσύνη ἐν τῷ τρόπῳ τῆς σωτηρίας ἡμῶν διεδείχθη, ἡ $_4$δύναμις ἐν τῷ γενέσθαι μὲν αὐτὸν ἐν ὁμοιώματι ἀνθρώπου $_5$καὶ σχήματι κατὰ τὸ ταπεινὸν τῆς 55 φύσεως ἡμῶν καὶ ἐλπισθῆναι $_6$δύνασθαι αὐτὸν καθ' ὁμοιότητα τῶν ἀνθρώπων $_7$τῷ θανάτῳ ἐγκρατηθῆναι, γενόμενον δὲ τὸ οἰκεῖον ἑαυτῷ $_8$καὶ κατὰ φύσιν ἐργάσασθαι· (7) οἰκεῖον δὲ φωτὶ μὲν ὁ ἀφανισμὸς $_9$τοῦ σκότους, ζωῇ δὲ ἡ τοῦ θανάτου καθαίρεσις. Ἐπεὶ $_{10}$οὖν τῆς εὐθείας ὁδοῦ παρενεχθέντες τὸ κατ' 60 ἀρχὰς τῆς $_{11}$ζωῆς ἐξετράπημεν καὶ τῷ θανάτῳ ἐγκατηνέχθημεν, τί τοῦ $_{12}$εἰκότος ἔξω παρὰ τοῦ μυστηρίου μανθάνομεν, εἰ ἡ καθαρότης $_{13}$τῶν ἐξ ἁμαρτίας μολυνθέντων ἐφάπτεται, καὶ ἡ ζωὴ $_{14}$τῶν τεθνηκότων, καὶ ἡ ὁδηγία τῶν πεπλανημένων, ὡς ἂν $_{15}$ὅ τε μολυσμὸς καθαρθείη, καὶ ἡ πλάνη θεραπευθείη, καὶ 65 εἰς $_{16}$τὴν ζωὴν τὸ τεθνηκὸς ἐπανέλθοι; |

(Sr 95) ΚΕ' $_{17}$Τὸ δὲ ἐν τῇ φύσει γενέσθαι ἡμῶν τὴν θεότητα τοῖς μὴ $_{18}$λίαν μικροψύχως κατανοοῦσι τὰ ὄντα οὐδένα ἂν ἐκ τοῦ $_{19}$εὐλόγου ξενισμὸν ἐπαγάγοι.—

—Τίς γὰρ οὕτω νήπιος τὴν ψυχὴν $_{20}$ὡς εἰς τὸ πᾶν βλέπων μὴ ἐν παντὶ πιστεύειν εἶναι τὸ $_{21}$θεῖον, καὶ 5 ἐνδυόμενον, καὶ ἐμπεριέχον, καὶ ἐγκαθήμενον; $_{22}$Τοῦ γὰρ ὄντος

every lofty and pious thought about God and to join one to another in order.

(6) It has been demonstrated, then, that the good, the wise, the just, the powerful, insusceptibility to corruption—all are demonstrated by the account of the economy concerning us: goodness is comprehended in choosing to save him who had perished, wisdom and justice are shown in the manner of our salvation, power in him being born "in the likeness" and "form"[227] of man in accordance with the humility of our nature, and causing [the enemy] to hope he was able to be under the sway of death like [other] men, and having been born [as a man], he worked what is proper to himself and in accordance with nature; (7) and the destruction of darkness is proper to light, and the overthrow of death [is proper] to life. Since, then, being led astray from the straight path, we were turned away from the life [we had] in the beginning, and were dragged down into death, what do we learn from the mystery that is beyond likelihood if purity lays hold of those who were defiled by sins, and life those who had died, and the guide those who had wandered astray, so that defilement might be purified, and the straying might be healed, and he who had died might return to life?

OBJECTION: *It is strange for God to be born in our nature.*

25 And the divinity being born in our nature would advance nothing strange, on reasonable grounds, to those who do not understand existing things very narrow-mindedly.

RESPONSE: *It is admitted that God is present everywhere in creation. What then is the scandal of his presence in human nature, if he is present everywhere?*

For who is so infantile in mind[228] that he does not believe, when looking at the universe, that the divine is in everything, and clothed [with it], and encompassing [it], and residing [in it]? For existing

[227]Phil 2.7.
[228]Lit. "soul" (ψυχὴν).

ἐξῆπται τὰ ὄντα καὶ οὐκ ἔνεστιν εἶναί τι μὴ ₂₃ἐν τῷ ὄντι τὸ εἶναι

(GNO 64) ἔχον. Εἰ οὖν ἐν αὐτῷ τὰ πάντα καὶ ἐν | πᾶσιν ἐκεῖνο, τί ἐπαισχύνονται τῇ οἰκονομίᾳ τοῦ μυστηρίου ₂τοῦ Θεὸν ἐν ἀνθρώπῳ γεγενῆσθαι διδάσκοντος τὸν ₃οὐδὲ νῦν ἔξω τοῦ ἀν-
10 θρώπου εἶναι πεπιστευμένον;—

—(2) Εἰ γὰρ ₄καὶ ὁ τρόπος τῆς ἐν ἡμῖν |

(Sr 96) τοῦ Θεοῦ παρουσίας οὐχ ὁ αὐτὸς ₅οὗτος ἐκείνῳ, ἀλλ' οὖν τὸ ἐν ἡμῖν εἶναι καὶ νῦν καὶ τότε ₆κατὰ τὸ ἴσον διωμολόγηται. Νῦν μὲν οὖν ἐγκέκραται ἡμῖν ₇ὥς συνέχων ἐν τῷ εἶναι τὴν φύσιν, τότε δὲ κατεμίχθη πρὸς ₈τὸ ἡμέτερον, ἵνα τὸ ἡμέτερον τῇ πρὸς
15 τὸ θεῖον ἐπιμιξίᾳ ₉γένηται θεῖον, ἐξαιρεθὲν τοῦ θανάτου καὶ τῆς

(PG 68) τοῦ ἀντικειμένου ₁₀τυραννίδος ἔξω | γενόμενον· ἡ γὰρ ἐκείνου ἀπὸ τοῦ ₁₁θανάτου ἐπάνοδος ἀρχὴ τῷ θνητῷ γένει τῆς εἰς τὴν ἀθάνατον ₁₂ζωὴν ἐπανόδου γίνεται.

ΚΣΤ'   ₁₃Ἀλλ' ἴσως τις ἐν τῇ τῆς δικαιοσύνης τε καὶ σοφίας ₁₄ἐξετάσει τῆς κατὰ τὴν οἰκονομίαν ταύτην θεωρουμένης ₁₅ἐνά-γεται πρὸς τὸ νομίσαι ἀπάτην τινὰ τὴν τοιαύτην μέθοδον ₁₆ἐπινενοῆσθαι ὑπὲρ ἡμῶν τῷ Θεῷ. Τὸ γὰρ μὴ γυμνῇ τῇ

18 γίνεται GNO : γίγνεται Srawley

things depend upon "the Existing One"²²⁹ and nothing can exist that does not have existence in the Existing One. If, then, all things are in him and he in all, why are they ashamed at the economy of the mystery, which teaches that God has come to be in man, who not even now is believed to be outside man?²³⁰

(2) For even if the manner of God's presence in us is not the same as it was in that [case], but still it is agreed he is equally in us now and then. Now he is mixed with us, as the one who holds together nature in existence, but then he was mingled with what is ours, so that by admixture with the divine, what is ours might become divine,²³¹ delivered from death and beyond the tyranny of the adversary. For his return from death becomes the beginning of the return to immortal life for the mortal race.

OBJECTION: *God used deceit to defeat the devil.*

26 But perhaps someone, in examining the justice and the wisdom seen in this economy, is led to deem such a method, devised by God on our behalf, a sort of deceit.²³² For the fact that God came to be

²²⁹Ex 3.14 (LXX), i.e., the name of God revealed in the burning bush in the Greek Old Testament. Christian thinkers connected this to Greek philosophy since the time of Justin Martyr (*Hortatory Address to the Greeks* 12).

²³⁰Cf. St Athanasius' argument about God's immanence in *On the Incarnation* 41–42. Many philosophically inclined pagans accepted the divine presence within all human beings, e.g., Plotinus, who wrote: "God . . . is outside of none, present unperceived to all; we break away from Him, or rather from ourselves." *Enneads* 6.9.7.

²³¹Cf. St Athanasius, *On the Incarnation* 57: "For he was incarnate that we might be made god" (PPS 44a:167). The *Discourse* was directly influenced by this work, but the same thought was expressed earlier and often in the tradition, e.g., by St Irenaeus ("the Word of God, our Lord Jesus Christ . . . did, through His transcendent love, become what we are, that He might bring us to be even what He is Himself"—*Against Heresies* 5, preface [ANF 1:526]) and Clement of Alexandria ("the Word of God became man, that thou mayest learn from man how man may become God"—*Exhortation to the Heathen* 1 [ANF 2:174]).

²³²St Gregory's defense of deceit strikes many readers as odd. Western thought was deeply influenced by St Augustine, who unequivocally condemned all instances of falsehood in his work *De Mendacio* (Aquinas concurred, cf. *Summa Theologiae* 2.110.3, which also relies on Aristotle, *Nicomachean Ethics* 4.7). But Chrysostom, Nyssen's younger contemporary, defends deception with good intent in *Six Books on the Priesthood* 1.8, and this is not an uncommon position in later eastern fathers (e.g., be

5 (Sr 97) [17]θεότητι, ἀλλ᾽ ὑπὸ τῆς ἀνθρωπίνης φύσεως | κεκαλυμμένῃ [18]ἀγνοηθέντα παρὰ τοῦ ἐχθροῦ τὸν Θεὸν ἐντὸς τοῦ κρατοῦντος [19]γενέσθαι ἀπάτῃ τίς ἐστι τρόπον τινὰ καὶ παραλογισμός, [20]ἐπείπερ ἴδιον τῶν ἀπατώντων ἐστὶ τὸ πρὸς ἕτερον [21]τὰς τῶν ἐπιβουλευομένων ἐλπίδας τρέπειν καὶ ἄλλο παρὰ [22]τὸ ἐλπισθὲν 10 κατεργάζεσθαι.

Ἀλλ᾽ ὁ πρὸς τὴν ἀλήθειαν [23]βλέπων πάντων μάλιστα καὶ τοῦτο τῆς δικαιοσύνης τε [24]καὶ τῆς σοφίας εἶναι συνθήσεται. (2) Δικαίου μὲν γάρ ἐστι τὸ [25]κατ᾽ ἀξίαν ἑκάστῳ νέμειν, σοφοῦ δὲ τὸ μήτε παρατρέπειν [26]τὸ δίκαιον μήτε τὸν ἀγαθὸν τῆς φιλαν-
15 (GNO 65) θρωπίας σκοπὸν | ἀποχωρίζειν τῆς κατὰ τὸ δίκαιον κρίσεως, ἀλλὰ συνάπτειν [2]ἀλλήλοις εὐμηχάνως ἀμφότερα, τῇ μὲν δικαιοσύνῃ [3]τὸ κατ᾽ ἀξίαν ἀντιδιδόντα, τῇ δὲ ἀγαθότητι τοῦ σκοποῦ [4]τῆς φιλανθρωπίας οὐκ ἐξιστάμενον. Σκοπήσωμεν τοίνυν [5]εἰ μὴ τὰ δύο ταῦτα τοῖς γεγονόσιν ἐνθεωρεῖται.—

—(3) Ἡ μὲν γὰρ [6]τοῦ
20 κατ᾽ ἀξίαν ἀντίδοσις, δι᾽ ἧς ὁ ἀπατεὼν ἀνταπατᾶται, [7]τὸ δίκαιον δείκνυσιν, ὁ δὲ σκοπὸς τοῦ γινομένου μαρτυρία [8]τῆς τοῦ ἐνεργοῦντος ἀγαθότητος γίνεται. Ἴδιον μὲν [9]γὰρ τῆς δικαιοσύνης τὸ ἐκεῖνα νέμειν ἑκάστῳ ὧν τις τὰς [10]ἀρχὰς καὶ τὰς αἰτίας προκατεβάλετο, ὥσπερ ἡ γῆ κατὰ [11]τὰ γένη τῶν καταβληθέντων
25 σπερμάτων καὶ τοὺς καρποὺς [12]ἀντιδίδωσι, σοφίας δὲ τὸ ἐν τῷ
(Sr 98) τρόπῳ τῆς τῶν | [13]ὁμοίων ἀντιδόσεως μὴ ἐκπεσεῖν τοῦ βελτίονος. (4) Ὥσπερ [14]γὰρ τῷ ἐδέσματι ὁμοίως παραμίγνυσι τὸ φάρμακον καὶ

25 ἀντιδίδωσι GNO : ἀντιδίδωσιν Srawley

within the power of him who held sway [over us], not in [his] naked divinity, but covered by human nature went unrecognized by the enemy, is a certain deception and some manner of misleading, since it is a property of those who use deception to divert the hopes of those they plot against to something else and to accomplish something other than what was hoped.

RESPONSE: *The economy is both just and wise, and the aim of the deception was to save and benefit man.*

But he who looks to the truth will concur that this, too, above all things belongs both to justice and to wisdom. (2) For it belongs to the just to render to each according to worth,[233] and to the wise not to pervert the just nor to separate the good aim of love for man from just judgment,[234] but skillfully joining both together, in justice recompensing according to worth, and in goodness not displacing the aim of love for man. Let us look,[235] then, if these two are seen in the things that have come to pass.

(3) For the recompense according to worth, by which the deceiver was deceived in turn, demonstrates the just, and the aim of what was done is a testimony of the goodness of him who effected it. For it is a property of justice to render to each those things whose beginnings and causes he sowed, just as the earth also returns fruits according to the kinds of seeds that were sown, and it belongs to wisdom, in [its] manner of recompensing like things, not to fall away from what is better. (4) For just as both the conspirator and he who

The Ladder of Divine Ascent 12.12 acknowledges a licit use of deception, in the step devoted to the sin of lying).

[233]Gregory uses the same definition in his *Homilies on the Beatitudes* (4.2; GNO VII/2:112), but later rejects it in favor of the broader view (also expressed in *Catechetical Discourse* 20.1–2): "It is impossible . . . for one kind of virtue, independently of the others, to be by itself perfect virtue. . . . Therefore every virtue is here [Mt 5.6] indicated by the word 'justice'" (*On the Beatitudes* 4.5; GNO VII/2:118, 119; trans. Hall). These correspond to the partial and universal notions of justice that Aristotle gives in *Nicomachean Ethics* 5.

[234]Cf. Jn 7.24.

[235]The verb form (Σκοπήσωμεν) of the noun translated as "aim" (σκοπός).

ὁ ₁₅ἐπιβουλεύων καὶ ὁ τὸν ἐπιβουλευθέντα ἰώμενος—ἀλλ' ὁ ₁₆μὲν
τὸ δηλητήριον, ὁ δὲ τοῦ δηλητηρίου ἀλεξητήριον—₁₇καὶ οὐδὲν
30 ὁ τρόπος τῆς θεραπείας τὸν σκοπὸν τῆς εὐεργεσίας ₁₈διελυ-
μήνατο—εἰ γὰρ καὶ παρ' ἀμφοτέρων φαρμάκου ₁₉μίξις ἐν
τροφῇ γίνεται, ἀλλὰ πρὸς τὸν σκοπὸν ἀποβλέψαντες ₂₀τὸν μὲν
ἐπαινοῦμεν, τῷ δὲ χαλεπαίνομεν—οὕτω ₂₁καὶ ἐνταῦθα τῷ μὲν
κατὰ τὸ δίκαιον λόγῳ ἐκεῖνα ὁ ἀπατεὼν ₂₂ἀντιλαμβάνει ὦν τὰ
35 σπέρματα διὰ τῆς ἰδίας προαιρέσεως ₂₃κατεβάλετο—ἀπατᾶται
γὰρ καὶ αὐτὸς τῷ τοῦ ἀνθρώπου ₂₄προβλήματι ὁ προαπατήσας
τὸν ἄνθρωπον τῷ ₂₅τῆς ἡδονῆς δελεάσματι—ὁ δὲ σκοπὸς τῶν
(GNO 66) γινομένων ἐπὶ | τὸ κρεῖττον τὴν παραλλαγὴν ἔχει.

(5) Ὁ μὲν γὰρ ἐπὶ διαφθορᾷ ₂τῆς φύσεως τὴν ἀπάτην ἐνήργησεν,
40 ὁ δὲ δίκαιος ἅμα καὶ ₃ἀγαθὸς καὶ σοφὸς ἐπὶ σωτηρίᾳ τοῦ
καταφθαρέντος τῇ ₄ἐπινοίᾳ τῆς ἀπάτης ἐχρήσατο, οὐ μόνον τὸν
ἀπολωλότα ₅διὰ τούτων εὐεργετῶν, ἀλλὰ καὶ αὐτὸν τὸν τὴν
(Sr 99) ἀπώλειαν ₆καθ' ἡμῶν ἐνεργήσαντα. Ἐκ γὰρ | τοῦ προσεγγίσαι
τῇ ζωῇ ₇μὲν τὸν θάνατον, τῷ φωτὶ δὲ τὸ σκότος, τῇ ἀφθαρσίᾳ
45 δὲ ₈τὴν φθοράν, ἀφανισμὸς μὲν τοῦ χείρονος γίνεται καὶ εἰς τὸ
₉μὴ ὂν μεταχώρησις, ὠφέλεια δὲ τοῦ ἀπὸ τούτων καθαιρο-
₁₀μένου.—
(PG 69)   —(6) Κα-| θάπερ γάρ, ἀτιμοτέρας ὕλης τῷ χρυσῷ κατα-
μιχθείσης, ₁₁τῇ διὰ τοῦ πυρὸς δαπάνῃ τὸ ἀλλότριόν τε καὶ
₁₂ἀπόβλητον οἱ θεραπευταὶ τοῦ χρυσοῦ καταναλώσαντες ₁₃πάλιν
50 ἐπανάγουσι πρὸς τὴν κατὰ φύσιν λαμπηδόνα τὴν ₁₄προτιμο-
τέραν ὕλην—οὐκ ἄπονος μέντοι γίνεται ἡ διάκρισις, ₁₅χρόνῳ
τοῦ πυρὸς τῇ ἀναλωτικῇ δυνάμει τὸ νόθον ₁₆ἐξαφανίζοντος,
πλὴν ἀλλὰ θεραπεία τίς ἐστι τοῦ χρυσίου ₁₇τὸ ἐκτακῆναι αὐτῷ
τὸ ἐπὶ λύμῃ τοῦ κάλλους ἐγκείμενον—(7) ₁₈κατὰ τὸν αὐτὸν
55 τρόπον, θανάτου, καὶ φθορᾶς, καὶ σκότους, ₁₉καὶ εἴ τι κακίας

45 γίνεται GNO : γίγνεται Srawley | 53 αὐτῷ GNO : αὐτὸ Srawley

heals the one who has been conspired against similarly mix a drug in food—but one is poison, and the other is a remedy for poison (and the manner of therapy in no way falsifies the aim of benefit, for even if mixing the drug in food happens in both cases, but looking at the aim, we praise one and blame the other)—so too here with the principle of the just: the deceiver receives in return those things whose seeds were sown by [his] own decision—for he who before had deceived man with the bait of pleasure is also himself deceived by the screen of man[236]—and the aim of what is done is an alteration to what is better.

The deception led to the harrowing of hades: the destruction of death, corruption, and darkness.

(5) For he [i.e., the devil] worked the deception for the corruption of [our] nature, but he who is at once just and good and wise used the artifice of deception for the salvation of the one who was corrupted, not only benefitting the one who was destroyed by these things, but also him who worked our destruction himself. For from the proximity of death to life, and darkness to light, and corruption to incorruption, the destruction of what is worse and [its] departure into nonbeing come to pass, and the profit of him who is purified from these things.

(6) For just as, when matter of no value is mixed with gold, the refiners[237] of the gold, consuming what is alien and worthless by the use of fire, lead the more valuable matter back again to its natural brilliance—indeed the separation is not without labor, with time [required] for the fire to make the base [matter] disappear by [its] consuming power, but, further, the melting out of what was embedded in it, damaging its beauty, is a sort of healing of the gold—(7) in the same manner, when death, and corruption, and darkness,

---

[236]Or "the projection [προβλήματι] of man." The word comes from προβάλλω, "what is put forward." This refers to the fact that the flesh of Christ obscured his divine identity from the devil (it ought not to be taken as a creeping Docetism).

[237]Lit. "healers" (θεραπευταὶ).

ἔκγονον τῷ εὑρετῇ τοῦ κακοῦ περιφυέντων, 20ὁ προσεγγισμὸς τῆς θείας δυνάμεως πυρὸς δίκην 21ἀφανισμὸν τοῦ παρὰ φύσιν κατεργασάμενος εὐεργετεῖ τῇ 22καθάρσει τὴν φύσιν, κἂν ἐπίπονος ἡ διάκρισις ᾖ—οὐκοῦν 23οὐδ᾽ ἂν παρ᾽ αὐτοῦ τοῦ 60 (GNO 67) ἀντικειμένου μὴ εἶναι δίκαιόν τε | καὶ σωτήριον τὸ γεγονὸς ἀμφιβάλοιτο, εἴπερ εἰς αἴσθησιν 2τῆς εὐεργεσίας ἔλθοι νῦν.

(8) Καθάπερ γὰρ οἱ ἐπὶ θεραπείᾳ 3τεμνόμενοί τε καὶ καιόμενοι (Sr 100) χαλεπαίνουσι τοῖς | θεραπεύουσι, 4τῇ ὀδύνῃ τῆς τομῆς δριμυσσόμενοι, εἰ δὲ τὸ ὑγιαίνειν 5διὰ τούτων προσγένοιτο καὶ ἡ τῆς 65 καύσεως ἀλγηδὼν 6παρέλθοι, χάριν εἴσονται τοῖς τὴν θεραπείαν ἐπ᾽ αὐτῶν 7ἐνεργήσασι· κατὰ τὸν αὐτὸν τρόπον ταῖς μακραῖς περιόδοις 8ἐξαιρεθέντος τοῦ κακοῦ τῆς φύσεως, τοῦ νῦν αὐτῇ 9καταμιχθέντος καὶ συμφυέντος, ἐπειδὰν ἡ εἰς τὸ ἀρχαῖον 10ἀποκατάστασις τῶν νῦν ἐν κακίᾳ κειμένων γένηται, 70 ὁμόφωνος 11ἡ εὐχαριστία παρὰ πάσης ἔσται τῆς κτίσεως, καὶ 12τῶν ἐν τῇ καθάρσει κεκολασμένων καὶ τῶν μηδὲ τὴν 13ἀρχὴν ἐπιδεηθέντων καθάρσεως.—

(Sr 101)   —(9) Ταῦτα | καὶ τὰ τοιαῦτα 14παραδίδωσι τὸ μέγα μυστήριον τῆς θείας ἐνανθρωπήσεως. 15Δι᾽ ὧν γὰρ κατεμίχθη τῇ ἀνθρωπότητι—διὰ πάντων 16τῶν τῆς φύσεως 75 ἰδιωμάτων γενόμενος, γενέσεώς τε καὶ 17ἀνατροφῆς, καὶ αὐξή-

_____

61–62 ἔλθοι νῦν. Καθάπερ γὰρ GNO : ἔλθοι. Νυνὶ γὰρ καθάπερ Srawley

and any other offspring of vice had grown around the inventor of evil, the approach[238] of the divine power, like fire accomplishing the disappearance[239] of what is against nature, benefits [our] nature by purification, though the separation is painful—therefore even the adversary himself would not dispute that what has come to pass is both just and saving, if indeed he might now come to a perception of the benefit.[240]

(8) For just as in the case of those who are healed with cuttings and cautery, they are indignant with [their] healers, cringing at the pain of the cut, but if through these things health should be regained and the pain of the cautery should be passed, they will be thankful to those who effected the healing in them; in the same manner, when the evil in nature, which is now mingled and growing with it, is taken out through long periods, when the restoration[241] to the ancient [state] of those who are now lying in vice comes to pass, there will be thanksgiving in unison from all creation,[242] both from those who have been chastised in purification and also from those who had no need of purification from the beginning.

(9) The great mystery of the divine incarnation teaches[243] these things and the like. For through these things mingling with humanity—through being born with all of the properties of [our] nature, both birth and nurture, and growth, and going out as far as the

[238]Or "proximity" (προσεγγισμὸς).

[239]Or "destruction" (ἀφανισμὸν).

[240]This is a far cry from a clear assertion that the devil will be saved. The grammar of the sentence is remarkably tentative. It is not at all clear that the devil will even perceive what has happened (in the past) as just and saving. It is not a certain affirmation that he will be saved in the future. Rather, this is a crowning rhetorical flourish in an argument defending the propriety of deception in Christ's saving work: even the devil himself—the one who was deceived—would not fault the means of salvation, if he came to view things in the proper light. See introduction pp. 38–40.

[241]Here St Gregory uses the word "*apokatastasis*" (ἀποκατάστασις). The word occurs once in the New Testament (Acts 3.21), and became associated with Origen and the idea that all will be saved. For the word's meaning and different uses in St Gregory of Nyssa, see Morwenna Ludlow, *Universal Salvation*, 38–44.

[242]Cf Phil 2.10–11.

[243]Or "transmits" (παραδίδωσι), the verb form of "tradition" (παράδοσις).

σεως, καὶ μέχρι τῆς τοῦ θανάτου πείρας [18]διεξελθών—τὰ προειρημένα πάντα κατείργασται, τόν [19]τε ἄνθρωπον τῆς κακίας ἐλευθερῶν καὶ αὐτὸν τὸν τῆς [20]κακίας εὑρετὴν ἰώμενος. Ἴασις γάρ ἐστιν ἀρρωστίας ἡ τοῦ [21]νοσήματος κάθαρσις, κἂν
80 ἐπίπονος ᾖ. |

(GNO 68) **ΚΖ'** Ἀκόλουθον δὲ πάντως τὸν πρὸς τὴν φύσιν ἡμῶν ἀνακιρνάμενον [2]διὰ πάντων δέξασθαι τῶν ἰδιωμάτων αὐτῆς [3]τὴν πρὸς ἡμᾶς συνανάκρασιν. Καθάπερ γὰρ οἱ τὸν ῥύπον [4]τῶν ἱματίων ἐκπλύνοντες οὐ τὰ μὲν ἐῶσι τῶν μολυσμάτων, [5]τὰ δὲ
5 ἀπορρύπτουσιν, ἀλλ' ἀπ' ἀρχῆς ἄχρι τέλους [6]ἐκκαθαίρουσι τῶν κηλίδων ἅπαν τὸ ὕφασμα, ὡς ἂν ὁμότιμον [7]ἑαυτῷ δι' ὅλου τὸ
(Sr 102) ἱμάτιον γένοιτο, κατὰ τὸ | ἴσον λαμπρυνθὲν [8]ἐκ τῆς πλύσεως· οὕτως, μολυνθείσης τῇ ἁμαρτίᾳ [9]τῆς ἀνθρωπίνης ζωῆς ἐν ἀρχῇ τε καὶ τελευτῇ, καὶ τοῖς διὰ [10]μέσου πᾶσιν, ἔδει διὰ πάντων
10 γενέσθαι τὴν ἐκπλύνουσαν [11]δύναμιν, καὶ μὴ τὸ μέν τι θεραπεῦσαι τῷ καθαρσίῳ, τὸ δὲ [12]περιϊδεῖν ἀθεράπευτον. (2) Τούτου χάριν, τῆς ζωῆς ἡμῶν δύο [13]πέρασιν ἑκατέρωθεν διειλημμένης —τὸ κατὰ τὴν ἀρχήν [14]φημι καὶ τὸ τέλος—καθ' ἑκάτερον εὑρίσκεται πέρας ἡ [15]διορθωτικὴ τῆς φύσεως δύναμις, καὶ τῆς
15 ἀρχῆς ἁψαμένη [16]καὶ μέχρι τοῦ τέλους ἑαυτὴν ἐπεκτείνασα καὶ τὰ διὰ μέσου [17]τούτων πάντα διαλαβοῦσα.
(PG 72) (3) Μιᾶς δὲ πᾶσιν ἀνθρώποις τῆς [18]εἰς τὴν ζωὴν | οὔσης παρόδου, πόθεν ἔδει τὸν εἰσιόντα πρὸς [19]ἡμᾶς εἰσοικισθῆναι τῷ βίῳ; Ἐξ οὐρανοῦ, φησὶ τυχὸν ὁ διαπτύων [20]ὡς αἰσχρόν τε καὶ ἄδοξον τὸ
20 εἶδος τῆς ἀνθρωπίνης [21]γενέσεως. Ἀλλ' οὐκ ἦν ἐν οὐρανῷ τὸ

experience of death—he has accomplished all that has been said before, both freeing man from vice and healing the inventor of vice himself.[244] For the healing of a disease is the purification of the sickness, even if it is painful.

Christ accepts all of the properties of our nature to cleanse and heal it entirely.

27 And it altogether follows the order [of the argument] for him who is mingled in our nature to accept all of its properties in [this] commingling with us. For just as those who wash out garments' filth do not leave some spots while they wash away the others, but from the beginning to the end they clean out the entire fabric from stains[245] so that the garment, made bright by washing, might thus be of the same worth equally throughout all of itself; thus, when human life was stained by sin both in [its] beginning and end and all that is in the middle, it was necessary for the cleansing power to be through all, and not to heal one thing by purification while overlooking the unhealed one. (2) Because of this, since our life is embraced by two limits on either side—I mean, the beginning and the end—the power to correct [our] nature is discovered in each limit, both touching the beginning and extending itself to the end and embracing all of those things in the middle.

(3) And since there is one entrance into life for all men, from whence must he who enters into us [come] to make [his] dwelling in life? Perhaps he who despises[246] the the form of human birth as both shameful and inglorious says, "From heaven."[247] But humanity

---

[244]This is the closest St Gregory comes to speaking of the salvation of the devil. But we must note that he claims to be repeating "all that has been said before," and previously he only tentatively expresses the possibility of the devil coming to perceive this benefit (26.7). See introduction, pp. 38–40.

[245]The image has an even readier application in Greek: the nouns "spots" (κηλί-δων) and "stains" (μολυσμάτων), and the verbs "wash out" (ἐκπλύνοντες), "wash away" (ἀπορρύπτουσιν), and "clean" (ἐκκαθαίρουσι) carry moral connotations in a non-laundering context.

[246]Lit. "he who spits upon" (ὁ διαπτύων).

[247]Cf. Jn 3.13. This view was attributed to Apollinaris, against whom St Gregory

ἀνθρώπινον, οὐδέ τις ₂₂ἐν τῇ ὑπερκοσμίῳ ζωῇ κακίας νόσος
ἐπεχωρίαζεν. Ὁ δὲ τῷ ₂₃ἀνθρώπῳ καταμιγνύμενος τῷ σκοπῷ
(GNO 69) τῆς ὠφελείας ἐποιεῖ- | τὸ τὴν συνανάκρασιν. Ἔνθα τοίνυν τὸ
κακὸν οὐκ ἦν, οὐδὲ ₂ὁ ἀνθρώπινος ἐπολιτεύετο βίος, πῶς ἐπι-
25 (Sr 103) ζητεῖ τις ἐκεῖθεν | ₃τῷ Θεῷ περιπλακῆναι τὸν ἄνθρωπον, μᾶλλον
δὲ οὐχὶ ἄνθρωπον, ₄ἀλλὰ ἀνθρώπου τι εἴδωλον καὶ ὁμοίωμα;
Τίς δ' ₅ἂν ἐγένετο τῆς φύσεως ἡμῶν ἡ διόρθωσις, εἰ τοῦ ἐπι-
γείου ₆ζῴου νενοσηκότος ἕτερόν τι τῶν οὐρανίων τὴν θείαν
₇ἐπιμιξίαν ἐδέξατο; Οὐκ ἔστι γὰρ θεραπευθῆναι τὸν κάμνοντα,
30 ₈μὴ τοῦ πονοῦντος μέρους ἰδιαζόντως δεξαμένου ₉τὴν ἴασιν.—

—(4) Εἰ
οὖν τὸ μὲν κάμνον ἐπὶ γῆς ἦν, ἡ δὲ θεία δύναμις ₁₀τοῦ κάμνοντος
μὴ ἐφήψατο, πρὸς τὸ ἑαυτῆς βλέπουσα ₁₁πρέπον, ἄχρηστος ἦν
τῷ ἀνθρώπῳ ἡ περὶ τὰ μηδὲν ἡμῖν ₁₂ἐπικοινωνοῦντα τῆς θείας
δυνάμεως ἀσχολία.—

—Τὸ μὲν γὰρ ₁₃ἀπρεπὲς ἐπὶ τῆς θεότητος ἴσον,
35 εἴπερ ὅλως θεμιτόν ἐστιν ₁₄ἄλλο τι παρὰ τὴν κακίαν ἀπρεπὲς
ἐννοεῖν. Πλὴν τῷ ₁₅μικροψύχως ἐν τούτῳ κρίνοντι τὴν θείαν
(Sr 104) μεγαλειότητα, ἐν ₁₆τῷ μὴ δέξασθαι τῶν τῆς φύσεως | ἡμῶν ἰδιω-
μάτων τὴν ₁₇κοινωνίαν, οὐδὲν μᾶλλον παραμυθεῖται τὸ ἄδοξον
οὐρανίῳ ₁₈σώματι ἢ ἐπιγείῳ συσχηματισθῆναι τὸ θεῖον. Τοῦ
40 γὰρ ₁₉ὑψίστου καὶ ἀπροσίτου κατὰ τὸ ὕψος τῆς φύσεως ἡ κτίσις
₂₀πᾶσα κατὰ τὸ ἴσον ἐπὶ τὸ κάτω ἀφέστηκε, καὶ ὁμοτίμως ₂₁αὐτῷ
τὸ πᾶν ὑποβέβηκε. Τὸ γὰρ καθ' ὅλου ἀπρόσιτον οὔ ₂₂τινι μέν
ἐστι προσιτόν, τῷ δὲ ἀπροσπέλαστον, ἀλλ' ἐπ' ₂₃ἴσης πάντων
τῶν ὄντων ὑπερανέστηκεν. (5) Οὔτε οὖν ἡ γῆ ₂₄πορρωτέρω τῆς

was not in heaven, nor did any sickness of vice make an inroad in the supercosmic life. Now he who was mingled with man effected the commingling with the aim of profit. How then does someone seek there—where there was no evil, and human life held no citizenship—man who was entwined with God, or rather not man, but some image and likeness of man? What correction of our nature would have come about if, while the earthly creature[248] was sick, someone else, among the heavenly ones, received the divine admixture? For it is not possible for the suffering one to be healed if the pained part does not receive healing individually.

(4) If, then, the suffering one was on earth, and the divine power did not touch the suffering one, looking [only] to what is befitting for himself, the divine power's occupation with things that share nothing in common with us would be useless for man.

For in the case of the divinity [all] is equally unbefitting, if indeed it is entirely allowable[249] to think of anything apart from vice as unbefitting. But for one who narrow-mindedly judges the divine greatness [to lie] in this, in not accepting fellowship with the properties of our nature, the dishonor is no more assuaged by the divine being conformed[250] to a heavenly body[251] than to an earthly one. For all creation is equally removed from [and] beneath the height of the most high, who is unapproachable according to the height of [his] nature, and all falls beneath, of equal value to him. For the wholly unapproachable[252] is not approachable to one, and to another unapproachable, but he stands over all existing things equally. (5) The

wrote his *Antirrheticus*. Cf. St Vincent of Lerins, *Commonitorium* 12.34: "[Apollinaris] says that this same flesh of the Lord was not received from the flesh of the holy Virgin Mary, but came down from heaven into the Virgin" (NPNF[2] 11:140).

[248]Lit. "animal," "living thing" (ζῷου).

[249]Or "pious" (θεμιτόν).

[250]See Phil 3.21 (and Rom 8.29).

[251]We cannot expect to find Cartesian dualism in the fourth century. St Paul spoke of "heavenly bodies" (1 Cor 15.40) and a "spiritual body" as opposed to a "psychic body" (1 Cor 15.44), and far later St John of Damascus thought that angels were bodiless when compared to us, but "only the Divinity is truly immaterial and incorporeal." *Exact Exposition* 2.3 (trans. Chase; cf. *On the Holy Images* 4).

[252]1 Tim 6.16.

45 ἀξίας ἐστίν, οὔτε ὁ οὐρανὸς πλησιαίτερος, ₂₅οὔτε τὰ ἐν ἑκατέρῳ
(GNO 70) τῶν στοιχείων ἐνδιαιτώμενα διαφέρει | τι ἀλλήλων ἐν τῷ μέρει
τούτῳ, ὡς τὰ μὲν ἐφάπτεσθαι τῆς ₂ἀπροσίτου φύσεως, τὰ δὲ
ἀποκρίνεσθαι, ἢ οὕτω γ' ἂν μὴ ₃διὰ πάντων ἐπ' ἴσης διήκειν τὴν
τὸ πᾶν ἐπικρατοῦσαν ₄δύναμιν ὑπονοήσαιμεν, ἀλλ' ἔν τισι
50 πλεονάζουσαν, ἐν ₅ἑτέροις ἐνδεεστέραν εἶναι, καὶ τῇ πρὸς τὸ
ἔλαττόν τε καὶ ₆πλέον καὶ μᾶλλον καὶ ἧττον διαφορᾷ σύνθετον
ἐκ τοῦ ₇ἀκολούθου τὸ θεῖον ἀναφανήσεται, αὐτὸ πρὸς ἑαυτὸ μὴ
₈συμβαῖνον, εἴπερ ἡμῶν μὲν πόρρωθεν ὑπονοοῖτο εἶναι τῷ ₉λόγῳ
τῆς φύσεως, ἑτέρῳ δέ τινι γειτνιῴη καὶ εὔληπτον ἐκ ₁₀τοῦ |
55 (Sr 105) σύνεγγυς γίνοιτο.—
        —(6) Ἀλλ' ὁ ἀληθὴς λόγος ἐπὶ τῆς ₁₁ὑψηλῆς ἀξίας
οὔτε κάτω βλέπει διὰ συγκρίσεως οὔτε ἄνω· ₁₂πάντα γὰρ κατὰ
τὸ ἴσον τὴν τοῦ παντὸς ἐπιστατοῦσαν ₁₃δύναμιν ὑποβέβηκεν,
ὥστε, εἰ τὴν ἐπίγειον φύσιν ἀναξίαν ₁₄τῆς πρὸς τὸ θεῖον οἰή-
σονται συμπλοκῆς, οὐδ' ἂν ἄλλη τις ₁₅εὑρεθείη τὸ ἄξιον ἔχουσα.
60 Εἰ δὲ ἐπ' ἴσης πάντα τῆς ἀξίας ₁₆ἀπολιμπάνεται, ἓν πρέπον ἐστὶ
τῷ Θεῷ τὸ εὐεργετεῖν τὸν ₁₇δεόμενον. Ὅπου τοίνυν ἦν ἡ νόσος,
ἐκεῖ φοιτῆσαι τὴν ἰωμένην ₁₈δύναμιν ὁμολογοῦντες, τί ἔξω τῆς
θεοπρεποῦς ὑπολήψεως ₁₉πεπιστεύκαμεν; |

(PG 73) ΚΗ'   ₂₀Ἀλλὰ κωμῳδοῦσι τὴν φύσιν ἡμῶν, καὶ τὸν τῆς γεννήσεως ₂₁τρόπον διαθρυλοῦσι, καὶ οἴονται διὰ τούτων ἐπιγέ-
λαστον ₂₂ποιεῖν τὸ μυστήριον, ὡς ἀπρεπὲς ὂν Θεῷ διὰ τοιαύτης
(GNO 71) ₂₃εἰσόδου τῆς τοῦ ἀνθρωπίνου βίου κοινωνίας ἐφάψα- | σθαι.

5 Ἀλλ' ἤδη περὶ τούτου καὶ ἐν τοῖς ἔμπροσθεν εἴρηται ₂λόγοις ὅτι
μόνον αἰσχρὸν τῇ ἑαυτοῦ φύσει τὸ κακόν ἐστι ₃καὶ εἴ τι πρὸς τὴν
κακίαν οἰκείως ἔχει, ἡ δὲ τῆς φύσεως ₄ἀκολουθία, θείῳ

---

54 γειτνιῴη GNO : γειτνιῶν Srawley

earth, then, is not further from [his] worth, nor is heaven nearer, nor do the things dwelling in each of the elements differ from each other in this respect, so that some are joined to[253] the unapproachable nature, but others are separated [from it], otherwise we might suspect the power holding sway over the universe not to pervade all things equally, but abounding in some, to be lacking in others, and by the difference of less and more and superior and inferior the divine will come to light in the order [of the argument] as composite, itself not congruous with itself, if indeed it is suspected to be far from us by reason of nature, but would be nearby some other and would be within easy grasp because of [its] proximity.

(6) But in the case of the lofty worth [of the divine], the true account looks neither upward nor downward in comparison; for all things equally fall beneath the power that presides over the universe, and so, if they will think the earthly nature unworthy of being intertwined with the divine, nothing else is found to have such worth. But if all things equally fall short of [his] worth, one thing is befitting for God: benefitting those in need. If, then, it is agreed that wherever there was sickness, there the healing power would resort, what have we believed that is outside God-befitting suppositions?

OBJECTION: *Human birth is unbefitting.*

28 But they mock our nature, and drone on about the manner of [our] birth, and think to make the mystery a laughingstock on account of these things, as if it were unbefitting for God to be joined with the communion of human life by such an entrance.

RESPONSE: *We have already refuted this objection.*[254]

But it was already said in the preceding arguments about this that the only thing that is shameful in its own nature is evil and anything that has a kinship with vice, but the order of nature, arranged by

---

[253]Or "touch" (ἐφάπτεσθαι).
[254]This objection has been raised and answered several times (cf. 9, 13, 16, and 25).

(Sr 106) βουλή- | ματι καὶ νόμῳ διαταχθεῖσα, πόρρω ₅τῆς κατὰ κακίαν ἐστὶ
διαβολῆς—ἢ οὕτω γ’ ἂν ἐπὶ τὸν δημιουργὸν ₆ἡ κατηγορία τῆς
10 φύσεως ἐπανίοι, εἴ τι τῶν περὶ ₇αὐτὴν ὡς αἰσχρόν τε καὶ
ἀπρεπὲς διαβάλλοιτο.

(2) Εἰ οὖν ₈μόνης κακίας τὸ θεῖον κεχώ-
ρισται, φύσις δὲ κακία οὐκ ₉ἔστι, τὸ δὲ μυστήριον ἐν ἀνθρώπῳ
γενέσθαι τὸν Θεόν, οὐκ ₁₀ἐν κακίᾳ λέγει, ἡ δὲ τοῦ ἀνθρώπου ἐπὶ
τὸν βίον εἴσοδος ₁₁μία ἐστί, δι’ ἧς παράγεται ἐπὶ τὴν ζωὴν τὸ
15 γεννώμενον, τίνα ₁₂νομοθετοῦσιν ἕτερον τρόπον τῷ Θεῷ τῆς εἰς
τὸν βίον ₁₃παρόδου οἱ ἐπισκεφθῆναι μὲν παρὰ τῆς θείας δυνάμεως ₁₄ἀσθενήσασαν ἐν κακίᾳ τὴν φύσιν εὔλογον κρίνοντες,
₁₅πρὸς δὲ τὸν τῆς ἐπισκέψεως τρόπον δυσαρεστούμενοι, ₁₆οὐκ
εἰδότες ὅτι πᾶσα πρὸς ἑαυτὴν ἡ κατασκευὴ τοῦ ₁₇σώματος
20 ὁμοτίμως ἔχει καὶ οὐδὲν ἐν ταύτῃ τῶν πρὸς τὴν ₁₈σύστασιν τῆς
ζωῆς συντελούντων ὡς ἄτιμόν τι ἢ πονηρὸν ₁₉διαβάλλεται;

(3) Πρὸς ἕνα γὰρ σκοπὸν ἡ τῶν ὀργανικῶν μελῶν ₂₀διασκευὴ
πᾶσα συντέτακται· ὁ δὲ σκοπός ἐστι τὸ διαμένειν ₂₁ἐν τῇ ζωῇ τὸ
ἀνθρώπινον. Τὰ μὲν οὖν λοιπὰ τῶν ὀργάνων ₂₂τὴν παροῦσαν |
25 (Sr 107) συνέχει τῶν ἀνθρώπων ζωήν, ἄλλα ₂₃πρὸς ἄλλην ἐνέργειαν
μεμερισμένα, δι’ ὧν ἡ αἰσθητική τε ₂₄καὶ ἡ ἐνεργητικὴ δύναμις
(GNO 72) οἰκονομεῖται, τὰ δὲ γεννητικὰ | τοῦ μέλλοντος ἔχει τὴν πρό-
νοιαν, δι’ ἑαυτῶν τῇ φύσει τὴν ₂διαδοχὴν ἀντεισάγοντα.—

—(4) Εἰ οὖν
πρὸς τὸ χρειῶδες βλέποις, ₃τίνος ἂν εἴη τῶν τιμίων εἶναι
30 νομιζομένων ἐκεῖνα δεύτερα; ₄Τίνος δὲ οὐκ ἂν προτιμότερα
κατὰ τὸ εὔλογον κρίνοιτο; ₅Οὐ γὰρ ὀφθαλμῷ, καὶ ἀκοῇ, καὶ
γλώσσῃ, ἢ ἄλλῳ τινὶ τῶν ₆αἰσθητηρίων πρὸς τὸ διηνεκὲς τὸ

divine counsel and law, is far from the charge[255] of vice—otherwise
the accusation against nature would fall back upon the creator,[256] if
anything about it were attacked as shameful and unbefitting.

(2) If, then, the divine is separated from vice alone, and nature is
not vice, and the mystery says that God was born in man, and not in
vice, and there is one entrance for man into life, through which the
one who is begotten is led into life, what other manner of passage
into life do they lay down[257] for God, since they judge it reasonable
for the nature that was sick with vice to be visited by the divine
power, though they are displeased with the manner of the visita-
tion, not knowing that all of the body's fashioning is of equal value
with itself and none of the things that contribute to the constitution
of life in this [i.e., the body] is attacked as something dishonorable
or wicked?

Each part of the body has a particular aim. The reproductive organs
battle death. Is this unbefitting?

(3) For all the construction of the bodily parts is arranged for one
aim; and the aim is the continuance of humanity in life. Therefore the
rest of the organs preserve the present life of men, others are appor-
tioned for another activity, through which the sensory and active
power is dispensed,[258] but the generative [organs] provide for the
future,[259] introducing through themselves the succession of nature.

(4) If, then, you look to what is necessary, which of the honorable [body parts] would be deemed to be secondary ones?[260] Which
would not be reasonably judged as more honorable? For it is not by
the eye, and ear, and tongue, or another one of the sensory [organs]

---

[255]Or "slander" (διαβολῆς), i.e., a specifically *false* charge.

[256]Lit. "demiurge"—a classical, not a biblical word, which suits the audience.

[257]Lit. "legislate" (νομοθετοῦσιν).

[258]The verb form of "economy" (οἰκονομεῖται); here used in a non-theological
sense.

[259]Lit. "have provision [πρόνοιαν—the same word can also mean 'providence']
for the future."

[260]Cf. 1 Cor 12.11–24.

γένος ἡμῶν διεξάγεται· [7]ταῦτα γάρ, καθὼς εἴρηται, τῆς παρούσης ἐστὶν ἀπολαύσεως, [8]ἀλλ᾽ ἐν ἐκείνοις ἡ ἀθανασία
35 συντηρεῖται τῇ ἀνθρωπότητι, [9]ὡς ἀεὶ καθ᾽ ἡμῶν ἐνεργοῦντα τὸν θάνατον [10]ἄπρακτον εἶναι τρόπον τινὰ καὶ ἀνήνυτον, πάντοτε πρὸς [11]τὸ λεῖπον διὰ τῶν ἐπιγινομένων ἑαυτὴν ἀντεισαγούσης [12]τῆς φύσεως. Τί οὖν ἀπρεπὲς περιέχει ἡμῶν τὸ μυστήριον, [13]εἰ διὰ τούτων κατεμίχθη ὁ Θεὸς τῷ ἀνθρωπίνῳ
40 βίῳ, δι᾽ ὧν [14]ἡ φύσις πρὸς τὸν θάνατον μάχεται;

(Sr 108) **ΚΘ᾽** [15]Ἀλλὰ μεταβάντες ἀπὸ τούτου δι᾽ ἑτέρων πάλιν | κακί-[16]ζειν ἐπιχειροῦσι τὸν λόγον καί φασιν· εἰ καλὸν καὶ πρέπον τῷ [17]Θεῷ τὸ γενόμενον, τί ἀνεβάλετο τὴν εὐεργεσίαν; Τί δὲ οὐκ [18]ἐν ἀρχαῖς οὔσης τῆς κακίας τὴν ἐπὶ τὸ πλέον αὐτῆς πρόοδον
5 [19]ὑπετέμετο;—

—(2) Πρὸς δὲ τοῦτο σύντομος ὁ παρ᾽ ἡμῶν ἐστι [20]λόγος
(PG 76) ὅτι σοφίᾳ | γέγονε καὶ τοῦ λυσιτελοῦντος τῇ φύσει [21]προμηθείᾳ ἡ πρὸς τὴν εὐεργεσίαν ἡμῶν ἀναβολή. Καὶ γὰρ [22]ἐπὶ τῶν σω-
(GNO 73) ματικῶν νοσημάτων, ὅταν τις διεφθορὼς χυμὸς | ὑφέρπῃ τοὺς πόρους, πρὶν ἅπαν ἐπὶ τὴν ἐπιφάνειαν ἐκκαλυφθῆναι [2]τὸ παρὰ
10 φύσιν ἐγκείμενον, οὐ καταφαρμακεύεται [3]τοῖς πυκνοῦσι τὸ σῶμα παρὰ τῶν τεχνικῶς μεθοδευόντων [4]τὰ πάθη, ἀλλ᾽ ἀναμένουσι τὸ ἐνδομυχοῦν ἅπαν [5]ἔξω γενέσθαι, καὶ οὕτω γυμνῷ τῷ πάθει τὴν ἰατρείαν προσάγουσιν. [6]Ἐπειδὴ τοίνυν ἅπαξ ἐνέσκηψε τῇ φύσει τῆς [7]ἀνθρωπότητος ἡ τῆς κακίας νόσος,
15 ἀνέμεινεν ὁ τοῦ παντὸς [8]θεραπευτὴς μηδὲν ὑπολειφθῆναι τῆς πονηρίας εἶδος [9]ἐγκεκρυμμένον τῇ φύσει.

that the continuation of our race is brought about. For these things, as has been said, belong to present enjoyment, but in those immortality is preserved for humanity, so that death, which is always acting against us, is in a certain manner of no avail and ineffectual, [since] nature is always thrusting itself into the breach through posterity. What unbefitting thing surrounds our mystery, if by these [organs] God was mixed with human life, through which nature battles death?

OBJECTION: *Why did God delay?*

29 But passing over this [objection] they take in hand different ones to reproach the account[261] again, and say: "If being born[262] was good and befitting for God, why did he postpone the benefit?[263] And why did he not cut off vice from its further progress while it was in [its] beginnings?"

RESPONSE: *For the healing to be effective, evil first had to run its course.*

(2) To this our concise argument is that the postponement of our benefit has happened by wisdom and forethought for what is profitable for [our] nature. For even in the case of bodily sicknesses, when some corrupt humor creeps in under the pores, those who skillfully treat diseases[264] do not prescribe drugs that close up the body before the unnatural secretion is entirely uncovered on the surface, but wait until what is lurking within becomes entirely external, and thus with the disease laid bare[265] they apply the healing. Thus accordingly once the sickness of vice fell upon the nature of humanity, the healer of all[266] waited until no form of wickedness remained hidden in [our] nature.

---

[261]Or "word" (λόγον), as in "the word of faith" or "the word of piety" (cf. 1.1).
[262]Or "what came to pass," "what happened" (τὸ γενόμενον).
[263]St Athanasius also addresses this objection in *Against the Arians* 1.29 and 2.68.
[264]Lit. "sufferings" (τὰ πάθη).
[265]Lit. "naked" (γυμνῷ).
[266]Or "of the universe" (τοῦ παντὸς).

—(3) Διὰ τοῦτο οὐκ εὐθὺς
(Sr 109) μετὰ | τὸν ₁₀φθόνον καὶ τὴν ἀδελφοκτονίαν τοῦ Κάϊν προσάγει
τῷ ₁₁ἀνθρώπῳ τὴν θεραπείαν· οὔπω γὰρ τῶν ἐπὶ Νῶε κατα-
φθαρέντων ₁₂ἡ κακία ἐξέλαμψεν, οὐδὲ τῆς Σοδομιτικῆς παρα-
20 νομίας ₁₃ἡ χαλεπὴ νόσος ἀπεκαλύφθη, οὐδὲ ἡ τῶν Αἰγυπτίων
₁₄θεομαχία, οὐδὲ ἡ τῶν Ἀσσυρίων ὑπερηφανία, οὐδὲ ἡ τῶν
₁₅Ἰουδαίων κατὰ τῶν ἁγίων τοῦ Θεοῦ μιαιφονία, οὐδὲ ἡ τοῦ
₁₆Ἡρῴδου παράνομος παιδοφονία, οὐδὲ τὰ ἄλλα πάντα ₁₇ὅσα τε
μνημονεύεται καὶ ὅσα ἔξω τῆς ἱστορίας ἐν ταῖς ₁₈καθεξῆς
25 γενεαῖς κατεπράχθη, πολυτρόπως τῆς τοῦ κακοῦ ₁₉ῥίζης ἐν ταῖς
τῶν ἀνθρώπων προαιρέσεσι βλαστανούσης. (4) ₂₀Ἐπεὶ οὖν πρὸς τὸ
(GNO 74) ἀκρότατον ἔφθασε μέτρον ἡ κακία, καὶ | οὐδὲν ἔτι πονηρίας
εἶδος ἐν τοῖς ἀνθρώποις ἀτόλμητον ἦν, ₂ὡς ἂν διὰ πάσης τῆς
ἀρρωστίας προχωρήσειεν ἡ θεραπεία, ₃τούτου χάριν οὐκ
30 ἀρχομένην, ἀλλὰ τελειωθεῖσαν ₄θεραπεύει τὴν νόσον.

Λ´   ₅Εἰ δέ τις ἐλέγχειν οἴεται τὸν ἡμέτερον λόγον, ὅτι καὶ
(Sr 110) ₆μετὰ τὸ προσαχθῆναι τὴν θεραπείαν ἔτι πλημ- | μελεῖται διὰ ₇τῶν
ἁμαρτημάτων ὁ ἀνθρώπινος βίος,—

—ὑποδείγματί τινι ₈τῶν γνω-
ρίμων ὁδηγηθήτω πρὸς τὴν ἀλήθειαν. Ὥσπερ γὰρ ₉ἐπὶ τοῦ
5 ὄφεως, εἰ κατὰ κεφαλῆς τὴν καιρίαν λάβοι, οὐκ ₁₀εὐθὺς συν-
νεκροῦται τῇ κεφαλῇ καὶ ὁ κατόπιν ὁλκός, ἀλλ' ₁₁ἡ μὲν τέθνηκε,

(3) Because of this he did not apply the healing to man immediately after the envy and fratricide of Cain;[267] for the vice of those
who were destroyed at the time of Noah had not yet burst forth,[268]
nor had the grievous sickness of the Sodomite lawlessness been
revealed,[269] nor the Egyptians' fight against God,[270] nor the arrogance of the Assyrians,[271] nor the Jews' bloodthirstiness against
God's saints,[272] nor Herod's lawless infanticide,[273] nor all the other
things that are remembered and all that were done outside the historical record in the following generations, the root of evil sprouting
diversely in the wills[274] of men. (4) When, then, vice reached the
uttermost measure, and no form of wickedness among men was
still unattempted, so that the healing might advance through all the
illness, for this reason he does not heal the sickness at the beginning,
but when it was completed.

OBJECTION: *Why has sin not ceased, if it was defeated?*

30 But if someone thinks to refute our account, [saying] that even
after the healing is applied, human life is still erring in sins,

RESPONSE: *The victory has been won; these are but the death
throes of vice.*

let him be guided to the truth by some illustration from well-known
things. For just as in the case of a snake, if it should receive a mortal
wound in the head, the hind coil does not also immediately die with
the head, but while the [head] is dead, the tail is still animate with

[267]Gen 4.1–15.
[268]Gen 6.1–6.
[269]Gen 18.20–20.29.
[270]Ex 1–15.
[271]Referring to the Assyrian captivity (2 Kg 15.29, 17.3–6, 18.11–12; 1 Chron 5.26).
In Isaiah the pride of Assyria is castigated (Is 10.12–19).
[272]Here "the saints" refers to the prophets. Cf. Mt 23.29–39; Lk 13.33–35; Acts
7.52; Heb 11.36–38; St Ignatius of Antioch, *Letter to the Magnesians* 8.1–2 and 9.2; the
apocryphal *Lives of the Prophets* may be the source of some of these traditions.
[273]Mt 2.16–18.
[274]Or "faculties of decision" (προαιρέσεσι).

τὸ δὲ οὐραῖον ἔτι ἐψύχωται τῷ ἰδίῳ θυμῷ ₁₂καὶ τῆς ζωτικῆς
κινήσεως οὐκ ἐστέρηται, οὕτως ἔστι καὶ ₁₃τὴν κακίαν ἰδεῖν τῷ
μὲν καιρίῳ πληγεῖσαν, ἐν δὲ τοῖς λειψάνοις ₁₄ἑαυτῆς ἔτι διο-
10 χλοῦσαν τὸν βίον.

(2) Ἀλλ' ἀφέντες καὶ ₁₅τὸ περὶ τούτων τὸν λόγον τοῦ μυστηρίου
μέμφεσθαι, τὸ μὴ ₁₆διὰ πάντων διήκειν τῶν ἀνθρώπων τὴν πίστιν ἐν αἰτίᾳ ₁₇ποιοῦνται. Καὶ τί δήποτε, φασίν, οὐκ ἐπὶ πάντας
(Sr 111) ἦλθεν ἡ ₁₈χάρις, ἀλλά | τινων προσθεμένων τῷ λόγῳ οὐ μικρόν
15 ἐστι ₁₉τὸ ὑπολειπόμενον μέρος, ἢ μὴ βουληθέντος τοῦ Θεοῦ
πᾶσιν ₂₀ἀφθόνως τὴν εὐεργεσίαν νεῖμαι ἢ μὴ δυνηθέντος
πάντως; ₂₁Ὧν οὐθέτερον καθαρεύει τῆς μέμψεως· οὔτε γὰρ
ἀβούλητον ₂₂εἶναι τὸ ἀγαθὸν προσήκει τῷ Θεῷ οὔτε ἀδύνατον.
Εἰ ₂₃οὖν ἀγαθόν τι ἡ πίστις, διὰ τί, φασίν, οὐκ ἐπὶ πάντας ἡ |
20 (GNO 75) χάρις;—

—(3) Εἰ μὲν οὖν ταῦτα καὶ παρ' ἡμῶν ἐν τῷ λόγῳ κατε-
₂σκευάζετο, τὸ παρὰ τοῦ θείου βουλήματος ἀποκληροῦσθαι ₃τοῖς
ἀνθρώποις τὴν πίστιν, τῶν μὲν καλουμένων, ₄τῶν δὲ λοιπῶν
(Sr 112) ἀμοιρούντων τῆς κλήσεως, καιρὸν εἶχε τὸ ₅τοιοῦτον ἔγ- | κλημα
κατὰ τοῦ μυστηρίου προφέρεσθαι· εἰ δὲ ₆ὁμότιμος ἐπὶ πάντας

23 εἶχε GNO : εἶχεν Srawley

its own spirit and is not deprived of vital motion, so too vice is seen to have been struck with a mortal wound, but in its remnants is still sorely vexing [our] life.

OBJECTION: *Why do all not believe?*

(2) But having given up complaining against the account of the mystery about these things, they regard as a fault the fact that the faith does not extend to all men. "And why in the world," it is said, "did grace not come to all, but while some assented to the word, the portion of those who were left behind is not small, either because God was not willing to bestow the benefit to all ungrudgingly or he was not at all able (neither of which is free from blame; for neither is it fitting for God to be unwilling [to do] the good nor [to be] unable)?[275] If, then, the faith is something good, why," it is said, "has grace not [come] to all?"

RESPONSE: *People have free will. Some choose not to believe.*

(3) If, then, these things were established by us in the discourse, that the faith is allotted to men by the divine will, some of whom are called, and the remainder have no portion in the calling, there would have been an opportunity for such an accusation to be brought against the mystery;[276] but if the calling is equal in honor for all, not

---

[275]Cf. Epicurus' classic argument: "God . . . either wishes to take away evils, and is unable; or He is able, and is unwilling; or He is neither willing nor able, or He is both willing and able. If He is willing and is unable, He is feeble, which is not in accordance with the character of God; if He is able and unwilling, He is envious, which is equally at variance with God; if He is neither willing nor able, He is both envious and feeble, and therefore not God; if He is both willing and able, which alone is suitable to God, from what source then are evils? or why does He not remove them?" Recorded in Lactantius, *On the Anger of God* 13.20–22 (ANF 7:271).

[276]St Justin Martyr defended free will with the same argument: "We have learned from the prophets, and we hold it to be true, that punishments, and chastisements, and good rewards, are rendered according to the merit of each man's actions. Since if it be not so, but all things happen by fate, neither is anything at all in our own power. For if it be fated that this man, e.g., be good, and this other evil, neither is the former meritorious nor the latter to be blamed. And again, unless the human race have the power of avoiding evil and choosing good by free choice, they are not accountable

25 (PG 77) ἡ κλῆσις, οὔτε ἀξίας, οὔτε ἡλικίας, ₇οὔτε τὰς κατὰ | τὰ ἔθνη διαφορὰς διακρίνουσα—διὰ τοῦτο ₈γὰρ παρὰ τὴν πρώτην ἀρχὴν τοῦ κηρύγματος ὁμόγλωσσοι ₉πᾶσι τοῖς ἔθνεσιν οἱ διακονοῦντες τὸν λόγον ἐκ θείας ₁₀ἐπιπνοίας ἀθρόως ἐγένοντο, ὡς ἂν μηδεὶς τῆς διδαχῆς ₁₁τῶν ἀγαθῶν ἀμοιρήσειε· πῶς ἂν
30 οὖν τις ἔτι κατὰ τὸ εὔλογον ₁₂τὸν Θεὸν αἰτιῷτο τοῦ μὴ πάντων ἐπικρατῆσαι τὸν λόγον;—
—(4) ₁₃Ὁ γὰρ τοῦ παντὸς τὴν ἐξουσίαν ἔχων δι' ὑπερβολὴν ₁₄τῆς εἰς τὸν ἄνθρωπον τιμῆς ἀφῆκέ τι καὶ ὑπὸ τὴν ἡμετέραν ₁₅ἐξουσίαν εἶναι, οὗ μόνος ἕκαστός ἐστι κύριος· τοῦτο δέ ₁₆ἐστιν ἡ προαίρεσις, ἀδούλωτόν τι χρῆμα καὶ αὐτεξούσιον,
35 ₁₇ἐν τῇ ἐλευθερίᾳ τῆς διανοίας κείμενον. Οὐκοῦν ἐπὶ τοὺς μὴ ₁₈προσαχθέντας τῇ πίστει δικαιότερον ἂν τὸ τοιοῦτον ἔγκλημα ₁₉μετατεθείη, οὐκ ἐπὶ τὸν κεκληκότα πρὸς συγκατάθεσιν. (5) ₂₀Οὐδὲ γὰρ ἐπὶ τοῦ Πέτρου κατ' ἀρχὰς τὸν λόγον ₂₁ἐν πολυανθρώπῳ τῶν Ἰουδαίων ἐκκλησίᾳ κηρύξαντος, ₂₂τρισχιλίων κατὰ ταὐτὸν
40 (Sr 113; παραδεξαμένων τὴν | πίστιν, πλεί- | ους ὄντες τῶν πεπιστευ-
GNO 76) κότων οἱ ἀπειθήσαντες ἐμέμψαντο ₂τὸν ἀπόστολον ἐφ' οἷς οὐκ ἐπείσθησαν. Οὐδὲ γὰρ ἦν εἰκός, ₃ἐν κοινῷ προτεθείσης τῆς χάριτος, τὸν ἑκουσίως ἀποφοιτήσαντα ₄μὴ ἑαυτόν, ἀλλ' ἕτερον τῆς δυσκληρίας ἐπαιτιᾶ- ₅σθαι.

---

29 ἀμοιρήσειε GNO : ἀμοιρήσειεν Srawley | 30 ἔτι after κατὰ τὸ εὔλογον Srawley

being distinguished by worth, nor age, nor differences of nationality—for because of this from the first beginning of the preaching, the ministers of the word were suddenly, by divine inspiration, speaking with the same tongue to all the nations,[277] so that no one might be without a portion of the good things of the teaching—how then can anyone still reasonably fault God that the word has not held sway over all?

(4) For he who has authority over the universe, because of the exceeding honor in which he held man, also left something to be under our authority, of which each [person] is the only master;[278] and this is the faculty of decision, something that is not enslaved and [is capable of] self-determination, lying in freedom of thought. Therefore it would be more just for such an accusation to be transferred to those who have not adhered to the faith, not to him who has called [them] to assent. (5) For when Peter preached the word at the beginning in the crowded assembly of Jews, when three thousand received the faith at the same time,[279] those who did not believe, who were more numerous than those who had believed, did not blame the apostle because he had not persuaded them. Nor was it likely, when grace was set forth before all,[280] for he who willingly deserted [grace] to accuse not himself, but another for [his] misfortune.

---

for their actions, of whatever kind they be." *First Apology* 43 (ANF 1:177). The early Church not only rejected pagan notions of fate (St Gregory himself wrote a work *Against Fate*), but also any form of irresistible predestination, though certain biblical passages could be construed this way (Origen goes through many of these passages in *On First Principles* 3.1, and St Gregory draws on some of these arguments in his *Life of Moses*). Augustine was the first person in Christian history to affirm such a notion of predestination, rather than to warn against this as a possible misconstrual of biblical texts.

[277]Cf. Acts 2.
[278]Or "lord" (κύριος).
[279]Acts 2.41.
[280]Lit. "in public" (ἐν κοινῷ).

ΛΑ΄ 6Ἀλλ᾿ οὐκ ἀποροῦσιν οὐδὲ πρὸς τὰ τοιαῦτα τῆς ἐρισ
τικῆς 7ἀντιλογίας. Λέγουσι γὰρ δύνασθαι τὸν Θεόν, εἴπερ 8ἐβού
λετο, καὶ τοὺς ἀντιτύπως ἔχοντας ἀναγκαστικῶς 9ἐφελκύ
σασθαι πρὸς τὴν παραδοχὴν τοῦ κηρύγματος.

5 Ποῦ 10τοίνυν ἐν τούτοις τὸ αὐτεξούσιον; Ποῦ δὲ ἡ ἀρετή;
Ποῦ δὲ 11τῶν κατορθούντων ὁ ἔπαινος; Μόνων γὰρ τῶν ἀψύχων
ἢ 12τῶν ἀλόγων ἐστὶ τῷ ἀλλοτρίῳ βουλήματι πρὸς τὸ δοκοῦν
13περιάγεσθαι, ἡ δὲ λογική τε καὶ νοερὰ φύσις, ἐὰν τὸ κατ᾿
14ἐξουσίαν ἀπόθηται, καὶ τὴν χάριν τοῦ νοεροῦ συναπώλεσεν.
10 15Εἰς τί γὰρ χρήσεται τῇ διανοίᾳ, τῆς τοῦ προαιρεῖσθαί 16τι τῶν
κατὰ γνώμην ἐξουσίας ἐφ᾿ ἑτέρῳ κειμένης;—

—(2) Εἰ δὲ 17ἄπρακτος ἡ
(Sr 114) προαίρεσις μείνειεν, ἠφάνισται | κατ᾿ ἀνάγκην 18ἡ ἀρετή, τῇ
ἀκινησίᾳ τῆς προαιρέσεως ἐμπεδηθεῖσα· ἀρετῆς 19δὲ μὴ οὔσης,
ὁ βίος ἠτίμωται, ἀφῄρηται τῶν κατορθούντων 20ὁ ἔπαινος, ἀκίν
15 δυνος ἡ ἁμαρτία, ἄκριτος ἡ κατὰ 21τὸν βίον διαφορά.

Τίς γὰρ ἂν ἔτι κατὰ τὸ εὔλογον ἢ διαβάλλοι 22τὸν ἀκόλαστον
(GNO 77) ἢ ἐπαινοίη τὸν σώφρονα; Ταύτης | κατὰ τὸ πρόχειρον οὔσης
ἑκάστῳ τῆς ἀποκρίσεως, τὸ 2μηδὲν ἐφ᾿ ἡμῖν τῶν κατὰ γνώμην
εἶναι, δυναστείᾳ δὲ 3κρείττονι τὰς ἀνθρωπίνας προαιρέσεις
20 πρὸς τὸ τῷ κρατοῦντι 4δοκοῦν περιάγεσθαι. Οὐκοῦν οὐ τῆς
ἀγαθότητος 5τοῦ Θεοῦ τὸ ἔγκλημα, τὸ μὴ πᾶσιν ἐγγενέσθαι τὴν
πίστιν, 6ἀλλὰ τῆς διαθέσεως τῶν δεχομένων τὸ κήρυγμα.

OBJECTION: *God could compel people to believe.*

31 But they are not at a loss for a contentious counterargument to such [claims]. For they say God, if he indeed willed it, was also able to draw by compulsion those who refused to receive the preaching.

RESPONSE: *Virtue is lost together with free will, and moral distinctions are confused.*

Where then is self-determination in these [circumstances]? Where is virtue? Where is praise for the upright? For it belongs only to inanimate or irrational things to be led around by an alien will to [its] purpose, and the rational and noetic nature, if it should lay aside [its] self-determination, destroys noetic grace along with it. For of what use will thought be if the authority to decide anything according to [one's] judgment[281] lies with someone else?

(2) And if the faculty of decision should remain impotent, virtue by necessity has been destroyed,[282] since it is impeded by the immobility of the faculty of decision; and when virtue does not exist, life has been dishonored, praise has been taken away from the upright, sin is without danger, [since] the difference in life is indistinguishable.

For who would still reasonably reject the incontinent or praise the chaste? [For] this answer is ready to hand for each: none of the things in accordance with [our] judgment are up to us, but by a superior power the human faculty of decision is led around to the purpose of him who holds sway. Therefore the accusation that the faith has not been engendered in all does not belong to God's goodness, but to the disposition of those who receive the preaching.

---

[281]Or "inclination," "will" (γνώμην).
[282]Or "has disappeared" (ἠφάνισται). Cf. Justin Martyr, *First Apology* 43.

ΛΒ' ₇Τί πρὸς τούτοις ἔτι παρὰ τῶν ἀντιλεγόντων προφέ-
(Sr 115) ρεται; ₈Τὸ μάλιστα μὲν μηδὲ ὅλως δεῖν εἰς θανάτου | πεῖραν
₉ἐλθεῖν τὴν ὑπερέχουσαν φύσιν, ἀλλὰ καὶ δίχα τούτου τῇ ₁₀πε-
ριουσίᾳ τῆς δυνάμεως δύνασθαι ἂν μετὰ ῥᾳστώνης τὸ ₁₁δοκοῦν
κατεργάσασθαι.—

5 (PG 80) —Εἰ δὲ καὶ πάν-| τως ἔδει τοῦτο γενέσθαι ₁₂κατά
τινα λόγον ἀπόρρητον, ἀλλ' οὖν τὸ μὴ τῷ ἀτίμῳ ₁₃τρόπῳ τοῦ
θανάτου καθυβρισθῆναι. Τίς γὰρ ἂν γένοιτο, ₁₄φησί, τοῦ διὰ
σταυροῦ θάνατος ἀτιμότερος;

(2) Τί οὖν καὶ ₁₅πρὸς ταῦτά φαμεν; Ὅτι τὸν θάνατον μὲν
10 ἀναγκαῖον ἡ γένεσις ₁₆ἀπεργάζεται. Τὸν γὰρ ἅπαξ μετασχεῖν
ἐγνωκότα τῆς ₁₇ἀνθρωπότητος διὰ πάντων ἔδει γενέσθαι τῶν
ἰδιωμάτων ₁₈τῆς φύσεως. Εἰ τοίνυν δύο πέρασι τῆς ἀνθρωπίνης
ζωῆς ₁₉διειλημμένης ἐν τῷ ἑνὶ γενόμενος τοῦ ἐφεξῆς μὴ προσήψατο, ₂₀ἡμιτελὴς ἂν ἡ πρόθεσις ἔμεινε, τοῦ ἑτέρου τῶν τῆς
15 ₂₁φύσεως ἡμῶν ἰδιωμάτων οὐχ ἁψαμένου.—

—(3) Τάχα δ' ἄν τις δι'
₂₂ἀκριβείας καταμαθὼν τὸ μυστήριον εὐλογώτερον εἴποι ₂₃μὴ διὰ
τὴν γένεσιν συμβεβηκέναι τὸν θάνατον, ἀλλὰ τὸ ₂₄ἔμπαλιν τοῦ
(Sr 116; θανάτου χάριν παραληφθῆναι τὴν | γένεσιν· οὐ | γὰρ τοῦ ζῆσαι
GNO 78) δεόμενος ὁ ἀεὶ ὢν τὴν σωματικὴν ὑποδύεται ₂γένεσιν, ἀλλ'
20 ἡμᾶς ἐπὶ τὴν ζωὴν ἐκ τοῦ θανάτου ₃ἀνακαλούμενος. Ἐπεὶ οὖν
ὅλης ἔδει γενέσθαι τῆς φύσεως ₄ἡμῶν τὴν ἐκ τοῦ θανάτου πάλιν

OBJECTION: *Christ could have accomplished our salvation without dying.*

32 What [objection] is still brought forth by the naysayers against these things? That, at best, it was not wholly necessary for the transcendent nature to come to the experience of death,[283] but even apart from this, [he] was able to accomplish [his] purpose with ease by an abundance of power.

OBJECTION: *If death was necessary, it did not need to be dishonorable.*

But even if it was altogether necessary for this to happen for some ineffable reason, at least he ought not to have been insulted by a dishonorable manner of death. For what death, it is said, would be more dishonorable than the one through the cross?

RESPONSE: *1) All of the properties of human nature must be assumed; 2) it is precisely his death that saves us from death; 3) the cross has a mystic and cosmic meaning.*

(2) What then do we say to these things? That birth makes death necessary. For he who had determined to partake of humanity once for all must pass through all the properties of [human] nature. If, then, since human life is embraced by two limits, while he came to be in one, he did not touch the subsequent [limit], his purpose would have remained half-finished, not having touched the other [limit] of the properties of our nature.

(3) But perhaps someone who studied the mystery with precision might more reasonably say that the death has not happened because of the birth, but on the contrary, the birth was accepted for the sake of the death; for the ever Existing One[284] did not plunge down into bodily birth because he was bound to live, but to recall us from death to life. Since, then, it was necessary for the whole of

---

[283]St Athanasius addressed the necessity for Christ's death in *On the Incarnation* 21–25.

[284]Cf. Ex 3.14 LXX.

ἐπάνοδον, οἱονεὶ χεῖρα τῷ ₅κειμένῳ ὀρέγων διὰ τοῦτο πρὸς τὸ ἡμέτερον ἐπικύψας ₆πτῶμα, τοσοῦτον τῷ θανάτῳ προσήγγισεν ὅσον τῆς νεκρότητος ₇ἅψασθαι καὶ ἀρχὴν δοῦναι τῇ φύσει τῆς ₂₅ ἀναστάσεως ₈τῷ ἰδίῳ σώματι, ὅλον τῇ δυνάμει συναναστήσας ₉τὸν ἄνθρωπον.

(4) Ἐπειδὴ γὰρ οὐκ ἄλλοθεν ἀλλ' ἐκ τοῦ ₁₀ἡμετέρου (Sr 117) φυράματος ὁ θεοδόχος ἄνθρωπος ἦν, ὁ διὰ | τῆς ₁₁ἀναστάσεως συνεπαρθεὶς τῇ θεότητι, ὥσπερ ἐπὶ τοῦ καθ' ₁₂ἡμᾶς σώματος ἡ τοῦ ἑνὸς τῶν αἰσθητηρίων ἐνέργεια πρὸς ₁₃πᾶσαν τὴν συναίσ- ₃₀ θησιν ἄγει τὸ ἡνωμένον τῷ μέρει, οὕτω ₁₄καθάπερ ἑνός τινος ὄντος ζῴου πάσης τῆς φύσεως, ἡ τοῦ ₁₅μέρους ἀνάστασις ἐπὶ τὸ πᾶν διεξέρχεται, κατὰ τὸ συνεχὲς ₁₆τε καὶ ἡνωμένον τῆς φύσεως ἐκ τοῦ μέρους ἐπὶ τὸ ὅλον ₁₇συνεκδιδομένη. Τί οὖν ἔξω τοῦ εἰκό- τος ἐν τῷ μυστηρίῳ ₁₈μανθάνομεν, εἰ κύπτει πρὸς τὸν πεπτω- ₃₅ κότα ὁ ἑστὼς ἐπὶ ₁₉τὸ ἀνορθῶσαι τὸν κείμενον;

(GNO 79) Ὁ δὲ σταυρὸς εἰ μέν τινα καὶ | ἕτερον περιέχει λόγον βαθύ- τερον, εἰδεῖεν ἂν οἱ τῶν κρυπτῶν ₂ἐπιΐστορες· ὃ δ' οὖν εἰς ἡμᾶς (Sr 118) ἐκ | παραδόσεως ἥκει, ₃τοιοῦτόν ἐστιν.

30 οὕτω GNO : οὕτως Srawley

our nature to return again from death, as if stretching out a hand to him who lay prostrate, by this bending down to our fallen corpse, he came so near to death as to touch death itself,[285] and to give to [our] nature the principle[286] of the resurrection in his own body, raising up with himself[287] the whole man[288] by [his] power.

(4) For since the God-receiving man,[289] who by the resurrection was raised to the divinity,[290] was not from anything else, but from our stock,[291] just as in the case of our body, the activity of one of the sensory organs leads to a joint sensation[292] with all that is united to [that] part, so, just as if all [our] nature were some one living being, the resurrection of the part passes through to all, distributing from the part to the whole, in accordance with the continuity and unity of nature. What then do we learn in the mystery that is beyond likelihood, if he who is standing bends to him who had fallen in order to set upright him who lay prostrate?

The Mystical Cross

But the cross, if it also embraces some other and deeper meaning,[293] those who are well-versed in hidden things might know; but what has come down to us from tradition is this.

[285]Or "the state of being dead," "mortality" (νεκρότητος).

[286]Or "beginning" (ἀρχὴν).

[287]Lit. "co-resurrecting" (συναναστήσας).

[288]On the concept of the "whole man" in St Gregory, along with its connection to notions of a "double creation," see *On the Making of Man* 16.16–18.

[289]I.e., Christ. See p. 102, n. 168 above.

[290]Cf. *Against Eunomius* 3.3, where St Gregory interprets Acts 2.33 as meaning that Christ was raised by the right hand of God, which he himself is, i.e., he raised himself (the dative "right hand" [τῇ δεξιᾷ] is taken by virtually all other readers and translators as locative: "exalted at [or 'to'] the right hand of God" rather than, as Gregory does, as an instrumental dative: "*by* the right hand").

[291]Lit. "lump" (φυράματος), cf. Rom 9.20 and 11.16; 1 Cor 5.7.

[292]This is an allusion to Aristotle's concept of "common sense" (*On the Soul* 3.1, especially 425a27), the mind's capacity to assimilate and categorize the disparate data of the five senses in one united and "common" perception.

[293]λόγον (or "word"). Cf. 1 Cor 1.18. On the deeper, or mystical meaning of the cross, see St Athanasius, *On the Incarnation* 25.

(5) Ἐπειδὴ πάντα κατὰ τὸν ὑψηλότερόν τε καὶ ₄θειότερον λόγον
40 ἐν τῷ εὐαγγελίῳ καὶ εἴρηται καὶ γεγένηται, ₅καὶ οὐκ ἔστιν τι ὅ
τι μὴ τοιοῦτόν ἐστιν, ᾧ οὐχὶ πάντως ₆μίξις τις ἐμφαίνεται τοῦ
θείου πρὸς τὸ ἀνθρώπινον, τῆς ₇μὲν φωνῆς ἢ τῆς πράξεως ἀν-
θρωπικῶς διεξαγομένης, τοῦ ₈δὲ κατὰ τὸ κρυπτὸν νοουμένου τὸ
θεῖον ἐμφαίνοντος, ₉ἀκόλουθον ἂν εἴη καὶ ἐν τῷ μέρει τούτῳ μὴ
45 τὸ μὲν βλέπειν, ₁₀παρορᾶν δὲ τὸ ἕτερον, ἀλλ᾽ ἐν μὲν τῷ θανάτῳ
καθορᾶν τὸ ₁₁ἀνθρώπινον, ἐν δὲ τῷ τρόπῳ πολυπραγμονεῖν τὸ
θειότερον.

(6) ₁₂Ἐπειδὴ γὰρ ἴδιόν ἐστι τῆς θεότητος τὸ διὰ πάντων ₁₃ἥκειν
καὶ τῇ φύσει τῶν ὄντων κατὰ πᾶν μέρος συμπαρεκτείνεσθαι
50 (Sr 119) —₁₄οὐ γὰρ ἄν τι διαμένοι | ἐν τῷ εἶναι, μὴ ἐν τῷ ὄντι ₁₅μένον· τὸ
δὲ κυρίως καὶ πρώτως ὂν ἡ θεία φύσις ἐστίν, ἣν ₁₆ἐξ ἀνάγκης
πιστεύειν ἐν πᾶσιν εἶναι τοῖς οὖσιν ἡ διαμονὴ ₁₇τῶν ὄντων
καταναγκάζει—τοῦτο διὰ τοῦ σταυροῦ διδασκόμεθα, ₁₈τετρα-
χῇ τοῦ κατ᾽ αὐτὸν σχήματος διῃρημένου, ₁₉ὡς ἐκ τοῦ μέσου καθ᾽
55 ὃ πρὸς ἑαυτὸν συνάπτεται, τέσσαρας ₂₀ἀριθμεῖσθαι τὰς προβο-
λάς, ὅτι ὁ ἐπὶ τούτου ἐν τῷ καιρῷ ₂₁τῆς κατὰ τὸν θάνατον
οἰκονομίας διαταθείς, ὁ τὸ πᾶν ₂₂πρὸς ἑαυτὸν συνδέων τε καὶ
(PG 81; συναρμόζων ἐστί, τὰς | διαφό- | ρους τῶν ὄντων φύσεις πρὸς
GNO 80) μίαν σύμπνοιάν τε καὶ ἁρμονίαν ₂δι᾽ ἑαυτοῦ συνάγων. (7) Ἐν γὰρ
60 τοῖς οὖσιν ἢ ἄνω τι νοεῖται, ₃ἢ κάτω, ἢ πρὸς τὰ κατὰ τὸ πλάγιον
(Sr 120) πέρατα διαβαίνει ἡ ἔννοια. ₄Ἂν τοίνυν λογίσῃ | τῶν ἐπουρανίων ἢ
τῶν ὑποχθονίων ₅ἢ τῶν καθ᾽ ἑκάτερον τοῦ παντὸς περάτων τὴν
σύστασιν, ₆πανταχοῦ τῷ λογισμῷ σου προαπαντᾷ ἡ θεότης,
μόνη ₇κατὰ πᾶν μέρος τοῖς οὖσιν ἐνθεωρουμένη καὶ ἐν τῷ εἶναι
65 ₈τὰ πάντα συνέχουσα.—

—(8) Εἴτε δὲ θεότητα τὴν φύσιν ταύτην
₉ὀνομάζεσθαι χρή, εἴτε λόγον, εἴτε δύναμιν, εἴτε σοφίαν, εἴτε

---

(5) Since all things in the gospel, both what has been said and what has happened, [have] a loftier and more divine meaning,[294] and there is nothing that is not like this, which is not altogether shown as some mixture of the divine with the human, the voice or action proceeding humanly, but the hidden understanding showing the divine, it would also follow the order in this part [of the gospel] not to look at one aspect while overlooking the other, but seeing what is human in the death, to take care to seek what is more divine in the manner [of his death].

(6) For since it is a property of the divinity to be present through all things and to extend through the nature of existing things in every part—for nothing would remain in existence if it did not remain in being; and being, properly and primarily, is the divine nature, which the permanence of existing things constrains one to believe by necessity is in all existing things—we are taught this by the cross—whose shape is divided in four parts, so that the projections, four in number, come into contact with itself in the middle—that he who was stretched upon this at the time of the economy of death is he who binds and frames the universe to himself, by himself bringing the different natures of existing things into one accord and harmony. (7) For among existing things, something is thought of above or below, or thought passes sideways to the limits. Therefore, if you take into account[295] the constitution of heavenly things or the things beneath the earth or those at either of the [lateral] limits of the universe,[296] everywhere the divinity meets your thought in advance, who alone is contemplated in existing things in every part, and who holds all things together in existence.

(8) And whether this nature ought to be named "divinity," or "Word," or "Power," or "Wisdom," or any other of the lofty [titles]

[294]λόγον.
[295]λογίσῃ.
[296]Here the image is not the geocentric Hellenic model of heavenly spheres surrounding the globe of the earth, but a more Old Testament poetic image of heaven above, hades beneath the earth, and the lateral extremes of the (horizontal, "flat") earth. In short, it is a cruciform vision: above, below, and to the sides.

[10]ἄλλο τι τῶν ὑψηλῶν τε καὶ μᾶλλον ἐνδείξασθαι δυναμένων [11]τὸ ὑπερκείμενον, οὐδὲν ὁ λόγος ἡμῶν περὶ φωνῆς ἢ [12]ὀνόματος ἢ τύπου ῥημάτων διαφέρεται. Ἐπεὶ οὖν πᾶσα [13]πρὸς αὐτὸν ἡ κτί-
70 σις βλέπει, καὶ περὶ αὐτόν ἐστι, καὶ δι' [14]ἐκείνου πρὸς ἑαυτὴν συμφυὴς γίνεται, τῶν ἄνω τοῖς κάτω [15]καὶ τῶν πλαγίων πρὸς ἄλληλα δι' ἐκείνου συμφυομένων, [16]ἔδει μὴ μόνον δι' ἀκοῆς ἡμᾶς πρὸς τὴν τῆς θεότητος [17]κατανόησιν χειραγωγεῖσθαι, ἀλλὰ καὶ τὴν ὄψιν γενέσθαι [18]τῶν ὑψηλοτέρων νοημάτων διδάσκαλον,
75 ὅθεν καὶ ὁ μέγας [19]ὁρμηθεὶς Παῦλος μυσταγωγεῖ τὸν ἐν Ἐφέσῳ λαόν, δύναμιν [20]αὐτοῖς ἐντιθεὶς διὰ τῆς διδασκαλίας πρὸς τὸ γνῶναι Τί [21]ἐστι τὸ βάθος καὶ τὸ ὕψος, τό τε πλάτος καὶ τὸ
(Sr 121) μῆκος. (9) Ἑκάστην [22]γὰρ τοῦ σταυροῦ προβολὴν ἰδίῳ | ῥήματι κατονομάζει, [23]ὕψος μὲν τὸ ὑπερέχον, βάθος δὲ τὸ ὑποκείμενον,
80 (GNO 81) πλάτος | τε καὶ μῆκος τὰς πλαγίας ἐκτάσεις λέγων. Καὶ σαφέστερον [2]ἑτέρωθι τὸ τοιοῦτον νόημα πρὸς Φιλιππησίους, οἶμαι, [3]ποιεῖ οἷς φησιν ὅτι Ἐν τῷ ὀνόματι Ἰησοῦ Χριστοῦ πᾶν [4]γόνυ κάμψει ἐπουρανίων καὶ ἐπιγείων καὶ καταχθονίων. [5]Ἐνταῦθα τὴν μέσην κεραίαν μιᾷ προσηγορίᾳ διαλαμβάνει,
85 [6]πᾶν τὸ διὰ μέσου τῶν ἐπουρανίων καὶ ὑποχθονίων ὀνομάσας [7]ἐπίγειον. (10) Τοῦτο μεμαθήκαμεν περὶ τοῦ σταυροῦ τὸ [8]μυστήριον.

Τὰ δὲ ἀπὸ τούτου τοιαῦτα κατὰ τὸ ἀκόλουθον [9]περιέχει ὁ λόγος, ὡς ὁμολογεῖσθαι καὶ παρὰ τῶν ἀπίστων [10]μηδὲν ἀλλό-
90 τριον εἶναι τῆς θεοπρεποῦς ὑπολήψεως. Τὸ [11]γὰρ μὴ ἐμμεῖναι τῷ θανάτῳ, καὶ τὰς διὰ τοῦ σιδήρου κατὰ [12]τοῦ σώματος

that are more able to indicate the transcendent, our discourse[297] makes no dispute about the expression or name or type of utterance. Since, then, all creation looks to him, and is about him, and through him has an innate affinity with itself, through him the things above having an innate affinity with the things below and those to the sides with each other, it was necessary not only to be guided[298] to an understanding of the divinity by our hearing, but that sight should also be a teacher of loftier thoughts, whence also the great Paul begins when he initiates[299] the people in Ephesus, through his teaching implanting in them the power to come to know "What is the depth and the height, the breadth and length."[300] (9) For each projection of the cross is named by its proper predication, calling "height" what rises above, and "depth" what lies below, both "length" and "breadth" what extends to the sides. And elsewhere, I think, he makes such a thought clearer to the Philippians, to whom he says that "at the name of Jesus Christ every knee will bow, of things in heaven, and things on earth, and things under the earth."[301] There in one designation he distinguishes the middle beam, naming "things on earth" all that is in the middle of the "things in heaven" and the "things under the earth." (10) This is the mystery we have learned about the cross.

The account contains such things in order after this that it is admitted even by the unbelievers that there is nothing alien to a God-befitting supposition. For he did not remain in death, and the

[297]Or "argument," "account" (λόγος).

[298]Lit. "led by the hand" (χειραγωγεῖσθαι).

[299]μυσταγωγεῖ, the verb form of "mystagogy" (μυσταγωγία). In the ancient Church, mystagogy completed the process of catechesis: after candidates were baptized, chrismated, and received the Eucharist for the first time, a series of homilies explained the sacraments' deeper meaning. This is the end of the proof section of the *Discourse*. The conclusion deals with the same subject matter as mystagogy proper (though here Gregory once more fields objections and engages in what appears to be apologetics, whereas traditional mystagogy is the instruction of the newly illumined in the meaning of the mysteries into which they had just been initiated).

[300]Eph 3.18.

[301]Phil 2.10. In Philippians, St Paul uses the subjunctive "every knee *should* bow" (κάμψῃ), but St Gregory uses future indicative: "every knee *will* bow" (κάμψει).

γενομένας πληγὰς μηδὲν ἐμπόδιον πρὸς τὸ $_{13}$εἶναι ποιήσασθαι,
κατ' ἐξουσίαν τε φαίνεσθαι μετὰ τὴν $_{14}$ἀνάστασιν τοῖς μαθη-
ταῖς, ὅτε βούλοιτο παρεῖναί τε αὐτοῖς $_{15}$μὴ ὁρώμενον καὶ ἐν
(Sr 122) μέσῳ | γίνεσθαι, μηδὲ τῆς εἰσόδου $_{16}$τῆς διὰ τῶν θυρῶν
95 προσδεόμενον, ἐνισχύειν τε τοὺς μαθητὰς $_{17}$τῇ προσφυσήσει τοῦ
Πνεύματος, ἐπαγγέλλεσθαί τε καὶ τὸ $_{18}$μετ' αὐτῶν εἶναι, καὶ
μηδενὶ μέσῳ διατειχίζεσθαι, καὶ τῷ $_{19}$μὲν φαινομένῳ πρὸς τὸν
οὐρανὸν ἀνιέναι, τῷ δὲ νοουμένῳ $_{20}$πανταχοῦ εἶναι, καὶ ὅσα
τοιαῦτα περιέχει ἡ ἱστορία, οὐδὲν $_{21}$τῆς ἐκ τῶν λογισμῶν
100 συμμαχίας προσδέεται πρὸς τὸ θεῖά $_{22}$τε εἶναι καὶ τῆς ὑψηλῆς
καὶ ὑπερεχούσης δυνάμεως. (11) Περὶ $_{23}$ὧν οὐδὲν οἶμαι δεῖν καθ'
ἕκαστον διεξιέναι, αὐτόθεν τοῦ $_{24}$λόγου τὸ ὑπὲρ τὴν φύσιν
ἐμφαίνοντος. |—
(GNO 82) —Ἀλλ' ἐπειδὴ μέρος τι τῶν μυστικῶν διδαγμά-
(PG 84) των καὶ ἡ $_{2}$κατὰ τὸ λουτρόν ἐστιν οἰ-| κονομία, ὃ εἴτε βάπτισμα,
105 εἴτε $_{3}$φώτισμα, εἴτε παλιγγενεσίαν βούλοιτό τις ὀνομάζειν,
οὐδὲν $_{4}$πρὸς τὴν ὀνομασίαν διαφερόμεθα, καλῶς ἂν ἔχοι καὶ
$_{5}$περὶ τούτου βραχέα διεξελθεῖν. |

---

94 γίνεσθαι GNO : γίγνεσθαι Srawley | μηδὲ GNO : μηδὲν Srawley

blows to [his] body with the iron[302] made no impediment to [his] existence, [and] after the resurrection he appeared to the disciples at will, when he wanted he was present with them and was in [their] midst unseen, not needing to enter through the doors, strengthening the disciples by breathing the Spirit,[303] promising to be with them,[304] and that nothing would separate [him from their] midst, and to the senses[305] going up to heaven,[306] while being everywhere present to the mind, and all such things that the history contains need no alliance from arguments to show them to be divine and belonging to the lofty and transcendent power. (11) There is no need to go through each of them in detail, I think, since the account itself is shown to be above nature.

But since the economy of washing[307]—which, whether one should want to call it baptism, or illumination, or regeneration, we make no dispute about the naming—is also some part of the mystic[308] teaching, it would be good to go through this shortly also.

---

[302]I.e., the nails and the spear at Christ's crucifixion.

[303]Jn 20.22.

[304]Mt 28.20.

[305]Lit. "in appearance" (φαινομένῳ), i.e., what is apparent "to the senses" (not in *mere* appearance).

[306]Lk 24.51; Acts 1.9–11.

[307]Tit 3.5.

[308]Or "sacramental" (μυστικῶν); perhaps "hidden" in the sense of the *disciplina arcani* (in the ancient Church, the sacraments were often not explained or discussed before a catechumen was initiated).

Δ'

(Sr 123) ΛΓ' Ἐπειδὰν γὰρ παρ' ἡμῶν τὸ ₆τοιοῦτον ἀκούσωσιν, ὅτι τοῦ θνητοῦ πρὸς τὴν ζωὴν μεταβαίνοντος, ₇ἀκόλουθον ἦν τῆς πρώτης γενέσεως ἐπὶ τὸν ₈θνητὸν παραγούσης βίον ἑτέραν γένεσιν ἐξευρεθῆναι, ₉μήτε ἀπὸ φθορᾶς ἀρχομένην, μήτε εἰς
5 φθορὰν καταλήγουσαν, ₁₀ἀλλ' εἰς ἀθάνατον ζωὴν τὸν γεγεννημένον παράγουσαν, ₁₁ἵν', ὥσπερ ἐκ θνητῆς γενέσεως θνητὸν ἐξ ἀνάγκης τὸ ₁₂γεγεννημένον ὑπέστη, οὕτως ἐκ τῆς μὴ παραδεχομένης ₁₃φθορὰν τὸ γεννώμενον κρεῖττον γένηται τῆς ἐκ τοῦ ₁₄θανάτου φθορᾶς· ἐπειδὰν οὖν τούτων καὶ τῶν τοιούτων ₁₅ἀκού-
10 σωσι καὶ προδιδαχθῶσι τὸν τρόπον, ὅτι εὐχὴ πρὸς ₁₆Θεόν, καὶ
(Sr 124) χάριτος οὐρανίας ἐπίκλησις, καὶ | ὕδωρ, καὶ πίστις ₁₇ἐστὶ δι' ὧν τὸ τῆς ἀναγεννήσεως πληροῦται μυστήριον, ₁₈δυσπειθῶς ἔχουσι πρὸς τὸ φαινόμενον βλέποντες, ὡς οὐ ₁₉συμβαῖνον τῇ ἐπαγγελίᾳ τὸ σωματικῶς ἐνεργούμενον. ₂₀Πῶς γάρ, φασίν, εὐχὴ καὶ δυνά-
15 μεως θείας ἐπίκλησις ἐπὶ ₂₁τοῦ ὕδατος γινομένη ζωῆς ἀρχηγὸς τοῖς μυηθεῖσι γίνεται;

10 ἀκούσωσι GNO : ἀκούσωσιν Srawley

PART 4

CONCLUSION

Baptism and the Eucharist

OBJECTION: *How do prayer and calling upon the divine power become the beginning of new and incorruptible life for those who are baptized?*

33 For when [the unbelievers] hear something like this from us, that when the mortal passed into life, it followed[309] that, since the first birth led to mortal life, another birth should be discovered, neither having its beginning from corruption nor ending in corruption, but leading him who has been begotten to immortal life, in order that, just as one who has been begotten by a mortal by necessity subsists as a mortal, so he who is begotten by one who does not admit of corruption becomes superior to the corruption of death—when, then, they hear of these things and the like, and have been taught beforehand the manner [of rebirth], that prayer to God, and calling upon[310] heavenly grace, and water, and faith are the things through which the mystery of regeneration is fulfilled, they are incredulous, since they look at the [outward] appearance, on the ground that the bodily activity does not correspond with the promise. For how, they say, do prayer and calling upon the divine power, performed over water, become the beginning of life to those who are initiated?

---

[309]Or "was in order" (ἀκόλουθον ἦν). This has logical, not only temporal force.

[310]ἐπίκλησις (*epiklēsis*), the word translated as "calling upon," came to be a technical term in later sacramental theology, referring to the act of calling down the Holy Spirit to change the bread and wine into Christ's body and blood in the divine liturgy.

—(2) ₂₂Πρὸς οὕς, εἴπερ μὴ λίαν ἔχοιεν ἀντιτύπως, ἁπλοῦς ἐξαρκεῖ ₂₃λόγος πρὸς τὴν τοῦ δόγματος ἀγαγεῖν συγκατάθεσιν. Ἀντερωτήσωμεν ₂₄γὰρ περὶ τοῦ τρόπου

(GNO 83) τῆς κατὰ σάρκα γεν- | νήσεως τοῦ πᾶσιν ὄντος προδήλου, πῶς

20 ἄνθρωπος ἐκεῖνο ₂γίνεται τὸ εἰς ἀφορμὴν τῆς συστάσεως τοῦ ζῴου καταβαλλόμενον. ₃Ἀλλὰ μὴν οὐδεὶς ἐπ' ἐκείνου λόγος ἐστὶν ὁ λογισμῷ ₄τινὶ τὸ πιθανὸν ἐφευρίσκων. Τί γὰρ κοινὸν

(Sr 125) ἔχει ὅρος ₅ἀνθρώπου πρὸς τὴν ἐν ἐκείνῳ θεωρουμένην | ποιότητα συγκρινόμενος; ₆Ἄνθρωπος λογικόν τι χρῆμα καὶ διανοητικόν

25 ₇ἐστι, νοῦ καὶ ἐπιστήμης δεκτικόν, ἐκεῖνο δὲ ὑγρᾷ τινι ἐνθεωρεῖται ₈ποιότητι, καὶ πλέον οὐδὲν τοῦ κατ' αἴσθησιν ₉ὁρωμένου καταλαμβάνει ἡ ἔννοια.—

—(3) Ἦν τοίνυν εἰκός ἐστιν ₁₀ἀπόκρισιν ἡμῖν γίνεσθαι παρὰ τῶν ἐρωτηθέντων ὅτι πῶς ₁₁ἐστι πιστὸν ἐξ ἐκείνου συστῆναι ἄνθρωπον, τοῦτο καὶ περὶ ₁₂τῆς διὰ τοῦ ὕδατος

30 γινομένης ἀναγεννήσεως ἐρωτηθέντες ₁₃ἀποκρινούμεθα. Ἐκεῖ τε γὰρ πρόχειρόν ἐστιν ἑκάστῳ τῶν ₁₄ἠρωτημένων εἰπεῖν ὅτι θείᾳ δυνάμει ἐκεῖνο ἄνθρωπος γίνεται, ₁₅ἧς μὴ παρούσης ἀκίνητόν ἐστιν ἐκεῖνο καὶ ἀνενέργητον. ₁₆Εἰ οὖν ἐκεῖ οὐ τὸ ὑποκείμενον ποιεῖ τὸν ἄνθρωπον, ₁₇ἀλλ' ἡ θεία δύναμις πρὸς ἀνθρώπου

35 φύσιν μεταποιεῖ τὸ ₁₈φαινόμενον, τῆς ἐσχάτης ἂν εἴη ἀγνωμοσύνης ἐκεῖ τοσαύτην ₁₉τῷ Θεῷ προσμαρτυροῦντας δύναμιν ἀτονεῖν ἐν τῷ ₂₀μέρει τούτῳ τὸ θεῖον οἴεσθαι πρὸς τὴν ἐκπλήρωσιν τοῦ ₂₁θελήματος.—

—(4) Τί κοινόν, φασίν, ὕδατι καὶ ζωῇ; Τί δὲ

(Sr 126) κοινόν, ₂₂πρὸς αὐτοὺς ἐροῦμεν, ὑγρότητι καὶ εἰκόνι Θεοῦ; | Ἀλλ'

40 (GNO 84) | οὐδὲν ἐκεῖ τὸ παράδοξον, εἰ Θεοῦ βουλομένου πρὸς τὸ ₂τιμιώ-

---

19 Srawley omits τοῦ | 26 πλέον GNO : πλεῖον Srawley | 28 γίνεσθαι GNO : γενέσθαι Srawley

RESPONSE: *Baptism is as comprehensible and incomprehensible as biological reproduction: if you believe in the latter, why not the former?*

(2) To these, unless they should be exceedingly stubborn, a simple argument suffices to lead them to assent to the teaching. For let us ask them in turn about the manner of carnal begetting, which is clear to all, how that which is sown for the origin of the composition of a living thing[311] becomes a man. But surely in that case, no account discovers a credible [explanation] by any sort of reasoning. For, when comparing [the two], what does the definition of man have in common with the quality contemplated in that [i.e., seed]? Man is something rational and intellectual, capable of thought and knowledge, but that [seed] is seen with a certain wet quality, and thought grasps nothing more than what is seen by the senses.

(3) The answer, then, which is likely to be given to us by those who were asked how it is believable that man is constituted from that, is this, which we will also answer when asked about the regeneration that comes about through water. For in that case, [the answer] is ready to hand for each of those who are asked, to say that by divine power that [seed] becomes a man, which, when it is not present, it is unchanged[312] and inactive. If, then, in that case, the underlying [matter][313] does not make man, but divine power remakes the visible[314] [matter] into human nature, it would be the uttermost foolishness when in that case they testify to such a power in God, to think the divine is too weak to fulfill [his] will in this matter.

(4) "What," they say, "does water have in common with life?" "But what," we ask them, "does wetness have in common with the image of God?" But in that case it is no surprise if, when God wills,

---

[311]"That which is sown for the beginning of the constitution of a living thing" refers to human seed. The same argument is used in Gregory's *On the Baptism of Christ* (NPNF² 5:520).

[312]Or "motionless" (ἀκίνητόν). See p. 100, n. 164.

[313]Or simply "matter" (ὑποκείμενον in an Aristotelian sense).

[314]Lit. "what is apparent" (τὸ φαινόμενον), meaning here "what is apparent" to the senses.

τατον ζῷον τὸ ὑγρὸν μεταβαίνει. Τὸ ἴσον καὶ ἐπὶ τούτου ₃φαμὲν
μηδὲν εἶναι θαυμαστόν, εἰ θείας δυνάμεως ₄παρουσία πρὸς
ἀφθαρσίαν μετασκευάζει τὸ ἐν τῇ φθαρτῇ ₅φύσει γενόμενον.|

(PG 85) ΛΔ'   ₆Ἀλλὰ ζητοῦσιν ἀπόδειξιν τοῦ παρεῖναι τὸ θεῖον ἐπὶ
₇ἁγιασμῷ τῶν γινομένων καλούμενον.—

—Ὁ δὲ τοῦτο ζητῶν ₈ἀνα-
γνώτω πάλιν τὰ κατόπιν ἐξητασμένα. Ἡ γὰρ κατασκευὴ ₉τοῦ
τὴν διὰ σαρκὸς ἡμῖν ἐπιφανεῖσαν δύναμιν ἀληθῶς ₁₀θείαν εἶναι
5 τοῦ παρόντος λόγου συνηγορία γίνεται·—
                                           —(2) ₁₁δειχθέντος γὰρ τοῦ
(Sr 127) Θεὸν εἶναι τὸν ἐν σαρκὶ φανερωθέντα, | ₁₂τοῖς διὰ τῶν γινομένων
θαύμασι τὴν φύσιν ἑαυτοῦ δείξαντα, ₁₃συναπεδείχθη τὸ παρεῖναι
τοῖς γινομένοις αὐτὸν κατὰ ₁₄πάντα καιρὸν ἐπικλήσεως. Ὥσπερ
γὰρ ἑκάστου τῶν ὄντων ₁₅ἔστι τις ἰδιότης ἡ τὴν φύσιν γνωρί-
10 ζουσα, οὕτως ἴδιον ₁₆τῆς θείας φύσεώς ἐστιν ἡ ἀλήθεια. Ἀλλὰ
μὴν ἀεὶ παρέσεσθαι ₁₇τοῖς ἐπικαλουμένοις ἐπήγγελται, καὶ ἐν
μέσῳ τῶν ₁₈πιστευόντων εἶναι, καὶ ἐν πᾶσι μένειν, καὶ ἑκάστῳ
συνεῖναι.—
            —₁₉Οὐκέτ' ἂν ἑτέρας εἰς τὸ παρεῖναι τὸ θεῖον τοῖς γινο-
μένοις ₂₀ἀποδείξεως προσδεοίμεθα, τὸ μὲν Θεὸν εἶναι διὰ τῶν
15 ₂₁θαυμάτων αὐτῶν πεπιστευκότες, ἴδιον δὲ τῆς θεότητος τὸ |
(GNO 85) ἀμίκτως πρὸς τὸ ψεῦδος ἔχειν εἰδότες, ἐν δὲ τῷ ἀψευδεῖ ₂τῆς

13 οὖν after Οὐκέτ' Srawley

he changes the wet [seed] into the most honorable living thing. Likewise also in this case we say that it is nothing wonderful if the presence of the divine power refashions what was born in corruptible nature into incorruption.

OBJECTION: *What proof is there of the divine presence when it is called upon in the rite of baptism?*

34 But they seek a demonstration that the divine is present when it is called upon for the sanctification of what takes place [in baptism].

RESPONSE: *Christ is divine, and he promised the divine presence is found in baptism. Since he is God, his promise is to be trusted.*

Now let him who asks this again remember [our] earlier inquiries. For the proof[315] [we gave] that the power manifested to us through the flesh is truly divine is an aid to the present argument.

(2) For when it was demonstrated that he who was manifested in the flesh is God,[316] demonstrating his own nature by the wonders that took place, along with this it was demonstrated that he is present in the things that take place every time he is called upon. For just as for each of the things that exist there is some property that is the distinguishing mark of its nature, so truth is a property of the divine nature. But surely he has promised always to be present with those who call upon [him],[317] and to be in the midst of those who believe,[318] and to abide with all,[319] and to be with each one.[320]

We shall no longer need another demonstration of the divine presence in what takes place [in baptism], if we have believed that he is God because of the wonders themselves, and have known that it is a property of the divinity to have no mingling with falsehood,

---

[315]Here Gregory again uses the rhetorical term for "proof" (κατασκευὴ). See p. 60, n. 6.
[316]Cf. 1 Tim 3.16.
[317]Mt 28.20.
[318]Mt 18.20.
[319]Jn 15.4.
[320]Jn 14.23.

ὑποσχέσεως παρεῖναι τὸ ἐπηγγελμένον οὐκ ἀμφιβάλλοντες.

(Sr 128) (3) $_3$Τὸ δὲ προηγεῖσθαι τὴν διὰ | τῆς εὐχῆς κλῆσιν τῆς $_4$θείας οἰκο-
νομίας περιουσία τίς ἐστι τῆς ἀποδείξεως τοῦ $_5$κατὰ Θεὸν
20 ἐπιτελεῖσθαι τὸ ἐνεργούμενον. Εἰ γὰρ ἐπὶ τοῦ $_6$ἑτέρου τῆς ἀνθρωποποιΐας εἴδους αἱ τῶν γεννώντων ὁρμαί, $_7$κἂν μὴ ἐπικληθῇ
παρ' αὐτῶν δι' εὐχῆς τὸ θεῖον, τῇ τοῦ $_8$Θεοῦ δυνάμει, καθὼς
ἐν τοῖς ἔμπροσθεν εἴρηται, διαπλάσσουσι $_9$τὸ γεννώμενον, ἧς
χωρισθείσης ἄπρακτός ἐστιν ἡ $_{10}$σπουδὴ καὶ ἀνόνητος, πόσῳ
25 μᾶλλον ἐν τῷ πνευματικῷ $_{11}$τῆς γεννήσεως τρόπῳ, καὶ Θεοῦ
παρέσεσθαι τοῖς γινομένοις $_{12}$ἐπηγγελμένου καὶ τὴν παρ' ἑαυτοῦ
δύναμιν ἐντεθεικότος $_{13}$τῷ ἔργῳ, καθὰ πεπιστεύκαμεν, καὶ τῆς
ἡμετέρας $_{14}$προαιρέσεως πρὸς τὸ σπουδαζόμενον τὴν ὁρμὴν
ἐχούσης, $_{15}$εἰ συμπαραληφθείη καθηκόντως ἡ διὰ τῆς εὐχῆς
30 συμμαχία, $_{16}$μᾶλλον ἐπιτελὲς ἔσται τὸ σπουδαζόμενον;—
—(4) Καθά-
$_{17}$περ γὰρ οἱ ἐπιφαῦσαι τὸν ἥλιον αὐτοῖς εὐχόμενοι τῷ Θεῷ
$_{18}$οὐδὲν ἀμβλύνουσι τὸ πάντως γινόμενον, οὐδὲ μὴν ἄχρηστον
$_{19}$εἶναί τις φήσει τὴν τῶν προσευχομένων σπουδήν, εἰ $_{20}$περὶ τοῦ
πάντως ἐσομένου τὸν Θεὸν ἱκετεύουσιν, οὕτως οἱ $_{21}$πεπεισμένοι
35 (Sr 129) κατὰ τὴν | ἀψευδῆ τοῦ ἐπαγγειλαμένου ὑπόσχεσιν $_{22}$πάντως
παρεῖναι τὴν χάριν τοῖς διὰ τῆς μυστικῆς $_{23}$ταύτης οἰκονομίας
(GNO 86) ἀναγεννωμένοις ἢ προσθήκην τινὰ | ποιοῦνται τῆς χάριτος, ἢ
τὴν οὖσαν οὐκ ἀποστρέφουσιν. $_2$Τὸ γὰρ πάντως εἶναι διὰ τὸ
Θεὸν εἶναι τὸν ἐπαγγειλάμενον $_3$πεπίστευται, ἡ δὲ τῆς θεό-
40 τητος μαρτυρία διὰ τῶν θαυμάτων $_4$ἐστίν· ὥστε διὰ πάντων τὸ
παρεῖναι τὸ θεῖον οὐδεμίαν $_5$ἀμφιβολίαν ἔχει.

38 εἶναι GNO : συνεῖναι Srawley

and do not reject that what is promised is present because of the truthfulness of the pledge.

(3) The fact that the call by prayer precedes the divine economy[321] is an abundant demonstration that what is enacted is accomplished by God. For if in the case of the other form of human reproduction[322] the parents' impulses, even though the divine is not called upon by them through prayer, by God's power—as it was said before—form the one who is begotten, without which [their] eagerness is ineffective and useless, how much more in the spiritual manner of begetting, since God has both promised he will be present in what takes place [in baptism] and has placed a power from himself in the act, as we have believed, and our faculty of decision is [directed] toward the impulse for which we are eager, if the aid[323] [that comes] through prayer is duly invited?

(4) For just as those who pray to God that the sun may shine on them do not at all obstruct what takes place, surely no one will say the eagerness of those who pray is useless, if they supplicate God about what will by all means be. So those who have been persuaded, according to the truthful pledge of what was promised, that grace is altogether present to those who are regenerated through this mystic economy,[324] either make some addition to the grace, or do not divert that which exists. For [the grace] by all means has been believed to be [present], because he who promised is God, and the testimony of [his] divinity is [given] by the wonders; so that the divine presence through all is not in doubt.

---

[321] I.e., baptism (in this context).

[322] Lit. "man-making" (ἀνθρωποποιΐας), normally the word for biological reproduction, but here St Gregory uses the word to make a striking point: both baptism and sexual intercourse are ways of making human beings (ἀνθρωποποιΐα), one spiritual and one biological. This is, of course, taken from the biblical image of the Christian being "born again" or "having been begotten by God . . . [whose] seed remains in him" (1 Jn 3.9). See introduction, pp. 28–29.

[323] Or "alliance" (συμμαχία).

[324] Here "mystic" (μυστικῆς) in the sense of the mystery, or sacrament, of baptism.

ΛΕ'   ₆Ἡ δὲ εἰς τὸ ὕδωρ κάθοδος καὶ τὸ εἰς τρὶς ἐν αὐτῷ
        ₇γενέσθαι τὸν ἄνθρωπον ἕτερον ἐμπεριέχει μυστήριον. ₈Ἐπειδὴ
(Sr 130) γὰρ ὁ τῆς σωτηρίας ἡμῶν τρόπος οὐ τοσοῦτον ἐκ | ₉τῆς κατὰ τὴν
        διδαχὴν ὑφηγήσεως ἐνεργὸς γέγονεν ὅσον ₁₀δι᾽ αὐτῶν ὧν ἐποίη-
     5 σεν ὁ τὴν πρὸς τὸν ἄνθρωπον ὑποστὰς ₁₁κοινωνίαν, ἔργῳ τὴν
(PG 88) ζωὴν ἐνερ-| γήσας, ἵνα διὰ τῆς ἀναληφθείσης ₁₂παρ᾽ αὐτοῦ καὶ
        συναποθεωθείσης σαρκὸς ἅπαν ₁₃συνδιασωθῇ τὸ συγγενὲς αὐτῇ
(Sr 131) καὶ ὁμόφυλον, ἀναγκαῖον | ₁₄ἦν ἐπινοηθῆναί τινα τρόπον, ἐν ᾧ τις
        ἦν συγγένειά τε καὶ ₁₅ὁμοιότης ἐν τοῖς γινομένοις παρὰ τοῦ
    10 ἑπομένου πρὸς τὸν ₁₆ἡγούμενον. Χρὴ τοίνυν ἰδεῖν ἐν τίσιν ὁ τῆς
        ζωῆς ἡμῶν ₁₇καθηγησάμενος ἐθεωρήθη, ἵνα, καθώς φησιν ὁ
        ἀπόστολος, ₁₈κατὰ τὸν ἀρχηγὸν τῆς σωτηρίας ἡμῶν κατορ-
        θωθῇ ₁₉τοῖς ἑπομένοις ἡ μίμησις.—
                    —(2) Ὥσπερ γὰρ παρὰ τῶν
        πεπαιδευμένων ₂₀τὰ τακτικὰ πρὸς τὴν ὁπλιτικὴν ἐμπειρίαν
    15 ἀνάγονται ₂₁οἱ δι᾽ ὧν βλέπουσι πρὸς τὴν εὔρυθμόν τε καὶ ἐνό-
        πλιον ₂₂κίνησιν παιδευόμενοι, ὁ δὲ μὴ πράττων τὸ προδεικνύ-
        μενον ₂₃ἀμέτοχος τῆς τοιαύτης ἐμπειρίας μένει, κατὰ τὸν αὐτὸν
(GNO 87) ₂₄τρόπον τῷ πρὸς τὴν σωτηρίαν ἡμῶν ἐξηγουμένῳ πάν- | τας οἷς
        ἴση πρὸς τὸ ἀγαθόν ἐστιν ἡ σπουδή, ὁμοίως ₂ἐπάναγκες διὰ
    20 μιμήσεως ἕπεσθαι, τὸ παρ᾽ αὐτοῦ προδειχθὲν ₃εἰς ἔργον ἄγον-
        τας. Οὐ γὰρ ἔστι πρὸς τὸ ἴσον καταντῆσαι ₄πέρας μὴ διὰ τῶν
        ὁμοίων ὁδεύσαντας.—
                    —(3) Καθάπερ γὰρ ₅οἱ τὰς τῶν λαβυρίνθων
(Sr 132) πλάνας διεξελθεῖν ἀμηχανοῦντες, ₆εἴ τινος | ἐμπείρως ἔχοντος
        ἐπιτύχοιεν, κατόπιν ἑπόμενοι ₇τὰς ποικίλας τε καὶ ἀπατηλὰς
    25 τῶν οἴκων ἀναστροφὰς ₈διεξέρχονται, οὐκ ἂν διεξελθόντες μὴ
        κατ᾽ ἴχνος ἑπόμενοι ₉τῷ προάγοντι, οὕτω μοι νόησον καὶ τὸν

15 βλέπουσι GNO : βλέπουσιν Srawley

Triple immersion: imitation of and participation in Christ's death and resurrection

35 Now the descent into the water and the triple immersion[325] of man in it contains another mystery. For since the manner of our salvation did not become operative[326] so much by the guidance of teaching as by the things which he who submitted to fellowship with man did, since he effected life in deed, so that, through the flesh assumed and deified by him, all that is congenial to it and related might be saved together, it was necessary for some manner to be devised by which there might be some kinship and similarity between him who leads and him who follows in what happens [in baptism]. It is necessary, then, to see what [qualities] are contemplated in the leader of our life, so that, as the apostle says, the imitation for those who follow may be set aright, in accordance with the "founder of our salvation."[327]

(2) For just as [soldiers]—who are trained in rhythmic and martial movement by the things which they see—are led to military experience by those who have been trained in tactics, while he who does not practice what is shown to him remains without a share in such an experience, in the same manner all those who have an equal eagerness for the good must likewise follow the leader of our salvation by imitation, carrying out in deed what was shown by him. For it is not possible to arrive at the same end unless one travels by the same [paths].

(3) For just as those who are at a loss to go through the wanderings of labyrinths, if they should meet someone who has experience, following after [him], go through the halls' intricate and deceptive turns, [but] would not have gone through [them] had they not followed in the footsteps of their leader, so too, I ask you, consider also

---

[325]Lit. "being in it thrice" (τὸ εἰς τρὶς ἐν αὐτῷ γενέσθαι).

[326]Or "effective," "active" (ἐνεργὸς).

[327]Cf. Heb 2.10. This term has been rendered variously in popular translations of the Bible: the ESV has "founder" (ἀρχηγὸν), while the KJV has the equally accurate but different "captain" (and the RSV the memorable "pioneer").

τοῦ βίου τούτου ₁₀λαβύρινθον ἀδιεξίτητον εἶναι τῇ ἀνθρωπίνῃ
φύσει, εἰ μὴ ₁₁τις τῆς αὐτῆς ὁδοῦ λάβοιτο δι' ἧς ὁ ἐν αὐτῷ γενόμενος ἔξω ₁₂κατέστη τοῦ περιέχοντος. (4) Λαβύρινθον δέ φημι τρο-
30 πικῶς ₁₃τὴν ἀδιέξοδον τοῦ θανάτου φρουράν, ᾗ τὸ δείλαιον τοῦ
ἀνθρώπου ₁₄γένος περιεσχέθη. Τί οὖν περὶ τὸν ἀρχηγὸν τῆς
₁₅σωτηρίας ἡμῶν ἐθεασάμεθα; Τριήμερον νέκρωσιν καὶ πάλιν
₁₆ζωήν. Οὐκοῦν χρή τι τοιοῦτον καὶ ἐν ἡμῖν ἐπινοηθῆναι
₁₇ὁμοίωμα. Τίς οὖν ἐστιν ἡ ἐπίνοια δι' ἧς καὶ ἐν ἡμῖν πλη-
35 ροῦται ₁₈τοῦ παρ' ἐκείνου γεγονότος ἡ μίμησις;—

—(5) Ἅπαν τὸ
₁₉νεκρωθὲν οἰκεῖόν τινα καὶ κατὰ φύσιν ἔχει χῶρον, τὴν γῆν, ₂₀ἐν ᾗ
κλίνεταί τε καὶ κατακρύπτεται. Πολλὴν δὲ πρὸς ₂₁ἄλληλα τὴν
(GNO 88) συγγένειαν ἔχει γῆ τε καὶ ὕδωρ, μόνα τῶν | στοιχείων βαρέα τε
ὄντα καὶ κατωφερῆ, καὶ ἐν ἀλλήλοις ₂μένοντα καὶ δι' ἀλλήλων
40 κρατούμενα. Ἐπεὶ οὖν τοῦ καθηγουμένου ₃τῆς ζωῆς ἡμῶν ὁ
θάνατος ὑπόγειος κατὰ τὴν ₄κοινὴν γέγονε φύσιν, ἡ τοῦ θανάτου μίμησις ἡ παρ' ἡμῶν ₅γινομένη ἐν τῷ γείτονι διατυποῦται
στοιχείῳ· (6) καὶ ὡς ἐκεῖνος ₆ὁ ἄνωθεν ἄνθρωπος ἀναλαβὼν τὴν
(Sr 133) νεκρότητα μετὰ ₇τὴν ὑπόγειον | θέσιν τριταῖος ἐπὶ τὴν ζωὴν
45 πάλιν ἀνέδραμεν, ₈οὕτω πᾶς ὁ συνημμένος κατὰ τὴν τοῦ
σώματος φύσιν ₉ἐκείνῳ πρὸς τὸ αὐτὸ κατόρθωμα βλέπων—τὸ
κατὰ τὴν ₁₀ζωὴν λέγω πέρας—ἀντὶ γῆς τὸ ὕδωρ ἐπιχεάμενος
καὶ ὑποδὺς ₁₁τὸ στοιχεῖον ἐν τρισὶ περιόδοις τὴν τριήμερον τῆς
₁₂ἀναστάσεως χάριν ἀπεμιμήσατο.—

—(7) Εἴρηται δὲ τὸ τοιοῦτον ₁₃καὶ
50 ἐν τοῖς φθάσασιν, ὅτι κατ' οἰκονομίαν ἐπῆκται τῇ ἀνθρωπίνῃ
₁₄φύσει παρὰ τῆς θείας προνοίας ὁ θάνατος, ὥστε ₁₅τῆς κακίας ἐν
(PG 89) τῇ διαλύσει | τοῦ σώματος καὶ τῆς ψυχῆς ₁₆ἐκρυείσης πάλιν διὰ

that the labyrinth of this life is without exit for human nature, unless someone should take the same way by which he who was in it got outside [its] confine. (4) And by "labyrinth" I mean figuratively[328] the exitless prison of death, in which the wretched race of man was confined. What then did we behold in the case of the founder of our salvation? Three-day death, and life once more. Therefore it is necessary to devise some such likeness in us also. What then is the device by which the imitation of what has come to pass with him is fulfilled also in us?

(5) In death[329] everything has a proper and natural place: the earth, in which it is laid and hidden. Now both earth and water have quite a kinship with one another, being the only elements that are heavy and tend downward, both remaining with each other and being held by each other.[330] Since, then, the death of the leader of our life led to [burial] underground, in accordance with the shared nature, the imitation of [his] death, which is done by us, is expressed[331] in the neighboring element; (6) and as he, the man from above,[332] assumed the state of death, [and] after being placed under the earth on the third day returned to life again, so everyone who is joined to him by the nature of the body—looking to the same success (I mean the purpose of life) when water, instead of earth, is poured on him, and when he is plunged into [this] element in three rounds—imitates the three-day grace of the resurrection.

(7) In what came before something like this has been said, that death has been introduced in human nature by divine providence as

---

[328]τροπικῶς, a rhetorical term used widely in the early Church by exegetes as different as Origen (e.g., *Commentary on Matthew* 11.17.56–60; SC 162:364) and Theodoret (e.g., *Commentary on the Psalms*, Ps 45.12; PG 80:1205C).

[329]Or "the state of death" (τὸ νεκρωθὲν).

[330]On the elements and their place in the cosmos in ancient thought, see p. 114, n. 223 above.

[331]This verb (διατυποῦται) is related to the word "type" (a τύπος is a seal *pressed* into a wax to form a seal, hence διατυποῦται is rendered "expressed"). Our baptism is a type of Christ's death and resurrection. The language of type is taken from St Paul (cf. Rom 5.14; 1 Cor 10.6, 11).

[332]Jn 3.31 (cf. 1 Cor 15.47).

τῆς ἀναστάσεως σῶον, καὶ ἀπαθῆ, καὶ $_{17}$ἀκέραιον, καὶ πάσης
τῆς κατὰ κακίαν ἐπιμιξίας ἀλλότριον $_{18}$ἀναστοιχειωθῆναι τὸν
55 ἄνθρωπον. Ἀλλ' ἐπὶ μὲν τοῦ $_{19}$καθηγουμένου τῆς σωτηρίας
ἡμῶν τὸ τέλειον ἡ κατὰ τὸν $_{20}$θάνατον ἔσχεν οἰκονομία, κατὰ τὸν
(Sr 134) ἴδιον | σκοπὸν ἐντελῶς $_{21}$πληρωθεῖσα—(8) διεστάλη τε γὰρ διὰ τοῦ
θανάτου τὰ ἡνωμένα $_{22}$καὶ πάλιν συνήχθη τὰ διακεκριμένα, ὡς
ἂν καθαρθείσης $_{23}$τῆς φύσεως ἐν τῇ τῶν συμφυῶν διαλύσει,
60 ψυχῆς τε $_{24}$λέγω καὶ σώματος, πάλιν ἡ τῶν κεχωρισμένων
(GNO 89) ἐπάνοδος | τῆς ἀλλοτρίας ἐπιμιξίας καθαρεύουσα γένοιτο—
ἐπὶ δὲ $_{2}$τῶν ἀκολουθούντων τῷ καθηγουμένῳ οὐ χωρεῖ τὴν
$_{3}$ἀκριβῆ μίμησιν δι' ὅλων ἡ φύσις, ἀλλ' ὅσον δυνατῶς ἔχει,
$_{4}$τοσοῦτον νῦν παραδεξαμένη, τὸ λεῖπον τῷ μετὰ ταῦτα $_{5}$τα-
65 μιεύεται χρόνῳ.—

—(9) Τί οὖν ἔστιν ὃ μιμεῖται; Τὸ τῆς ἐμμιχθείσης
$_{6}$κακίας ἐν τῇ τῆς νεκρώσεως εἰκόνι τῇ γενομένῃ $_{7}$διὰ τοῦ ὕδατος
τὸν ἀφανισμὸν ἐμποιῆσαι, οὐ μὴν τελείως $_{8}$ἀφανισμόν, ἀλλά
τινα διακοπὴν τῆς τοῦ κακοῦ συνεχείας, $_{9}$συνδραμόντων δύο
πρὸς τὴν τῆς κακίας ἀναίρεσιν, τῆς τε $_{10}$τοῦ πλημμελήσαντος
70 μεταμελείας καὶ τῆς τοῦ θανάτου $_{11}$μιμήσεως, δι' ὧν ἐκλύεταί
πως ὁ ἄνθρωπος τῆς πρὸς τὸ $_{12}$κακὸν συμφυΐας, τῇ μεταμελείᾳ
(Sr 135) μὲν εἰς μῖσός | τε καὶ ἀλλοτρίωσιν $_{13}$τῆς κακίας χωρῶν, τῷ δὲ
θανάτῳ τοῦ κακοῦ τὸν $_{14}$ἀφανισμὸν ἐργαζόμενος.—

—(10) Ἀλλ' εἰ μὲν ἦν
δυνατὸν ἐν τελείῳ $_{15}$τῷ θανάτῳ γενέσθαι τὸν μιμούμενον, οὐδ'
75 ἂν μίμησις, $_{16}$ἀλλὰ ταυτότης τὸ γινόμενον ἦν, καὶ εἰς τὸ παν-
τελὲς τὸ $_{17}$κακὸν ἐκ τῆς φύσεως ἡμῶν ἠφανίζετο, ὥστε, καθώς
φησιν $_{18}$ὁ ἀπόστολος, Ἐφάπαξ ἀποθανεῖν τῇ ἁμαρτίᾳ. Ἐπεὶ
δέ, $_{19}$καθὼς εἴρηται, τοσοῦτον μιμούμεθα τὴν ὑπερέχουσαν $_{20}$δύ-
ναμιν ὅσον χωρεῖ ἡμῶν ἡ πτωχεία τῆς φύσεως, τὸ ὕδωρ $_{21}$τρὶς
80 ἐπιχεάμενοι καὶ πάλιν ἀναβάντες ἀπὸ τοῦ ὕδατος, τὴν $_{22}$σωτή-
ριον ταφὴν καὶ ἀνάστασιν τὴν ἐν τριημέρῳ γενομένην $_{23}$τῷ
(GNO 90) χρόνῳ ὑποκρινόμεθα, τοῦτο λαβόντες κατὰ διά- | νοιαν ὅτι, ὡς

78–79 ὑπερέχουσαν δύναμιν GNO : ὑπερεχούσης δυνάμεως Srawley

an economy,[333] so that, by vice flowing out in the dissolution of body and soul, man might be recreated[334] again by the resurrection sound, and impassible, and uncontaminated, and alien to any admixture of vice. But in the case of the leader of our salvation the economy of death was perfected, entirely fulfilled in accordance with [its] proper aim—(8) for by death united things were separated, and things that had been divided were brought together again, so that, when nature was cleansed by the dissolution of things that grow together (I mean soul and body), the return of things that had been separated might be purified of alien admixture—but in the case of those who follow the leader, nature is not capable of an entirely precise imitation, but as much as it is able, now admitting such things, the rest is stored up for a time after these things.

(9) What then is it that is imitated? Producing the destruction of the mixture of vice by the image of death[335] that takes place through the water, not indeed a complete destruction, but some break in the continuity of evil, two things concur to the destruction of vice, the repentance of the wrongdoer and the imitation of death, by which man is somehow released from an innate affinity toward evil, by repentance progressing to hatred and estrangement from vice, and by death working the destruction of evil.

(10) But if it was possible for the imitating to be complete death, it would not be an imitation, but an identical occurrence, and evil would have completely disappeared[336] from our nature, so as "to die once for all to sin," as the apostle says.[337] But since, as has been said, we imitate the transcendent power as much as the poverty of [our] nature allows, by the water being poured on [us] thrice and ascending from the water again, we act out the saving burial and the resurrection that took place in three days' time, having this

---

[333]Or "dispensation" (οἰκονομίαν).
[334]Lit. "re-elemented" (ἀναστοιχειωθῆναι).
[335]Or "mortification" (νεκρώσεως).
[336]Or "been destroyed" (ἠφανίζετο).
[337]Rom 6.10. In Romans this is said of Christ, not believers.

ἡμῖν ἐν ἐξουσίᾳ τὸ ὕδωρ ἐστί, καὶ ἐν αὐτῷ ₂γενέσθαι, καὶ ἐξ
αὐτοῦ πάλιν ἀναδῦναι, κατὰ τὸν αὐτὸν ₃τρόπον ἐπ' ἐξουσίας ἦν
85 ὁ τοῦ παντὸς ἔχων τὴν δεσποτείαν, ₄ὡς ἡμεῖς ἐν τῷ ὕδατι,
οὕτως ἐκεῖνος ἐν τῷ θανάτῳ ₅καταδυείς, πάλιν ἐπὶ τὴν ἰδίαν
ἀναλύειν μακαριότητα.—

　　　　　—(11) Εἰ ₆οὖν τις πρὸς τὸ εἰκὸς βλέποι καὶ
κατὰ τὴν ἐν ἑκατέρῳ ₇δύναμιν τὰ γινόμενα κρίνοι, οὐδεμίαν ἐν
(Sr 136) τοῖς | γινομένοις ₈εὑρήσει διαφοράν, ἑκατέρου κατὰ τὸ τῆς
90 φύσεως μέτρον ₉ἐξεργαζομένου τὰ κατὰ δύναμιν. Ὡς γὰρ ἔστιν
ἀνθρώπῳ ₁₀τὸ ὕδωρ πρὸς τὸ ἀκινδύνως ἐπιθιγγάνειν, εἰ βούλοιτο, ₁₁ἀπειροπλασίως τῇ θείᾳ δυνάμει κατ' εὐκολίαν ὁ θάνατος
₁₂πρόκειται καὶ ἐν αὐτῷ γενέσθαι καὶ μὴ τραπῆναι πρὸς πάθος.

(12) ₁₃Διὰ τοῦτο τοίνυν ἀναγκαῖον ἡμῖν τὸ ἐν τῷ ὕδατι ₁₄προμελετῆσαι
95 τὴν τῆς ἀναστάσεως χάριν, ὡς ἂν εἰδείημεν ₁₅ὅτι τὸ ἴσον ἡμῖν εἰς
εὐκολίαν ἐστὶν ὕδατί τε βαπτισθῆναι ₁₆καὶ ἐκ τοῦ θανάτου πάλιν
ἀναδῦναι. Ἀλλ' ὥσπερ ἐν τοῖς ₁₇κατὰ τὸν βίον γινομένοις τινά
(Sr 137; τινῶν ἐστιν ἀρχικώτερα, ὧν ₁₈ἄνευ οὐκ ἂν τὸ γινόμενον κατορ- |
PG 92) θωθείη, καίτοι εἰ πρὸς τὸ ₁₉πέρας ἡ ἀρχὴ κρίνοιτο, | ἀντ'
100 οὐδενὸς εἶναι δόξει τοῦ πράγματος ₂₀ἡ ἀρχὴ συγκρινομένη τῷ
τέλει—τί γὰρ ἴσον ἄνθρωπος ₂₁καὶ τὸ πρὸς τὴν σύστασιν τοῦ
ζῴου καταβαλλόμενον; ₂₂Ἀλλ' ὅμως, εἰ μὴ ἐκεῖνο εἴη, οὐδ' ἂν
(GNO 91) τοῦτο γένοιτο—οὕτω | καὶ τὸ κατὰ τὴν μεγάλην ἀνάστασιν,
μεῖζον ὂν τῇ φύσει, ₂τὰς ἀρχὰς ἐντεῦθεν καὶ τὰς αἰτίας ἔχει· οὐ
105 γάρ ἐστι δυνατὸν ₃ἐκεῖνο γενέσθαι, εἰ μὴ τοῦτο προκαθ-
ηγήσαιτο. (13) Μὴ ₄δύνασθαι δέ φημι δίχα τῆς κατὰ τὸ λουτρὸν
ἀναγεννήσεως ₅ἐν ἀναστάσει γενέσθαι τὸν ἄνθρωπον, οὐ πρὸς
τὴν ₆τοῦ συγκρίματος ἡμῶν ἀνάπλασίν τε καὶ ἀναστοιχείωσιν
₇βλέπων—πρὸς τοῦτο γὰρ δεῖ πάντως πορευθῆναι τὴν φύσιν

98 ἀρχικώτερα GNO : ἀρχηγικώτερα Srawley | 103 οὕτω GNO : οὕτως Srawley

in mind, that, as the water is within our power,[338] both to be in it and to emerge from it again, in the same manner it was within the power of him who has mastery over the universe, as we [sink down] in the water, so he submerges in death, to return again to his own blessedness.

(11) If, then, one should look to what is likely and judge the things that take place according to the power in each,[339] he will find no difference in what takes place, each accomplishing the things that are in its power according to the measure of [its] nature. For as it is [possible] for man to touch water without danger, if he should want, with infinitely greater ease death lies within the divine power, both to be in it and not to undergo a change toward passibility.

(12) Because of this, therefore, it was necessary for us to rehearse the grace of the resurrection in the water, so that we might know that it is equally easy for us to be baptized in water and to emerge again from death. But just as in life some events are more primary than some others, without which what takes place would not succeed, and yet if the beginning were judged by the end, the beginning of the matter, compared with the end, seems to be of no account—for what equality is there between man and what is sown for the constitution of [this] living thing? But likewise, if that [seed] should not exist, neither would this one come into being—so too what takes place in the great resurrection, which is greater by nature, has [its] beginnings and causes from this source; for it is not possible for that to happen, if this had not led the way. (13) It is not possible, I mean, for man to be in the resurrection without the "washing of regeneration"[340] (not looking to the re-forming and re-creation[341] of our compound [nature][342]—for to this [our] nature must by all means proceed,

[338]Or "authority" (ἐξουσίᾳ).

[339]I.e., the actual death and resurrection of the God-man and the mimetic triple immersion of baptism, which correspond to the divine power and human capacity, respectively.

[340]Cf. Tit 3.5.

[341]Lit. "re-elementing" (ἀναστοιχείωσιν).

[342]I.e., the bodily resurrection, which by necessity happens to all.

110 (Sr 138) ₈οἰκείαις ἀνάγκαις κατὰ | τὴν τοῦ τάξαντος οἰκονομίαν ₉συνωθουμένην, κἂν προσλάβῃ τὴν ἐκ τοῦ λουτροῦ χάριν, ₁₀κἂν ἄμοιρος μείνῃ τῆς τοιαύτης μυήσεως—ἀλλὰ τὴν ἐπὶ τὸ ₁₁μακάριόν τε καὶ θεῖον καὶ πάσης κατηφείας κεχωρισμένον ₁₂ἀποκατάστασιν.—

—(14) Οὐ γὰρ ὅσα δι' ἀναστάσεως τὴν ἐπὶ ₁₃τὸ εἶναι
115 πάλιν ἐπάνοδον δέχεται πρὸς τὸν αὐτὸν ἐπάνεισι ₁₄βίον, ἀλλὰ πολὺ τὸ μέσον τῶν τε κεκαθαρμένων καὶ τῶν ₁₅τοῦ καθαρσίου προσδεομένων ἐστίν. Ἐφ' ὧν γὰρ κατὰ τὸν ₁₆βίον τοῦτον ἡ διὰ τοῦ λουτροῦ προκαθηγήσατο κάθαρσις, ₁₇πρὸς τὸ συγγενὲς τούτοις ἡ ἀναχώρησις ἔσται· τῷ δὲ ₁₈καθαρῷ τὸ ἀπαθὲς
120 προσῳκείωται, ἐν δὲ τῇ ἀπαθείᾳ τὸ ₁₉μακάριον εἶναι οὐκ ἀμφιβάλλεται. Οἷς δὲ προσεπωρώθη ₂₀τὰ πάθη καὶ οὐδὲν προσήχθη τῆς κηλῖδος καθάρσιον, οὐχ ₂₁ὕδωρ μυστικόν, οὐκ ἐπίκλησις θείας δυνάμεως, οὐχ ἡ ἐκ ₂₂μεταμελείας διόρθωσις, ἀνάγκη πᾶσα καὶ τούτους ἐν τῷ ₂₃καταλλήλῳ γενέσθαι. (15) Κατάλ-
125 (Sr 139;   ληλον δὲ τῷ κεκιβδηλευ-| μένῳ | χρυσίῳ τὸ χωνευτήριον, ὡς τῆς
GNO 92)   ἐμμιχθείσης αὐτοῖς κακίας ₂ἀποτακείσης μακροῖς ὕστερον αἰῶσι καθαρὰν ἀποσωθῆναι ₃τῷ Θεῷ τὴν φύσιν. Ἐπεὶ οὖν ῥυπτική τίς ἐστι δύναμις ₄ἐν τῷ πυρὶ καὶ τῷ ὕδατι, οἱ διὰ τοῦ ὕδατος τοῦ ₅μυστικοῦ τὸν τῆς κακίας ῥύπον ἀποκλυσάμενοι τοῦ

being impelled by its own laws,[343] in accordance with the economy of him who arranges it, should it receive the grace of the washing, or should it remain without a share in such an initiation—but to the restoration[344] to the blessed and divine [state], separated from all sorrow).

(14) For not all who receive a return to existence again by the resurrection return to the same life, but there is a great interval[345] between those who have been purified and those who are in need of purification. For those for whom the purification through washing led the way beforehand in this life, the return will be to that which is akin to these things, and impassibility[346] is proper to purity, and it is not doubted that blessedness exists in impassibility.[347] But for those whose passions have solidified, and have not been brought to the purification of defilement—no mystic[348] water, no calling upon the divine power, no correction by repentance—it is also altogether necessary for them to come to be in an appropriate [state]. (15) And the furnace is appropriate for gold that has been alloyed with dross, so that, the vice mingled in them being melted, after long ages [its] nature might be restored[349] pure to God. Since, then, there is some purgative power in fire and in water,[350] those who have washed away the filth of vice by the mystic[351] water do not need other forms

---

[343]Lit. "necessities" (ἀνάγκαις). In the plural, it can mean "laws of nature" (cf. Xenophon, *Memorabilia* 1.1.11).

[344]Lit. "apokatastasis" (ἀποκατάστασιν). See introduction pp. 38–58.

[345]Perhaps an echo of the great "chasm" between Lazarus and the rich man (Lk 16.26). St Gregory discusses this passage in several of his works. See introduction, pp. 51–52, 54 n. 131, 55, 56.

[346]Or "dispassion," "passionlessness" (τὸ ἀπαθὲς).

[347]Or "dispassion," "passionlessness" (τῇ ἀπαθείᾳ).

[348]Or "sacramental" (μυστικόν), i.e., pertaining to the mystery.

[349]The verb rendered "might be restored" (ἀποσωθῆναι) is more closely related to the standard biblical verb "to save" (σῴζω) than to the noun *apokatastasis* (ἀποκατάστασις), rendered above as "restoration."

[350]See Mt 3.10–12; Lk 3.9, 16–17 (cf. Mal 3.2–3); also see Ps 65.12.

[351]Or "sacramental" (μυστικοῦ), i.e., pertaining to the mystery.

130 ₆ἑτέρου τῶν καθαρσίων εἴδους οὐκ ἐπιδέονται, οἱ δὲ ταύτης
₇ἀμύητοι τῆς καθάρσεως ἀναγκαίως τῷ πυρὶ καθαρίζονται.

ΛΣΤ'   ₈Μὴ γὰρ εἶναι δυνατὸν ὅ τε κοινὸς δείκνυσι λόγος ₉καὶ ἡ
τῶν γραφῶν διδασκαλία ἐντὸς τοῦ θείου γενέσθαι ₁₀χοροῦ τὸν
μὴ καθαρῶς πάντας τοὺς ἐκ κακίας σπίλους ₁₁ἀπορρυψάμενον.
Τοῦτό ἐστιν ὃ μικρὸν ὂν καθ' ἑαυτὸ ₁₂μεγάλων ἀγαθῶν ἀρχή τε
5 (Sr 140) καὶ ὑπόθεσις γίνεται. Μικρὸν | δέ ₁₃φημι τῇ εὐκολίᾳ τοῦ κατορ-
θώματος. Τίς γὰρ πάρεστι ₁₄πόνος τῷ πράγματι, πιστεῦσαι
πανταχοῦ τὸν θεὸν εἶναι, ἐν ₁₅πᾶσι δὲ ὄντα παρεῖναι καὶ τοῖς
ἐπικαλουμένοις τὴν ₁₆ζωτικὴν αὐτοῦ δύναμιν, παρόντα δὲ τὸ
οἰκεῖον ποιεῖν; (2) Ἴδιον ₁₇δὲ τῆς θείας ἐνεργείας ἡ τῶν δεομένων
10 ἐστὶ σωτηρία· ₁₈αὕτη δὲ διὰ τῆς ἐν ὕδατι καθάρσεως ἐνεργὸς
γίνεται· ὁ δὲ ₁₉καθαρθεὶς ἐν μετουσίᾳ τῆς καθαρότητος ἔσται,
τὸ δὲ ἀληθῶς ₂₀καθαρὸν ἡ θεότης ἐστίν. Ὁρᾷς ὅπως μικρόν τι τὸ
κατὰ ₂₁τὴν ἀρχήν ἐστι καὶ εὐκατόρθωτον, πίστις καὶ ὕδωρ, ἡ
μὲν ₂₂ἐντὸς τῆς προαιρέσεως ἡμῶν ἀποκειμένη, τὸ δὲ σύντροφον
15 ₂₃τῇ ἀνθρωπίνῃ ζωῇ. Ἀλλὰ τὸ ἐκ τούτων ἀναφυόμενον ₂₄ἀγαθὸν
(PG 93) ὅσον | καὶ οἷον, ὡς πρὸς αὐτὸ τὸ θεῖον ἔχειν τὴν ₂₅οἰκειότητα. |

(GNO 93;   ΛΖ'   Ἀλλ' ἐπειδὴ διπλοῦν τὸ ἀνθρώπινον, ψυχῇ τε καὶ
Sr 141)   ₂σώματι συγκεκραμένον, δι' ἀμφοτέρων ἀνάγκη τοῦ πρὸς ₃τὴν
ζωὴν καθηγουμένου τοὺς σῳζομένους ἐφάπτεσθαι. ₄Οὐκοῦν ἡ
(Sr 142) ψυχὴ μὲν διὰ πίστεως πρὸς αὐτὸν ἀνακραθεῖσα | ₅τὰς ἀφορμὰς
5 ἐντεῦθεν τῆς σωτηρίας ἔχει—ἡ γὰρ πρὸς τὴν ₆ζωὴν ἕνωσις

of cleansing, but those who are not initiates in this purification are necessarily purified by fire.[352]

The Greatness of Baptism and Purgation after Death

36 For both the teaching of the Scriptures and common reason show that it is not possible to be in the divine chorus for him who has not entirely[353] washed away all the blemishes of vice. This [i.e., baptism], which is little in itself, becomes the beginning and foundation of great blessings.[354] And by "little," I mean the ease of the correction. For what difficulty is there with the matter, to believe God is everywhere, and being in all things he is also present with those who call upon his life-giving power, and being present he does what is proper to him? (2) And what is proper for the divine activity[355] is the salvation of those who are in need; and this becomes active by purification in water; and he who is purified will be a participant in purity, and the divinity is truly pure. You see how little a thing it is in the beginning and how easily it is effected: faith and water, one lying within our decision, and the other habitual to human life. But how great and what a good it is that grows up out of these, that [we] might have familiarity[356] with the divine itself.

The Eucharist

37 But since humanity is twofold, being a commixture of both soul and body, it is necessary for those who are being saved to lay hold of him who leads to life through both. Therefore the soul, which is mingled with him by faith, has the means[357] of salvation from him—for union with life has a fellowship with life—but the body

---

[352]See 1 Cor 3.15. This passage was used by the Latin side at the Council of Florence (1431–49).
[353]Or "purely" (καθαρῶς).
[354]Or "good things" (ἀγαθῶν).
[355]Or "energy" (ἐνεργείας).
[356]Or "a relationship" (οἰκειότητα).
[357]Or "origins" (ἀφορμὰς).

145 SAINT GREGORY OF NYSSA

τὴν τῆς ζωῆς κοινωνίαν ἔχει—τὸ δὲ σῶμα ἕτερον ₇τρόπον ἐν
μετουσίᾳ τε καὶ ἀνακράσει τοῦ σῴζοντος ₈γίνεται.

(2) Ὥσπερ γὰρ οἱ δηλητήριον δι' ἐπιβουλῆς λαβόντες ₉ἄλλῳ
φαρμάκῳ τὴν φθοροποιὸν δύναμιν ἔσβεσαν—χρὴ δὲ ₁₀καθ'
10 ὁμοιότητα τοῦ ὀλεθρίου καὶ τὸ ἀλεξητήριον ἐντὸς ₁₁τῶν
ἀνθρωπίνων γενέσθαι σπλάγχνων, ὡς ἂν δι' ἐκείνων ₁₂ἐφ' ἅπαν
καταμερισθείη τὸ σῶμα ἡ τοῦ βοηθοῦντος δύναμις—₁₃οὕτω
τοῦ διαλύοντος τὴν φύσιν ἡμῶν ἀπογευσάμενοι ₁₄πάλιν
ἀναγκαίως καὶ τοῦ συνάγοντος τὸ διαλελυμένον ₁₅ἐπεδεήθημεν,
15 ὡς ἂν ἐν ἡμῖν γενόμενον τὸ τοιοῦτον ἀλεξητήριον ₁₆τὴν προ-
εντεθεῖσαν τῷ σώματι τοῦ δηλητηρίου ₁₇βλάβην διὰ τῆς οἰκείας
ἀντιπαθείας ἀπώσαιτο.—

—(3) Τί οὖν ἐστι ₁₈τοῦτο; Οὐδὲν ἕτερον ἢ
(Sr 143) ἐκεῖνο τὸ σῶμα ὃ τοῦ τε | θανάτου ₁₉κρεῖττον ἐδείχθη καὶ τῆς
ζωῆς ἡμῖν κατήρξατο. Καθάπερ ₂₀γὰρ Μικρὰ ζύμη, καθὼς
20 φησιν ὁ ἀπόστολος, ὅλον τὸ ₂₁φύραμα πρὸς ἑαυτὴν ἐξομοιοῖ,
οὕτω τὸ ἀθανατισθὲν ὑπὸ ₂₂τοῦ Θεοῦ σῶμα ἐν τῷ ἡμετέρῳ
(GNO 93) γενόμενον ὅλον πρὸς ἑαυτὸ | μεταποιεῖ καὶ μετατίθησιν. Ὡς
γὰρ τῷ φθοροποιῷ πρὸς τὸ ₂ὑγιαῖνον ἀναμιχθέντι ἅπαν τὸ
ἀνακραθὲν συνηχρειώθη, ₃οὕτω καὶ τὸ ἀθάνατον σῶμα ἐν τῷ
25 ἀναλαβόντι αὐτὸ γενόμενον ₄πρὸς τὴν ἑαυτοῦ φύσιν καὶ τὸ πᾶν
μετεποίησεν.—

(Sr 144)   —(4) ₅Ἀλλὰ μὴν οὐκ ἔστιν ἄλλως ἐντός τι γενέσθαι | τοῦ
σώματος, ₆μὴ διὰ βρώσεως ἢ πόσεως τοῖς σπλάγχνοις
καταμιγνύμενον. ₇Οὐκοῦν ἐπάναγκες κατὰ τὸν δυνατὸν τῇ
φύσει ₈τρόπον τὴν ζωοποιὸν δύναμιν τῷ σώματι δέξασθαι.
30 Μόνου ₉δὲ τοῦ θεοδόχου σώματος ἐκείνου ταύτην δεξαμένου
τὴν ₁₀χάριν, ἄλλως δὲ δειχθέντος μὴ εἶναι δυνατὸν ἐν ἀθανασίᾳ
₁₁γενέσθαι τὸ ἡμέτερον σῶμα, μὴ διὰ τῆς πρὸς τὸ ἀθάνατον
₁₂κοινωνίας ἐν μετουσίᾳ τῆς ἀφθαρσίας γινόμενον, σκοπῆσαι
₁₃προσήκει πῶς ἐγένετο δυνατὸν τὸ ἓν ἐκεῖνο σῶμα ₁₄ταῖς τοσαύ-

21 οὕτω GNO : οὕτως Srawley | 24 συνηχρειώθη, οὕτω GNO : συνηχρείωται, οὕτως
Srawley | 27 ἢ GNO : καὶ Srawley

comes into participation and mingling with the savior in a different manner.

(2) For just as those who took some poison by treachery quench the destructive power with another drug—and, like the fatal [drug], the defensive [drug] must be within man's inward parts, so that through them the power of the thing helping might be distributed to the entire body—so, having tasted[358] of that which dissolves our nature, we also necessarily were in need of something to bring together again what had been dissolved, so that such a defensive [drug] working in us might drive out the damage of the poison that was previously placed in [our] body by the proper antidote.[359]

(3) What then is this? Nothing else than that body which was shown superior to death and brought about the beginning of life for us. For just as "a little leaven," as the apostle says, assimilates "the whole lump"[360] to itself, so the body that was made immortal by God, coming to be in us, remakes and transfers the whole to itself. For as by the mixture of a destructive [drug] with a healthy [body] all of the mixture becomes useless, so too the immortal body, coming to be in him who receives it, remakes all into its own nature.

(4) But surely there is no other way for something to come to be inside a body, unless it is mingled with the inner parts by food or drink. Therefore it is necessary for the body to receive the life-giving power in the manner that is possible for [its] nature. But since only that God-receiving body[361] admitted this grace,[362] and it was shown not to be otherwise possible for our body to become immortal unless it becomes a participant in incorruption by fellowship with immortality, it is fitting to consider how it was possible for that one body to be ever distributed to so many myriads of the faithful in all

[358]Cf. Gen 2.16–3.24.

[359]St Ignatius of Antioch likewise calls the Eucharist "the medicine of immortality, an antidote [ἀντίδοτος] which prevents death, yet enables us to live at all times in Jesus Christ." *Ephesians* 20.2 (PPS 49:41—St Gregory uses a different Greek word: ἀντιπαθείας).

[360]Gal 5.9.

[361]See p. 102, n. 168.

[362]I.e., "the life-giving power."

35 ταις τῶν πιστῶν μυριάσι κατὰ πᾶσαν τὴν οἰκουμένην [15]εἰς ἀεὶ
καταμεριζόμενον ὅλον ἑκάστῳ διὰ τοῦ [16]μέρους γίνεσθαι καὶ
αὐτὸ μένειν ἐφ᾽ ἑαυτοῦ ὅλον.

(5) Οὐκοῦν [17]ὡς ἂν πρὸς τὸ ἀκόλουθον ἡμῖν ἡ πίστις βλέπουσα |
(Sr 145) μηδεμίαν [18]ἀμφιβολίαν περὶ τοῦ προκειμένου νοήματος ἔχοι,
40 [19]μικρόν τι προσήκει παρασχολῆσαι τὸν λόγον εἰς τὴν φυσιο-
λογίαν [20]τοῦ σώματος. Τίς γὰρ οὐκ οἶδεν ὅτι ἡ τοῦ σώματος
[21]ἡμῶν φύσις αὐτὴ καθ᾽ ἑαυτὴν ἐν ἰδίᾳ τινὶ ὑποστάσει [22]ζωὴν οὐκ
ἔχει, ἀλλὰ διὰ τῆς ἐπιρρεούσης αὐτῇ δυνάμεως [23]συνέχει τε
ἑαυτὴν καὶ ἐν τῷ εἶναι μένει, ἀπαύστῳ κινήσει [24]τό τε λεῖπον
45 (GNO 95) πρὸς ἑαυτὴν ἐφελκομένη καὶ τὸ περιττεῦον | ἀπωθουμένη;
(6) Καὶ ὥσπερ τις ἀσκὸς ὑγροῦ τινος πλήρης [2]ὤν, εἰ κατὰ τὸν
(PG 96) πυθμένα τὸ ἐγκείμενον ὑπεξίοι, οὐκ ἂν [3]φυλάσσοι τὸ περὶ τὸν |
ὄγκον ἑαυτοῦ σχῆμα, μὴ ἀντεισιόντος [4]ἄνωθεν ἑτέρου πρὸς τὸ
κενούμενον, ὥστε τὸν ὁρῶντα [5]τὴν ὀγκώδη τοῦ ἀγγείου τούτου
50 περιοχὴν εἰδέναι μὴ ἰδίαν [6]εἶναι τοῦ φαινομένου, ἀλλὰ τὸ εἰσ-
ρέον ἐν αὐτῷ γινόμενον [7]σχηματίζειν τὸ περιέχον τὸν ὄγκον,
(Sr 146) οὕτω καὶ ἡ τοῦ σώματος [8]ἡμῶν κατασκευὴ ἴδιον | μὲν πρὸς τὴν
ἑαυτῆς σύστασιν [9]οὐδὲν ἡμῖν γνώριμον ἔχει, διὰ δὲ τῆς ἐπεισ-
αγομένης δυνάμεως [10]ἐν τῷ εἶναι μένει.—
—(7) Ἡ δὲ δύναμις αὕτη
55 τροφὴ καὶ ἔστι [11]καὶ λέγεται. Ἔστι δὲ οὐχ ἡ αὐτὴ πᾶσι τοῖς
τρεφομένοις [12]σώμασι, ἀλλά τις ἑκάστῳ κατάλληλος παρὰ τοῦ
τὴν φύσιν [13]οἰκονομοῦντος ἀποκεκλήρωται. Τὰ μὲν γὰρ τῶν
ζῴων [14]ῥιζωρυχοῦντα τρέφεται, ἑτέροις ἐστὶν ἡ πόα τρόφιμος,
[15]τινῶν δὲ ἡ τροφὴ σάρκες εἰσίν, ἀνθρώπῳ δὲ κατὰ τὸ προη-
60 [16]γούμενον ἄρτος, καὶ εἰς τὴν τοῦ ὑγροῦ διαμονὴν καὶ συν-
[17]τήρησιν πότον γίνεται οὐκ αὐτὸ μόνον τὸ ὕδωρ, ἀλλ᾽ οἴνῳ
[18]πολλάκις ἐφηδυνόμενον, πρὸς τὴν τοῦ θερμοῦ τοῦ ἐν ἡμῖν

36 ἑκάστῳ GNO : ἑκάστου Srawley | 56 σώμασι GNO : σώμασιν Srawley

the inhabited world, the whole being in each through the portion [received], and itself remaining whole in itself.[363]

(5) Therefore it is fitting for the argument[364] to digress a little into the physiology of the body, so that, looking to the order [of the argument], our faith might have no doubt about the proposed thought. For who has not known that the nature of our body itself, in itself, does not have life in its own subsistence, but it holds itself together and remains in existence by an influx of power into it, that draws to itself what it lacks by a ceaseless motion, and casts out what is superfluous?[365] (6) And just as a wineskin[366] that is full of some liquid, if the contents leaked out at the bottom, would not keep the shape around its volume unless a different [liquid] enters from above into the empty [space], so that he who looks at the circumference of the volume of this vessel knows that it is not a property of what he sees,[367] but that what enters into it gives shape to the circumference of the volume, so too the fashioning of our body has no property for its own composition that is recognizable for us, but remains in existence by the power introduced [into it].

(7) Now this power itself both is and is called nourishment. And it is not the same in all nourished bodies, but to each something appropriate has been allotted by him who arranges the economy of nature.[368] For some of the animals are nourished by rooting, for others grass is nourishing, and the nourishment of some is flesh, but for man bread takes precedence, and for the maintenance and preservation of moisture, for drink, there is not only water by itself,

---

[363]This paradox is similarly expressed in the Byzantine liturgy at the fraction of the consecrated Lamb. The priest says, "Broken and distributed is the Lamb of God: broken, yet not divided; ever eaten, though never consumed, but sanctifying them that partake thereof."

[364]Or "discourse" (λόγον).

[365]I.e., the human body is sustained by the digestive system, through the intake of food and the excretion of waste.

[366]Or "waterskin" (ἀσκὸς); not necessarily a wine container, but certainly a leather container for liquids (ἀσκὸς means "skin" or "hide"), which does not keep its shape when empty.

[367]Lit. "the appearance" (τοῦ φαινομένου).

[368]Lit. "him who economizes nature" (τοῦ τὴν φύσιν οἰκονομοῦντος).

19συμμαχίαν. Οὐκοῦν ὁ πρὸς ταῦτα βλέπων δυνάμει πρὸς 20τὸν
ὄγκον τοῦ ἡμετέρου σώματος βλέπει· ἐν ἐμοὶ γὰρ ἐκεῖνα 21γενό-
65 μενα αἷμα καὶ σῶμα γίνεται, καταλλήλως διὰ τῆς 22ἀλλοιωτικῆς
(Sr 147) δυνάμεως πρὸς τὸ τοῦ σώματος εἶδος τῆς 23τροφῆς | μεθιστα-
μένης.
(8) 24Τούτων ἡμῖν τοῦτον διευκρινηθέντων τὸν τρόπον ἐπανακ-
τέον 25πάλιν πρὸς τὰ προκείμενα τὴν διανοίαν. Ἐζητεῖτο 26γὰρ
70 (GNO 96) πῶς τὸ ἓν ἐκεῖνο σῶμα τοῦ Χριστοῦ πᾶσαν ζωοποιεῖ | τὴν τῶν
ἀνθρώπων φύσιν, ἐν ὅσοις ἡ πίστις ἐστίν, πρὸς 2πάντας μερι-
ζόμενον καὶ αὐτὸ οὐ μειούμενον. Τάχα τοίνυν 3ἐγγὺς τοῦ
εἰκότος λόγου γινόμεθα. Εἰ γὰρ παντὸς σώματος 4ἡ ὑπόστασις
(Sr 148) ἐκ τῆς τροφῆς γίνεται, αὕτη δὲ | βρῶσις καὶ 5πόσις ἐστίν—ἔστι
75 δὲ ἐν τῇ βρώσει ἄρτος, ἐν δὲ τῇ πόσει τὸ 6ὕδωρ ἐφηδυσμένον τῷ
οἴνῳ—ὁ δὲ τοῦ Θεοῦ Λόγος, καθὼς 7ἐν τοῖς πρώτοις διῄρηται,
ὁ καὶ Θεὸς ὢν καὶ Λόγος, τῇ ἀνθρωπίνῃ 8συνανεκράθη φύσει
καὶ ἐν τῷ σώματι τῷ ἡμετέρῳ 9γενόμενος οὐκ ἄλλην τινὰ
παρεκαινοτόμησε τῇ φύσει τὴν 10σύστασιν, ἀλλὰ διὰ τῶν
80 συνήθων τε καὶ καταλλήλων 11ἔδωκε τῷ καθ᾽ ἑαυτὸν σώματι
τὴν διαμονήν, βρώσει καὶ 12πόσει περικρατῶν τὴν ὑπόστασιν, ἡ
δὲ βρῶσις ἄρτος ἦν· (9) 13ὥσπερ τοίνυν ἐφ᾽ ἡμῶν, καθὼς ἤδη
πολλάκις εἴρηται, ὁ 14τὸν ἄρτον ἰδὼν τρόπον τινὰ τὸ σῶμα τὸ
ἀνθρώπινον βλέπει, 15ὅτι ἐν τούτῳ ἐκεῖνο γενόμενον τοῦτο γίνε-
85 ται, οὕτω 16κἀκεῖ τὸ θεοδόχον σῶμα τὴν τροφὴν τοῦ ἄρτου πα-
ραδεξάμενον 17λόγῳ τινὶ ταὐτὸν ἦν ἐκείνῳ, τῆς τροφῆς, καθὼς
18εἴρηται, πρὸς τὴν τοῦ σώματος φύσιν μεθισταμένης· τὸ 19γὰρ
πάντων ἴδιον καὶ ἐπ᾽ ἐκείνης τῆς σαρκὸς ὡμολογήθη 20ὅτι ἄρτῳ
(Sr 149) κἀκεῖνο τὸ σῶμα διεκρατεῖτο, | τὸ δὲ σῶμα τῇ 21ἐνοικήσει τοῦ

71 ἐστίν GNO : ἐστί Srawley | 84 γενόμενον GNO : γινόμενον Srawley

but it is often sweetened with wine, as an aid for the heat in us.[369] Therefore he who looks at these things sees the bulk of our body in potential; for in me these become blood and body, the nourishment correspondingly changed into the form of [my] body by [a nutritive] power of alteration.

(8) Having made these distinctions in this manner, we must recall [our] thought to the preceding [objections] again. For it was asked how that one body of Christ gives life to all men's nature, in whomever the faith is, being distributed to all and itself not being diminished. Perhaps, then, we are near a likely account. For if the subsistence of all the body comes from nourishment, and this is food and drink—and there is bread for eating, and water sweetened with wine for drinking—and the Word of God, as has been narrated in the previous [sections], being both God and Word, was commingled with human nature and, being in a body [like] ours, he did not innovate some other constitution for [our] nature, but through habitual and appropriate things he maintained[370] his own body, securing [its] substance with food and drink, and the food was bread; (9) therefore just as it is in our case, as was already often said, he who is looking at bread sees, in some manner, the human body, for the bread, being in the body, becomes the body,[371] so too in that case the God-receiving body,[372] receiving the nourishment of bread was, in some sense, identical with that [bread], since the nourishment, as has been said, was changed into the nature of [his] body; for the property of all [human bodies] is also admitted in the case of that flesh, for that body was also supported by bread, and the body, by the

[369]Heat was key to ancient theories of digestion (stretching back at least to Hippocrates): food was digested in the stomach by heat, and it was then sent through the small intestine to the liver, from whence it entered the bloodstream. Then, the blood carried it to the various appendages, where it became flesh (this was the consensus view until the circulation of blood was discovered by Harvey in the seventeenth century).

[370]Lit. "gave maintenance" or "continuation" (ἔδωκε . . . τὴν διαμονήν).

[371]Lit. "for that being in this, becomes this" (ὅτι ἐν τούτῳ ἐκεῖνο γενόμενον τοῦτο γίνεται). For clarity, these pronouns are replaced by their antecedents.

[372]See p. 102, n. 168.

90 Θεοῦ Λόγου πρὸς τὴν θεϊκὴν ἀξίαν μετεποιήθη. ₂₂Καλῶς οὖν
καὶ νῦν τὸν τῷ Λόγῳ τοῦ Θεοῦ ἁγιαζόμενον ₂₃ἄρτον εἰς σῶμα
(GNO 97) τοῦ Θεοῦ Λόγου μεταποιεῖσθαι πιστεύομεν· | (10) καὶ γὰρ ἐκεῖνο
τὸ σῶμα ἄρτος τῇ δυνάμει ἦν, ἡγιάσθη δὲ ₂τῇ ἐπισκηνώσει τοῦ
Λόγου τοῦ σκηνώσαντος ἐν τῇ σαρκί. ₃Οὐκοῦν ὅθεν ὁ ἐν
95 ἐκείνῳ τῷ σώματι μεταποιηθεὶς ἄρτος ₄εἰς θείαν μετέστη δύνα-
(PG 97) μιν, διὰ τοῦ αὐτοῦ καὶ | νῦν τὸ ἴσον ₅γίνεται. Ἐκεῖ τε γὰρ ἡ τοῦ
Λόγου χάρις ἅγιον ἐποίει τὸ ₆σῶμα ᾧ ἐκ τοῦ ἄρτου ἡ σύστασις
ἦν, καὶ τρόπον τινὰ καὶ ₇αὐτὸ ἄρτος ἦν, ἐνταῦθά τε ὡσαύτως ὁ
(Sr 150) ἄρτος, καθώς ₈φησιν ὁ ἀπόστολος, | Ἁγιάζεται διὰ Λόγου Θεοῦ
100 καὶ ἐντεύξεως, ₉οὐ διὰ βρώσεως προϊὼν εἰς τὸ σῶμα γενέσθαι
τοῦ ₁₀Λόγου, ἀλλ᾽ εὐθὺς πρὸς τὸ σῶμα διὰ τοῦ Λόγου μετα-
(Sr 151) ποιούμενος, ₁₁καθὼς εἴρηται | ὑπὸ τοῦ Λόγου ὅτι Τοῦτό ἐστι τὸ
₁₂σῶμά μου.—
        —(11) Πάσης δὲ σαρκὸς καὶ διὰ τοῦ ὑγροῦ τρεφομένης
—₁₃οὐ γὰρ ἂν δίχα τῆς πρὸς τοῦτο συζυγίας τὸ ἐν ἡμῖν ₁₄γεῶδες
105 ἐν τῷ ζῆν διαμένοι—ὥσπερ διὰ τῆς στερρᾶς τε καὶ ₁₅ἀντιτύπου

indwelling of the Word of God, was remade into the divine dignity. We rightly believe, then, that even now the bread that is sanctified by the Word of God is remade into the body of the Word of God; (10) for that body was also bread in potential, and was sanctified by the tabernacling of the Word who tabernacled in the flesh.[373] Therefore the means by which the bread, which was remade into that body, was changed to divine power, is the same [means] by which the like thing also happens. For in that case the grace of the Word made the body holy, whose constitution was from bread, and, in some manner, was also itself bread; likewise here the bread, as the apostle says, "is sanctified by the Word of God and prayer,"[374] not proceeding to become the body of the Word through eating, but immediately being remade into the body by the Word, as was said by the Word: "This is my body."[375]

(11) Now since all flesh is also nourished by moisture—for without being conjoined with this, what is earthly in us would not continue in life—just as we support the solid [part] of the body with

---

[373]Cf. Jn 1.14: "And the word became flesh, and tabernacled [ἐσκήνωσεν] among [or 'in'] us." Most translations have "dwelt" or "made his dwelling," but the verb comes from the word σκῆνος, "tent," which refers to the portable tabernacle of the Old Testament.

[374]1 Tim 4.5. St Gregory interprets this verse uniquely. No modern translation capitalizes "word," but throughout this passage St Gregory has referred to the Word of God, the second person of the Trinity, and he seems to understand the verse this way also. Most read this passage as a rejection of a proto-Encratite group, which denied the goodness of the material world: "forbidding to marry, [commanding others] to abstain from foods, which God created to be received [lit. 'for reception,' εἰς μετάλημψιν] with thanksgiving [μετὰ εὐχαριστίας] by the faithful and those who know the truth. For every creation of God is good, and nothing is to be rejected, if it is taken with thanksgiving [μετὰ εὐχαριστίας]" (1 Tim 4.3–4, my translation). St Gregory seems to understand this all in a eucharistic sense: the word "thanksgiving" may also simply mean "Eucharist," and the word "reception" (μετάλημψιν) is used to describe the reception of the Eucharist in Greek liturgical texts. Finally, St Paul says that this is to be received by "the faithful," by St Gregory's time a long-established technical term for those who are baptized, who remain for the entirety of the liturgy, and who receive the Eucharist.

[375]Mt 26.26; Mk 14.22; Lk 22.19; 1 Cor 11.24. For more on the Eucharist in Gregory and other fathers, see introduction, pp. 31–32.

τροφῆς τὸ στερρὸν τοῦ σώματος ὑποστηρίζομεν, 16τὸν αὐτὸν
τρόπον καὶ τῷ ὑγρῷ τὴν προσθήκην ἐκ τῆς 17ὁμογενοῦς ποιού-
μεθα φύσεως, ὅπερ ἐν ἡμῖν γενόμενον διὰ 18τῆς ἀλλοιωτικῆς
δυνάμεως ἐξαιματοῦται καὶ μάλιστά γε 19εἰ διὰ τοῦ οἴνου λάβοι
110 τὴν δύναμιν πρὸς τὴν εἰς τὸ θερμὸν 20μεταποίησιν.—

—(12) Ἐπεὶ οὖν καὶ
τοῦτο τὸ μέρος ἡ θεοδόχος 21ἐκείνη σὰρξ πρὸς τὴν σύστασιν
ἑαυτῆς παρεδέξατο, ὁ δὲ 22φανερωθεὶς Θεὸς διὰ τοῦτο κατέμιξεν
(Sr 152) ἑαυτὸν τῇ ἐπικήρῳ 23φύσει, ἵνα τῇ τῆς | θεότητος κοινωνίᾳ συνα-
(GNO 98) ποθεωθῇ τὸ ἀν- | θρώπινον, τούτου χάριν πᾶσι τοῖς πεπιστευ-
115 κόσι τῇ οἰκονομίᾳ 2τῆς χάριτος ἑαυτὸν ἐνσπείρει διὰ τῆς
σαρκὸς ἧς ἡ 3σύστασις ἐξ οἴνου τε καὶ ἄρτου ἐστίν, τοῖς σώμασι
τῶν 4πεπιστευκότων κατακιρνάμενος, ὡς ἂν τῇ πρὸς τὸ ἀθά-
5νατον ἑνώσει καὶ ὁ ἄνθρωπος τῆς ἀφθαρσίας μέτοχος 6γένοιτο.
Ταῦτα δὲ δίδωσι τῇ τῆς εὐλογίας δυνάμει πρὸς 7ἐκεῖνο μετα-
120 στοιχειώσας τῶν φαινομένων τὴν φύσιν. |

(Sr 153) ΛΗ'   8Οὐδὲν οἶμαι τοῖς εἰρημένοις ἐνδεῖν τῶν περὶ τὸ
μυστήριον 9ζητουμένων, πλὴν τοῦ κατὰ τὴν πίστιν λόγου, ὃν δι'
10ὀλίγου μὲν καὶ ἐπὶ τῆς παρούσης ἐκθησόμεθα πραγματείας,

---

116 ἐστίν GNO : ἐστί Srawley

solid and firm[376] nourishment, in the same manner, we also make an addition to the moisture from a kindred nature, the very thing that, passing into us, by a power of alteration, becomes blood, especially if through the wine it should receive the power to be remade into heat.

(12) Since, then, that God-receiving flesh[377] also received this part for its own composition, and the God who was made manifest mingled himself with perishable nature for this: in order that humanity might be deified by communion with the divinity,[378] because of this, by the economy of grace he sows himself in all the faithful[379] through the flesh whose composition [derives] from wine and bread, mixing with the bodies of the faithful, so that, by union with the immortal, man might become a partaker of incorruption. And he gives these things by the power of blessing, changing[380] the nature of those things that appear [to the senses] to that [immortal nature].[381]

Correct faith in the Trinity is necessary for baptism.

38 In what has been said, I think none of the questions about the mystery are omitted, except an account of the faith, which we will also briefly expound in the present study, but for those who seek a

---

[376]Here ἀντιτύπου refers simply to solid or "firm" food (as opposed to drink), but the same word can also mean "a figure (or 'type') of something else." This is the way it is used in Scripture, when the ark of Noah is called "an antitype [ἀντίτυπον] of baptism, which now saves us" (1 Pet 3.21). It is a word associated with the Eucharist by Gregory's brother, who calls the eucharistic offering of bread and wine "antitypes" in the formula immediately preceding the epiclesis, which calls down the Holy Spirit to bless, sanctify, and show the gifts to be Christ's body and blood.

[377]See p. 102, n. 168.

[378]St Gregory consistently uses the verb form of "apotheosis" (ἀποθέωσις), which is familiar to a pagan audience.

[379]More literally, "those who have believed" (τοῖς πεπιστευκόσι) here and below.

[380]Lit. "re-elementing" (μεταστοιχειώσας).

[381]St Gregory is referring to an experienced fact more than a eucharistic theory: what is changed is not the phenomenal aspect of the bread and wine—the senses detect no difference. See introduction, pp. 31–32.

$_{11}$τοῖς δὲ τὸν τελεώτερον ἐπιζητοῦσι λόγον ἤδη $_{12}$προεξεθέμεθα ἐν
5 ἑτέροις πόνοις, διὰ τῆς δυνατῆς ἡμῖν $_{13}$σπουδῆς ἐν ἀκριβείᾳ τὸν
λόγον ἁπλώσαντες, ἐν οἷς πρός $_{14}$τε τοὺς ἐναντίους ἀγωνιστικῶς
συνεπλάκημεν καὶ καθ' $_{15}$ἑαυτοὺς περὶ τῶν προσφερομένων ἡμῖν
ζητημάτων ἐπεσκεψάμεθα. (2) $_{16}$Τῷ δὲ παρόντι λόγῳ τοσοῦτον
εἰπεῖν περὶ τῆς $_{17}$πίστεως καλῶς ἔχειν ᾠήθημεν ὅσον ἡ τοῦ
10 εὐαγγελίου $_{18}$περιέχει φωνή, τὸ τὸν γεννώμενον κατὰ τὴν πνευ-
ματικὴν $_{19}$ἀναγέννησιν εἰδέναι παρὰ τίνος γεννᾶται καὶ ποῖον
(Sr 154) γίνεται | $_{20}$ζῷον· μόνον γὰρ τοῦτο τὸ τῆς γεννήσεως εἶδος κατ'
$_{21}$ἐξουσίαν ἔχει ὅτιπερ ἂν ἕληται τοῦτο γενέσθαι.

ΛΘ' Τὰ μὲν $_{22}$γὰρ λοιπὰ τῶν τικτομένων τῇ ὁρμῇ τῶν ἀπογεννώντων $_{23}$ὑφίσταται, ὁ δὲ πνευματικὸς τόκος τῆς ἐξουσίας
ἤρτηται $_{24}$τοῦ τικτομένου. Ἐπειδὴ τοίνυν ἐν τούτῳ ἐστὶν ὁ
κίνδυνος, $_{25}$ἐν τῷ μὴ διαμαρτεῖν τοῦ συμφέροντος, κατ' ἐξουσίαν |
5 (GNO 99) προκειμένης παντὶ τῆς αἱρέσεως, καλῶς ἔχειν φημὶ τὸν $_{2}$πρὸς
τὴν γέννησιν τὴν ἰδίαν ὁρμῶντα προδιαγνῶναι τῷ $_{3}$λογισμῷ,
τίς αὐτῷ λυσιτελήσει πατὴρ καὶ ἐκ τίνος ἄμεινον $_{4}$αὐτῷ συ-
(PG 100) στῆναι τὴν φύσιν· εἴρηται γὰρ ὅτι κατ' ἐξουσίαν | $_{5}$τοὺς
γεννήτορας ὁ τοιοῦτος αἱρεῖται τόκος.—

—(2) Διχῇ τοίνυν $_{6}$τῶν ὄντων
10 (Sr 155) μεμερισμένων εἰς τὸ κτιστὸν | καὶ τὸ ἄκτιστον, $_{7}$καὶ τῆς μὲν
ἀκτίστου φύσεως τὸ ἄτρεπτόν τε καὶ ἀμετάθετον $_{8}$ἐν ἑαυτῇ
κεκτημένης, τῆς δὲ κτίσεως πρὸς τροπὴν ἀλλοιουμένης, $_{9}$ὁ
κατὰ λογισμὸν τὸ λυσιτελοῦν προαιρούμενος $_{10}$τίνος αἱρήσεται
μᾶλλον γενέσθαι τέκνον, τῆς ἐν $_{11}$τροπῇ θεωρουμένης ἢ τῆς

more complete account, we have already previously expounded in other works, explaining the account with precision, with [all] the care of which we are capable, in which we wrestled contentiously with [our] opponents,[382] and considered the questions proposed to us on their own terms. (2) But in the present discourse we thought it good to say as much about the faith as the language[383] of the gospel contains: he who is begotten by the spiritual regeneration knows by whom he is begotten and what sort of living thing he becomes; for this is the only form of begetting that has "the authority to become"[384] whatever this one chooses.

39 For the rest of those who are born are given substance by the impulse of their parents,[385] but the spiritual birth is dependent on the authority of him who is born. Since, then, the danger is in this, lest he should miss what is beneficial, since the choice lies within everyone's authority, I say it is good for him who is eager[386] for his own begetting to determine beforehand by thinking what father would be profitable for him, and from whom it is better for [his] nature to be constituted; for it has been said that such a birth chooses [its] parents at will.

(2) Therefore, since existing things have been divided in two, into the created and the uncreated[387]—and while the uncreated nature possesses in itself changelessness and immutability, the created is altered by change—of whom will he who chooses what is profitable in accordance with reason[388] choose to become the child, of the one

---

[382]This may contain a clue to help us date the work, but it is not entirely clear which writings he refers to here. See introduction, p. 18.

[383]Lit. "voice" or "sound" (φωνή), a favored word to denote Scripture in St Gregory's writings.

[384]Jn 1.12.

[385]Or their "begetters" (ἀπογεννώντων); cf. Jn 1.13.

[386]Or "feels an impulse" (ὁρμῶντα), the same word as the noun (ὁρμή) used to describe biological parents' sexual desire—further emphasis on the decisive role the person who is baptized plays in his decision to be reborn.

[387]This is the more fundamental, and Christian division (compared to the division at 6.2).

[388]Elsewhere "reasoning," or "thought" (λογισμὸν).

15 ἀμετάστατόν τε καὶ παγίαν καὶ [12]ἀεὶ ὡσαύτως ἔχουσαν ἐν τῷ
ἀγαθῷ κεκτημένης τὴν φύσιν;—

—(3) [13]Ἐπεὶ οὖν ἐν τῷ Εὐαγγελίῳ τὰ
τρία παραδέδοται πρόσωπά [14]τε καὶ ὀνόματα δι' ὧν ἡ γέννησις
τοῖς πιστεύουσι γίνεται, [15]γεννᾶται δὲ κατὰ τὸ ἴσον ὁ ἐν τῇ
Τριάδι γεννώμενος παρὰ [16]Πατρός τε καὶ Υἱοῦ καὶ Πνεύματος
20 Ἁγίου—οὕτω γάρ φησι [17]περὶ τοῦ Πνεύματος τὸ Εὐαγγέλιον
ὅτι Τὸ γεγεννημένον ἐκ [18]τοῦ Πνεύματος πνεῦμά ἐστιν, καὶ ὁ
Παῦλος ἐν Χριστῷ [19]γεννᾷ, καὶ Ὁ Πατὴρ πάντων ἐστὶ
(Sr 156) Πατήρ—ἐνταῦθά μοι [20]νηφέτω τοῦ ἀκροατοῦ ἡ διάνοια, | μὴ
τῆς ἀστατούσης φύσεως [21]ἑαυτὸν ἔκγονον ποιήσῃ, ἐξὸν τὴν
25 ἄτρεπτόν τε καὶ [22]ἀναλλοίωτον ἀρχηγὸν ποιήσασθαι τῆς ἰδίας
ζωῆς.—

(GNO 100)   —(4) Κατὰ | γὰρ τὴν διάθεσιν τῆς καρδίας τοῦ προσιόντος τῇ
οἰκονομίᾳ [2]καὶ τὸ γινόμενον τὴν δύναμιν ἔχει, ὥστε τὸν μὲν
[3]ἄκτιστον ὁμολογοῦντα τὴν ἁγίαν Τριάδα εἰς τὴν ἄτρεπτόν [4]τε
καὶ ἀναλλοίωτον εἰσελθεῖν ζωήν, τὸν δὲ τὴν κτιστὴν [5]φύσιν ἐν
30 τῇ Τριάδι διὰ τῆς ἠπατημένης ὑπολήψεως βλέποντα, [6]ἔπειτα
ἐν αὐτῇ βαπτιζόμενον, πάλιν τῷ τρεπτῷ τε [7]καὶ ἀλλοιουμένῳ
ἐγγεννηθῆναι βίῳ· τῇ γὰρ τῶν γεννώντων [8]φύσει κατ' ἀνάγκην
ὁμογενές ἐστι καὶ τὸ τικτόμενον.—

—(5) Τί [9]οὖν ἂν εἴη λυσιτελέστερον,
εἰς τὴν ἄτρεπτον ζωὴν εἰσελθεῖν [10]ἢ πάλιν τῷ ἀστατοῦντι καὶ
35 ἀλλοιουμένῳ ἐγκυματοῦσθαι [11]βίῳ; Ἐπεὶ οὖν παντὶ δῆλόν ἐστι
τῷ καὶ ὁπωσοῦν διανοίας [12]μετέχοντι, ὅτι τὸ ἑστὼς τοῦ μὴ
ἑστῶτος παρὰ πολὺ τιμιώτερον, [13]καὶ τοῦ ἐλλιποῦς τὸ τέλειον,
καὶ τοῦ δεομένου τὸ μὴ [14]δεόμενον, καὶ τοῦ διὰ προκοπῆς ἀνιόν-
τος τὸ μὴ ἔχον εἰς [15]ὅ τι προέλθῃ, ἀλλ' ἐπὶ τῆς τελειότητος τοῦ
40 (Sr 157) ἀγαθοῦ μένον [16]ἀεί, ἐπάναγκες ἂν εἴη | ἓν ἐξ ἀμφοτέρων αἱρεῖσθαι

---

21 ἐστιν GNO : ἐστι Srawley | 24 ἑαυτὸν GNO : ἑαυτὴν Srawley

contemplated in change, or the one that has a nature possessing immutability and stability and is ever likewise in the good?

(3) Since, then, it has been handed down in the gospel that there are three persons[389] and names through which the begetting takes place among the faithful, and he who is begotten by the Trinity is equally begotten by the Father and the Son and the Holy Spirit—for thus the gospel says about the Spirit, that "what has been begotten from the Spirit is spirit,"[390] and Paul begets "in Christ,"[391] and [says that] the "Father of all"[392] is the Father—here, I ask, let the thought of the hearer be sober, lest he make himself the offspring of an unstable nature, when it is possible to make the unchangeable and unalterable [nature] the author of his own life.

(4) For what happens [in baptism] has power according to the disposition of the heart of him who approaches the economy [of baptism], so that he who confesses the holy Trinity to be uncreated enters into unchangeable and unalterable life, but he who, through a deceptive supposition, sees a created nature in the Trinity, and then is baptized into it, is again begotten into a changeable and alterable life; for the one who is born is also by necessity akin[393] to the nature of [his] begetters.[394]

(5) What then would be more profitable, to enter into the unchangeable life, or to be tossed about again in an unstable and alterable life? Since, then, it is clear to all who partake of thought in any way whatever, that the stable is by far more valuable than what is not stable, and the perfect than what is deficient, and what is in no need than what is in need, and what has no advance, but remains always in the perfection of the good, than what ascends through a progression. He who has a mind at all must by all means choose one

[389]Πρόσωπά.
[390]Jn 3.6.
[391]Cf. 1 Cor 4.15.
[392]Eph 4.6.
[393]Or "of the same kind," literally "homogenous" (ὁμογενές).
[394]For other fathers' attitude toward Arian baptism, see introduction, p. 30, n. 53.

πάντως ₁₇τόν γε νοῦν ἔχοντα, ἢ τῆς ἀκτίστου φύσεως εἶναι πιστεύειν ₁₈τὴν ἁγίαν Τριάδα καὶ οὕτως ἀρχηγὸν διὰ τῆς πνευ-
ματικῆς ₁₉γεννήσεως ποιεῖσθαι τῆς ἰδίας ζωῆς, ἤ, εἰ ἔξω τῆς τοῦ
πρώτου, ₂₀καὶ ἀληθινοῦ, καὶ ἀγαθοῦ Θεοῦ φύσεως (τῆς τοῦ
45 Πατρὸς ₂₁λέγω), νομίζοι εἶναι τὸν Υἱὸν ἢ τὸ Πνεῦμα τὸ Ἅγιον,
μὴ συμπαραλαμβάνειν ₂₂τὴν εἰς ταῦτα πίστιν ἐν τῷ καιρῷ τῆς
(GNO 101) γεν- | νήσεως, μήποτε λάθῃ τῇ ἐλλιπεῖ φύσει καὶ δεομένῃ τοῦ
₂ἀγαθύνοντος ἑαυτὸν εἰσποιῶν καὶ τρόπον τινὰ πάλιν εἰς ₃τὸ
ὁμογενὲς ἑαυτὸν εἰσαγάγῃ, τῆς ὑπερεχούσης φύσεως ₄ἀπο-
50 στήσας τὴν πίστιν.—
        —(6) Ὁ γάρ τινι τῶν κτιστῶν ἑαυτὸν ὑποζεύξας
(Sr 158) ₅λέληθεν εἰς ἑαυτὸν καὶ οὐκ εἰς τὸ θεῖον τὴν | ἐλπίδα ₆τῆς σωτη-
ρίας ἔχων. Πᾶσα γὰρ ἡ κτίσις τῷ κατὰ τὸ ἴσον ₇ἐκ τοῦ μὴ ὄντος
εἰς τὸ εἶναι προήκειν οἰκείως πρὸς ἑαυτὴν ₈ἔχει, καὶ ὥσπερ ἐπὶ
τῆς τῶν σωμάτων κατασκευῆς πάντα ₉τὰ μέλη πρὸς ἑαυτὰ
55 συμφυῶς ἔχει, κἂν τὰ μὲν ὑποβεβηκότα, ₁₀τὰ δὲ ὑπερανεστῶτα
τύχῃ, οὕτως ἡ κτιστὴ φύσις ₁₁ἥνωται πρὸς ἑαυτὴν κατὰ τὸν
(PG 101) λό-| γον τῆς κτίσεως καὶ ₁₂οὐδὲν ἡ κατὰ τὸ ὑπερέχον καὶ ἐνδέον ἐν
ἡμῖν διαφορὰ διΐστησιν ₁₃αὐτὴν τῆς πρὸς ἑαυτὴν συμφυΐας· ὧν
γὰρ ἐπ' ἴσης ₁₄προεπινοεῖται ἡ ἀνυπαρξία, κἂν ἐν τοῖς ἄλλοις τὸ
60 διάφορον ₁₅ᾖ, οὐδεμίαν κατὰ τὸ μέρος τοῦτο τῆς φύσεως παραλ-
₁₆λαγὴν ἐξευρίσκομεν.—
        —(7) Εἰ οὖν κτιστὸς μὲν ὁ ἄνθρωπος, ₁₇κτιστὸν
δὲ καὶ τὸ Πνεῦμα καὶ τὸν μονογενῆ Θεὸν εἶναι ₁₈νομίζοι,
μάταιος ἂν εἴη ἐν ἐλπίδι τῆς ἐπὶ τὸ κρεῖττον μεταστάσεως
₁₉πρὸς ἑαυτὸν ἀναλύων. Ὅμοιον γὰρ ταῖς τοῦ ₂₀Νικοδήμου ὑπο-
65 λήψεσίν ἐστι τὸ γινόμενον, ὃς περὶ τοῦ ₂₁δεῖν ἄνωθεν γεν-

52 ἑαυτὸν GNO : αὐτὸ Srawley

of the two, either to believe the holy Trinity belongs to the uncreated nature and thus to make [the Trinity] the author of his own life by a spiritual begetting, or, if he should deem the Son or the Holy Spirit to be outside the first, and true, and good nature of God (I mean of the Father), not to include faith in these [persons] at the time of begetting [i.e., baptism], lest it should escape his notice that he is giving himself in adoption to a nature that is deficient and in need of someone to make it good, and in some manner introduce himself again to what is akin to himself, by deserting faith in the transcendent nature.

(6) For one who puts himself under bondage to any created things is unaware that he has [his] hope of salvation in himself and not in the divine. For all creation, in that it equally proceeds from nonbeing into existence, has a kinship[395] with itself, and just as in the case of the fashioning of bodies, all the parts have an innate affinity with themselves, while some happen to be lower and others to be higher, thus created nature is united with itself in the order[396] of creation, and the difference of the superior and inferior in us does not separate[397] it from an innate affinity with itself; for in the case of those things which were thought of before as equally [proceeding from] nonexistence, though there may be a difference in other things, we discover in this part no variation of nature.

(7) If then man is created, and he should also deem the Spirit and the only begotten God[398] [i.e., Christ] to be created, hope for a change for the better would be vain, since he returns to himself.[399] For what happens is similar to the suppositions of Nicodemus, who, learning from the Lord about the necessity of being born again,[400]

[395]Or "familiarity" (οἰκείως).

[396]λόγον.

[397]Here "separate" (δϊστησιν) is related to the word διάστημα, which is often a technical word for St Gregory.

[398]Jn 1.18 (variant).

[399]I.e., he is baptized into a created nature like his own; no transformation can take place. See introduction, p. 30, n. 53.

[400]Or "of being begotten [γεννηθῆναι] from above [ἄνωθέν]."

νηθῆναι παρὰ τοῦ Κυρίου μαθὼν διὰ τὸ ₂₂μήπω χωρῆσαι τοῦ
(Sr 159) μυστηρίου τὸν λόγον ἐπὶ τὸν | μητρῷον ₂₃κόλπον τοῖς λογισμοῖς
κατεσύρετο. Ὥστε εἰ μὴ πρὸς τὴν ₂₄ἄκτιστον φύσιν, ἀλλὰ πρὸς
(GNO 102) τὴν συγγενῆ καὶ ὁμόδουλον | κτίσιν ἑαυτὸν ἀπάγοι, τῆς
70 κάτωθεν, οὐ τῆς ἄνωθέν ἐστι ₂γεννήσεως. Φησὶ δὲ τὸ εὐαγγέλιον ἄνωθεν εἶναι τῶν ₃σῳζομένων τὴν γέννησιν.

Μ' ₄Ἀλλ' οὔ μοι δοκεῖ μέχρι τῶν εἰρημένων αὐτάρκη τὴν
₅διδασκαλίαν ἡ κατήχησις ἔχειν. Δεῖ γάρ, οἶμαι, καὶ τὸ ₆μετὰ
τοῦτο σκοπεῖν, ὃ πολλοὶ τῶν προσιόντων τῇ τοῦ ₇βαπτίσματος
χάριτι παρορῶσι, δι' ἀπάτης ἑαυτοὺς παράγοντες ₈καὶ τῷ
5 δοκεῖν μόνον, οὐχὶ τῷ ὄντι γεννώμενοι.
Ἡ ₉γὰρ διὰ τῆς ἀναγεννήσεως γινομένη τῆς ζωῆς ἡμῶν
μεταποίησις ₁₀οὐκ ἂν εἴη μεταποίησις, εἰ ἐν ᾧ ἐσμεν δια-
μένοιμεν. ₁₁Τὸν γὰρ ἐν τοῖς αὐτοῖς ὄντα οὐκ οἶδα πῶς ἔστιν
₁₂ἄλλον τινὰ γεγενῆσθαι νομίσαι, ἐφ' οὗ μηδὲν τῶν γνωρισ-
10 ₁₃μάτων μετεποιήθη. Τὸ γὰρ ἐπὶ ἀνακαινισμῷ καὶ μεταβολῇ
₁₄τῆς φύσεως ἡμῶν τὴν σωτήριον παραλαμβάνεσθαι γέννησιν
(Sr 160) ₁₅παντὶ δῆλόν ἐστιν. (2) Ἀλλὰ μὴν ἡ ἀνθρωπότης αὐτὴ καθ' | ₁₆ἑαυτὴν
μεταβολὴν ἐκ τοῦ βαπτίσματος οὐ προσίεται, οὔτε ₁₇τὸ λογικόν,
οὔτε τὸ διανοητικόν, οὔτε τὸ ἐπιστήμης δεκτικόν, ₁₈οὐδὲ ἄλλο τι
15 τῶν χαρακτηριζόντων ἰδίως τὴν ἀνθρωπίνην ₁₉φύσιν ἐν
μεταποιήσει γίνεται. Ἦ γὰρ ἂν πρὸς τὸ ₂₀χεῖρον ἡ μεταποίησις
εἴη, εἴ τι τούτων ὑπαμειφθείη τῶν ἰδίων ₂₁τῆς φύσεως. Εἰ οὖν ἡ
ἄνωθεν γέννησις ἀναστοιχείωσίς ₂₂τις τοῦ ἀνθρώπου γίνεται,
ταῦτα δὲ τὴν μεταβολὴν οὐ ₂₃προσίεται, σκεπτέον τίνος μετα-
20 ποιηθέντος ἐντελὴς τῆς ₂₄ἀναγεννήσεως ἡ χάρις ἐστίν.

20 ἐστίν GNO : ἐστί Srawley

because he was not yet capable [of understanding] the meaning[401] of the mystery, was led back to thoughts of a mother's womb. Therefore, if he should lead himself not to the uncreated nature, but rather to a creature, akin and alike a slave, he belongs to [the birth] from below, not to the birth from above.[402] And the gospel says the birth of the saved is from above.

Moral transformation must follow after baptism.

40 But up to this point in what has been said, the catechesis does not seem to me to have a sufficient teaching on its own. For it is also necessary, I think, to consider what is after this, which many of those who approach the grace of baptism overlook, misleading themselves through deception and being begotten only in seeming and not in reality.

For the remaking of our life that takes place through regeneration would not be a remaking if we should remain in the [state in which] we are. For I do not know how one could deem him who is among the same things to have become someone else, none of whose characteristics were remade; for it is clear to all that the saving birth is received for the renewal and change of our nature. (2) But truly humanity itself does not admit a change in itself in baptism, neither the rational faculty, nor the faculty of thought, nor the capacity for knowledge, nor is any other one of the things that properly characterize human nature remade. For it would be a remaking for the worse, if any of these properties of [our] nature were replaced. If, then, the rebirth[403] is a sort of recreation[404] of man, and these [properties] do not admit of change, one must consider by what sort of remaking the grace of regeneration is complete.

---

[401]Or "account" (λόγον).

[402]As in John 3, the word ἄνωθέν is ambiguous: it can mean "above" or "again"—rebirth, or birth from above.

[403]Or "birth [or 'begetting'] from above" (ἡ ἄνωθεν γέννησις).

[404]Lit. "re-elementing" (ἀναστοιχείωσις).

—(3) Δῆλον
ὅτι τῶν πονηρῶν ₂₅γνωρισμάτων ἐξαλειφθέντων τῆς φύσεως
(GNO 103) ἡμῶν ἡ πρὸς τὸ | κρεῖττον μετάστασις γίνεται. Οὐκοῦν εἰ,
καθώς φησιν ὁ ₂προφήτης, λουσάμενοι τῷ μυστικῷ τούτῳ λου-
τρῷ καθαροὶ ₃τὰς προαιρέσεις γενοίμεθα τὰς πονηρίας τῶν ψυ-
25 χῶν ₄ἀποκλύσαντες, κρείττους γεγόναμεν καὶ πρὸς τὸ κρεῖττον ₅μετεποιήθημεν. Εἰ δὲ τὸ μὲν λουτρὸν ἐπαχθείη τῷ ₆σώ-
ματι, ἡ δὲ ψυχὴ τὰς ἐμπαθεῖς κηλῖδας μὴ ἀπορρύψαιτο, ₇ἀλλ᾽ ὁ
μετὰ τὴν μύησιν βίος συμβαίνοι τῷ ἀμυήτῳ βίῳ, ₈κἂν τολμηρὸν
εἰπεῖν ᾖ, λέξω καὶ οὐκ ἀποτραπήσομαι, ὅτι ₉ἐπὶ τούτων τὸ ὕδωρ
30 (Sr 161) ὕδωρ ἐστίν, οὐδαμοῦ τῆς δωρεᾶς | τοῦ ₁₀ἁγίου Πνεύματος ἐπιφα-
νείσης τῷ γιγνομένῳ, ὅταν μὴ μόνον ₁₁τὸ κατὰ τὸν θυμὸν αἶσχος
(PG 104) ὑβρίζῃ τὴν θείαν | μορφὴν ἢ ₁₂τὸ κατὰ πλεονεξίαν πάθος, καὶ ἡ
ἀκόλαστος καὶ ἀσχήμων ₁₃διάνοια, καὶ τῦφος, καὶ φθόνος, καὶ
ὑπερηφανία, ἀλλὰ καὶ ₁₄τὰ ἐξ ἀδικίας κέρδη παραμένῃ αὐτῷ καὶ
35   —ἡ ἐκ μοιχείας ₁₅αὐτῷ κτηθεῖσα γυνὴ ταῖς ἡδοναῖς αὐτοῦ καὶ
μετὰ τοῦτο ₁₆ὑπηρετῆται.—

—(4) Ἐὰν ταῦτα καὶ τὰ τοιαῦτα ὁμοίως
πρότερόν τε ₁₇καὶ μετὰ ταῦτα περὶ τὸν βίον τοῦ βαπτισθέντος ᾖ,
τί ₁₈μεταπεποίηται ἰδεῖν οὐκ ἔχω, τὸν αὐτὸν βλέπων ὅνπερ καὶ
₁₉πρότερον. Ὁ ἠδικημένος, ὁ σεσυκοφαντημένος, ὁ τῶν ἰδίων
(GNO 104) ₂₀ἀπωσθεὶς οὐδεμίαν ὁρῶσιν ἐφ᾽ ἑαυτῶν τὴν τοῦ λελου- | μένου
μεταβολήν. Οὐκ ἤκουσαν καὶ παρὰ τούτου τὴν τοῦ ₂Ζακχαίου
φωνὴν ὅτι Εἴ τινά τι ἐσυκοφάντησα, ἀποδίδωμι ₃τετραπλα-
σίονα. Ἃ πρὸ τοῦ βαπτίσματος ἔλεγον, τὰ αὐτὰ ₄καὶ νῦν περὶ
αὐτοῦ διεξέρχονται, ἐκ τῶν αὐτῶν ὀνομάτων ₅κατονομάζουσι

(3) It is clear that when wicked characteristics are blotted out from our nature, there is a change for the better. If, then, as the prophet says, "being washed" by this mystic[405] washing our faculty of decision is "purified," "having washed away the wickednesses of [our] souls,"[406] we became better and were remade for the better. Now if the washing is applied to the body, and the soul has not expunged the stains of the passions, but life after initiation should be on a par with uninitiated life, though it may be daring to say, I will say it and not be deterred, that in these cases the water is water, since the gift of the Holy Spirit is nowhere manifest in what takes place, when not only the shame of anger mutilates the divine form, or the passion of greed, and unbridled and unseemly thought, and vanity, and envy, and arrogance, but also things gained by injustice remain with him, and the woman he acquired for himself through adultery serves his pleasures even after this.[407]

(4) If these things and the like should similarly surround the life of him who is baptized both before and after, I am unable to see what has been remade, since I see him the same as before. He who has suffered injustice, he who has been falsely accused, he who was thrust out from his own things, in their own case they see no change in him who has been washed. They did not hear also from this one the saying of Zacchaeus: "If I have [taken anything] from anyone by false accusation, I give back fourfold."[408] The things which they said before baptism, the same things they also relate about him now, they call him by the same names: greedy, desiring things that belong

---

[405]Or "sacramental" (μυστικῷ).

[406]Cf. Is 1.16.

[407]Cf. *Life of Moses* 2.125–29 (the catalogue of post-baptismal sins and their seeming ability to invalidate one's baptism are quite similar). These bold words resemble the near-contemporary teaching of St Cyril of Jerusalem: "For although your body might be here, if your mind is not, nothing is gained. Once Simon Magus also entered into the water; he was baptized but not enlightened. And while he plunged his body into the water, he did not enlighten his heart with the Spirit. And his body descended and ascended. But his soul was not buried with Christ, nor raised up." *Procatechesis* 1–2 (PPS 57:65). See introduction pp. 30–31.

[408]Lk 19.8.

45 πλεονέκτην, τῶν ἀλλοτρίων ἐπιθυμητήν, ₆ἀπὸ συμφορῶν ἀνθρωπίνων τρυφῶντα. Ὁ τοίνυν ἐν τοῖς ₇αὐτοῖς ὤν, ἔπειτα ἐπι-
(Sr 162) θρυλῶν ἑαυτῷ διὰ | τοῦ βαπτίσματος ₈τὴν πρὸς τὸ κρεῖττον
μεταβολήν, ἀκουσάτω τῆς Παύλου ₉φωνῆς ὅτι Εἴ τις δοκεῖ
εἶναί τι, μηδὲν ὤν, φρεναπατᾷ ἑαυτόν. ₁₀Ὁ γὰρ μὴ γέγονας, οὐκ
50 εἶ.—
        —(5) Ὅσοι ἔλαβον αὐτόν, φησὶ ₁₁περὶ τῶν ἀναγεννηθέντων τὸ
εὐαγγέλιον, ἔδωκεν αὐτοῖς ₁₂ἐξουσίαν τέκνα θεοῦ γενέσθαι.
Τὸ τέκνον γενόμενόν τινος ₁₃ὁμογενὲς πάντως ἐστὶ τῷ γεννή-
σαντι. Εἰ οὖν ἔλαβες τὸν ₁₄Θεὸν καὶ τέκνον ἐγένου Θεοῦ, δεῖξον
διὰ τῆς προαιρέσεως ₁₅καὶ τὸν ἐν σοὶ ὄντα Θεόν, δεῖξον ἐν
55 σεαυτῷ τὸν γεννήσαντα. ₁₆Ἐξ ὧν τὸν Θεὸν γνωρίζομεν, δι᾿
ἐκείνων προσήκει δειχθῆναι ₁₇τοῦ γενομένου υἱοῦ Θεοῦ τὴν πρὸς
τὸν Θεὸν οἰκειότητα. ₁₈Ἐκεῖνος Ἀνοίγει τὴν χεῖρα καὶ ἐμπι-
πλᾷ πᾶν ζῷον ₁₉εὐδοκίας, ὑπερβαίνει ἀνομίας, μετανοεῖ ἐπὶ
(GNO 105) κακίαις· | Χρηστὸς Κύριος τοῖς σύμπασι, μὴ ὀργὴν ἐπάγων
60 καθ᾿ ₂ἑκάστην ἡμέραν· Εὐθὴς Κύριος ὁ Θεός, καὶ οὐκ ἔστιν
ἀδικία ₃ἐν αὐτῷ, καὶ ὅσα τοιαῦτα σποράδην παρὰ τῆς γραφῆς
₄διδασκόμεθα. (6) Ἐὰν ἐν τούτοις ᾖς, ἀληθῶς ἐγένου τέκνον
₅Θεοῦ· εἰ δὲ τοῖς τῆς κακίας ἐπιμένεις γνωρίσμασι, μάτην
₆ἐπιθρυλεῖς σεαυτῷ τὴν ἄνωθεν γέννησιν. Ἐρεῖ πρὸς σὲ ἡ

to others, living in luxury off of human misfortunes. Therefore let him who is in the midst of the same things [and] then babbles to himself about the change for the better through baptism hear the voice of Paul, that "if anyone thinks himself to be something, when he is nothing, he deceives himself."[409] For that which you have not become, you are not.

(5) "As many as received him," the evangelist says about those who have been regenerated, "to them he gave authority to become children of God."[410] One who has become someone's child is altogether akin to him who begot [him]. If, then, you received God and became a child of God, show by your decision the God who is in you, show in yourself him who begot [you]. From these things we recognize God, through them it is fitting for him who has become a son of God to show [his] relationship[411] with God. He "opens [his] hand and fills every living thing with [his] good pleasure";[412] "he passes over iniquity";[413] "he repents of vices";[414] "the Lord is good to all,"[415] "not bringing his anger upon [us] each day";[416] "upright is the Lord God, and there is not unrighteousness in him";[417] and all such things we are taught by [passages] scattered throughout the Scripture. (6) If you are amidst these things, truly you have become a child of God; but if you remain in the midst of vicious characteristics, in vain do you babble to yourself about being born again.[418] Prophecy will tell you that you are "a son of man,"[419] not "a son of

[409]Gal 6.3.
[410]Jn 1.12.
[411]Or "familiarity" (οἰκειότητα).
[412]Ps 144.16.
[413]Cf. Mic 7.18 LXX.
[414]Joel 2.13.
[415]Ps 144.9.
[416]Ps 7.12b LXX.
[417]Ps 91.16.
[418]Or "the birth [or 'begetting'] from on high" (τὴν ἄνωθεν γέννησιν).

[419]This title is used numerous times in Scripture. In Ezekiel, God refers to the prophet dozens of times by this epithet, while in Daniel 7 it refers to a mysterious figure related to the Ancient of Days, which is interpreted by later Christian tradition—and by Christ himself (Mt 26.64; Mk 14.62; Lk 22.69)—as referring to the

65 7προφητεία ὅτι Υἱὸς ἀνθρώπου εἶ, οὐχὶ υἱὸς Ὑψίστου· 8ἀγαπᾷς
ματαιότητα, ζητεῖς ψεῦδος· οὐκ ἔγνως πῶς θαυμαστοῦται
(Sr 163) 9ἄνθρωπος, ὅτι οὐκ ἄλλως εἰ μὴ ὅσιος | γένηται.

(7) 10Ἀναγκαῖον ἂν εἴη τούτοις προσθεῖναι καὶ τὸ λειπόμενον, 11ὅτι
οὔτε τὰ ἀγαθὰ τὰ ἐν ἐπαγγελίαις τοῖς εὖ βεβιωκόσι 12προ-
70 κείμενα τοιαῦτά ἐστιν ὡς εἰς ὑπογραφὴν λόγου ἐλθεῖν. 13 Πῶς
γὰρ Ἃ οὔτε ὀφθαλμὸς εἶδεν, οὔτε οὖς ἤκουσεν, οὔτε 14ἐπὶ
καρδίαν ἀνθρώπου ἀνέβη; Οὔτε μὴν ἡ ἀλγεινὴ τῶν
15πεπλημμεληκότων ζωὴ πρός τι τῶν τῇδε λυπούντων τὴν
16αἴσθησιν ὁμοτίμως ἔχει, ἀλλὰ κἂν ἐπονομασθῇ τι τῶν ἐκεῖ
5 (GNO 106) 17κολαστηρίων τοῖς ὧδε γνωριζομένοις ὀνόμασιν, οὐκ ἐν | ὀλίγῳ
τὴν παραλλαγὴν ἔχει· πῦρ γὰρ ἀκούων ἄλλο τι 2παρὰ τοῦτο
(PG 105) νοεῖν ἐδιδάχθης ἐκ τοῦ προσκεῖσθαί τι τῷ πυρὶ 3ἐκείνῳ | ὃ ἐν
τούτῳ οὐκ ἔστιν· τὸ μὲν γὰρ οὐ σβέννυται, τούτου 4δὲ πολλὰ
παρὰ τῆς πείρας ἐξεύρηται τὰ σβεστήρια· 5πολλὴ δὲ τοῦ σβεν-
80 νυμένου πρὸς τὸ μὴ παραδεχόμενον 6σβέσιν ἡ διαφορά. Οὐκοῦν
ἄλλο τι καὶ οὐχὶ τοῦτό ἐστιν.—
—(8) 7Πάλιν σκώληκά τις ἀκούσας μὴ
διὰ τῆς ὁμωνυμίας πρὸς 8τὸ ἐπίγειον τοῦτο θηρίον ἀποφερέσθω
τῇ διανοίᾳ· ἡ γὰρ 9προσθήκη τοῦ ἀτελεύτητον εἶναι ἄλλην τινὰ
φύσιν παρὰ 10τὴν γινωσκομένην νοεῖν ὑποτίθεται. Ἐπεὶ οὖν

78 ἔστιν GNO : ἔστι Srawley

the Most High";[420] you "love vanity,"[421] you "seek falsehood";[422] you have not come to know how man is "made wonderful,"[423] that it is no way other than by becoming holy.

Eternal recompense awaits us.

(7) It is necessary to add to these things the remaining [truth] also, that the good things in the promises that lie before those who have lived well are such that they cannot be hinted at by word. For how [can one describe] "things that eye has not seen, nor ear heard, nor has it entered into man's heart"?[424] Nor indeed is the painful life of transgressors comparable to any of the things that pain the senses here, but even though some of the punishments there are called by the names known here, the difference is not slight: for when you hear "fire,"[425] you have been taught to think of it as something other than this, because of something added to that fire, which is not in this one: for the [former] "is not quenched,"[426] but many things have been discovered by experience that quench this one; and there is much difference between the [fire] that is quenched and that which does not admit of being quenched. Therefore it is something else and not this.

(8) Again when you hear of some "worm"[427] do not be carried off in thought by the similarity of the name[428] to this earthly beast; for the addition "that does not die"[429] suggests some nature other than

Messiah. St Gregory uses "son of man" in the former sense, meaning "a human being" (and here, a *mere* human being).

[420]Mk 5.7; Lk 1.32 (this entire phrase is used only twice in Scripture, both times referring to Christ).

[421]Ps 4.3.

[422]Ibid.

[423]Ps 4.4: "Know also that the Lord has made wonderful his holy one."

[424]1 Cor 2.9 (cf. Is 64.4).

[425]Mk 9.43–48.

[426]Ibid.

[427]Ibid.

[428]Lit. "homonymy" (ὁμωνυμίας).

[429]Or "is endless" (ἀτελεύτητον).

85 ταῦτα πρόκειται ₁₁τῇ ἐλπίδι τοῦ μετὰ ταῦτα βίου, καταλλήλως
(Sr 164) ἐκ τῆς ₁₂ἑκάστου προαιρέσεως | κατὰ τὴν δικαίαν τοῦ Θεοῦ
κρίσιν ₁₃ἀναφυόμενα τῷ βίῳ, σωφρονούντων ἂν εἴη μὴ πρὸς τὸ
₁₄παρὸν ἀλλὰ πρὸς τὸ μετὰ τοῦτο βλέπειν, καὶ τῆς ἀφράστου
₁₅μακαριότητος ἐν τῇ ὀλίγῃ ταύτῃ καὶ προσκαίρῳ ζωῇ ₁₆τὰς
90 ἀφορμὰς καταβάλλεσθαι καὶ τῆς τῶν κακῶν πείρας ₁₇δι' ἀγαθῆς
προαιρέσεως ἀλλοτριοῦσθαι, νῦν μὲν κατὰ τὸν ₁₈βίον, μετὰ
ταῦτα δὲ κατὰ τὴν αἰωνίαν ἀντίδοσιν.

the one known [to us]. Since, then, these things are set forth for [our] hope for the afterlife,[430] which are, according to the just judgment of God, the corresponding products of decision in [one's] life, it would be prudent not to look to the present but to what is after this, and to lay down the foundations of ineffable blessedness in this short and temporary life, and by a good decision to estrange [ourselves] from the experience of evils now in life, and after these things in an eternal recompense.

---

[430]Lit. "the life after these things" (τοῦ μετὰ ταῦτα βίου).

Greek-English Glossary

The translation strives for terminological precision and consistency (using the same English word for the same Greek word, when possible, allows the reader to determine the meaning by its use). Below are the main ways that many key Greek terms are translated, along with secondary translations, which are necessary at times either because a word bears more than one meaning, or because English usage required a different rendering.

αἱρέω—to decide, *sometimes* to choose

αἵρεσις—heresy

αἴσθησις— perception; sense, sensation, sense perception

αἰσθητός—sensory; sense perceptible

αἴτιος—cause; *rarely* fault *(30.2.13; cf. 30.3.30)*

ἀκολουθία/ἀκόλουθον —order; *often* order [of the argument] *(see p. 61, n. 11)*

ἀλλοιούμενον—alterable (*once* altered)

ἀλλοίωσις—alteration

ἀλλότριος—alien; *once plural:* things that belong to others (40.4.45)

ἀλλοτρίωσις—alienation *or* estrangement

ἀναγέννησις—regeneration

ἀναγωγικῶς—by way of ascent, lit. "anagogically"

ἀνάκρασις—mingling

ἄνθρωπος—man (*sometimes an individual, but more often meaning "mankind"*; ἀνήρ *is never used); once plural* human beings *(8.4.25) referring to Adam and Eve, otherwise* men

ἀντιδιαιρέω—to distinguish

ἀντιδιαστολή—distinction

ἀντίδοσις—recompense

ἀξία/ἄξιος—worth/worthy; *sometimes* dignity

ἀπάτη—deception *or* deceit

ἀπόδειξις—demonstration; proof

ἀποκατάστασις—restoration

ἀπολογία—defense

ἅπτω—to join; to fasten; to touch; to lay hold

ἀρχή—beginning; principle

αὐτεξουσία—self-determination; *sometimes* free will *(with footnote identifying the term)*

ἀφανίζω/ἀφανισμός—to destroy/destruction; to disappear/disappearance ἀφορμή—*most often plural:* means; origins; foundations; *once* pretext *(22.1.4)*

βίος—life

βούλημα/βούλησις—intention; will; *once* counsel *(28.1.8; cf. 8.19.170)*

γνώμη—intention *(6.11.108; 17.1.6)*; judgment *(31.1.11; 31.2.18)*

γνώρισμα—characteristic; *once this word translates* χαρακτηριζόμενα *(Pr.6.51); verb* to characterize *is always* χαρακτηρίζω

γυμνός—naked *or* laid bare

δείκνυμι—to demonstrate; to show; *once* displayed *(Pr.4.34) and* appear *(13.3.25)*

δημιουργέω/δημιουργία/ δημιουργός—to create/creation/ creator *(lit.* demiurge; *see n. 57 on p. 73); once* to craft *(5.3.34)*

διαίρεσις/διαιρέω—division/to divide; distinction/to distinguish

διακρίνω/διάκρισις—to divide/divi- sion; to distinguish/distinction; to separate/separation

διάνοια—thought; thinking; *once* meaning *(8.4.28); once* spirit *(18.5.45); once* τὴν διάνοιαν φέρει *rendered as* brings to mind *(20.1.3)*

διαστολή—distinction

διηγέομαι/διήγησις—to nar- rate/narrative; *once* description *(8.12.12); once* tales *(18.5.47)*

δόγμα—teaching *or* doctrine

δοκέω—to seem; *once the plu- ral participle:* those who hold opinions

τὸ δοκοῦν—good pleasure; purpose; *once* what pleased [the devil] *(6.7.75)*

δύναμαι—to be able; to be empowered

δύναμις—power; ability; *sometimes* potential *in Aristotelian sense* twice host/hosts *(4.2.10/4.4.24, quoting Ps 32.6)*

δόξα—glory; opinion; *once* ἄδοξον *as* dishonor *(27.4.38)*

εἶδος—form

εἴδωλον—image *in a neutral sense, or (false, pagan)* idol

εἰκών—image

εἱρμός—sequence; *once* chain *(6.3.21)*

ἑκουσίως—willingly *(see p. 57 and n. 33 on p. 66)*

ἐνέργεια—activity

ἐνεργὸς—active; operative

ἔννοια—notion *or* thought

ἐξουσία—authority; power; κατ᾽ ἐξουσίαν *rendered as* at will; *once* τὸ κατ᾽ ἐξουσίαν *rendered as* self- determination *(31.1.8–9)*

ἔξω/ἔξωθεν/ἐκτός—outside; with- out; *sometimes* beyond *or* apart from

ἐπιμιξία—admixture

ἐπίνοια—concept *(sometimes a technical term for St Gregory esp. in* Against Eunomius*);* artifice *or* device

ἔργον—work; *once* deed *(35.2.20)*

ἕτερος/ἑτερότητος—different/dif- ference; other *or* another

εὐεργεσία/εὐεργετέω/εὐεργέτης—
benefit (*or* beneficence)/to
benefit/benefactor

ζητέω—to seek; to ask

ζήτημα—inquiry *or* question

ζωή—life

ζῷον—living thing; *once* creature
(27.3.28)

θαυμάζω/θαύματος—to wonder/
wonder; miracle

θέλημα/θέλω—will/to will

θεοπρεπής—God-befitting; befitting God; befitting for God (*see
n. 15 on p. 62*)

θεωρέω/θεωρία—to contemplate/
contemplation; to see (*the etymological meaning*)

ἱστορέω/ἱστορία/ἱστορικός—to
record/record; history/historical;
once historical record (29.3.24)

κακία—vice; *twice* κατὰ κακίαν
rendered as vicious (6.9.97; 9.2.19)

κακός—evil; *once* illness (17.2.14);
likewise ἐν κακοῖς *once rendered*
ill (20.4.30)

κατάληψις—apprehension; comprehension; grasp

κατανοέω—to understand; *sometimes* to consider *or* perceived

κατανόησις—understanding; *once*
observation (6.2.7)

κατασκευή/κατασκέω—proof/to
prove (*rhetorical sense); or*
fashioning/to fashion (*a near
synonym of* what is made/to
make)

κατήχησις—catechesis

κίνησις—motion *or* movement;
more generally change (*see n. 164
on p. 100*)

κοινωνία—fellowship; communion

κόσμος—world; cosmos

κρεῖττον—superior *or* better

κριτήριον—criterion

λογισμός—reasoning (*once* reason*);
sometimes* thought/thinking *or*
arguments

λόγος—discourse; argument; word
(*and* Word); account; principle;
rarely idea (15.6.57, 15.7.61);
once sense (37.9.86); *once* scale
(16.8.73)

μαρτυρέω/μαρτυρία—to testify/tes-
timony; to bear witness/witness

μέσος—mean; middle; *once* interval
(35.14.116)

μεταποιέω—to remake; *once*
reclaiming (20.3.22)

μετουσία—participation

μίξις—mixing *or* mixture

μίμημα/μίμησις—imitation *or* copy

νόημα—thought

νομίζω—to deem

οἰκεῖος—proper; (*one's*) own; *in
the etymological sense:* at home;
οἰκείως ἔχει *rendered as* has a
kinship

οἰκειότης—relationship; familiarity

ὁμολογέω/ὁμολογία—to admit/
admission; to agree/agreement;
to confess/confession

ὁρμή—impulse; *once* rush (1.4.23)

οὐσία—being; *sometimes* essence

πάθος—passion *(the proper Nyssene sense, cf. 16)*; suffering; *sometimes* experience *or* possibility

τὸ πᾶν—the universe

πέρας—limit *or more rarely* end; purpose; *once* completion *(20.4.31)*

πονηρία/πονηρός—wickedness; wicked

προαίρεσις—decision *or* choice; faculty of decision *(see n. 33 on p. 66)*; *sometimes* will *or* free will *(with footnote identifying the term)*

προαιρετικός—capable of decision

πρόληψις—presupposition

πρόνοια—providence

πρός τι—relational

ῥοπή—inclination

σημεῖον—sign

σκοπός—aim

συγγένεια/συγγενής—kinship/akin *or* kindred; congenial

συγκρίνω—to compare

συζεύγνυμι/σύζευξις—to conjoin *or* join/coinjoined *or* joined *(so too* διαζεύγνυμαι/διάζευξις—to disjoin/disjoined)

συμφυής—innate *or* innate affinity

συμφύω—to grow together *or* with; to have an innate affinity

συνανάκρασις—commingling

συνδρομή/σύνδρομος—concourse/concurrent

σύστασις—constitution *or* composition

σχετικός—relational

τάξις—arrangement

ταπεινότης/τὸ ταπεινόν—humiliation *or* humility

τεχνικός/τεχνικῶς—skillful/skillfully; artful/artfully; technical/technically

τροπή—change

τρόπος—manner

ὑπερέχουσα—transcendent

ὕπαρξις—existence; *likewise* ἀνυπαρξία rendered as nonexistence

ὑπόδειγμα—illustration

ὑποκείμενον—subject *or* underlying subject; *once* what lies below *(32.9.79)*

ὑπόληψις—supposition

ὑπονοέω/ὑπόνοια—to conjecture/conjecture

ὑπόστασις—*general sense:* substance; *specific Christian sense is transliterated:* hypostasis *(for a person of the Trinity)*

φαινόμενον/φαίνω—appearance *or* phenomenon/to appear; *once* φαινομένῳ rendered as to the senses *(32.10.97); once* τὸ φαινόμενον *rendered* as the visible [matter] *(33.3.35) and once* τοῦ φαινομένου *rendered as* what he sees *(37.6.50)*

φαντασία—fantasy; mere appearance *(21.4.31; 21.5.43); once* manifestation *(23.3.43)*

χαρακτηρίζω—to characterize

χωρίζω—to separate

ὠφέλεια/ὠφελέω—profit/to profit

Select Bibliography

Editions and Translations of the *Catechetical Discourse*

An Address on Religious Instruction. Translated by Cyril C. Richardson. In *Christology of the Later Fathers*. Edited Edward R. Hardy and Cyril C. Richardson. Louisville, KY: The Westminster Press, 1954. Pp. 268–325.

The Catechetical Oration of Gregory of Nyssa. Edited by John Herbert Srawley. Cambridge: Cambridge University Press, 1903.

The Catechetical Oration of St. Gregory of Nyssa. Translated by John Herbert Srawley. London: Society for Promoting Christian Knowledge, 1917.

Discours catéchétique. Translated by Raymond Winling. Sources Chrétiennes, N° 453. Paris: Les Édition du Cerf, 2000.

The Great Catechism. Translated by William Moore and Henry Austin Wilson. NPNF² 5:471–509.

Grégoire de Nysse: Discours Catéchétique. Translated by Louis Méridier. Paris: Libraire Alphonse Picard et Fils, 1908.

Oratio Catechetica: Opera Dogmatica Minora, Pars IV. Edited by Ekkehard Mühlenberg. Gregorii Nysseni Opera, Volumen III, Pars IV. Leiden: Brill, 1996.

Other Works by St Gregory of Nyssa[1]

Against Usury. Translated by Richard McCambley. http://www.lectio-divina.org/images/nyssa/On%20Usury.pdf
> *Contra usurarios oratio*. GNO IX:195–207. PG 46:433–52.

Concerning Almsgiving. Translated by Richard McCambley. http://www.lectio-divina.org/images/nyssa/On%20Almsgiving.pdf.
> *De beneficentia*. GNO IX:93–108. PG 46:453–69.

Discourse on the Holy Pascha. Translated by Stuart George Hall. In *The Easter Sermons of Gregory of Nyssa: Translation and Commentary*. Edited by

---

[1]Following each English translation is an entry with the Latin title and its place in the GNO and PG.

Andreas Spira and Christoph Klock. Cambridge, MA: The Philadelphia Patristic Foundation, Ltd., 1981. Pp. 5–23.

   In sanctum Pascha. GNO IX:245–70. PG 46:652–81.

First Homily on the Forty Martyrs of Sebaste (Ia and Ib). Translated by Johan Leemans. In '*Let us Die that We May Live': Greek Homilies on Christian Martyrs from Asia Minor, Palestine and Syria (c. AD 350–AD 450).* London: Routledge, 2003. Pp. 91–107.

      In XL Martyres Ia, Ib. GNO X/1:137–42, 145–56. PG 46:749–56, 757–772.

Homilies on the Beatitudes: An English Version with Commentary and Supporting Studies. Translated by Stuart George Hall. Leiden: Brill, 2000.
      De beatitudinibus. GNO VII/2:75–170. PG 44:1193–1301.

The Letters: Introduction, Translation and Commentary. Translated by Anna M. Silvas. Leiden: Brill, 2007.

      Epistulae. GNO VIII/2. PG 46:1000–1100.

      Epistula canonica ad Letoium episcopum. GNO III/5. PG 45:221–36.

The Life of Moses. Translated by Abraham J. Malherbe and Everett Ferguson. Classics of Western Spirituality. Mahwah, NJ: Paulist Press, 1978.
      De vita Moysis. GNO VII/1. PG 44:297–429.

The Life of Macrina. In Anna M. Silvas. *Macrina the Younger, Philosopher of God.* Turnhout, Belgium: Brepols Publishers, 2008. Pp. 109–48.
      Vita s. Macrinae. VIII/1:370–414. PG 46:960–1000.

Life of Gregory the Wonderworker. In *Saint Gregory Thaumaturgus: Life and Works.* Translated by Michael Slusser. The Fathers of the Church, Volume 98. Washington, DC: The Catholic University of America Press, 1998. Pp. 41–90.

      De vita Gregorii Thaumaturgi. GNO X/1:3–57. PG 46:893–957.

On the Baptism of Christ. Translated by William Moore and Henry Austin Wilson. NPNF² 5:518–24.

      In diem luminum. GNO IX:221–42. PG 46:577–600.

On Infants' Early Deaths. Translated by William Moore and Henry Austin Wilson. NPNF² 5:372–81.

      De infantibus praemature abreptis. GNO III/2:67–97. PG 46:161–92.

On "Then Also the Son Himself Will Be Subjected to the One Who Subjected All Things to Him." In Rowan A. Greer. *One Path for All: Gregory of Nyssa*

    on the Christian Life and Human Destiny. Eugene, OR: Cascade Books,
    2015. Pp. 118–32.
        In illud: Tunc et ipse Filius. GNO III/2:3–28. PG 44:1304–25.
On the Three-day Period of the Resurrection of our Lord Jesus Christ. Trans-
    lated by Stuart George Hall. In *The Easter Sermons of Gregory of Nyssa:
    Translation and Commentary*. Edited by Andreas Spira and Christoph
    Klock. Cambridge, MA: The Philadelphia Patristic Foundation, Ltd.,
    1981. Pp. 31–50.
        *De tridui inter mortem et resurrectionem domini nostri Iesu Christi
        spatio*. GNO IX:273–306. PG 46:600–28.
On the Soul and the Resurrection. In Anna M. Silvas. *Macrina the Younger,
    Philosopher of God*. Turnhout, Belgium: Brepols Publishers, 2008. Pp.
    171–246.
        De anima et resurrectione. GNO III/3. PG 46:12–160.
On Virginity. In *St. Gregory of Nyssa: Ascetical Works*. Translated by Virginia
    Callahan. The Fathers of the Church Series, Volume 58. Washington,
    DC: The Catholic University of America Press, 1967. Pp. 1–75.
        De virginitate. GNO VIII/1:247–343. PG 46:317–416.

Primary Sources[2]

The Acts of the Council of Constantinople of 553, Volumes 1 and 2. Translated
    by Richard Price. Liverpool: Liverpool University Press, 2012.
Ambrose of Milan. *The Mysteries*. In *Theological and Dogmatic Works*.
    Translated by Roy J. Deferrari . The Fathers of the Church, Volume 44.
    Washington, DC: The Catholic University of America Press, 1963. Pp.
    3–30.
_____. *The Sacraments*. In *Theological and Dogmatic Works*. Translated by
    Roy J. Deferrari . The Fathers of the Church, Volume 44. Washington,
    DC: The Catholic University of America Press, 1963. Pp. 265–328.
Anastasius of Sinai. [Greek original:] *Anastasii Sinaitae Viae dux*. Edited
    by Karl-Heinz Uthemann. Corpus Christianorum Series Graeca 8.
    Leuven: Brepols University Press, 1981.
Athanasius the Great. *Four Discourses Against the Arians*. Translated by
    Archibald Robertson. NPNF[2] 4:306–447.

---

[2]English translations are listed here, when available. Some works exist only in the
original, or in another modern language, and are listed accordingly.

_____. *On the Incarnation*. Translated by John Behr. Popular Patristics Series Number 44a. Yonkers, NY: St Vladimir's Seminary Press, 2011.

Augustine. *The First Catechetical Instruction (De Catechizandis Rudibus)*. Translated by Joseph P. Christopher. Ancient Christian Writers, Number 2. Westminster, MD: The Newman Bookshop, 1946.

Barsanuphius. *Barsanuphius and John: Letters*, Volume 2. Translated by John Chryssavgis. Washington, DC: The Catholic University of America Press, 2007.

Basil the Great. *Exegetic Homilies*. Translated by Agnes Clare Way. The Fathers of the Church, Volume 46. Washington, DC: The Catholic University of America Press, 1963.

Cyril of Jerusalem. *Lectures on the Christian Sacraments: The Procatechesis and the Five Mystagogical Catecheses ascribed to St Cyril of Jerusalem*. Translated by Maxwell E. Johnson. Popular Patristics Series, Number 57. Yonkers, NY: St Vladimir's Seminary Press, 2017.

_____. *The Works of Saint Cyril of Jerusalem, Volume 1: Procatechesis and Catecheses 1–12*. Translated by Leo P. McCauley and Anthony A. Stephenson. The Fathers of the Church, Volume 61. Washington, DC: The Catholic University of America Press, 1969.

_____. *The Works of Saint Cyril of Jerusalem, Volume 2: Catecheses 13–18 and Mystagogical Lectures*. Translated by Leo P. McCauley and Anthony A. Stephenson. The Fathers of the Church, Volume 64. Washington, DC: The Catholic University of America Press, 1970.

Ephraim the Syrian. *The Nisibene Hymns*. Translated by J. T. Sarsfield Stopford. NPNF[2] 13:165–219.

Gregory the Great. *Forty Gospel Homilies.* Translated by David Hurst. Collegeville, MN: Cistercian Publications, 1990.

Gregory of Nazianzus. *The Epigrams of Saint Gregory the Theologian*. Translated by W. R. Paton. In *The Greek Anthology*, Volume 2. The Loeb Classical Library, Number 68. New York, NY: G. P. Putnam's Sons, 1917. Pp. 339–508.

_____. *Select Orations of Saint Gregory Nazianzen.* Translated by Charles Gordon Browne. NPNF[2] 7:185–434.

Gregory Palamas. *Saint Gregory Palamas: The Homilies*. Translated by Christopher Veniamin. Waymart, PA: Mount Thabor Publishing, 2009.

Ignatius. *Ignatius of Antioch: The Letters.* Translated by Alistair Stewart. Popular Patristics Series, Number 49. Yonkers, NY: St Vladimir's Seminary Press, 2013.

Irenaeus, *Against Heresies.* Translated by Alexander Roberts and William Rambaut. ANF 1:307–567.

Jerome. *The Letters of St. Jerome.* Translated by W. H. Fremantle. NPNF² 6:1–295.

John Chrysostom. *Baptismal Instructions.* Translated by Paul William Harkins. Ancient Christian Writers, Number 31. Mahwah, NJ: Paulist Press, 1962.

————. *Homilies of St. John Chrysostom, Archbishop of Constantinople, on the Gospel According to St. Matthew.* Translated by George Prevost. NPNF¹ 10.

John of Damascus. *Writings: The Fount of Knowledge—Philosophical Chapters, On Heresies, An Exact Exposition of the Orthodox Faith.* Translated by Frederic H. Chase, Jr. The Fathers of the Church Patristic Series, Volume 37. Washington, DC: Catholic University of America Press, 1958.

Julian the Apostate. *Against the Galileans.* In *The Works of the Emperor Julian, Volume 3.* Translated by Wilmer C. Wright. Loeb Classical Library, Number 157. Cambridge, MA: Harvard University Press, 1923. Pp. 318–427.

Justin Martyr. *The First and Second Apologies.* Translated by Leslie William Barnard. Ancient Christian Writers, Number 56. Mahwah, NJ: Paulist Press, 1997.

Mark of Ephesus. [Greek original and Latin translation:] *Marci archiepiscopi Ephesii oratio prima de igne purgatorio.* In *Documents Relatifs au Concile de Florence I: La Question du Purgatoire à Ferrare, Documents I-VI.* Edited by Louis Petit. Repr. Turnhout, Belgium: Brepols, 1990. Pp. 39–60. [Russian translation: *Первое слово св. Марка Ефесскаго об очистительном огне.* Translated by Archimandrite Ambrose (Pogodin). In *Святой Марк Эфесский и Флорентийская уния.* Jordanville, NY: Holy Trinity Monastery, 1963. Pp. 59–73.]

————. [Greek original and Latin translation:] *Marci archiepiscopi Ephesii oratio altera de igne purgatorio.* In *Documents Relatifs au Concile de Florence I: La Question du Purgatoire à Ferrare, Documents I-VI.* Edited by Louis Petit. Repr. Turnhout, Belgium: Brepols, 1990. Pp. 108–151. [Russian translation: *Второе слово св. Марка Ефесскаго объ очистительномъ огнѣ*. Translated by Archimandrite Ambrose (Pogodin). In *Святой Марк Эфесский и Флорентийская уния*. Jordanville, NY: Holy Trinity Monastery, 1963. Pp. 116–150.]

Maximus the Confessor. *St. Maximus the Confessor's Questions and Doubts*. Translated by Despina D. Prassas. DeKalb, IL: Northern Illinois University Press, 2009.

_____. *Various Texts on Theology, the Divine Economy, and Virtue and Vice*. In *The Philokalia*, Volume 2. Translated by G. E. H. Palmer, Philip Sherrard, Kallistos Ware. London: Faber and Faber Ltd., 1981. Pp. 164–284.

Origen, *Commentary on the Epistle to the Romans, Books 1–5*. Translated by Thomas P. Scheck. The Fathers of the Church, Volume 103. Washington, DC: The Catholic University of America Press, 2001.

_____. *On First Principles*. Translated by John Behr. Oxford: Oxford University Press, 2017.

Photius. [Greek original and French translation:] *Bibliothèque*, Tome V. Edited and translated by René Henry. Paris: Société d'Édition "Les Belles Lettres," 1967.

_____. *Mystagogy of the Holy Spirit*. Translated by Joseph P. Farrell. Brookeline, MA: Holy Cross Orthodox Press, 2005.

Pseudo-Hermogenes. *On Invention*. In *Invention and Method: Two Rhetorical Treatises from the Hermogenic Corpus*, trans. George A. Kennedy. Atlanta, GA: Society of Biblical Literature, 2005. Pp. 3–200.

Romanos the Melodist. [Greek original and French translation:] *Hymnes, IV: Nouveau Testament (XXXII-XLV)*. Translated by José Grosdidier de Matons. Sources chrétiennes 128. Paris: Les Édition du Cerf, 1967

Theodore Agallianus. *De Providentia*. In *Catalogue of the Greek Manuscripts in the Library of the Laura on Mount Athos*, ed. Sophronios Eustratiades and Spyridon, Harvard Theological Studies 12. Cambridge, MA: Harvard University Press, 1925. Pp. 421–34.

Theodore of Mopsuestia. *Commentary of Theodore of Mopsuestia on the Nicene Creed*. Translated and edited by A. Mingana. Woodbrooke Studies 5. Cambridge: W. Heffer and Sons Limited, 1932.

_____. *Commentary of Theodore of Mopsuestia on the Lord's Prayer and on the Sacraments of Baptism and the Eucharist*. Translated and edited by A. Mingana. Woodbrooke Studies 6. Cambridge: W. Heffer and Sons Limited, 1933.

Secondary Sources

Alfeyev, Hilarion. *Christ the Conqueror of Hell: The Descent into Hades from an Orthodox Perspective.* Crestwood, NY: St Vladimir's Seminary Press, 2009.

Allen, Prudence. *The Concept of Woman: The Aristotelian Revolution, 750 B.C.–A.D. 1250*, 2nd edition. Grand Rapids, MI: Eerdmans, 1997.

Aulén, Gustaf. *Christus Victor: A Historical Study of the Three Main Types of the Idea of Atonement.* Translated by A. G. Herbert. London: Society for the Promotion of Christian Knowledge, 1953.

Azkoul, Michael. *St. Gregory of Nyssa and the Tradition of the Fathers.* Lewiston, NY: The Edwin Mellen Press, 1995.

Baghos, Mario. "Reconsidering *Apokatastasis* in St Gregory of Nyssa's *On the Soul and Resurrection* and the *Catechetical Oration*." In *Cappadocian Legacy: A Critical Appraisal.* Edited by Doru Costache and Philip Kariatlis. Sydney, Australia: St Andrew's Orthodox Press, 2013. Pp. 411–440.

Bonazzi, Mauro. "The Platonist Appropriation of Stoic Epistemology" In *From Stoicism to Platonism: The Development of Philosophy, 100 BCE–100 CE.* Edited by Troels Engberg-Pedersen. Cambridge: Cambridge University Press, 2017. Pp. 120–41.

Bouteneff, Peter. "Christ and Salvation." In *The Cambridge Companion to Orthodox Christian Theology.* Edited by Mary B. Cunningham and Elizabeth Theokritoff. Cambridge: Cambridge University Press, 2008. Pp. 93–106.

The Brill Dictionary of Gregory of Nyssa. Edited by Lucas Francisco Mateo-Seco and Giulio Maspero. Translated by Seth Cherney. Leiden: Brill, 2010.

Cherniss, Harold Fredrik. *The Platonism of Gregory of Nyssa.* Berkeley, CA: University of California Press, 1930.

Constas, Nicholas. "The Last Temptation of Satan: Divine Deception in Greek Patristic Interpretation of the Passion Narrative." *Greek Orthodox Theological Review* 47:1–4 (2002): 237–74.

Daley, Brian E. *The Hope of the Early Church: A Handbook of Patristic Eschatology.* Grand Rapids, MI: Baker Academic, 2010.

Daniélou, Jean. "Apocatastase." In *L'être et le temps chez Grégoire de Nysse.* Leiden: Brill, 1970. Pp. 205–26.

_____. "Enchaînement." Ibid. Pp. 18–50.

Dyson, Henry. *Prolepsis and Ennoia in the Early Stoa*. Berlin: Walter de Gruyter, 2009.

Ferguson, Everett. *Baptism in the Early Church: History, Theology, and Liturgy in the First Five Centuries*. Grand Rapids, MI: William B. Eerdmans Publishing Co., 2009.

Handbook of Classical Rhetoric in the Hellenistic Period (330 B.C.–A.D. 400). Edited by Stanley E. Porter. Leiden: Brill, 1997.

Hart, David Bentley. *That All Shall Be Saved: Heaven, Hell, and Universal Salvation*. New Haven, CT: Yale University Press, 2019.

Hart, Mark. "Gregory of Nyssa's Ironic Praise of the Celibate Life." *Heythrop Journal* 33 (1992): 1–19.

Hombergen, Daniel. *The Second Origenist Controversy: A New Perspective on Cyril of Scythopolis' Monastic Biographies as Historical Sources for Sixth-Century Origenism*. Rome: Centro Studi S. Anselmo, 2001.

Karras, Valerie. "A Re-evaluation of Marriage, Celibacy, and Irony in Gregory of Nyssa's *On Virginity*." *Journal of Early Christian Studies* 13.1 (2005): 111–21.

Kees, Reinhard. *Die Lehre Von Der* Oikonomia *Gottes in Der* Oratio catechetica *Gregors Von Nyssa*. Leiden: Brill, 1995.

Ludlow, Morwenna. *Gregory of Nyssa, Ancient and (Post)modern*. Oxford: Oxford University Press, 2007.

_____. *Universal Salvation: Eschatology in the Thought of Gregory of Nyssa and Karl Rahner*. Oxford: Oxford University Press, 2000.

McClymond, Michael J. *The Devil's Redemption: A New History and Interpretation of Christian Universalism*, Volumes 1 and 2. Grand Rapids, MI: Baker Academic, 2018.

McGuckin, John. "St Gregory of Nyssa on the Dynamics of Salvation." In *Seeing the Glory Studies in Patristic Theology*. Collected Studies of John A. McGuckin, Volume 2. Yonkers, NY: St Vladimir's Seminary Press, 2017. Pp. 217–48.

Radde-Gallwitz, Andrew. *Gregory of Nyssa's Doctrinal Works: A Literary Study*. Oxford: Oxford University Press, 2018.

Ramelli, Ilaria. *The Christian Doctrine of Apokatastasis: A Critical Assessment from the New Testament to Eriugena*. Leiden: Brill, 2013.

_____. "In Illud: Tunc et ipse Filius . . . : Gregory of Nyssa's Exegesis, its Derivations from Origen, and Early Patristic Interpretations Related to Origen's." *Studia Patristica* 44 (2010): 259–74.

Riviére, Jean. *The Doctrine of the Atonement: A Historical Essay*, Volumes 1 and 2.Translated by Luigi Cappadelta. London: Kegan, Paul, Trench, Trübner & Co., Ltd., 1909.

Sandbach, F. H. "Ennoia and Prolepsis in the Stoic Theory of Knowledge." *Classical Quarterly* 24 (1930): 45–51.

Teselle, Eugene. "The Cross as Ransom." *Journal of Early Christian Studies* 4.2 (1996): 147–70.

Tsirplanis, Constantine. "The Concept of Universal Salvation in Saint Gregory of Nyssa." *Patristic and Byzantine Review* 28 (2010): 79–94.

Ware, Kallistos. "Dare we Hope for the Salvation of All? Origen, St Gregory of Nyssa and St Isaac the Syrian." In *The Inner Kingdom.* The Collected Works of Kallistos Ware, Volume 1. Crestwood, NY: St Vladimir's Seminary Press, 2001. Pp. 193–215.

Weiswurm, Alcuin Alois. *The Nature of Human Knowledge According to Saint Gregory of Nyssa.* Washington, D.C.: CUA Press, 1952.

Winling, Raymond. "La résurrection du Christ comme principe explicatif et comme élément structurant dans le *Discours catéchétique* de Grégoire de Nysse." *Studia Patristica* 23 (1989): 74–80.

ST VLADIMIR'S SEMINARY PRESS
1-800-204-2665 • www.svspress.com

We hope this book has been enjoyable and edifying for your spiritual journey toward our Lord and Savior Jesus Christ.

One hundred percent of the net proceeds of all SVS Press sales directly support the mission of St Vladimir's Orthodox Theological Seminary to train priests, lay leaders, and scholars to be active apologists of the Orthodox Christian Faith. However, the proceeds only partially cover the operational costs of St Vladimir's Seminary. To meet our annual budget, we rely on the generosity of donors who are passionate about providing theological education and spiritual formation to the next generation of ordained and lay servant leaders in the Orthodox Church.

 Donations are tax-deductible and can be made at www.svots.edu/donate. We greatly appreciate your generosity.

To engage more with St Vladimir's Orthodox Theological Seminary, please visit:

www.svots.edu
online.svots.edu
www.svspress.com
www.instituteofsacredarts.com